Dictionary of
BABY NAMES

Dictionary of
BABY NAMES

**GEDDES&
GROSSET**

This edition published 2005 by
Geddes & Grosset, David Dale House,
New Lanark, ML11 9DJ, Scotland

© 2000 Geddes & Grosset,

First edition printed 2000
Reprinted 2001, 2002, 2003
This edition printed 2005, with additions

Cover illustrations by Jane Molineaux, Simon Girling and Associates.
Baby photograph by Suza Scalora, courtesy of PhotoDisc Inc.

ISBN 1 84205 529 1

Printed and bound in Poland

POLSKABOOK

A

Aamor *see* AENOR.

Aaron a masculine first name meaning 'mountaineer, enlightener' (*Hebrew*). In the Old Testament, Aaron, who was an older brother of Moses, became the first High Priest of the Israelites. A contracted diminutive is Arn.

Abán a masculine first name meaning 'little abbot', from *aba*, 'abbot' (*Irish Gaelic*). The anglicised form is Abban.

Abban the anglicised masculine form of ABÁN.

Abbie a feminine diminutive form of ABIGAIL, also used independently.

Abbot or **Abbott** a surname, meaning 'father of the abbey' (*Old English*), used as a masculine first name.

Abby a feminine diminutive form of ABIGAIL, also used independently.

Abdul or **Abdullah** a masculine first name meaning 'servant of Allah' (*Arabic*).

Abe (1) a masculine first name meaning 'father' (*Aramaic*). (2) a masculine diminutive form of ABRAHAM and ABRAM.

Abel a masculine first name meaning 'breath, fickleness, vanity' (*Hebrew*). In the Bible it is the name of the second son of Adam and Eve, who was killed by his brother, Cain.

Abelard a masculine first name meaning 'nobly resolute' (*Germanic*).

Aberah a feminine variant form of AVERAH.

Abiathar a masculine first name meaning 'father of plenty' or 'excellence' (*Hebrew*). In the Old Testament he was a priest and the only survivor of a massacre of the priesthood ordered by King Saul.

Abiel a masculine first name meaning 'father of strength' (*Hebrew*).

Abigail a feminine first name meaning 'my father's joy' or 'hand maid' (*Hebrew*). In the Old Testament Abigail was the woman who brought provisions to David and his followers and who later married David. Diminutive forms are Abbie, Abby and Gail.

5

Abijah a masculine first name meaning 'to whom Jehovah is a father' (*Hebrew*). It is a name often found in the Old Testament, most notably that of a king of Judah who ruled for two years, and that of the second son of Samuel, who, with his brother JOEL, ruled Israel. A diminutive form is Bije.

Abner a masculine first name meaning 'father of light' (*Hebrew*). In the Old Testament Abner was the chief of King Saul's army who declined to fight Goliath.

Abra a feminine first name meaning 'mother of multitudes' (*Hebrew*).

Abraham a masculine first name meaning 'father of a multitude' (*Hebrew*). In the Old Testament Abraham is the first of the patriarchs, and he is regarded as the founder of Israel. He was originally named ABRAM. Abraham Lincoln (1809–65) was the sixteenth President of the United States. Diminutive forms are Abe, Bram, Ham.

Abram a masculine first name meaning 'father of elevation' (*Hebrew*). It was the original name of ABRAHAM. Diminutive forms are Abe, Bram.

Absalom a masculine first name meaning 'my father is peace' (*Hebrew*). In the Old Testament he was the third and favourite son of King David. He killed his half-brother for raping his sister Tamar but was eventually pardoned. He led a rebellion against his father but was defeated by JOAB, who killed him.

Acacia the name of a plant, possibly meaning 'immortality and resurrection' (*Greek*), used as a feminine first name.

Acantha a feminine first name meaning 'thorny, spiny' (*Greek*).

Ace a masculine first name meaning 'unity, unit' (*Latin*).

Achilles a masculine first name that may come from a river name and that of the legendary Greek hero who joined the Greek attack on Troy. He was killed when an arrow from the bow of Paris was guided by Apollo to his heel, his only vulnerable part.

Ackerley a surname, meaning 'from the acre meadow' (*Old English*), used as a masculine first name.

Ackley a surname, meaning 'from the oak tree meadow' (*Old English*), used as a masculine first name.

Ada (1) a feminine diminutive of ADELA or names beginning with Adal, also used independently. (2) a variant form of ADAH. Ada, Countess Lovelace (1815–52), was the only legitimate daughter of Lord Byron and she worked with Charles Babbage, inventor of the Analytical Engine, a forerunner of the computer. The computing language ADA was named in her honour.

Adabel or **Adabela** or **Adabella** feminine variant forms of ADABELLE.

Adabelle a feminine first name meaning 'joyful and beautiful', a combination of ADA and BELLE. Variant forms are Adabel, Adabela and Adabella.

Adah a feminine first name meaning 'ornament' (*Hebrew*). In the Old Testament Adah was one of the two wives of Lamech, the son of Methusalah. A variant form is ADA.

Adair (1) a masculine first name, the root of which is Irish Gaelic *doire*, 'oak wood', and the origin of the name may be 'dweller by the oak wood', or perhaps 'attendant of the oak grove', since the oak was a sacred tree in Celtic lore, tended by the druids. (2) a Scottish masculine form of EDGAR.

Adalard a masculine first name meaning 'noble and brave' (*Germanic*).

Adalia a feminine first name from an early Saxon tribal name, the origin of which is unknown (*Germanic*).

Adam a masculine first name meaning 'man, earth man, red earth' (*Hebrew*). In the Bible Adam was the first man on earth and the father of the human race.

Adamina a feminine form of ADAM (*Latin*).

Adamnan a masculine first name, probably a diminutive form of Adam, 'little Adam' (*Gaelic*). The Gaelic form is both Adhamhán and Adomnán. St Adamnan, a seventh-century abbot of Iona, wrote his famous *Life of St Columba*.

Adar a feminine first name meaning 'fire' (*Hebrew*). As the name in the Jewish calendar for the twelfth month of the Biblical year and the sixth month of the civil year, it is a name sometimes given to girls born in that period.

Addie feminine diminutive of ADELAIDE.

Addison a surname, meaning 'Adam's son', used as a masculine first name (*Old English*).

Adeel a masculine variant form of ADIL.

Adela a feminine first name meaning 'of noble birth; a princess' (*Germanic*). A diminutive form is DELLA.

Adelaide a feminine first name meaning 'of noble birth; a princess' (*Germanic*). A diminutive form is Addie.

7

Adelbert *see* ALBERT.

Adèle or **Adele** the French feminine form of ADELA, now also used as an English form.

Adelfia a feminine variant form of ADELPHIA.

Adelheid a feminine first name meaning 'noble kind' (*Germanic*). A diminutive form is Heidi.

Adeline or **Adelina** a feminine first name meaning 'of noble birth; a princess' (*Germanic*). A diminutive form is Aline.

Adelpha a feminine variant form of ADELPHIA.

Adelphia a feminine first name meaning 'sisterly, eternal friend of mankind' (*Greek*). Variant forms are Adelfia, Adelpha.

Adeon a masculine first name that has been related to Welsh *adain*, 'wing' (*Welsh*), although perhaps it is a form of AEDDAN.

Aderyn a feminine first name from *aderyn*, 'bird' (*Welsh*).

Adhnúall (pronounced *a-nooall*) a masculine first name from *adnúall*, 'sweet of sound' (*Irish Gaelic*). In Celtic legend, this was the name of one of the hounds of FIONN macCumhaill.

Adil a masculine first name meaning 'honest' (Arabic). A variant form is Adeel.

Adin a masculine first name meaning 'sensual' (*Hebrew*). In the Old Testament Adin was one of the patriarchal heads of Israel.

Adina a feminine first name meaning 'voluptuous, ripe, mature' (*Hebrew*).

Adlai a masculine first name meaning 'God is just' (*Hebrew*). In the Bible Adlai was the overseer of King David's herds. A more recent bearer of the name was the American lawyer and Democrat politician Adlai Ewing Stevenson (1900–1968) who was twice defeated in the presidential elections.

Adler a masculine first name meaning 'eagle, perceptive one' (*Germanic*).

Adney a masculine first name meaning 'island-dweller' (*Old English*).

Adolf the German masculine form of ADOLPH.

Adolfa or **Adolfina** feminine variant forms of ADOLPHA.

Adolph or **Adolphus** a masculine first name meaning 'noble wolf; noble hero' (*Germanic*). A diminutive form is Dolph.

Adolpha a feminine first name meaning 'noble she-wolf, she who will give her life for her young', the feminine form of Adolf (*Germanic*). Variant forms are Adolfa, Adolfina, Adolphina.

Adolphe the French masculine form of ADOLPH.

Adolphina a variant feminine form of ADOLPHA.

Adon or **Adonai** a masculine first name meaning 'lord', a sacred word for God (*Hebrew*).

Adonia a feminine first name meaning 'beautiful goddess of the resurrection; eternal renewal of youth' (*Greek*).

Adoniram a masculine first name meaning 'lord of height' (*Hebrew*).

Adonis a name meaning 'lord' and that of the Greek god, borrowed from the Phoenicians, who was a favourite of VENUS. William Shakespeare (1654–1616) wrote a poem, *Venus and Adonis* (1593), that tells of the passion of Venus for the youthful Adonis and the killing of the latter by a wild boar.

Adora a feminine first name meaning 'adored and beloved gift' (*Latin*).

Adorabella a feminine first name meaning 'beautiful gift', a combination of ADORA and BELLA.

Adorna a feminine first name meaning 'adorned with jewels' (*Latin*).

Adrian a masculine first name meaning 'of the Adriatic' in Italy (*Latin*). It was the name adopted by several popes, including Adrian IV (Nicholas Breakspear) (*c*.1100–1159), the only English pope (1154–59). Variant forms are Adrien, HADRIAN.

Adrianne a feminine form of ADRIAN.

Adriel a masculine first name meaning 'from God's congregation' (*Hebrew*). In the Old Testament Adriel married Merab, SAUL's oldest daughter, although she had previously been promised to DAVID.

Adrien a masculine variant form of ADRIAN. It is sometimes used as a feminine first name.

Adrienne a feminine form of Adrian. Adrienne Corrie is British actress.

Adwen a masculine first name meaning 'fiery' (*Cornish*), a name related to the Gaelic AED.

Aeb or **Aebh** feminine variant forms of AOBH.

Aebhric (pronounced *ive-rick*) an Irish Gaelic masculine first name of unknown meaning. It was the name of the monk of Erris who wrote down the story of the *Children of Lír*. English forms are Evric, Everett.

Aebill a variant feminine form of AíBELL.

Aed (pronounced *aigh*) a masculine first name meaning 'fiery one', from *áed*, 'fire' (*Scottish and Irish Gaelic*). A common name among the Gaels, and said to have been the most frequent personal name in early

9

Ireland. It was so common that most who had the name had a further descriptive name or nickname, like Aed Finn (Gaelic *fionn*, 'fair') or Aed Ruad (Gaelic *ruadh*, 'red'). It was the name given to several high kings of Ireland and a king of the Scots, son of Kenneth MacAlpin. The name is also found as Aedh, Aodh.

Aedammair (pronounced *ay-dammar*) a diminutive and feminine form of AED (*Irish Gaelic*). Traditionally Aedammair was the first Irish nun.

Aedán (pronounced *ay-dann*) a diminutive form of Aed, with the -an suffix (*Scottish and Irish Gaelic*). The Anglicised forms are AIDAN and Edan. An early king of Dalriada was named Aedán, as were twenty-three other saints of the Gaelic Church.

Aeddan a masculine first name derived from *aed*, 'fire' (Welsh). Aeddan was a warrior of the Old Welsh, featuring in the sixth-century poem 'Y Gododdin'.

Aedh a variant masculine form of AED.

Aednat a feminine diminutive form of Aed (*Irish Gaelic*). A variant form is AODHNAIT.

Aefa an anglicised feminine form of AOIFE.

Ael (pronounced *ale*) a masculine first name meaning 'rocky', from *ail*, 'rock' (*Breton*). A name with a similar meaning to Peter.

Aelda or **Aeldra** a feminine variant form of ALDORA.

Aelheran (pronounced *ale-eran*) a masculine first name meaning 'iron-browed', from *ael*, 'brow', and *haearn*, 'iron' (*Welsh*). A saint's name, preserved in Llanaelhaearn in Caernarfonshire.

Aelwen a feminine first name meaning 'fair-browed' (*Welsh*).

Aelwyn a masculine first name meaning 'fair-browed' (*Welsh*), the masculine form of Aelwen.

Aeneas a masculine first name meaning 'commended' (*Greek*). In Virgil's *Aeneid*, Aeneas was a Trojan hero who escaped when Troy was taken and sailed for Italy. After numerous adventures he was driven by a tempest to Carthage where DIDO fell in love with him. On orders from Zeus, however, he sailed for Italy. In the New Testament Aeneas was healed by Peter after suffering paralysis for eight years. A variant form is Eneas.

Aengus *see* ANGUS.

Aenor (pronounced *ay-nor*) a feminine first name from the Breton name Aamor, probably from a root-word meaning 'bright' (*Irish Gaelic*).

Aerfen a feminine first name meaning 'renowned in battle' (*Welsh*). This was the name of an early Welsh goddess, whose cult was linked to the River Dee in North Wales.

Aeron a masculine first name the meaning of which is unclear; but possibly *aeron*, 'berry' (*Welsh*). It is also the name of an early Welsh wargod, derived from the Brythonic *agroná*, 'slaughter'. Some scholars have identified it with the Scottish river name Ayr, but this has also been disputed.

Aeronwen a feminine variant form of AERONWY.

Aeronwy a feminine first name meaning 'the berry stream' (*Welsh*). The name comes from the River Aeron in Ceredigion. A variant form is Aeronwen.

Aethelbert a variant form of ETHELBERT.

Aethelred a variant form of ETHELRED.

Afonso the Portuguese masculine form of ALPHONSO.

Afra a variant feminine form of APHRA.

Africa the name of the continent used as a feminine first name.

Agatha a feminine first name meaning 'good; kind' (*Greek*). St Agatha (202–251) was an early Christian martyr. Dame Agatha Christie (1890–1976) was a prolific writer of detective stories. A diminutive form is Aggie or Aggy.

Agave a feminine first name meaning 'illustrious, famous' (*Greek*). In Greek mythology, Agave was a daughter of CADMUS who was driven mad by the gods because of her ill-treatment of SEMELE.

Aggie or **Aggy** a feminine diminutive form of AGATHA, AGNES.

Agnes a feminine first name meaning 'chaste, pure' (*Greek*). St Agnes was a fourth-century Christian martyr and patron saint of young girls. Agnes was a very popular name in Scotland until the late twentieth century. 'Black Agnes' Randolph, Countess of Dunbar, was a fourteenth-century heroine of the Scottish warsof independence. Diminutive forms are Aggie, Aggy, Agneta, Nessa, Nessie.

Agnès the French feminine form of AGNES.

Agnese the Italian feminine form of AGNES.

Agneta a feminine variant form of AGNES.

Agostino the Italian masculine form of AUGUSTINE.

Agroná *see* AERON.

Agustín the Spanish masculine form of AUGUSTINE.

Ahern a masculine first name meaning 'horse lord, horse owner' (*Irish Gaelic*).

Ahmad or **Ahmed** a masculine first name meaning 'praiseworthier' (*Arabic*). It is one of the names applied to MOHAMMED.

Ahren a masculine first name meaning 'eagle' (*Germanic*).

Aíbell a feminine first name meaning 'radiance', 'spark' (Irish Gaelic). This was the name of an old Irish goddess, later viewed as a fairy queen, with her mound at Craigeevil, near Killaloe in County Clare. She figures in numerous legends. Variant forms of the name are Aebill, Aoibheall; anglicised to Aibinn or Eevin.

Aibinn a feminine anglicised form of AíBELL.

Aibgréne (pronounced *a-grenya*) a feminine first name meaning 'radiance of the sun', from *grian*, 'sun' (*Irish Gaelic*). The name of a daughter born to Deirdre and Naoise, in the Legend of the Sons of Usna, who married the king of Tir nan Og.

Aibhlinn (pronounced *ave-linn*) a feminine first name, an Irish and Scottish Gaelic form of AVELINE (Norman French), anglicised into EVELYN.

Aibreán (pronounced *ap-reeann*) the Irish Gaelic feminine form of APRIL.

Aidan the anglicised masculine form of AEDÁN. A variant form is Edan. St Aidan (d. 651) was an Irish missionary in Northumbria who founded a monastery on Lindisfarne (Holy Island). Aidan Quinn is an American film actor.

Aideen (1) a feminine form of AED (Irish Gaelic). Aideen was the wife of the legendary warrior Oscar, grandson of Fionn macCumhaill. (2) an anglicised feminine form of Irish ETAIN.

Aife a feminine variant of AOIFE.

Aiken (1) a Scottish male diminutive form of ADAM, shortened to Ad, with the diminutive suffix -kin added. Aiken Drum is the hero of a familiar Scottish nursery song. (2) or **Aitken** the Scottish form of ATKIN, a surname meaning 'son of Adam' (*Old English*), used as a masculine first name.

Ailaw a feminine first name meaning 'melodious' (Welsh).

Ailbe a masculine or feminine variant of AILBHE; Ailbe Grùadbrecc, 'of the freckled cheeks', was wife to Fionn MacCumhaill after Gráinne.

Ailbhe (pronounced *al-veh*) a masculine or feminine first name meaning 'white', from *albho*,'white' (*Irish Gaelic*). Twelve warriors of the Fianna bore this name. AILBE is a variant form.

Ailean a feminine Scots Gaelic form of ALAN.

Aileen an anglicised Scottish feminine form of Gaelic Eibhlinn, Helen (*see* EILEEN). The form Aileen is also used on the Isle of Man.

Ailill (pronounced *al-yill*) a masculine first name probably derived from Gaelic *ail*, 'rock' (Irish Gaelic), although an alternative is 'sprite', as in Old Welsh *ellyll*. An anglicised version is Aleel. It was a well-known name in ancient Ireland; the name of Queen Medb's consort, and numerous other kings and heroes.

Ailis an Irish Gaelic feminine form of ALICE.

Ailsa a feminine first name that comes from Ailsa Craig, the rocky isle off the Ayrshire coast also known as Paddy's Milestone. The name's derivation is probably from the Old Norse proper name Ael, with -ey, 'island'.

Aimée the French feminine form of AMY.

Aindrea a Scottish Gaelic masculine form of ANDREW.

Áine (pronounced *an-yeh*) a feminine first name meaning 'brightness' (*Irish Gaelic*). This was the name of an early fertility goddess, who later was viewed as a fairy queen. There are many legends around her, including her bewitchment of Maurice, Earl of Desmond, who however gained control of her by seizing hold of her cloak. Although often anglicised as Annie or Anne, the names have quite separate sources.

Aingeall (pronounced *an-gheeall*) a feminine first name meaning 'angel' (Irish and Scottish Gaelic). *See also* MELANGELL.

Ainnle (pronounced *ann-leh*) an Irish Gaelic masculine first name the meaning of which is unclear. In Celtic legend, it was the name of one of the three sons of Usna, brother to Naoise, Deirdre's lover. All three were famed warriors.

Ainsley a masculine or feminine variant form of AINSLIE. Ainsley Gotto became famous in an Australian political scandal.

Ainslie a place name, from *Aenes lie*, 'Aene's meadow' or 'meadow of the respected one' (*Old English*), then a surname, now increasingly used as a masculine or feminine first name. A variant form is AINSLEY.

Aisha or **Aishah** a feminine first name meaning 'prospering' (*Arabic*). Variant forms are Asia, Ayisah, Aysha, Ayshia.

Aisleen a feminine or masculine variant of AISLING.

Aisling (pronounced *ash-ling*) a feminine or masculine first name from *aisling*, 'dream' (*Irish and Scots Gaelic*), not used as a personal name until modern times. Variant forms are Aisleen, Aislinn, Ashling.

Aislinn a feminine or masculine variant of AISLING.

Ajay a masculine first name meaning 'unconquerable' (*Sanskrit*).

Akash a masculine first name meaning 'sky' (*Sanskrit*).

Akshar a masculine first name meaning 'not forgotten' (*Sanskrit*).

Al masculine diminutive of ALAN, ALBERT, etc. Al Pacino is an American film actor who came to stardom in *The Godfather* and whose original name was Alberto.

Alain the French masculine form of ALAN.

Alair (pronounced *allar*) a masculine first name meaning 'cheerful', 'vital', from *alair*, 'cheerful' (*Irish Gaelic*).

Alan a masculine first name meaning 'rock-like, steadfast', from *ailinn* 'rock' (Scottish Gaelic). *Ailean nan Sop*, 'Alan of the Straws' is a well-known character in Scottish Highland folk-tales. A popular name in Scotland since the time of the early Stewarts, when Alan FitzWalter, High Steward of Scotland, assumed the surname which was ultimately to be that of the royal line. In his case the name probably came from Brittany, although the root is the same. Other forms are ALLAN, ALLEN. *See* ALUN.

Alanna (1) a feminine first name meaning 'o child', from the Gaelic *a leanbh* (Irish Gaelic). (2) a feminine form of ALAN. Variant forms are Alana, Alannah, Lana.

Alard a masculine variant form of ALLARD.

Alaric a masculine first name meaning 'noble ruler; all-rich' (*Germanic*).

Alarica a feminine variant form of ALARICE.

Alarice feminine form of ALARIC (*Germanic*). Variant forms are Alarica, Alarise.

Alarise a feminine variant form of ALARICE.

Alasdair the Scottish Gaelic masculine form of ALEXANDER. This name was made popular by three kings of Scotland, especially Alexander III (died 1293). Other forms are ALASTAIR, ALISTAIR, ALISTER. Diminutive forms are Al, Aly, Ally.

Alastair a masculine variant form of ALASDAIR. Alastair Stewart was a British TV newscaster.

Alaw a feminine first name meaning 'melodious' (Welsh).

Alban (1) a masculine first name meaning 'Scot' (Scottish Gaelic). The name comes from the Gaelic name for Scotland, Alba. (2) a Welsh masculine first name that comes from St Alban, the Roman soldier who was the first British Christian martyr, in AD 303, and was venerated among the Brythonic tribes. The Latin name is Albanus, from *alba*, 'mountain'. (3) a masculine first name meaning 'white', or of Alba in Italy (*Latin*).

Albanus the Latin masculine form of ALBAN.

Albern a masculine first name meaning 'noble warrior' (*Old English*).

Albert a masculine first name meaning 'all-bright; illustrious' (*Germanic*). Albert the Great (Albertus Magnus) (1206–80) was a Dominican friar, bishop and philosopher and the teacher of St Thomas Aquinas. Albert Brooks is an American film actor and director. Diminutive forms are Al, Bert, Bertie.

Alberta feminine form of ALBERT.

Albin *see* ALBAN.

Albina a feminine first name meaning 'white, very fair' (*Latin*). Variant forms are Albinia, Alvina, Aubina, Aubine.

Albinia a feminine variant form of ALBINA.

Albrecht a German masculine form of ALBERT.

Alcina a feminine first name meaning 'strong-minded one', from a legendary woman who could make gold from stardust (*Greek*).

Alcott the surname, meaning 'old cottage or hut' (*Old English*), used as a masculine first name.

Alcyone a feminine first name that comes from the name of a woman in Greek mythology who drowned herself from grief at her husband's death and who was turned into a kingfisher. Variant forms are Halcyone, Halcyon.

Alda a feminine first name meaning 'wise and rich' (*Germanic*). Variant forms are Eada, Elda.

Alden a surname, meaning 'old or trustworthy friend' (*Old English*), used as a masculine first name.

Alder a surname, meaning 'alder tree' (*Old English*) or 'old, wise and rich' (*Germanic*), used as a masculine first name .

Aldis (1) a surname, meaning 'old house' (*Old English*), used as a masculine first name. (2) a feminine diminutive form of some names beginning with Ald-.

Aldo a masculine first name meaning 'old' (*Germanic*). Aldo Ray (1926–91) was an American film actor. A variant form is ALDOUS.

Aldora a feminine first name meaning 'of noble rank' (*Old English*). Variant forms are Aelda, Aeldra.

Aldous a masculine variant form of ALDO. Aldous Huxley (1894–1963) was an English novelist and essayist whose best-known novel was *Brave New World* (1932).

Aldrich a surname, meaning 'old, wise ruler' (*Old English*), used as a masculine first name.

Aldwin or **Aldwyn** a masculine variant form of ALVIN.

Alec a Scottish masculine diminutive form of ALEXANDER, sometimes used as a name in its own right. Alec Baldwin is an American actor.

Aled the name of a river in Denbighshire (*Welsh*) used as a masculine first name. Aled Jones was a celebrated boy singer. A variant form is Aleid.

Aleda a feminine variant from of ALIDA.

Aleel an anglicised masculine form of AILILL.

Aleid a masculine variant form of ALED.

Aleria a feminine first name meaning 'like an eagle' (*Latin*).

Aleron a masculine first name meaning 'eagle' (*Latin*).

Aleta a feminine variant form of ALIDA.

Alethea a feminine first name meaning 'truth' (*Greek*).

Alex (1) a masculine diminutive of ALEXANDER, now used independently. (2) a feminine diminutive of ALEXANDRA, now used independently. A variant form is Alix.

Alexa feminine diminutive of ALEXANDRA.

Alexander a masculine first name, the anglicised form of *Iskander*, 'defender of men' (*Greek*), made famous by Alexander the Great (*c.*360–330 BC). It was the name adopted by several popes and became a popular name in Scotland, since three of the country's most effective medieval kings bore this name. Diminutive forms are Alec, Alex, Alick, Lex, Sandy. *See also* ALASDAIR.

Alexandra and **Alexandrina** feminine forms of ALEXANDER. Diminutive forms are Alex, Alexa, Lexie, Lexy, Sandie, Sandra, Sandy.

Alexas a masculine variant of Alexis that was used by William Shakespeare (1564–1616) for the character of Cleopatra's duplicitous minister in his play *Antony and Cleopatra*.

Alexia a feminine form of ALEXIS.

Alexina feminine form of ALEXANDER.

Alexis a masculine or feminine first name meaning 'help, defence'

(*Greek*). A variant form is ALEXAS.

Alf or **Alfie** masculine diminutive forms of ALFRED.

Alfonsine feminine form of ALPHONSE (*Germanic*). Variant forms are Alphonsina, Alphonsine, Alphonza.

Alfonso a Spanish and Italian form of ALPHONSO.

Alford a surname, meaning 'old ford' (*Old English*), used as a masculine first name.

Alfred a masculine first name meaning 'good or wise counsellor' (*Germanic*). Alfred Molina is an English actor. Diminutive forms are Alf, Alfie.

Alfreda feminine form of ALFRED. Diminutive forms are Alfie, Allie. Variant forms are Elfreda, Elfreida, Elfrida, Elva, Elga, Freda.

Alger a masculine first name meaning 'elf spear' (*Old English*). Alger Hiss (1904–96) was an American politician who was imprisoned for perjury associated with alleged spying activities.

Algernon a masculine first name meaning 'whiskered' (*Old French*). A diminutive form is Algie, Algy.

Algie or **Algy** a masculine diminutive form of ALGERNON.

Ali a masculine first name meaning 'noble' or 'excellent' (*Arabic*).

Alice or **Alicia** a feminine first name meaning 'of noble birth; a princess' (*Germanic*). William Shakespeare (1564–1616) used the name Alice for the character of the French princess's attendant who acts as interpreter between the princess and King Henry V in his play *King Henry V*. Variant forms are Ailis, Alison, Alys, Alyssa, Eilis. A diminutive form is Allie or Ally.

Alick a masculine diminutive of ALEXANDER, now sometimes used independently as a first name.

Alida (1) a feminine first name meaning 'little bird'; 'small and lithe' (*Latin*). (2) a Hungarian form of ADELAIDE. Variant forms are Aleda, Aleta, Alita. Diminutive forms are Leda, Lita.

Aliénor a French feminine form of ELEANOR.

Alima a feminine first name meaning 'learned in music and dancing' (*Arabic*).

Aline a feminine contraction of ADELINE.

Alison (1) a Scottish feminine form of ALICE and a former diminutive of it now used entirely in its own right. Variant forms are Allison, Alyson and Alysoun. The diminutive form is Allie or Ally. Alison Cockburn wrote a version of *The Flowers of the Forest*. (2) a masculine first name meaning 'son of ALICE'; 'son of a nobleman' (*Old English*).

Alistair a masculine variant form of ALASDAIR.

Alister a masculine variant form of ALASDAIR.

Alita a feminine variant form of ALIDA.

Alix a feminine variant form of ALEX.

Allaid (pronounced *allay*) a masculine first name from the Ossian poems of James Macpherson (1736–96), from *allaid*, 'untamed', 'wild-living' (*Old Scottish Gaelic*).

Allan or **Allen** masculine variant forms of ALAN.

Allard a masculine first name meaning 'noble and brave' (*Old English*). A variant form is Alard.

Allegra a word for 'cheerful' or 'blithe' used as a feminine first name (*Italian*).

Allie a feminine diminutive of ALICE, ALISON.

Allison a feminine variant form of ALISON.

Ally (1) a feminine diminutive of ALICE, ALISON. Ally Sheedy is an American film actress.(2) a masculine diminutive of ALASDAIR. Ally McCoist is a Scottish footballer and presenter.

Alma a feminine first name meaning 'loving, nurturing' (*Latin*). Alma Cogan was an English singer.

Almha (pronounced *al-wah*) a feminine first name from the name of a Celtic goddess associated with strength and healing (*Irish Gaelic*).

Almira a feminine first name meaning 'lofty; a princess' (*Arabic*).

Almo a masculine first name meaning 'noble and famous' (*Old English*).

Aloha a word for 'welcome' used as a feminine first name (*Hawaiian*).

Alonso a Spanish form of ALPHONSO. William Shakespeare (1564–1616) used the name for the king of Naples, the enemy of Prospero, in his play *The Tempest*. A diminutive form is Lonnie.

Alonzo *see* ALPHONSO.

Aloysius a Latin form of LEWIS.

Alpha a masculine or feminine first name meaning 'first one' (*Greek*).

Alpheus a masculine first name meaning 'exchange' (*Hebrew*). In the New Testament Alpheus was the father of James the Less, one of Christ's Apostles.

Alphonse the French masculine form of ALPHONSO.

Alphonsina or **Alphonsine** feminine variant forms of ALFONSINE.

Alphonso or **Alphonsus** a masculine first name meaning 'all-ready; willing' (*Old German*). St Alphonsus Liguori (1696–1787), one of the Doctors of the Roman Catholic Church, was a priest who founded an order of missionary preachers working with the rural poor.

Alphonza a feminine variant form of ALFONSINE.

Alpin a masculine first name of uncertain meaning but possibly 'blond' (*Scottish Gaelic*). Alpin was the father of Kenneth, first king of both the Pictish and Scottish nations.

Alroy a masculine first name meaning 'red-haired' (*Scottish Gaelic*).

Alston a surname, meaning 'old stone' (*Old English*), used as a masculine first name.

Alta a feminine first name meaning 'tall in spirit' (*Latin*).

Althea a feminine first name meaning 'healing' (*Greek*). A diminutive form is Thea.

Altman a masculine first name meaning 'old, wise man' (*Germanic*).

Alton a surname, meaning 'old stream or source' (*Old English*), used as a masculine first name.

Alula a feminine first name meaning 'winged one' (*Latin*) or 'first' (*Arabic*).

Alun the name of a North Wales river, whose origin means 'flowing among rocks', used as a masculine first name. The personal name may be from the river or may go back directly to the root-form *ail*, 'rock'. Alun of Dyfed figures in the *Mabinogion* tales. The name was taken as a bardic name by the nineteenth century Welsh bard John Blackwell. *See also* ALAN.

Alura a feminine first name meaning 'divine counsellor' (*Old English*).

Alva (1) the name of a Scottish town, from Gaelic *ail*, 'rock', *magh*, 'plain' (Scottish Gaelic), used as a feminine first name but probably has also picked up associations with ALMHA. (2) a feminine first name meaning 'white' (*Latin*).

Alvah a masculine first name meaning 'exalted one' (*Hebrew*).

Alvin a masculine first name meaning 'winning all' (*Old English*). A variant form is Aldwin or Aldwyn.

Alvina or **Alvine** a feminine first name meaning 'beloved and noble friend' (*Germanic*). A diminutive form is Vina.

Alwyn the name of the River Alwen in Wales, used as a masculine first name. Its derivation is from *ail*, 'rock', and *wyn*, 'white' (*Welsh*), a reminder of the Welsh song 'David of the White Rock'.

Aly a masculine diminutive form of Alasdair. Aly Bain is a celebrated Shetland fiddle player.

Alys the Welsh feminine form of ALICE.

Alyson or **Alysoun** feminine variant forms of ALISON.

Alyssa a feminine variant form of ALICE or ALICIA.

Alyth a place name, meaning 'steep place', used as a feminine first name.

Alzena a feminine first name meaning 'woman, purveyor of charm and virtue' (*Arabic*).

Amabel a feminine first name meaning 'lovable' (*Latin*). A diminutive form is MABEL.

Amadea the feminine form of AMADEUS.

Amadeus a masculine first name meaning 'lover of God' (*Latin*).

Amado the Spanish form of AMATO.

Amairgein a masculine variant form of AMAIRGIN.

Amairgin (pronounced *a-mar-yin*) a masculine first name meaning 'wondrously born' (*Irish Gaelic*). This name is borne by numerous figures in the early legends of Ireland. Alternative forms include Amairgein and Amargen and the anglicised form is Amorgin.

Amalghaidh the Gaelic masculine form of AULAY.

Amalia (1) a feminine first name meaning 'work' (*Germanic*). (2) an Italian and Greek form of AMELIA.

Amalinda a feminine variant form of AMELINDA.

Amanda a feminine first name meaning 'worthy of love' (*Latin*). Amanda Donohoe is a British-born film actress. Diminutive forms are Manda, Mandy.

Amargen a masculine variant form of AMAIRGIN.

Amariah a masculine first name meaning 'whom Jehovah promised' (*Hebrew*).

Amaryllis a feminine first name meaning 'sparkling' (*Greek*). It became a name for a shepherdess or country girl in pastoral poetry.

Amasa a masculine first name meaning 'a burden' (*Hebrew*). In the Old Testament Amasa was the nephew of King DAVID and the commander of the army of ABSALOM.

Amber the name of a gemstone used as a feminine first name.

Ambert a masculine first name meaning 'shining bright light' (*Germanic*).

Ambrin or **Ambreen** the Arabic word for ambergris used as a feminine first name.

Ambrogio the Italian masculine form of AMBROSE.

Ambrose a masculine first name meaning 'immortal' (*Greek*). The Welsh form is EMRYS and the Latin form Ambrosius. It was the name of St Ambrose of Milan (339–397), one of the Doctors of the Roman Catholic Church, and as such was widely venerated beyond his territory of Lombardy.

Ambrosia or **Ambrosina** feminine variant forms of AMBROSINE.

Ambrosine feminine form of Ambrose. Variant forms are Ambrosia, Ambrosina.

Ambrosius the Latin masculine form of AMBROSE. See also EMRYS.

Amédée the French masculine form of AMADEUS.

Amelia a feminine first name meaning 'busy, energetic' (*Germanic*). A diminutive form is Millie.

Amélie the French feminine form of AMELIA.

Amelinda a feminine first name meaning 'beloved and pretty' (*Spanish*). Variant forms are Amalinda, Amelinde.

Amelinde a feminine variant form of AMELINDA.

Amena a feminine first name meaning 'honest, truthful' (*Gaelic*).

Amerigo an Italian variant form of ENRICO.

Amery a masculine variant form of AMORY.

Amethyst the name of the semiprecious gemstone used as a feminine first name (*Greek*).

Amin a masculine first name meaning 'honest' (*Arabic*).

Amina the feminine form of Amin.

Aminta or **Amintha** or **Aminthe** a feminine first name meaning 'protector', a shepherdess in Greek mythology (*Greek*).

Amit a masculine first name meaning 'limitless' (*Sanskrit*).

Amlodd (pronounced *am-loth*) a masculine first name from Welsh Arthurian legend of uncertain meaning. Amlodd was the grandfather of King Arthur.

Ammon a masculine first name meaning 'hidden' (*Egyptian*).

Amorgin the anglicised masculine form of AMAIRGIN.

Amory a masculine first name meaning 'famous ruler' (*Germanic*). Variant forms are Amery, Emery, Emmery.

Amos a masculine first name meaning 'bearer of a burden' (*Hebrew*). Amos was a Hebrew prophet of the eighth century BC and the first to have a Book of the Bible called after him.

Amy a feminine first name meaning 'beloved' (*Old French*). Amy Madigan is an American film actress.

Ana a feminine variant form of ANU.

Anaïs (pronounced *an-eye-ees*) a feminine first name meaning 'productive' (*Greek*). Anaïs Nin was a French writer.

Anand a masculine first name meaning joy (*Sanskrit*) and the name of a Hindu god.

Ananda or **Anandi** the feminine form of Anand.

Anann a feminine variant form of ANU.

Anarawd (pronounced *ana-rodd*) a masculine first name meaning 'most eloquent', from *iawn*, 'most', 'highly', and *huawdl*, 'eloquent' (*Welsh*), as in modern Welsh *hwyl*.

Anastasia a feminine first name meaning 'rising up, resurrection' (*Greek*). Diminutive forms are Stacey, Stacy, Stacie, Stasia.

Anastasius a masculine form of ANASTASIA. It was the name adopted by several popes.

Anatholia or **Anatola** feminine forms of Anatole (*Greek*. A variant form is Anatolia.

Anatole a masculine first name meaning 'from the East' (*Greek*).

Anatolia a feminine variant form of ANATHOLIA.

Andie a masculine diminutive of ANDREW. It is now being used as a feminine first name. Andie MacDowall is an American film actress.

Anderson the surname, meaning 'son of Andrew' (from 'manly') (*Greek*), used as a masculine first name.

Andrasta a feminine first name meaning 'invincible' (*Brythonic*). Andrasta was a goddess of the Celtic tribes in what is now England

André the French masculine form of ANDREW, becoming popular as an English-language form.

Andrea a feminine form of ANDREAS or ANDREW. A variant form is ANDRINA; the Italian form of ANDREW.

Andreas Greek, Latin, German and Welsh masculine forms of ANDREW.

Andrés the Spanish masculine form of ANDREW. It was the original name of the Cuban-born American film actor Andy Garcia.

Andrew a masculine first name meaning 'strong; manly; courageous' (*Greek*). It early became a popular name for boys in Scotland because of the cult of the Apostle St Andrew as the nation's patron saint (as well as that of Russia). Many famous people have borne this name including the famous sailors Sir Andrew Barton (died 1511) and Sir Andrew Wood (*c*.1455–1515), and the philanthropic millionaire Andrew Carnegie (1835–1919) who made his fortune in the United States. The variant form ANDRO is occasionally found. Diminutive forms are Andy, Andie, Andy, Dandie, Drew.

Andrewina a variant form of ANDRINA.

Andrina or **Andrine** a female form of ANDREW, popular when it was common for girls to be given a feminised version of their father's name. Another form is Andrewina.

Andro a masculine variant form of ANDREW. Andro Linklater is a British author.

Andy a diminutive form of ANDREW, ANDRES. Andy Garcia is a Cuban-born American film actor.

Aneirin or **Aneurin** (pronounced *an-eye-rin*) a masculine first name, perhaps a Welsh form of the Latin *Honorius*, or alternatively derived from the Welsh root forms *an*, 'very', *eur*, 'golden', with the diminutive ending *-an*. Aneirin was one of the earliest Welsh poets, author of 'Y Gododdin'. Aneurin Bevan, Welsh Labour politician, introduced the National Health Service into Britain in the 1940s. A diminutive form is Nye.

Anemone a feminine first name meaning 'windflower', the name of the garden plant used as a feminine first name (*Greek*).

Angel (1) a feminine diminutive of ANGELA (*Greek*). (2) a masculine form of ANGELA. Thomas Hardy (1840–1928) used the name for his character Angel Clare in his novel *Tess of the D'Urbervilles*.

Angela or **Angelina** a feminine first name meaning 'messenger' (*Greek*).

Angelica a feminine first name meaning 'lovely; angelic' (*Greek*). A variant form is ANJELICA.

Angelo a masculine Italian form of ANGEL. William Shakespeare (1564–1616) used the name for the character of the hypocritical deputy of the Duke of Vienna in his play *Measure for Measure* and for that of a goldsmith in *The Comedy of Errors*.

Angharad (pronounced *ang-harrad*) a feminine first name meaning 'the well-loved one' (*Welsh*). In the seventh century Angharad was the wife of Rhodri Mawr.

Angus a masculine first name meaning 'the unique one' or 'only choice', anglicised from *aon*, 'one' and *gus*, 'strength' (*Scottish Gaelic*). The

Gaelic form is Aonghas, from a Pictish name Oengus. A Pictish king of this name died in AD 761, and his name is preserved in the former county of Angus. The form Oengus also figures in Old Irish literature, notably in the character of Angus Og, the god of youth. A diminutive form is Gus.

Anil a masculine first name meaning 'wind' (*Sanskrit*) and the name of a Hindu god.

Anila the feminine form of ANIL.

Anish a masculine first name meaning 'masterless' (*Sanskrit*).

Anisha the feminine form of ANISH.

Anita the feminine Spanish diminutive of ANN, now used independently as an English-language form. A diminutive form is Nita.

Anjelica a feminine variant form of ANGELICA. Anjelica Huston is an American film actress.

Anluan a masculine first name meaning 'great hound', probably with the sense of great warrior (*Irish Gaelic*).

Ann a feminine first name meaning 'grace' (*Hebrew*). A variant form is HANNAH. A diminutive form is Annie.

Anna the feminine Latin form of ANN. In the New Testament it is the name of a Jewish prophetess who witnessed the presentation of Jesus in the Temple.

Annabel or **Annabelle** or **Annabella** a feminine first name meaning 'lovable' (possibly from AMABEL). Diminutive forms are Bella, Belle. Annabella Sciorra is an American film actress.

Annan a Scottish place name, meaning 'water' or 'waters' (*Scottish Gaelic*), used as a masculine first name.

Anne the French feminine form of ANN now commonly used as an English-language form. St Anne was the mother of the Virgin Mary.

Anneka a feminine Dutch diminutive of ANNA.

Annette a French diminutive of ANN, used as an English-language form. Annette Bening is an American actress and wife of Warren Beatty.

Annie a feminine diminutive form of ANN.

Annika a feminine Swedish diminutive of ANNA.

Annis or **Annice** a medieval feminine diminutive of AGNES.

Annona a feminine variant form of ANONA.

Annunciata a feminine first name from the Italian form of *nuntius*, 'bringer of news', i.e. the angel Gabriel, who delivered the announcement of the Virgin Mary's conception, a name often given to children born on 25 March, Lady Day (*Latin*).

Annwr (pronounced *ann-ur*) a Welsh feminine form of ANEIRIN. In Arthurian legend, Annwr attempted to seduce Arthur.

Annwyl (pronounced *ann-ul*) a masculine first name meaning 'very dear' (*Welsh*).

Anona a feminine first name meaning 'annual crops', hence the Roman goddess of crops (*Latin*). A variant form is Annona. Diminutive forms are Nonnie, Nona.

Anora a feminine first name meaning 'light, graceful' (*Old English*).

Anscom a masculine first name meaning 'one who dwells in a secret valley', 'a solitary person' (*Old English*).

Anselm or **Ansel** a surname, meaning 'god helmet', i.e. under the protection of God (*Germanic*), used as a masculine first name. St Anselm of Canterbury (1033–1109) was one of the Doctors of the Roman Catholic Church.

Anselma feminine form of ANSELM. A variant form is Arselma.

Ansley a surname, meaning 'clearing with a hermitage or solitary dwelling' (*Old English*), used as a masculine first name.

Anson a surname, meaning 'son of Agnes or Anne' (*Old English*), used as a masculine first name.

Anstice a surname, meaning 'resurrected' (*Greek*), used as a masculine first name.

Anthea a feminine first name meaning 'flowery' (*Greek*).

Anthony a masculine variant form of ANTONY. It is the name of several saints, including St Anthony of Padua (1195–1231), who is the patron saint of the poor, and St Anthony of Thebes (250–340), the founder of Christian monasticism. The diminutive form is Tony.

Antoine the French masculine form of ANTHONY, now used independently as an English-language form. A variant form is Antwan.

Antoinette feminine diminutive of ANTONIA, now used as an English-language form. A diminutive form is Toinette.

Anton a German masculine form of ANTONY, now used as an English-language form. Anton Lesser is an English actor.

Antonia feminine form of ANTONY. Lady Antonia Fraser is an English historian and biographer. Diminutive forms are Toni, Tonia, Tonie, Tony.

Antoninus a Roman family name meaning 'priceless; praiseworthy' (*Lat-*

25

in) used as a first name. St Antoninus (1389–1459) was archbishop of Florence and one of the founders of modern theology.

Antonio the Italian and Spanish masculine form of ANTONY. William Shakespeare (1564–1616) used the name for characters in several of his plays, most notably for that of the merchant in *The Merchant of Venice* from whom Shylock demands his pound of flesh and that of the usurping Duke of Milan in *The Tempest*.

Antony a masculine first name meaning 'priceless; praiseworthy' (*Latin*) from the Roman family name ANTONINUS. William Shakespeare (1564–1616) used this form of the name for Mark Antony (Marcus Antonius) in his plays *Julius Caesar* and *Antony and Cleopatra*. A variant form is Anthony. A diminutive form is Tony.

Antwan a masculine variant form of ANTOINE.

Anu (pronounced *an-oo*) a feminine first name meaning 'wealth', 'abundance of riches' (*Irish Gaelic*). In Celtic mythology, the semi-mythical Tuatha Dé Danann were 'the tribe of Anu'. She was a goddess of both good and evil, a figure of great power. Alternative forms are Ana, Anann. The name has no connection with Anne.

Anup a masculine first name meaning 'incomparable' (*Sanskrit*).

Anwell a masculine first name meaning 'beloved' (*Gaelic*).

Anwen a feminine first name meaning 'very beautiful or fair' (*Welsh*).

Anyon a masculine first name meaning 'anvil' (*Gaelic*).

Aobh (pronounced *ave*) a feminine first name meaning 'radiant, attractive', from Old Gaelic *oíb*, 'attractiveness'. In Celtic mythology, Aobh was the mother of the legendary Children of Lir, who were turned into swans. Variant forms of the name are AEB, AEBH.

Aodh a variant masculine form of AED.

Aodhagán (pronounced *ayd-a-gann*) a masculine first name meaning 'little AED'. The root is *aed*, 'fiery' (*Irish Gaelic/Manx*). Aodhagán O Raithile was a notable lyric poet of the seventeenth century. The anglicised form is Egan.

Aodhnait a feminine variant form of AEDNAT.

Aoibheall a feminine variant form of AÍBELL.

Aoibhín (pronounced *aiv-een*) a feminine first name meaning 'shining one' (*Irish Gaelic*). This was the name of numerous Irish princesses. *See also* AOIFE, EAVAN.

Aoife (pronounced *ay-fa*) an ancient feminine first name, stemming from

Old Irish Gaelic *aoibhinn*, 'of radiant beauty'. Nowadays it is often wrongly assumed to be a form of EVE and often anglicised into EVA. In Celtic mythology, Aoife was a Scottish 'Amazon' who bore a son to Cuchulainn, whom the hero was later to unwittingly kill in battle. The name was borne by numerous other women of legend and history. A variant form is Aife. The anglicised form is Aefa.

Aonghas (pronounced *inn-ess*) a masculine first name. The Scots Gaelic masculine form of ANGUS.

Aphra a feminine first name meaning 'dust' (*Hebrew*) or 'woman from Carthage' (*Latin*). Aphra Behn (1640–89) was an English playwright and novelist. A variant form is Afra.

April the name of the month, *Aprilis* (*Latin*), used as a feminine first name.

Ara a feminine first name meaning 'spirit of revenge', and the name of the goddess of destruction and vengeance (*Greek*).

Arabella or **Arabela** a feminine first name meaning 'a fair altar' (*Latin*). Diminutive forms are Bella, Belle.

Araminta a feminine first name meaning 'beautiful, sweet-smelling flower' (*Greek*). A diminutive form is Minta.

Archard a masculine first name meaning 'sacred and powerful' (*Germanic*).

Archer a surname, meaning 'professional or skilled bowman' (*Old English*), used as a masculine first name.

Archibald a masculine first name meaning 'very bold; holy prince' (*Germanic*). In parts of Scotland it was often erroneously identified with Gillespie (*see* GILLEASBUIG). A diminutive form is Archie or Archy. It is also a widely established surname in Scotland and northern England.

Archie or **Archy** a masculine diminutive form of ARCHIBALD. The American writer Don Marquis used the name for archy and mehitabel, his famous cockroach and cat whose stories were written by archy on a typewriter the shift key of which he could not operate.

Ardal a masculine first name meaning 'high valour' (*Irish Gaelic*). Ardal O'Hanlon is an Irish comedian.

Ardán (pronounced *ar-dann*) a masculine first name derived from *ardàn*, 'pride' (*Old Irish Gaelic*). In Celtic mythology, Ardán is the third son of Usna and brother of Naoise, Deirdre's lover. In the tale he is referred to as 'fierce', or 'unyielding': it is certainly a warrior name.

Ardath a feminine first name meaning 'field of flowers' (*Hebrew*). Variant forms are Aridatha, Ardatha.

Arddun (pronounced *arth-un*) a feminine first name meaning 'beautiful one' (*Welsh*).

Ardella or **Ardelle** or **Ardelis** a feminine first name meaning 'enthusiasm, warmth' (*Hebrew*).

Arden (1) a masculine first name meaning 'burning, fiery' (*Latin*). (2) a surname, meaning 'dwelling place' or 'gravel' or 'eagle valley' (*Old English*), used as a masculine first name.

Ardley a masculine first name meaning 'from the domestic meadow' (*Old English*).

Ardolph a masculine first name meaning 'home-loving wolf rover' (*Old English*).

Arduinna a feminine first name, of unknown meaning, of a Gaulish goddess of the Ardennes forest whose symbolic animal was a boar. A hunting goddess, her name has been linked with Greek Diana.

Areta or **Aretha** a feminine first name meaning 'excellently virtuous' (*Greek*). Variant forms are Aretta, Arette, Aretas.

Aretas a feminine variant form of ARETA.

Aretta or **Arette** feminine variant forms of ARETA.

Argante (pronounced *ar-ganta*) a masculine or feminine Old Gaelic or Welsh first name of unknown meaning. It was the name of a Celtic goddess of the underworld.

Argenta or **Argente** or **Argente** a feminine first name meaning 'silver' or 'silvery coloured' (*Latin*).

Argus a masculine first name meaning 'all-seeing, watchful one', from Argus Panoptes, a character from Greek mythology with a hundred eyes all over his body (*Greek*).

Argyle or **Argyll** the Scottish place name, meaning 'land or district of the Gaels' (*Scottish Gaelic*), used as a masculine first name.

Aria the Italian word for 'beautiful melody', from *aer*, 'breeze' (*Latin*), used as a feminine first name.

Ariadne a feminine first name meaning 'very holy' (*Greek*). In Greek mythology, Ariadne was a daughter of the king of Crete who saved Theseus from the labyrinth.

Arianrhod a feminine first name meaning 'silver disc' (*Welsh*). This is the name of a goddess from the *Mabinogion* cycle of tales, associated with the moon, beauty, inspiration and poetry.

Arianna an Italian feminine form of ARIADNE.

Arianne a French feminine form of ARIADNE.

Aric a masculine first name meaning 'sacred ruler' (*Old English*). Diminutive forms are Rick, Rickie, Ricky.

Ariel a masculine first name meaning 'God's lion' (*Hebrew*). In the Old Testament Ariel was one of the men used by Ezra to seek for leaders of the Jewish church. William Shakespeare (1564–1616) used the name for the character of the spirit of the air in *The Tempest*. It is occasionally used as a feminine first name.

Ariella or **Arielle** feminine forms of ARIEL.

Aries a masculine name meaning 'the ram' (*Latin*), the sign of the Zodiac for 21 March to 19 April.

Arjun a masculine first name meaning 'bright' (*Sanskrit*).

Arlan a Cornish masculine first name. It was the name of a legendary early saint of Cornwall, his name perhaps a corruption of Allen or Elwin, also Cornish saints.

Arleen a feminine variant form of ARLENE.

Arlen a masculine first name meaning 'pledge' (*Irish Gaelic*).

Arlene or **Arlena** (1) a Gaulish feminine first name, perhaps from the place name Arles. (2) the feminine form of ARLEN. (3) a feminine variant form of CHARLENE, MARLENE. Variant forms are Arleen, Arlina, Arline, Arlyne.

Arlie or **Arley** or **Arly** a surname, meaning 'eagle wood' (*Old English*), used as a masculine first name.

Arlina or **Arline** or **Arlyne** feminine variant forms of ARLENE.

Armand a French masculine form of HERMAN.

Armel a masculine first name meaning 'stone prince or chief' (*Breton Gaelic*).

Armelle the feminine form of ARMEL.

Armilla a feminine first name meaning 'bracelet' (*Latin*).

Armin a masculine first name meaning 'military man' (*Germanic*).

Armina or **Armine** feminine forms of ARMIN. Variant forms are Erminie, Erminia.

Armstrong a surname, meaning 'strong in the arm' (*Old English*), used as a masculine first name.

Arn (1) a masculine diminutive of ARNOLD, ARNULF. (2) a contraction of AARON.

Arnalda feminine form of ARNOLD (*Germanic*).

Arnall a surname variant form of ARNOLD (*Germanic*) used as a masculine first name.

Arnaud or **Arnaut** French forms of ARNOLD.

Arnatt or **Arnett** surname variant forms of ARNOLD used as masculine first names.

Arne a masculine first name meaning 'eagle' (*Old Norse*). A diminutive form is Arnie.

Arnie a masculine diminutive form of ARNE or ARNOLD.

Arno a masculine diminutive form of ARNOLD, ARNULF.

Arnold a masculine first name meaning 'strong as an eagle' (*Germanic*) or 'eagle meadow' (*Old English*). Arnold Bennett (1867–1931) was an English novelist. Arnold Schwarzenegger is an Austrian-born body-builder and film star. Diminutive forms are Arn, Arnie, Arno, Arny.

Arnott a surname variant form of ARNOLD used as a masculine first name.

Arnulf a masculine first name meaning 'eagle wolf' (*Germanic*). Diminutive forms are Arn, Arno.

Arny a masculine diminutive form of ARNOLD.

Arphad a masculine variant form of ARVAD.

Arselma a feminine variant form of ANSELMA.

Art an Irish Gaelic masculine first name, probably from the same Indo-European root as *arctos*, 'bear' (*Greek*). The bear was celebrated for its strength. In Irish legend, the best-known Art is a somewhat tragic hero, Art Oenfer, 'the lonely', son of CONN of the Hundred Battles and father of CORMAC macAirt.

Artair the Gaelic masculine form of ARTHUR.

Artemas a masculine form of ARTEMIS (*Greek*). In the New Testament Artemas was one of Paul's companions on part of his journeys.

Artemis in Greek mythology the name of the virgin goddess of hunting and the moon, the derivation of which is unknown. The Roman equivalent is DIANA.

Arthen a Welsh masculine first name cognate with Art, it was the name of a local god in Wales and given also to a ninth-century king of Ceredigion.

Arthur a masculine first name that has been linked to *arctos*, 'bear' (*Greek*) but also to a Celtic root form *ar*, 'plough', and to Brythonic *arddhu*, 'very black'. It was the name of the legendary leader of British resistance to the invading Anglo-Saxons. Its earliest appearance is in Welsh documents. The Gaelic form is ARTAIR. In the north of Scotland, it may also be a form of the Old Norse name Ottar.

Arturo the Italian and Spanish masculine forms of ARTHUR.

Arun a masculine first name meaning 'brownish red' (*Sanskrit*).

Aruna the feminine form of ARUN.

Arundel an English place name, meaning 'a valley where nettles grow' (*Old English*), used as a masculine first name.

Arva a feminine first name meaning 'ploughed land, pasture' (*Latin*).

Arvad a masculine first name meaning 'wanderer' (*Hebrew*). A variant form is Arpad.

Arval or **Arvel** a masculine first name meaning 'greatly lamented' (*Latin*).

Arvid a masculine first name meaning 'eagle wood' (*Norse*).

Arvin a masculine first name meaning 'people's friend' (*Germanic*).

Arwel a Welsh masculine first name, the meaning of which is uncertain.

Arwen a variant form of ARWYN.

Arwenna a feminine form of ARWYN.

Arwyn a masculine first name meaning 'muse' (*Welsh*). A variant form is Arwen.

Asa a masculine first name meaning 'healer, physician' (*Hebrew*). In the Old Testament Asa was the third king of Judah after its division into two kingdoms. Asa Briggs is an English historian and writer.

Asaf or **Asaph** (pronounced *ass-af*) a Welsh masculine first name. It was the name of the early Welsh saint who is commemorated in the North Wales bishopric of St Asaph, which is a variant form.

Asahel a masculine first name meaning 'made of God' (*Hebrew*). In the Old Testament Asahel was a nephew of King DAVID.

Asaph (1) a masculine variant form of ASAF. (2) a masculine first name meaning 'a collector' (*Hebrew*). In the Old Testament Asaph was a musician.

Ascot or **Ascott** an English place name and surname, meaning 'eastern cottages' (*Old English*), used as a masculine first name.

Ash a masculine or feminine first name from *aesc*, meaning 'ash tree' (*Old English*). The ash tree was widely worshipped among the Celtic peoples; ash, oak and thorn were a powerful triad. *See also* ROWAN.

Asha a feminine first name meaning 'hope' (*Sanskrit*).

Ashburn a surname, meaning 'stream where the ash trees grow' (*Old English*), used as a masculine first name.

Ashby an English place name, meaning 'ash-tree farmstead' (*Old English*), used as a masculine first name.

Asher a masculine first name meaning 'happy, fortunate' (*Hebrew*). In the Old Testament Asher was the founder of one of the Twelve Tribes of Israel.

Ashford an English place name, meaning 'ford by a clump of ash trees' (*Old English*), used as a masculine first name.

Ashia a feminine first name, possibly derived from Ash or Asia. Ashia Hansen is an English athlete.

Ashley or **Ashleigh** the surname, meaning 'ash wood or glade' (*Old English*), used as a masculine or feminine first name. Ashley Judd is an American actress.

Ashlin a masculine first name meaning 'ash-surrounded pool' (*Old English*).

Ashling a feminine or masculine variant of AISLING.

Ashraf a masculine first name meaning 'nobler' (*Arabic*).

Ashton an English place name, meaning 'ash-tree farmstead' (*Old English*), used as a masculine first name.

Asia a feminine variant form of AISHA.

Aslam a masculine first name meaning 'more sound' (*Arabic*).

Asma a feminine first name meaning 'more important' (*Arabic*).

Asphodel a daffodil-like plant, the origin of whose name is obscure, used as a feminine first name (*Greek*).

Asshur a masculine first name meaning 'martial, warlike' (*Semitic*). In the Old Testament Asshur was a son of Shem and forefather of the Assyrians.

Astra feminine diminutive of ASTRID.

Astrid a feminine first name meaning 'fair god' (*Norse*). A diminutive is Astra.

Atalanta or **Atalante** the name of a mythological character who agreed to marry the man who could outrun her (*Greek*). A variant form is Atlanta.

Atalya a feminine first name meaning 'guardian' (*Spanish*).

Athanasius a masculine first name meaning 'immortal' (*Greek*). St Athanasius of Alexandria (*c.*295–373) was one of the Doctors of the Roman Catholic Church.

Athena or **Ahthene** or **Athenée** a feminine first name from that of the goddess of wisdom in Greek mythology. Her Roman counterpart is MINERVA (*Greek*).

Atherton a surname, meaning 'noble army's place' (*Old English*), used as a masculine first name.

Athol or **Athole** or **Atholl** a place name in the Perthshire district that is now used as a masculine first name. It comes from *ath*, 'ford' (*Scottish Gaelic*) and Fotla, the name of one of the seven sons of the legendary founder of the Picts, Cruithne.

Athracht (pronounced *ath-rach*) a feminine first name from *athrach*, 'change' (*Irish Gaelic*), perhaps describing the change of life from that of an aristocratic girl to that of a female hermit. It was the name of a sixth-century Irish saint.

Atlanta a feminine variant form of ATALANTA.

Atlee or **Atley** or **Atley** a surname, meaning 'at the wood or clearing' (*Old English*), used as a masculine first name.

Atwater or **Atwatter** a surname, meaning 'by the water' (*Old English*), used as a masculine first name.

Atwell a surname, meaning 'at the spring or well of' (*Old English*), used as a masculine first name.

Auberon a masculine first name meaning 'noble bear' (*Germanic*). A variant form is OBERON. A diminutive form is Bron.

Aubin a surname, meaning 'blond one' (*French*), used as a masculine first name.

Aubina a feminine variant form of ALBINA.

Aubrey a masculine first name meaning 'ruler of spirits' (*Germanic*).

Aude (pronounced *awd-a*) (1) a Cornish feminine first name. In the French *Chanson de Roland*, Aude is a Breton princess betrothed to Roland. When Charlemagne wished instead to wed her to his son, she fell dead. (2) the name also exists in Old Norse: Aude 'the Deep-Minded' was the founder of a colony on Iceland in the eleventh century.

Audrey a feminine first name meaning 'noble might' (*Old English*). William Shakespeare (1564–1616) used the name for the character of a country wench in his comedy *As You Like It*.

August (1) the Polish and German masculine form of AUGUSTUS. (2) the eighth month of the year, named after the Roman emperor AUGUSTUS, used as a masculine first name.

Augusta feminine form of AUGUSTUS. Diminutive forms are Gussie, Gusta.

Auguste the French masculine form of AUGUSTUS.

Augustin the German and French masculine forms of AUGUSTINE.

Augustine a masculine first name meaning 'belonging to AUGUSTUS' (*Lat-*

in). A diminutive form is Gus. As the first archbishop of Canterbury, St Augustine (died 604) had great prestige in Britain; it is he rather than St Augustine of Hippo (354–430), one of the Doctors of the Roman Catholic Church, who is commemorated.

Augustus a masculine first name meaning 'exalted; imperial' (*Latin*). It was adopted by Octavius Caesar as his imperial name when he became the first emperor of Rome (27 BC). A diminutive form is Gus.

Aulay a Scottish masculine first name. The Gaelic form is Amalghaidh, a version of Old Norse Olaf. The MacAulay clan claims a Viking origin.

Aura or **Aure** or **Aurea** a feminine first name meaning 'breath of air' (*Latin*). A variant form is Auria.

Aurelia feminine form of AURELIUS.

Aurelius a masculine first name meaning 'golden' (*Latin*).

Auria a feminine variant form of AURA.

Aurora a feminine first name meaning 'morning redness; fresh; brilliant' (*Latin*).

Austell (pronounced *oss-tell*) a Cornish or Breton masculine first name from a saint's name of uncertain origin but perhaps linked with the place name Aust on the Bristol Channel. It is preserved in St Austell in Cornwall and Llanawastl in Wales.

Austin a masculine contraction of AUGUSTINE.

Autumn the name of the season, the origin of which is uncertain, used as a feminine first name.

Ava a feminine first name the origin of which is uncertain, perhaps a Germanic diminutive of names beginning Av-. Ava Gardner (1922–90) was a famous American film star.

Aveline a Norman French feminine first name, the Latin form of which, EVALINA, was used by the English writer Fanny Burney (1752–1840) for the heroine of her eponymous first novel. It evolved into EVELYN and the Irish and Scottish form is AIBHLINN.

Avera or **Averah** a feminine first name meaning 'transgressor' (*Hebrew*). A variant form is Aberah.

Averil or **Averill** a feminine English form of AVRIL.

Avery a surname, derived from ALFRED (*Old English*), used as a masculine first name.

Avice or **Avis** a feminine first name meaning possibly 'bird' (*Latin*).

Avril the French feminine form of APRIL.

Awsten (pronounced *ow-sten*) the Welsh masculine form of Augustine.

Axel a masculine first name meaning 'father of peace' (*Germanic*).

Axton a masculine first name meaning 'stone of the sword fighter' (*Old English*).

Ayisah a feminine variant form of Aisha.

Aylmer a surname, meaning 'noble and famous' (*Old English*), used as a masculine first name.

Aylward a surname, meaning 'noble guardian' (*Old English*), used as a masculine first name.

Aysha or **Ayshia** a feminine variant form of Aisha.

Azaliea or **Azalia** or **Azalee** feminine variant forms of the name of the azalea plant, supposed to prefer dry earth, used as a feminine first name.

Azaria feminine form of Azarias.

Azarias a masculine first name meaning 'helped by God' (*Hebrew*).

Azim a masculine first name meaning 'determined' (*Arabic*).

Azima or **Azimah** the feminine form of Azim.

Azura or **Azure** a feminine first name meaning 'blue as the sky' (*French*).

B

Bab or **Babs** feminine diminutive forms of BARBARA.

Baibín (pronounced *ba-been*) an Irish Gaelic feminine form of BARBARA. Báirbre is a variant form.

Bailey or **Baillie** a surname, meaning 'bailiff or steward' (*Old French*), used as a masculine first name and occasionally as a feminine name. A variant form is Bayley.

Bainbridge a surname, meaning 'bridge over a short river' (*Old English*), used as a masculine first name.

Báirbre a feminine variant form of BAIBÍN.

Baird a Scottish surname, meaning 'minstrel or bard', used as a masculine first name. A variant form is Bard.

Bala a masculine or feminine first name meaning 'infant' (*Sanskrit*).

Baldemar a masculine first name meaning 'bold and famous prince' (*Germanic*).

Baldovin the Italian masculine form of BALDWIN.

Baldric or **Baldrick** a surname, meaning 'princely or bold ruler' (*Germanic*), used as a masculine first name. A variant form is Baudric.

Baldwin a masculine first name meaning 'bold friend' (*Germanic*).

Balfour a surname from a Scottish place name, meaning 'village with pasture' (*Gaelic*), used as a masculine first name.

Ballard a surname, meaning 'bald' (*Old English*, *Old French*), used as a masculine first name.

Balor an Irish Gaelic masculine first name. Balor of the Evil Eye was a king of the Fomorians, early invaders of Ireland, whose baleful eye was never opened except on the field of battle, where it rendered his enemies powerless.

Balthasar or **Balthazar** a masculine first name meaning 'Baal defend the king' (*Babylonian*). In the Bible Balthasar was one of the Magi, the three wise men from the east who paid homage to the infant Jesus, presenting him with gifts. William Shakespeare (1564–1616) used the name for characters in four of his plays, including that of an attendant on Don Pedro in his comedy *Much Ado About Nothing.*

Balu a masculine first name meaning 'young' (*Sanskrit*).

Bambi a variant form of the word for *bambino*, 'child' (*Italian*) used as a feminine first name.

Banba or **Banbha** an Irish Gaelic feminine first name. This very ancient name can also refer to the land of Ireland itself; the original Banba came to be seen as a tutelary goddess of Ireland. *See also* ERIN.

Bancroft a surname, meaning 'bean place' (*Old English*), used as a masculine first name.

Banquo a masculine first name that comes from *ban*, 'white', and *cú*, 'hound' (*Scottish Gaelic*), suggesting a nickname origin. The name is familiar from the character that William Shakespeare (1564–1616) created in his play *Macbeth* for Macbeth's one-time comrade.

Baptist a masculine first name meaning 'a baptiser, purifier' (*Greek*).

Baptista feminine form of BAPTIST.

Baptiste a French masculine form of BAPTIST.

Barbara a feminine first name meaning 'foreign, strange' (*Greek*). The popularity of the story of St Barbara, killed about AD 200 by her father for refusing to renounce Christianity, spread the name. Barbara Hershey is an American film actress. A variant form is BARBRA. Diminutive forms are Bab, Babs, Barb, Barbie.

Barbe a Breton feminine first name and that of a mythical saint who is nevertheless venerated in Brittany, probably as a legacy from an earlier Celtic fire goddess in a similar mode to BRIDGET.

Barbie a feminine diminutive form of BARBARA. It has gained currency by the development of the well-known Barbie doll.

Barbra a feminine variant form of BARBARA that has been popularised by the American singer and actress Barbra Streisand.

Barclay a surname, meaning 'birch wood' (*Old English*), used as a masculine first name. Variant forms are Berkeley, Berkley.

Bard (1) a masculine variant form of BAIRD or BARDOLPH. (3) a masculine or feminine first name from the word for 'poet' or 'singer' in all the Celtic languages. This was an honoured profession in all Celtic communities. *See also* TADG.

Bardolph or **Bardolf** a masculine first name meaning 'bright wolf' (*G manic*). A diminutive form is Bard.

Barlow a surname, meaning 'barley hill' or 'barley clearing' (*Old English*), used as a masculine first name.

Barnaby or **Barnabas** a masculine first name meaning 'son of consolation and exhortation' (*Hebrew*). A diminutive form is Barney. In the New Testament Barnabas who took part with Paul in missionary activity.

Barnard a masculine variant form of BERNARD. A diminutive form is Barney.

Barnet or **Barnett** a surname, meaning 'land cleared by burning' (*Old English*), used as a masculine first name.

Barney a masculine diminutive form of BARNABY, BARNARD or BERNARD.

Barnum a surname, meaning 'homestead of a warrior' (*Old English*), used as a masculine first name.

Baron the lowest rank of the peerage used as a masculine first name. A variant form is Barron.

Barr a masculine first name meaning 'crest', 'top', perhaps signifying 'supreme' (*Scottish Gaelic*). St Barr is the same person as St Finbarr of Cork; his name is preserved in that of the Scottish island of Barra.

Barratt or **Barrett** a surname, meaning 'commerce' or 'trouble' or 'strife' (*Old French*), used as a masculine first name.

Barrfind (pronounced *barr-finn*) a masculine first name meaning 'fair-haired', 'fair-crested'. The name is a turned-about form of FINBARR.

Barrie a surname, which may have come from a Norman immigrant who gave his name to Barry in Angus but has also been traced back to *bearrach*, 'spear' (*Scottish Gaelic*), used as a masculine first name. The variant form is Barry.

Barron a masculine variant form of BARON.

Barry the masculine variant form of BARRIE. Barry Levinson is an American film director.

Bart a masculine diminutive form of BARTHOLOMEW, BARTLEY, BARTON, BARTRAM.

Barthold a variant form of BERTHOLD.

Bartholomew a masculine first name meaning 'a warlike son' (*Hebrew*). Bartholomew was one of Christ's Apostles. Diminutive forms are Bart, Bat.

Bartley a surname, meaning 'a birch wood or clearing' (*Old English*), used as a masculine first name. A diminutive form is Bart.

Barton the surname, meaning 'farm or farmyard' (*Old English*), used as a masculine first name. A diminutive form is Bart.

Bartram a masculine variant form of BERTRAM.

Barzillai a masculine first name meaning 'man of iron' (*Hebrew*).

Basil a masculine first name meaning 'kingly, royal' (*Greek*). St Basil the Great of Caesarea (329–379) was one of the Doctors of the Roman Catholic Church.

Basile the French masculine form of BASIL.

Basilia feminine form of BASIL.

Basilio the Italian and Spanish masculine form of BASIL.

Bat a masculine diminutive form of BARTHOLOMEW.

Bathilda a feminine first name meaning 'battle commander' (*Germanic*).

Bathilde the French feminine form of BATHILDA.

Bathsheba a feminine first name meaning 'daughter of plenty' (*Hebrew*). In the Old Testament Bathsheba was the wife of Uriah. She committed adultery with David and later married him. She was the mother of Solomon and Jedidiah. Thomas Hardy (1840–1928) used the name for Bathsheba Everdene, the heroine of his novel *Far from the Madding Crowd* (1874).

Batiste the French masculine form of BAPTIST.

Battista the Italian masculine form of BAPTIST.

Baudouin the French masculine form of BALDWIN.

Baudric a masculine variant form of BALDRIC.

Bautista the Spanish masculine form of BAPTIST.

Baxter a surname, meaning 'baker' (*Old English*), used as a masculine first name.

Bayley a masculine variant form of BAILEY.

Bea a feminine diminutive form of BEATRICE, BEATRIX.

Beal or **Beale** or **Beall** a surname variant form of BEAU (*French*) used as a masculine first name.

Beaman (1) a masculine first name meaning 'bee keeper' (*Old English*). (2) a variant form of BEAUMONT (*French*).

Beara (pronounced *bay-ara*) an Irish Gaelic feminine first name, that of a legendary Irish princess.

Bearrach a feminine variant form of BERRACH.

Beata a feminine first name meaning 'blessed, divine one' (*Latin*). A diminutive form is Bea.

Beatha (pronounced *bay-ha*) a feminine first name, probably from *beatha*, 'life' (*Irish Gaelic*). A variant form is Bethan. In old Scotland this was also a male name: Macbeth, eleventh-century king of Scots, means literally 'son of life'.

Beathag a feminine variant form of BETHÓC.

Beatie a feminine diminutive form of BEATRICE.

Beatrice or **Beatrix** a feminine first name meaning 'woman who blesses' (*Latin*). William Shakespeare (1564–1616) used the name for the heroine of his comedy *Much Ado About Nothing*. Diminutive forms are Bea, Beatie, Beaty, Bee, Trix, Trixie. The Welsh form is Betrys.

Beaty a feminine diminutive form of BEATRICE.

Beau (1) a masculine first name meaning 'handsome' (*French*). (2) a diminutive form of BEAUFORT, BEAUMONT. Beau Bridges is an American actor and son of Lloyd Bridges.

Beaufort a surname, meaning 'beautiful stronghold' (*French*), used as a masculine first name. A diminutive form is Beau.

Beaumont a surname, meaning 'beautiful hill' (*French*), used as a masculine first name. A diminutive form is Beau.

Beavan or **Beaven** masculine variant forms of BEVAN.

Bébhionn a feminine variant form of BÉIBHINN.

Bec or **Becca** (1) a feminine first name meaning 'little one', from *beag*, 'little' (*Irish Gaelic*). Bec was a goddess of wisdom. (2) a feminine diminutive of REBECCA.

Beckie or **Becky** feminine diminutive forms of REBECCA.

Becuma an Irish Gaelic feminine first name, from that of the wife of Conn of the Hundred Battles. Becuma loved the king's son, Art, but married Conn for his power.

Beda a feminine first name meaning 'maid of war' (*Old English*).

Bedivere the anglicised masculine form of BEDWYR.

Bedwyr (pronounced *bedd-uwir*) a Welsh masculine first name from that of the knight who was with King Arthur at his death, in the Round Table story of Celtic legend. Its anglicised form is Bedivere.

Bee a feminine diminutive form of BEATRICE.

Béfind a feminine variant form of BÉIBHINN.

Béibhinn (pronounced *bay-vin*) a feminine first name meaning 'fair woman' (*Irish Gaelic*). Related Gaelic forms are Béfind, Bébhionn. This name is found in numerous Gaelic love poems and was also the name of the mother of king Brian Boruma. In an anglicised form as Bevin or Bevan, it has been used as a boy's name. In the form Bhéibhinn, the first sound is 'v' and it has been confused with the unrelated Vivien/Vivian, a Norman-French name from Latin *vivere*, 'to live'.

Bel a masculine variant form of BELENUS.

Belenus or **Belenos** a Gaulish masculine first name, perhaps from a Celtic root word meaning 'bright'. This was the name of one of the chief gods of the pre-Christian Celts. It is found in other forms such as Bel, Belus.

Belinda a feminine first name used by the English architect and dramatist Sir John Vanbrugh (1664–1726) in his play *The Provok'd Wife* (1697). Its origin is uncertain, possibly 'beautiful woman' (*Italian*).

Bella or **Belle** (1) a feminine first name meaning 'beautiful' (*French, Italian*). (2) the feminine diminutive suffix of ANNABELLA, ARABELLA, ISABELLA used as a name in its own right.

Bellamy a surname, meaning 'handsome friend' (*Old French*), used as a masculine first name.

Belus a masculine variant form of BELENUS.

Ben a diminutive form of BENEDICT, BENJAMIN, also used independently as a masculine first name.

Bena a feminine first name meaning 'wise one' (*Hebrew*).

Benedetto the Italian masculine form of BENEDICT.

Benedict or **Benedick** a masculine first name meaning 'blessed' (*Latin*). Benedict was the name adopted by many popes as well as of St Benedict (480–546) who founded the Benedictine monastic order. William Shakespeare (1564–1616) used the form Benedick for the hero of his comedy *Much Ado About Nothing*. A variant form is Bennet. Diminutive forms are Ben, Bennie, Benny.

Benedicta a feminine form of BENEDICT, a contracted form of which is Benita. A diminutive form is Dixie.

Benedikt the German masculine form of BENEDICT.

Benita (1) feminine form of BENITO. (2) a contracted form of BENEDICTA.

Benito a Spanish masculine form of BENEDICT.

Benjamin a masculine first name meaning 'son of the right hand' (*Hebrew*). In the Old Testament he was the youngest son of Jacob and Rachel and patriarch of one of the Twelve Tribes of Israel. Diminutive forms are Ben, Benjie, Bennie, Benny.

Benji or **Benjie** a masculine diminutive form of BENJAMIN.

Bennet a masculine variant form of BENEDICT.

Bennie or **Benny** a masculine diminutive form of BENEDICT, BENJAMIN.

Benoît the French masculine form of BENEDICT.

Benson a surname, meaning 'son of BEN', used as a masculine first name.

Bentley a surname from a Yorkshire place name, meaning 'woodland clearing where bent-grass grows' (*Old English*), used as a masculine first name.

Beppe or **Beppo** a diminutive form of GIUSEPPE, occasionally used independently as a masculine first name.

Berchan a Scottish Gaelic masculine first name and that of a tenth-century holy man who compiled a 'Prophecy' or history of the kingdom of the Picts and Scots.

Berc'hed the Breton feminine form of BRIDGET.

Berenice a feminine first name meaning 'bringing victory' (*Greek*). A variant form is Bernice. A diminutive form is Bunny.

Beriana a feminine variant form of BURYAN.

Berkeley or **Berkley** masculine variant forms of BARCLAY.

Bernadette feminine form of BERNARD. St Bernadette of Lourdes (1844–79) was a French peasant girl who saw a vision of the Virgin Mary telling her of a fresh water spring below the ground. The site in Lourdes is now a place of pilgrimage.

Bernard a masculine first name meaning 'strong or hardy bear' (*Germanic*). St Bernard of Clairvaux (1091–1153) was one of the Doctors of the Roman Catholic Church. A variant form is Barnard. Diminutive forms are Barney, Bernie.

Bernardin a French masculine form of BERNARD.

Bernardino an Italian masculine diminutive form of BERNARD.

Bernardo a Spanish and Italian masculine form of BERNARD. William Shakespeare (1564–1616) used the name for a minor character in his tragedy *Hamlet*. Bernardo Bertolucci is an Italian film director.

Bernhard or **Bernhardt** a German masculine form of BERNARD.

Bernice a feminine variant form of BERENICE. In the New Testament Bernice was a daughter of King Herod Agrippa I and sister of Drusilla. Bernice Rubens is an English novelist who won the Booker Prize in 1970 for her fourth novel.

Bernie a masculine diminutive form of BERNARD.

Berrach an Irish Gaelic feminine first name, the source of which is uncertain. In Celtic mythology, Berrach Breac, 'the freckled', third wife of Fionn macCumhaill, was said to be the most generous woman in Ireland. A variant form is Bearrach.

Bert masculine diminutive forms of ALBERT, BERTRAM, EGBERT, GILBERT, HUBERT, etc.

Berta a German, Italian and Spanish feminine form of BERTHA.

Bertha a feminine first name meaning 'bright; beautiful; famous' (*Germanic*). A diminutive form is Bertie.

Berthe the French feminine form of BERTHA.

Berthilda or **Berthilde** or **Bertilda** or **Bertilde** a feminine first name meaning 'shining maid of war' (*Old English*).

Berthold a masculine first name meaning 'bright ruler' (*Germanic*). Variant forms are Barthold, Bertold, Berthoud. Diminutive forms are Bert, Bertie.

Bertie (1) masculine diminutive forms of ALBERT, BERTRAM, EGBERT, GILBERT, HERBERT, etc. (2) a feminine diminutive form of BERTHA.

Bertold or **Berthoud** masculine variant forms of BERTHOLD.

Bertram a masculine first name meaning 'bright; fair; illustrious' (*Germanic*). William Shakespeare (1564–1616) used the name for one of the main characters in his comedy *All's Well That Ends Well*. A variant form is Bartram. Diminutive forms are Bert, Bertie.

Bertrand the French masculine form of BERTRAM. Bertrand Tavernier is a French film director.

Berwyn a Cornish and Welsh masculine first name. Berwyn was an early Celtic saint whose name is preserved in the Berwyn Range of mountains in North Wales and in Merioneth.

Beryl a feminine first name meaning 'jewel' (*Greek*), the name of the gemstone used as a feminine first name.

Bess or **Bessie** feminine diminutive forms of ELIZABETH.

Bet a feminine diminutive form of ELIZABETH.

Beth a feminine diminutive form of ELIZABETH, BETHANY, now used independently.

Bethan (1) (pronounced *bay-han*) a feminine first name, probably from *beatha*, 'life' (*Irish Gaelic*). A variant form is Beatha. In old Scotland this was also a male name: Macbeth, eleventh-century king of Scots, means literally 'son of life'. (2) a Welsh feminine diminutive form of ELIZABETH or ELIZABETH-ANN, also often used as a name in its own right.

Bethany a place name near Jerusalem, the home of Lazarus in the New Testament and meaning 'house of poverty', used as a feminine first name (*Aramaic*).

Bethóc (pronounced *bay-ock*) a feminine first name that is related to Bethan, from beatha, 'life' (*Scottish Gaelic*). It was the name of the daughter of Somerled, Lord of Argyll. A variant form is Beathag.

Betrys the Welsh feminine form of BEATRICE.

Betsy or **Bette** or **Bettina** or **Betty** feminine diminutive forms of ELIZA-BETH. Bette Davis (1908–89) was a famous American film actress of the 1930s onwards. Bette Midler is an American singer and film actress.

Beulah a feminine first name meaning 'married' (*Hebrew*).

Beuno (pronounced *by-no*) a Welsh masculine first name, that of a seventh-century Welsh saint whose name is preserved in St Beuno's Well, the subject of a poem by the English poet and Jesuit priest Gerald Manley Hopkins (1844–89).

Bev a feminine diminutive form of BEVERLEY.

Bevan (1) an anglicised form of Béibhinn used as a masculine first name. (2) a surname, meaning 'son of EVAN' (*Welsh*), used as a masculine first name. Variant forms are Beavan, Beaven, Bevin.

Beverley or **Beverly** a place name, meaning 'beaver stream' (*Old English*), used as a masculine or feminine first name. Beverley Nichols was an English journalist. Beverly d'Angelo is an American film actress. A diminutive form is Bev.

Bevin (1) a surname, meaning 'drink wine', used as a masculine first name. (2) a variant form of BEVAN.

Bevis a masculine first name meaning 'bull' (*French*). Bevis of Hampton was a hero of English medieval romance.

Beynon a masculine first name meaning 'son of Einion' (*Welsh*).

Bharat a masculine first name meaning 'being maintained' (*Sanskrit*) and the Hindu name for India.

Bharati the feminine form of BHARAT.

Bhaskar a masculine first name meaning 'sun' (*Sanskrit*).

Bhéibhinn (pronounced *vay-vin*) a feminine variant form of BÉIBHINN.

Bianca the Italian feminine form of BLANCH, now also used independently as an English-language form, inspired by Bianca Jagger, the Nicaraguan-born first wife of the pop singer Mick Jagger. William Shakespeare (1564–1616) used the name for a courtesan in his tragedy *Othello* and the sister of the heroine in *The Taming of the Shrew*. The name was also used for one of the main characters in the popular television soap opera *Eastenders*.

Biddy or **Biddie** a feminine diminutive form of BRIDGET.

Bije a masculine diminutive form of ABIJAH.

Bile (pronounced *bee-la*) a masculine first name meaning 'noble warrior' (*Irish Gaelic/Pictish*). In Irish legend, Bile was a leader of the Milesians, one of the early invading groups. In Scotland he was the father of the Pictish king Bridei, whom St Columba visited.

Bill a masculine diminutive form of WILLIAM.

Billie (1) a masculine diminutive form of WILLIAM. (2) a feminine diminutive form of WILHELMINA.

Billy a masculine diminutive form of WILLIAM.

Bina or **Binah** or **Bine** a feminine first name meaning 'bee' (*Hebrew*).

Bing a surname, meaning 'a hollow' (*Germanic*), used as a masculine first name.

Binnie a feminine diminutive form of SABINA.

Birch a surname, from the birch tree (*Old English*), used as a masculine first name. A variant form is Birk.

Birgit or **Birgitta** the Swedish feminine form of BRIDGET. A diminutive form is BRITT.

Birk a masculine variant form of BIRCH.

Bishop a surname, meaning 'one who worked in a bishop's household' (*Old English*), used as a masculine first name.

Bjork an Icelandic feminine first name made famous by the popularity of the Icelandic pop singer Bjork Gudmunsdottir.

Björn a masculine first name meaning 'bear' (*Old Norse*). Björn Borg is a Swedish tennis champion.

Black a surname, meaning 'dark-complexioned' or 'dark-haired' (*Old English*), used as a masculine first name. A variant form is BLAKE.

Bladud a Brythonic Celtic masculine first name from that of a mythical king from old British tales, allegedly founder of the city of Bath and father of King Lear.

Blair a place name and surname, from *blár*, meaning 'a field', 'battleground' (*Scottish Gaelic*), used as a masculine first name.

Blaise a Breton and Cornish masculine first name that may derive from *blas*, 'taste' (*Breton*). It is preserved in St Blazey in Cornwall, and in

France was the name of the religious philosopher Blaise Pascal (1623–62). A variant form is BLEISE, in Celtic legend the tutor of the magician Myrddyn, 'Merlin'.

Bláithin (pronounced *bla-hin*) a feminine first name meaning 'flower', 'blossom', from *bláth*, 'flower' (*Irish Gaelic*). A name of the same meaning is BLÁTHNAT. *See also* BLODWEN.

Blake a variant form of Black; alternatively, 'pale' or 'fair-complexioned' (*Old English*). Blake Edwards is an American film director and Blake Morrison is an English poet.

Blánaid a variant form of BLÁTHNAT.

Blanca the Spanish feminine form of BLANCH.

Blanch or **Blanche** a feminine first name meaning 'white' (*Germanic*). Blanch of Castille (*c*.1188–1252) was the daughter of Alfonso VIII, king of Castile, and Eleanor, daughter of Henry II of England, and the niece of King John. She married King Louis VIII of France and from her were descended the royal houses of Valois, Bourbon and Orleans as well as Edward III of England.

Blane an Irish and Scottish Gaelic masculine first name from that of St Bláan, whose name is preserved in Scottish towns such as Dunblane and Blanefield.

Blathnáid and **Bláthnaid** variant forms of BLÁTHNAT.

Bláthnat (pronounced *bla-na*) a feminine first name meaning 'little flower' (*Irish Gaelic*). Variant Gaelic forms are Blánaid, Bláthnaid and Bláthnaid. In Celtic mythology, she was the wife of the chieftain Cú Roí and betrayed him to his enemy Cuchulainn. She was killed by Ferchertne, his faithful bard, who clasped her to him and leapt from a clifftop.

Bleddyn (pronounced *bleth-in*) a masculine first name meaning 'wolf-like', from *blaidd*, 'wolf' (*Welsh*). Bleddyn ap Cynfryn was a prince in the eleventh century.

Bleise a masculine variant form of BLAISE. In Celtic legend Bleise was the tutor of the magician Myrddyn, 'Merlin'.

Bliss a surname, meaning 'happiness or joy', used as a feminine first name (*Old English*).

Blodeuedd (pronounced *blod-wedd*) a feminine first name meaning 'flower face' (*Welsh*). In Celtic mythology she was a beautiful woman created by the mages GWYDION and Math to be the wife of the hero Lleu

Llaw Gyffes but who betrays him and is ultimately turned into an owl; the story is in the Mabonogion cycle.

Blodwen a feminine first name meaning 'white flower', from *blodau*, 'flowers', *ven*, 'white' (*Welsh*).

Blossom a feminine first name meaning 'like a flower' (*Old English*). Blossom Dearie is an American singer.

Blyth or **Blythe** a surname, meaning 'cheerful and gentle', used as a masculine or feminine first name (*Old English*). Blythe Danner is an American actress and the mother of the actress Gwyneth Paltrow.

Boas or **Boaz** a masculine first name meaning 'fleetness' (*Hebrew*). In the Old Testament Boaz was a landowner of Bethlehem in Judah.

Bob or **Bobby** a masculine diminutive form of ROBERT.

Bobbie or **Bobby** a feminine diminutive form of ROBERTA, now used independently.

Boniface a masculine first name meaning 'doer of good' (*Latin*). St Boniface (672–745) was an English missionary in Germany. It was also the name adopted by several popes.

Bonita a feminine first name meaning 'pretty' (*Spanish*) or 'good' (*Latin*). A diminutive form is BONNIE.

Bonnie or **Bonny** (1) the Scots adjective *bonnie*, 'pretty', reimported from North America as a feminine first name. In the USA it was made famous or notorious by the girl gangster Bonnie Parker. Bonnie Langford is an English actress. (2) a diminutive form of BONITA.

Booth a surname, meaning 'hut' or 'shed' (*Old Norse*), used as a masculine first name.

Boris a masculine first name meaning 'small' (*Russian*). Boris Karloff (1887–1969) was an English-born film actor known for his roles in horror films. Boris Johnson is an English journalist.

Botolf or **Botolph** a masculine first name meaning 'herald wolf' (*Old English*).

Bourn or **Bourne** masculine variant forms of BURN.

Bowen a surname, meaning 'son of OWEN' (*Welsh*), used as a masculine first name.

Bowie a surname, meaning 'yellow-haired' (*Scottish Gaelic*), used as a masculine first name.

Boyce a surname, meaning 'a wood' (*Old French*), used as a masculine first name.

Boyd a surname, meaning 'light-haired' (*Scots Gaelic*), used as a masculine first name.

Boyne the name of an Irish river, meaning 'white cow' (*Irish Gaelic*), used as a masculine first name.

Brad a masculine diminutive form of BRADLEY, now used independently. Brad Dourif and Brad Pitt are American film actors.

Bradford a place name and surname, meaning 'place at the broad ford' (*Old English*), used as a masculine first name.

Bradley a surname, meaning 'broad clearing' or 'broad wood' (*Old English*), used as a masculine first name. A diminutive form is Brad or Bradd.

Brady an Irish surname, of unknown meaning, used as a masculine first name.

Braham a surname, meaning 'house or meadow with broom bushes', used as a masculine first name.

Bram a masculine diminutive form of ABRAM, ABRAHAM.

Bramwell a surname, meaning 'from the bramble spring' (*Old English*), used as a masculine first name.

Bran a Celtic masculine first name meaning 'raven' or 'crow' (*Gaelic*), the name of a god who was believed to possess powers of life and death. The name occurs in legends of all the Celtic countries.

Brand a masculine first name meaning 'firebrand' (*Old English*).

Brandee or **Brandi** or **Brandie** a variant form of BRANDY.

Brandon (1) a surname, meaning 'broom-covered hill' (*Old English*), used as a masculine first name. (2) a variant form of BRENDAN.

Brandubh (pronounced *bran-doov*) a masculine first name meaning 'black raven' (*Irish /Scottish Gaelic*). It was a name borne by a number of provincial kings. An anglicised form is Branduff.

Branduff the anglicised masculine form of BRANDUBH.

Brandy the name of the alcoholic spirit distilled from grapes used as a feminine first name. A variant form is Brandee, Brandi, Brandie.

Brangaine (pronounced *bran-gy-ana*) an Irish Gaelic feminine form of BRONWEN. In legend, Brangaine was the nurse of Iseult who gave her and Trystan a love potion.

Branwen (1) a feminine first name meaning 'raven-haired beauty' (*Welsh*). (2) a variant form of BRONWEN.

Breanna or **Breanne** a variant form of BRIANA.

Bree a feminine diminutive form of BRIDGET.

Bregeen (pronounced *bregh-een*) an Irish feminine first name meaning 'little BRIDGET'.

Brenda a feminine first name, from *brandr*, meaning 'brand' or 'sword' (*Old Norse*). Brenda Blethyn is an English actress.

Brendan or **Brendon** a masculine first name perhaps derived originally from the Old Gaelic *bran*, 'raven', although a link with Welsh *brenhyn*, 'prince', has also been proposed. This was the name of the energetic and far-travelled St Brendan of Clonfert, 'Brendan the Navigator' (died AD 577), who, according to some, traversed the Atlantic in his coracle. An alternative form is BRANDON.

Brenna a feminine first name meaning 'raven-haired beauty' (*Irish Gaelic*).

Brent a surname, meaning 'a steep place' (*Old English*), used as a masculine first name.

Bret or **Brett** a masculine first name meaning 'a Breton', from Breizh, the Breton name for Brittany. Bret Harte (1836–1902) was an American writer who was for a time the American consul in Glasgow. It is also now used as a feminine first name; Brett Butler is an American comedienne.

Brewster a surname, meaning 'brewer' (*Old English*), used as a masculine first name.

Brian (pronounced *breye–an*, the Gaelic pronunciation is *bree-an*) a masculine first name, possibly Breton in origin, from a root-word *bri*, 'dignity, pride'. It gained great prestige from Brian Boruma, 'of the cattle taxes', high king of Ireland (*c.*941–1014), victor and victim of the Battle of Clontarf, at which Viking rule in Ireland was broken, and progenitor of the O'Briens. Variant forms are Brion and Bryan. The Belfast-born Canadian writer Brian Moore (1921–99) used the Gaelic pronunciation of the name.

Briana or **Brianna** (pronounced *bree-ana*) a feminine form of BRIAN. A variant form is Breanna or Breanne.

Brice a surname, from *ap-Rhys*, 'son of Rhys', 'the burning or ardent one' (*Welsh*), used as a first name. The fifth-century Gaulish St Brice or Bricius was bishop of Tours. A variant form is Bryce.

Bríd (pronounced *breeth*) the original Irish Gaelic form of BRIDGET.

Bride an anglicised form of BRÍD and variant form of BRIDGET. The name appears in Scotland as that of a sixth-century St Bride.

Bridei an original Pictish form of BRUDE.

Bridget a anglicised feminine first name from the Irish BRÍD, a name associated with *brígh*, 'power, virtue' (*Irish Gaelic*) and a name of power in the old Celtic world, when it belonged to a goddess. Assimilated into the Christian tradition, the goddess became a venerated saint; indeed there are sixteen or more St Bridgets, of whom the fifth-century St Bridget of Kildare is the best known. The name has numerous variant forms: Brigid and Brigit are the most frequent, with diminutive forms Biddy, Biddie, Bree (Ireland) and Bridie (Scotland). The Breton name Berc'hed is another form. For centuries it was the most popular girl's name in Ireland, as synonymous with an Irish girl as Patrick was with a boy.

Bridie a Scottish feminine diminutive form of BRIDGET.

Brieuc a Breton masculine variant form of BRIOC.

Brigham a surname, meaning 'homestead by a bridge' (*Old English*), used as a masculine first name. Brigham Young (1801–77). was an American Mormon leader who led the Mormon migration to Utah and founded Salt Lake City.

Brigid a feminine variant form of BRIDGET.

Brigide a Spanish, Italian and French feminine form of BRIDGET.

Brigit a feminine variant form of BRIDGET.

Brigitte a French feminine form of BRIDGET. Brigitte Bardot is a French film actress and animal rights campaigner.

Brioc a Welsh masculine first name and that of the sixth-century St Brioc who is also known in Brittany as St Brieuc.

Brion a masculine variant form of BRIAN.

Briony a feminine variant form of BRYONY.

Brisen (pronounced *bree-sen*) a Welsh feminine first name and the name of a witch from the Arthurian legends.

Britney a feminine first name popular in the USA. Possibly a contracted form of BRITTANY. Britney Spears is an American pop singer.

Britt a feminine diminutive form of BIRGIT, now used independently. Britt Eklund is a Swedish film actress.

Brittany the anglicised name of a French region, meaning 'land of the figured, or tattooed folk', used as a feminine first name.

Brochfael (pronounced *broch-file*) a Welsh masculine first name and that of a legendary king, mentioned in the songs of the minstrel Taliesin.

Brock a surname, meaning 'badger' (*Old English*), used as a masculine first name.

Broderic or **Broderick** a surname, meaning 'son of RODERICK' (*Welsh*), used as a masculine first name. Broderick Crawford (1911–86) was a noted American film actor.

Brodie or **Brody** a surname, meaning 'ditch' (*Scots Gaelic*), used as a masculine first name.

Brógán (pronounced *broh-gawn*) an Irish Gaelic masculine first name of uncertain derivation, this was the name of a number of early holy men, including St Brógán who acted as a scribe for St Patrick.

Bron a masculine diminutive form of AUBERON, OBERON.

Brona and **Bronach** variant feminine forms of BRÓNAGH.

Brónagh (pronounced *broh-na*) a feminine first name meaning 'sorrowing', from *brónach*, 'sorrowful' (*Irish Gaelic*). A Celtic equivalent of the name Dolores. Variant forms are Brona, Bronach.

Brongwyn a feminine variant form of BRONWEN.

Bronwen a feminine first name meaning 'white-breast' from *bron*, 'breast', *ven*, 'white' (*Welsh*). Variant forms are Brongwyn, Bronwyn and Branwen. *See also* BRANGAINE.

Bronwyn a feminine variant form of BRONWEN.

Brook or **Brooke** a surname, meaning 'stream', used as a masculine or feminine first name. Brooke Shields is an American actress. A variant form is Brooks.

Brooklyn the name of an area of New York City used as a masculine or feminine first name.

Brooklynn or **Brooklynne** a feminine form of Brooklyn.

Brooks a variant masculine or feminine form of BROOK.

Bruce a surname from Bruis or Brux in Normandy used as a masculine first name. The founder of the family came from Normandy with William the Conqueror; a descendant in Scotland was granted a lordship by King David I. It became a popular first name from the nineteenth century, especially in Australia. Bruce Lee (1940–73) was an American actor and kung fu expert.

Brude the anglicised masculine form of the Pictish Bruide or Bridei, who was the king of the Picts whom St Columba visted in AD 565.

Bruide one of the original Pictish forms of BRUDE.

Brunella feminine form of BRUNO.

Brunhilda or **Brunhilde** a feminine first name meaning 'warrior maid' (*Germanic*).

Bruno a masculine first name meaning 'brown' (*Germanic*). St Bruno (*c.*1032–1101) was the founder of the Carthusian monastic order. Bruno Kirby is an American film actor.

Bryan a masculine variant form of BRIAN. Bryan Brown is an Australian film actor.

Bryce a masculine variant form of BRICE.

Brychan (pronounced *bree-chan*) a masculine first name meaning 'freckled one' (*Welsh*). It was the name of a fifth-century chief whose name is preserved in Brecon and Castell Brychan, Aberystwyth.

Bryn (pronounced *brinn*) a masculine first name meaning 'hill' (*Welsh*). It is not connected with the name Brian.

Brynmawr a masculine variant form of BRYNMOR.

Brynmor a masculine first name from *bryn*, 'hill', and *mor*, 'great' (*Welsh*). A variant form is Brynmawr.

Bryony the name of a climbing plant used as a feminine first name (*Greek*). A variant form is Briony.

Buan (pronounced *bwan*) a masculine or feminine first name meaning 'lasting', 'enduring' (*Irish Gaelic*).

Buck a masculine first name meaning 'stag; he-goat; a lively young man' (*Old English*).

Buckley a surname, meaning 'stag or he-goat meadow' (*Old English*), used as a masculine first name.

Budd or **Buddy** the informal term for a friend or brother used as a masculine first name.

Buddug the Welsh masculine form of BUDOC.

Budoc a Cornish masculine first name that has the same form as Boudicca and is probably from the same root, *buad*, 'victory'. It is the name of the patron saint of Cornwall; his name is preserved in St Budeaux. The Welsh name Buddug is cognate with Budoc.

Buena a feminine first name meaning 'good' (*Spanish*).

Bunny a feminine diminutive form of BERENICE.

Bunty a feminine diminutive meaning 'lamb', now used as a feminine first name.

Buona a feminine first name meaning 'good' (*Italian*).

Burchard a masculine variant form of BURKHARD.

Burdon a surname, meaning 'castle on a hill or valley with a cowshed' (*Old English*), used as a masculine first name.

Burford a surname, meaning 'ford by a castle' (*Old English*), used as a masculine first name.

Burgess a surname, meaning 'citizen or inhabitant of a borough' (*Old French*), used as a masculine first name.

Burhan a masculine first name meaning 'proof' (*Arabic*).

Burk or **Burke** a surname, meaning 'fort or manor' (*Old French*), used as a masculine first name.

Burkhard a masculine first name meaning 'strong as a castle' (*Germanic*). A variant form is Burchard.

Burl a masculine first name meaning 'cup bearer' (*Old English*). Burl Ives is an American folksinger and actor.

Burleigh or **Burley** a masculine first name meaning 'dweller in the castle by the meadow' (*Old English*).

Burn or **Burne** a surname, meaning 'brook or stream' (*Old English*), used as a masculine first name. Variant forms are Bourn, Bourne, Byrne.

Burnett a surname, meaning 'brown-complexioned' or 'brown-haired' (*Old French*), used as a masculine first name.

Burt a masculine diminutive form of BURTON, now used independently. Burt Reynolds is an American film actor.

Burton a surname, meaning 'farmstead of a fortified place' (*Old English*), used as a masculine first name. A diminutive form is BURT.

Buryan a Cornish feminine first name meaning 'gift', probably related to Gaelic *beir*, 'gift'. Buryan or BERIANA was a Cornish saint. The name Veryan is probably from the same source.

Buster an informal term of address for a boy or young man, now used as a masculine first name. Buster Keaton (1895–1966) was a famous American silent film comedy actor.

Byrne a masculine variant form of BURN.

Byron a surname, meaning 'at the cowsheds' (*Old English*), used as a masculine first name.

C

Cabhán (pronounced *ca-vann*) the original Irish Gaelic form of CAVAN. It is a name similar in sound to Caoimhín (KEVIN) but unrelated.

Cadan (pronounced *cad-an*) a masculine first name meaning 'wild goose' (*Irish Gaelic*). It was the name of a mythical hero of early legend.

Caddick or **Caddock** a surname, meaning 'decrepit' (*Old French*), used as a masculine first name.

Caddie or **Caddy** a feminine diminutive form of CAROL, CAROLA, CAROLE, CAROLINE, CAROLYN.

Cadell a masculine first name, meaning 'battle spirit', from *cad*, 'battle' (*Welsh*). It was a warrior's name.

Cadence a feminine first name meaning 'rhythmic' (*Latin*).

Cadenza the Italian feminine form of CADENCE.

Cadfael (pronounced *cad-file*) a masculine first name meaning 'battle prince' (*Welsh*). The name has been made famous by the Brother Cadfael stories by Ellis Peters.

Cadmus a masculine first name meaning 'man from the east' (*Greek*). In Greek mythology, he was a Phoenician prince who founded Thebes with five warriors he had created.

Cadog or **Cadoc** a masculine first name from *cad*, 'battle' (*Welsh*). It was used as a warrior's name, but the most famous Cadog (505–570) was a saint whose name is preserved in places such as Llangattock.

Cadogan the anglicised masculine form of CADWGAN.

Cadwaladr a masculine first name meaning 'leader in battle', from *cad*, 'battle'; *gwaladr*, 'leader' (*Welsh*). It was the name of legendary heroes and of the sixth-century prince of Gwynedd, Cadwaladr Fendigaid, 'blessed', who died in Rome in the later seventh century. It is also found in the anglicised form of Cadwallader.

Cadwallader the anglicised masculine form of CADWALADR.

Cadwallon a masculine first name, from *cad*, 'battle', and *gallon*, 'scatterer', 'ruler' (*Welsh*).

Cadwgan (pronounced *cad-o-gan*) a masculine first name deriving from *cad*, 'battle' (*Welsh*). Cadwgan was a tenth-century Welsh chieftain associated with Glamorgan, where there is a hill called Moel Cadwgan. The anglicised form is Cadogan.

Cáel (pronounced *kyle*) a masculine first one meaning 'slender one' (*Irish Gaelic*). In Celtic mythology, he was a hero of the Fianna and lover of Créd.

Cáelfind (pronounced *kyle-finn*) a feminine first name meaning 'slender and fair', from *caol*, 'slender' and *fionn*, 'fair' (*Irish Gaelic*). A variant Gaelic form is CAOILAINN. This name was borne by a number of holy women. The anglicised form is Keelin, Keelan or Ceelin.

Caerwyn (pronounced *carr-win*) a masculine first name meaning 'white fort' (*Welsh*).

Caesar a masculine first name meaning 'long-haired' (*Latin*); the Roman title of 'emperor' used as a masculine first name.

Cahal a masculine variant form of CATHAL.

Cahir the anglicised masculine form of Irish Gaelic CATHAÍR.

Cai *see* CEI

Cailean the Scottish Gaelic masculine form of COLIN.

Cain a masculine first name meaning 'possession' (*Hebrew*). In the Bible it is the name of the first son of Adam and Eve, who killed his younger brother, Abel.

Cainche or **Caince** (pronounced *cann-hya*) a feminine first name meaning 'melody', 'songbird' (*Irish Gaelic*). In Celtic mythology, she was a daughter of FIONN macCumhaill, who bears a son to Fionn's enemy Goll macMorna.

Cairbre (pronounced *carr-bra*) a masculine first name that probably means 'charioteer' (*Irish Gaelic*). In Celtic mythology, the great warriors had their personal charioteers, who were not themselves fighting men. A frequent name in Old Irish sources, it is applied to a high king, Cairbre Lifechair, 'of the Liffey', in the tales of the Fenian Cycle.

Cairenn or **Caireann** (pronounced *carr-enn*) an Irish Gaelic feminine first name perhaps taken into the Celtic languages from the Latin *carina*, 'dear'. It was the name of the mother of the early Irish high king Niall of the Nine Hostages, founder of the Ui Neills. She was not the wife of Niall's father but a concubine, traditionally a slave from Britain. It is sometimes anglicised to Carina and Karen.

Cáit (pronounced *kawt*) a shortened Irish Gaelic feminine form of CAITLÍN.

Caitlín (pronounced *kawt-leen*) an Irish Gaelic feminine form of Norman-French Cateline, a form of Catherine. The anglicised version is Cathleen or Kathleen.

Caius a masculine first name meaning 'rejoice' (*Latin*). A variant form is GAIUS.

Cal (1) a feminine diminutive form of CALANDRA, CALANTHA. (2) a masculine diminutive form of CALUM, CALVIN.

Calandra a feminine first name meaning 'lark' (*Greek*). Diminutive forms are Cal, Callie, Cally.

Calandre the French feminine form of CALANDRA.

Calandria the Spanish feminine form of CALANDRA.

Calantha a feminine first name meaning 'beautiful blossom' (*Greek*). Diminutive forms are Cal, Callie, Cally.

Calanthe the French feminine form of CALANTHA.

Calder a masculine or feminine first name from a Scots Gaelic compound meaning 'stream by the hazels', a location name from several parts of Scotland that has become a surname and an occasional first name.

Caldwell a surname, meaning 'cold spring or stream' (*Old English*), used as a masculine first name.

Cale a masculine diminutive form of CALEB.

Caleb a masculine first name meaning 'a dog' (*Hebrew*). In the Old Testament Caleb was one of the spies dispatched by Moses to spy out Canaan. A diminutive form is Cale.

Caledonia the Roman name for Scotland (*Latin*) used as a feminine first name.

Caley (1) a masculine first name meaning 'thin, slender' (*Irish Gaelic*). (2) a diminutive form of CALUM.

Calgacus a masculine first name said to mean 'sword wielder' (*Latin*). It was the name given by the Roman historian Tacitus (AD *c*.55–*c*.120) to the the commander of the Caledonian tribes at the battle of Mons Graupius, AD 83 and is the oldest recorded name of an inhabitant of what is now Scotland.

Calhoun a surname, meaning 'from the forest' (*Irish Gaelic*), used as a masculine first name.

Calla a feminine first name meaning 'beautiful' (*Greek*).

Callan an anglicised masculine form of the Irish Gaelic CULANN.

Callie a feminine diminutive form of CALANDRA, CALANTHA.

Calliope a feminine first name meaning 'lovely voice' (*Greek*). In Greek mythology Calliope was the muse of poetry.

Callista feminine form of CALLISTO.

Callisto a masculine first name meaning 'most fair or good' (*Greek*).

Callum a masculine variant form of CALUM.

Cally (1) a feminine diminutive form of CALANDRA, CALANTHA. (2) a masculine diminutive form of CALUM.

Calum (1) the Scottish Gaelic masculine form of *columba*, the Latin word for 'dove'. (2) a diminutive form of MALCOLM. A variant form is Callum. Diminutive forms are Cal, Cally, Caley.

Calumina a feminine form of CALUM.

Calvert a surname, meaning 'calf herd' (*Old English*), used as a masculine first name.

Calvin a masculine first name meaning 'little bald one' (*Latin*). Calvin Klein is an American dress designer. A diminutive form is Cal.

Calvina a feminine form of CALVIN.

Calvino Italian and Spanish masculine forms of CALVIN.

Calypso a feminine first name meaning 'concealer' (*Greek*). In Greek mythology, Calypso was the name of the sea nymph who held Odysseus captive for seven years. A variant form is Kalypso.

Cameron a Scottish surname, from *cam*, 'hooked' and *sron*, 'nose' (*Scots Gaelic*), used as a masculine or feminine first name. Originally probably only given to boys whose mothers' maiden name was Cameron, it is now in general use and increasingly given to girls as well, the American actress Cameron Diaz being an example.

Camila the Spanish feminine form of CAMILLA.

Camilla a feminine first name meaning 'votaress, attendant at a sacrifice' (*Latin*).

Camille the French masculine and feminine form of CAMILLA.

Campbell (pronounced *cam-bell*) a Scottish surname, from *cam*, 'crooked', and *beul*, 'mouth' (*Scots Gaelic*) or from *champ*, 'field' and *bel*, 'beautiful' (*French*), used as a masculine first name. Its use as a first name probably began in the same way as Cameron.

Candace a feminine variant form of CANDICE.

Candie a feminine diminutive form of CANDICE, CANDIDA.

Candice a feminine first name, the meaning of which is uncertain but possibly 'brilliantly white' or 'pure and virtuous' (*Latin*). It was the name of an Ethiopian queen.Candice Bergen is an American actress. Variant forms are Candace, Candis.

Candida a feminine first name meaning 'shining white' (*Latin*). George Bernard Shaw (1856–1950) used the name for the eponymous heroine of his play *Candida* (1903). Diminutive forms are Candie, Candy.

Candis a feminine variant form of CANDICE.

Candy (1) a feminine diminutive form of CANDICE, CANDIDA. (2) a name used in its own right, from candy, the American English word for a sweet.

Canice an anglicised masculine form of the Irish Gaelic *Coinneach*, 'KENNETH'. Kilkenny Cathedral is dedicated to St Canice, and shows the same name in a different form: *cill*, 'church', Coinneaich, 'of Kenneth'.

Canute a masculine first name meaning 'knot' (*Old Norse*), the name of a Danish king of England (1016–35). Variant forms are Cnut, Knut.

Caoilainn a variant Irish Gaelic form of CÁELFIND.

Caoilfhinn (pronounced *kyle-finn*) a feminine first name meaning 'slender fair one' from *caol*, 'slender', *fionn*, 'fair' (*Irish Gaelic*). Anglicised forms of the name are Kaylin, Keelan. *See also* CÁELFIND.

Caoimhe *see* KEVA.

Caoimhín *see* KEVIN.

Caomh (pronounced *kave*) a masculine first name, from *caomh*, 'gentle', 'noble' (*Irish Gaelic*). It was the name of an Irish legendary warrior and progenitor of the O'Keeffes.

Cara (1) a feminine first name meaning 'friend' (*Irish Gaelic*). *See also* Cera. (2) a feminine first name meaning 'dear, darling' (*Italian*). A variant form is Carina.

Caractacus *see* CARADOG.

Caradoc the anglicised form of the Welsh CARADOG.

Caradog a masculine first name meaning 'beloved' (*Welsh*). It was the name of an early Welsh chieftain who fought against the Romans in the first century AD. The Romans rendered the name as 'Caractacus'. The Irish form is Cárthach, and an anglicised form is Caradoc. Caer Caradoc (Caradoc's fort) is a hill in Shropshire. A variant form is Cradoc.

Cardew a surname meaning 'black fort' (*Welsh*), used as a masculine first name.

Cardigan see CEREDIG.

Carey (1) a feminine first name from a place and river name Cary that occurs in Somerset and in central Scotland, and may be from the Celtic root *car*, 'dark', which is also the source of Kerry in Ireland. An association may also have grown up with Latin *cara*, 'dear'. The phrase 'Mother Carey's chickens' is from Latin *mata cara*, meaning the Virgin Mary. (2) a variant masculine form of CARY.

Cari a feminine variant form of CERI.

Caridad (pronounced *car-ee-dath*) the Spanish feminine form of CHARITY.

Carina (1) a feminine variant form of CARA. (2) an anglicised feminine form of CAIRENN.

Carissa a feminine first name meaning 'dear one' (*Latin*).

Carl (1) an anglicised German and Swedish masculine form of CHARLES. (2) an anglicised masculine form of Irish Gaelic CERBHALL. (3) a masculine diminutive form of CARLTON, CARLIN, CARLISLE, CARLO, CARLOS.

Carla feminine form of CARL. A variant form is Carlin. Diminutive forms are Carlie, Carley, Carly.

Carleton a masculine variant form of CARLTON.

Carley or **Carly** feminine diminutive forms of CARLA.

Carlie a feminine diminutive form of CARLA, CARLIN.

Carlin a feminine variant form of CARLA. Diminutive forms are Carlie, Carley, Carly.

Carlisle a masculine diminutive form of CARL.

Carlo the Italian masculine form of CHARLES.

Carlos the Spanish masculine form of CHARLES.

Carlotta the Italian feminine form of CHARLOTTE.

Carlton a place name and surname, meaning 'farm of the churls' (a rank of peasant) (*Old English*), used as a masculine first name. Variant forms are Carleton, Charlton, Charleton. A diminutive form is CARL.

Carly a feminine diminutive form of CARLA, CARLIN, now used independently. Carly Simon is an American singer.

Carlyn a feminine variant form of CAROLINE.

Carmel a feminine first name meaning 'garden' (*Hebrew*).

Carmela a Spanish and the Italian feminine forms of CARMEL.

Carmelita a Spanish feminine diminutive form of CARMEL.

Carmen a Spanish feminine form of CARMEL.

Carmichael a Scottish place name and surname, meaning 'fort of

MICHAEL', used as a masculine first name.

Carnation the name of a flower, meaning 'flesh colour' (*Latin/French*), used as a feminine first name.

Caro a feminine diminutive form of CAROL, CAROLINE.

Carol (1) a shortened masculine form of Carolus, the Latin form of CHARLES. (2) the feminine form of CHARLES. A variant form is Caryl. Diminutive forms are Caro, Carrie, Caddie.

Carola a feminine variant form of CAROLINE. Diminutive forms are Carrie, Caro, Caddie.

Carole (1) the French feminine form of CAROL. (2) a contracted form of CAROLINE. Diminutive forms are Caro, Carrie, Caddie.

Carolina the Italian and Spanish feminine forms of CAROLINE.

Caroline or **Carolyn** the feminine form of Carolus, the Latin form of CHARLES. Caroline of Brunswick (1768–1821) was the wife of George IV. She was tried for adultery in 1820. A variant form is Carlyn. Diminutive forms are Caro, Carrie, Caddie.

Caron (1) (pronounced *carr-on*) a Welsh masculine first name from the name of a saint, found in the place name Tregaron, in Ceredigion. (2) a feminine variant form of KAREN.

Caronwyn a feminine first name meaning 'beautiful loved one', from *caru*, 'to love', and *gwyn*, 'white, fair' (*Welsh*).

Carr a place name and surname, meaning 'overgrown marshy ground' (*Old Norse*), used as a masculine first name. Variant forms are Karr, Kerr.

Carrie a feminine diminutive form of CAROL, CAROLA, CAROLE, CAROLINE, CAROLYN. Carrie Fisher is an American actress and writer.

Carrick a place name, from *caraig*, 'rock or crag' (*Gaelic*), used as a masculine first name.

Carroll the anglicised masculine form of Irish Gaelic CERBHALL.

Carson a surname, of uncertain meaning but possibly 'marsh dweller' (*Old English*), used as a masculine first name.

Carter a surname, meaning 'a driver or maker of cars' (*Old English*) or 'son of ARTHUR' (*Scots Gaelic*), used as a masculine first name.

Cárthach the Irish masculine form of Welsh CARADOG.

Cartimandua a feminine first name from the Latinised Brythonic name of the first-century AD queen of the Brigantes, in what is now northern England.

Carver (1) a masculine first name meaning 'great rock' (*Cornish Gaelic*). (2) a surname, meaning 'sculptor' (*Old English*), used as a masculine first name.

Carwen (pronounced *carr-wen*) a feminine first name meaning 'white love', from *caru*, 'to love' and *ven*, 'white' (*Welsh*).

Carwyn the masculine form of CARWEN.

Cary a masculine form of CAREY. Cary Elwes is an English actor, son of the artist Dominic Elwes. Cary Grant was the adopted name of Archibald Leach.

Caryl (1) a feminine first name deriving from *caru*, 'to love' (*Welsh*). (2) a feminine variant form of Carol.

Caryn a feminine variant form of KAREN.

Carys a feminine first name meaning 'loved', from *caru*, 'to love' (*Welsh*).

Casey (1) a surname, meaning 'vigilant in war' (*Irish Gaelic*), increasingly being used as a masculine or feminine first name. (2) a place name, Cayce in Kentucky, where the hero Casey Jones was born, used as a masculine first name. (3) a variant feminine form of CASSIE, which is also used independently.

Cashel a place name, meaning 'circular stone fort' (*Irish Gaelic*), used as a masculine first name.

Casimir the English masculine form of KASIMIR.

Caspar or **Casper** the Dutch masculine form of JASPER, now also used as an English-language form. In the Bible Caspar was one of the Magi, the three wise men from the east who paid homage to the infant Jesus, presenting him with gifts.

Cass (1) a feminine diminutive form of CASSANDRA. (2) a masculine diminutive form of CASSIDY, CASSIAN, CASSIUS.

Cassandra a feminine first name meaning 'she who inflames with love' (*Greek*). In Greek mythology, Cassandra was a princess, the daughter of King Priam of Troy and Hecuba, whose prophecies of doom were not believed. Diminutive forms are Cass, Cassie.

Cassia a feminine variant form of KEZIA.

Cassian a masculine first name from the Roman family name CASSIUS.

Cassidy a surname, meaning 'clever' (*Irish Gaelic*), used as a masculine first name. A diminutive form is Cass.

Cassie a feminine diminutive form of CASSANDRA.

Cassius a Roman family name, of uncertain meaning, possibly 'empty' (*Latin*), used as a masculine first name. The American boxer Cassius Marcellus Clay changed his name to Muhammad Ali. A diminutive form is Cass.

Cassivellaunus the Latinised form of a Celtic masculine first name, that of a first-century tribal king of southern Britain who fought against Julius Caesar's invading troops.

Castor a masculine first name meaning 'beaver' (*Greek*). In Greek mythology, Castor was the mortal one of the twins born to Zeus and Leda.

Caswallon a hero of the Welsh *Mabinogion* tales who conquers Britain. The name may be modelled at least in part on CASSIVELLAUNUS.

Catalina the Spanish feminine form of KATHERINE.

Caterina the Italian feminine form of KATHERINE.

Cath a feminine diminutive form of CATHERINE.

Cathaír (pronounced *ka-har*) a masculine first name, probably derived from *cath*, 'battle', and meaning 'battle-lord' (*Irish Gaelic*). The anglicised form is Cahir.

Cathal (pronounced *ka-hal*) a masculine first name meaning 'strong battler', from *cath*, 'battle' (*Irish Gaelic*). Cathal Brugha (1874–1922) was a leader of the 1916 Easter Rising and was killed in the Irish Civil War in 1922. A variant form is Cahal.

Cathán (pronounced *ka-hann*) a masculine first name meaning 'warrior', from *cath*, 'battle' (*Irish Gaelic*). The name of a descendant of NIALL of the Nine Hostages, who was the founder of the O'Kanes.

Catharina or **Catharine** or **Catherina** feminine variant forms of CATHERINE.

Cathbad (pronounced *cath-bat*) a masculine first name incorporating the stem *cath*, 'battle' (*Irish Gaelic*). This was the name of a celebrated druid who warned the men of Ulster of the baneful future awaiting the baby DEIRDRE. It has been anglicised to Cuthbert.

Cathella a feminine first name formed from the combination of parts of CATHERINE and ISABELLA. It is very much a Scottish and Irish name.

Catherine the French feminine form of KATHERINE, now used as an English-language form. It is the name of several saints, including the fourth-century martyr St Catherine of Alexandria who was tortured on a spiked wheel, and St Catherine of Siena (1347–80), the patron saint of Italy. Diminutive forms are Cath, Cathie, Cathy.

Cathie or **Cathy** feminine diminutive forms of CATHERINE.

Cathleen an anglicised feminine form of CAITLÍN.

Cato a Roman family name, meaning 'wise one' (*Latin*), used as a masculine first name.

Catrin the Welsh feminine form of KATHERINE, CATRIONA.

Catrine a feminine variant form of CATRIONA.

Catriona the Scottish and Irish Gaelic feminine form of KATHERINE. *Catriona*, the novel by Robert Louis Stevenson (1850–94), sequel to *Kidnapped*, popularised the name. Variant forms are Catrine, Katrine, Katrina, Katriona. Diminutive forms are Riona, TRINA.

Cavan the name of the Irish county, derived from Gaelic *cabhán*, 'grassy hill' or 'grassy hollow', referring to a hilly countryside (*Irish Gaelic*), used as a masculine first name. A variant form is Kavan.

Ceallach a masculine or feminine first name meaning 'bright-headed' (*Irish Gaelic*). Ceallach Cualand was the father of St KENTIGERN, or MUNGO, of Glasgow. An alternative form is Cellach, and the anglicised form is Kelly.

Ceara a variant form of CERA.

Cecil a masculine first name stemming from *seisyllt*, 'sixth' (*Welsh*), which could mean 'sixth child', like Latin Sextus, but its use as a first name seems to come from the fame of the surname Cecil in England, where it is the family name of the marquesses of Salisbury. It was the first name of the English writer and poet laureate C. Day Lewis (104–72), the father of Daniel Day Lewis.

Cecile the French feminine form of CECILY, CECILIA.

Cécile the French masculine form of CECIL.

Cecily or **Cecilia** the feminine form of CECIL. St Cecilia was a third-century Roman martyr who became the patron saint of music. Diminutive forms are Celia, Cis, Cissie, Cissy. A variant form is Cicely.

Cedric a masculine first name adapted by the Scottish writer Sir Walter Scott (1771–1832) for a character in *Ivanhoe* from the Saxon Cerdic, the first king of Wessex. Sir Cedric Hardwicke (1893–1964) was an English actor who appeared in many films.

Ceelin an anglicised feminine form of CÁELFIND.

Cei (pronounced *kay*) a Welsh masculine first name, possibly from the common Latin name Caius, which would have been frequently found in Roman Britain. In Welsh legend, he was a companion to King ARTHUR and steward of his household. It is also found as Cai. His name has been anglicised to Sir KAY in the English Arthurian tales.

Ceinwen (pronounced *kyne-wen*) a feminine first name meaning 'fine white one', from *cein*, 'elegant', 'fine', *ven*, 'white' (*Welsh*). Her name is preserved in St Keyne's Well, near Liskeard.

Ceiriog (pronounced *kye-riog*) a Welsh masculine first name from a river name of North Wales.

Celandine the name of either of two unrelated flowering plants, meaning 'swallow', used as a feminine first name (*Greek*).

Celeste a feminine first name meaning 'heavenly' (*Latin*). Celeste Holm is an American actress.

Celestine (1) a feminine diminutive form of Celeste. (2) a masculine name adopted by several popes, one of whom, Celestine V (1209–96), was the first pope to abdicate.

Celia a feminine first name meaning 'heavenly' (*Latin*), a diminutive form of CECILIA. William Shakespeare (1564–1616) used the name for Rosalind's cousin in his play *As You Like It*.

Céline the French feminine form of SELINA.

Cellach a masculine variant form of CEALLACH.

Cemlyn a place name, meaning 'bending lake', used as a masculine first name.

Cendrillon a feminine first name meaning 'from the ashes', the fairytale heroine (*French*); the anglicised form is CINDERELLA.

Cennydd (pronounced *kennith*) the Welsh masculine form of KENNETH. The Welsh St Cennydd, whose name is cognate with Irish CINÁED, is preserved in Senghennydd in Glamorgan.

Cephas a masculine first name meaning 'a stone' (*Aramaic*).

Cera (pronounced *kee-ra*) an Irish Gaelic feminine first name that goes a long way back in Irish legend to the wife of Nemed, leader of the Nemedians, the third set of invaders of ancient Ireland. It was also borne by three saints. An alternative form is Ceara. It is liable to be confused with CARA.

Cerbhall (pronounced *kerr-wal*) a masculine first name meaning 'brave in battle' (*Irish Gaelic*). It was a name borne by several kings in the Gaelic period, and by the fifth President of the Irish Republic, Cearbhall O Dálaigh. Anglicised forms include Carroll and Carl, athough in this latter form it is likely to be confused with German Carl or Karl.

Ceredig (pronounced *ker-ee-dig*) a masculine first name meaning 'lovable', 'kind one' (*Welsh*). Ceredig was a sixth-century king of the Strath-clyde Britons. Ceredigion in Wales is called after another Ceredig, son of the semi-legendary fifth-century king Cynedda. The anglicised form is Cardigan.

Ceri (pronounced *kerri*) a Cornish and Welsh masculine or feminine first name meaning 'loved', from *caru*, 'to love' (*Welsh*). Ceri Richards (1903–77) was a distinguished twentieth-century artist. Feminine variant forms are Cari, Kari. A diminutive form is Cerian.

Cerian a feminine diminutive form of CERI.

Ceridwen (pronounced *ker-idwen*) a feminine first name from *cerdd*, 'poetry', and *ven*, 'white' (Welsh). It was the name of the Welsh poetic muse, mother of the minstrel Taliesin.

Cernunnos (pronounced *ker-nunnos*) a masculine first name meaning 'horned one' (*Gaulish*). He was an important god of the continental Celts, portrayed with the body of a man and the head of a stag.

Cerys (pronounced *kerr-ees*) a feminine first name meaning 'love' (*Welsh*).

César the French masculine form of CAESAR.

Cesare the Italian masculine form of CAESAR.

Cethern or **Cethren** (pronounced *ke-hern*) a masculine first name meaning 'long-lived' (*Irish Gaelic*).

Chad a masculine first name the meaning of which is uncertain, possibly 'warlike, bellicose' (*Old English*). St Chad (died 672) was the first bishop of Lichfield.

Chaim a masculine variant form of HYAM.

Chance (1) the abstract noun for the quality of good fortune used as a masculine first name. (2) a variant form of CHAUNCEY.

Chancellor a surname, meaning 'counsellor or secretary' (*Old French*), used as a masculine first name.

Chancey a masculine variant form of CHAUNCEY.

Chander the masculine form of CHANDRA.

Chandler a surname, meaning 'maker or seller of candles' (*Old French*), used as a masculine first name.

Chandra a feminine first name meaning 'moon brighter than the stars' (*Sanskrit*).

Chanel (pronounced *sha-nelle*) the surname of the French couturier and perfumier Coco Chanel (1883–1971) used as a feminine first name. A variant form is Shanel or Shanelle.

Chantal (pronounced *shawn-tal*) a French place name used as a feminine first name.

Chapman a surname, meaning 'merchant' (*Old English*), used as a masculine first name.

Charis (pronounced *ka-rees*) a feminine first name meaning 'grace' (*Greek*).

Charity the abstract noun for the quality of tolerance or generosity used as a feminine first name. It was a popular Puritan name.

Charlene a relatively modern feminine diminutive form of CHARLES, used as a feminine first name. A variant form is Charline.

Charles a masculine first name meaning 'strong; manly; noble-spirited' from *Carl*, 'man' (*Germanic*). It has long been a popular name and a royal one. Diminutive forms are Charlie, Charley, CHAS, CHUCK.

Charlie or **Charley** masculine and feminine diminutive forms of CHARLES, CHARLOTTE. Charlie Dimmock is a popular TV gardener.

Charline a feminine variant form of CHARLENE.

Charlotte a feminine form of CHARLES (*Germanic*). It was the name of George IV's only legitimate child. Diminutive forms are Charlie, Charley, Lottie.

Charlton or **Charleton** masculine variant forms of CARLTON. Charlton Heston is an American film actor.

Charmian a feminine first name meaning 'little delight' (*Greek*). A modern variant form is CHARMAINE.

Charmaine (1) a feminine diminutive form of the abstract noun for the quality of pleasing or attracting people used as a feminine first name. (2) a variant form of CHARMIAN.

Chas a masculine diminutive form of CHARLES.

Chase a surname, meaning 'hunter' (*Old French*), used as a masculine first name.

Chauncey or **Chaunce** a surname, of uncertain meaning, possibly 'chancellor' (*Old French*), used as a masculine first name. Variant forms are Chance, Chancey.

Chelsea a place name, meaning 'chalk landing place' (*Old English*), used as a feminine first name.

Cher (pronounced *sher*) or **Chérie** or **Cherie** (pronounced *sher-ee*) a feminine first name meaning 'dear, darling' (*French*). Cher is an American singer and actress; Cherie Blair is a barrister and the wife of Prime Minister Tony Blair. Variant forms are Cherry, Sheree, Sheri, Sherrie, Sherry.

Cherry (1) the name of the fruit used as a feminine first name. (2) a form of CHÉRIE. A variant form is CHERYL.

Cheryl (1) a feminine variant form of CHERRY. (2) a combining form of Cherry and BERYL. A variant form is Sheryl.

Chester a place name, meaning 'fortified camp' (*Latin*), used as a masculine first name.

Cheyenne (pronounced *shy-ann*) the name of the North American Indian nation, the meaning of which is uncertain, used as a masculine or feminine first name.

Chiara (pronounced *kee-ara*) the Italian feminine form of CLARA.

Chilton a place name and surname, meaning 'children's farm' (*Old English*), used as a masculine first name.

Chiquita (pronounced *chi-keeta*) a feminine first name meaning 'little one' (*Spanish*).

Chloë or **Chloe** a feminine first name meaning 'a green herb, a young shoot' (*Greek*). In the New Testament Chloe was a woman in whose house there was a correspondant of Paul's. In a Greek pastoral poem of the fourth or fifth century AD, it is the name of a shepherdess loved by Daphnis and became a generic name among poets and romance writers for a rustic maiden.

Chloris a feminine first name meaning 'green' (*Greek*). A variant form is Cloris.

Chris a masculine or feminine diminutive form of CHRISTIAN, CHRISTINE, CHRISTOPHER. Chris O'Donnell is an American film actor.

Chrissie (1) a Scottish feminine diminutive form of CHRISTIANA, CHRISTINE. (2) an Irish masculine diminutive form of CHRISTOPHER.

Christabel a feminine first name formed by the combination of the names CHRISTINE and BELLA made by Samuel Taylor Coleridge (1772–1834) for a poem of this name.

Christian a masculine or feminine first name meaning 'belonging to Christ, a believer in Christ' (*Latin*). John Bunyan (1628–88) used the name for the pilgrim hero of his allegory, *The Pilgrim's Progress* (1678). Christian Slater is an American actor. Diminutive forms are Chris, Christie, Christy.

Christiana the feminine form of CHRISTIAN. A variant form is Christina.

Christie (1) a surname, meaning 'Christian', used as a masculine first name. (2) a masculine diminutive form of CHRISTIAN, CHRISTOPHER. (3) a feminine diminutive form of CHRISTIAN, CHRISTINE. A variant form is Christy.

Christina a feminine variant form of CHRISTIANA.

Christine a French feminine form of CHRISTINA, now used as an English-language form. Christine Keeler was an English call-girl who helped bring about the downfall of Harold Macmillan's Conservative government in 1963. Diminutive forms are Chris, Chrissie, Christie, Christy, Teenie, Tina.

Christmas a masculine first name meaning 'festival of Christ' (*Old English*). Christmas Humphrys was an eminent English judge.

Christoph the German masculine form of CHRISTOPHER.

Christopher a masculine first name meaning 'bearing Christ' (*Greek*). St Christopher was a third-century martyr about whom little is known. Until 1969 he was the patron saint of travellers. Christopher Lambert is a French film actor. Diminutive forms are Chris, Christie, Christy, Kester, Kit.

Christy a masculine and feminine variant form of CHRISTIE. Christy Brown was an Irish writer who suffered from cerebral palsy and who wrote a best-selling autobiography, *My Left Foot*.

Chrystal a feminine variant form of CRYSTAL.

Chuck a masculine diminutive form of Charles. Chuck Norris is an American film actor.

Churchill a place name and surname, meaning 'church on a hill' (*Old English*), used as a masculine first name.

Ciabhán (pronounced *keea-vann*) a masculine first name meaning 'full-haired' (*Irish Gaelic*). In Irish legend, Ciabhán 'of the flowing locks' was the lover of Clídna, with whom he eloped from the land of the sea-god, Manannan. The anglicised form is Keevan.

Cian a masculine first name meaning 'ancient' (*Irish Gaelic*). Anglicised forms are Kean, Keane.

Ciara (pronounced *keera*) a feminine first name meaning 'dark one', from *ciar*, 'dark' (*Irish Gaelic*). Anglicised forms of the name include Keera, Keira, Kira.

Ciarán or **Ciaran** (pronounced *keer-ann*) a masculine first name meaning 'little dark one', from *ciar*, 'dark' (Irish Gaelic), with the diminutive suffix -an. Among several saints to bear the name, perhaps the most celebrated is the founder of the abbey of Clonmacnoise in AD 547, the year of his death. Anglicised forms include Kieran. *See also* KERR.

Cicely a feminine variant form of CECILIA.

Cilla a feminine diminutive form of PRISCILLA (*French*). Cilla Black is an English singer and TV host.

Cináed (pronounced *kin-aith*) a masculine name borne by kings of the Northern Irish Picts. It has been linked to Gaelic Coinneach, KENNETH, but this link is uncertain.

Cinderella a feminine first name from the anglicised form of CENDRILLON, the fairytale heroine. Diminutive forms are Cindie, Cindy, Ella.

Cindi or **Cindie** or **Cindy** a feminine diminuntive form of CINDERELLA, CYNTHIA, LUCINDA, now often used independently. Cindy Crawford is an American model.

Cinzia (prounced *chint-sia*) the Italian feminine form of CYNTHIA.

Cis or **Cissie** or **Cissy** feminine diminutive forms of CECILY.

Claiborne a masculine variant form of CLAYBORNE. A diminutive form is Clay.

Claire the French feminine form of CLARA, now used widely as an English form.

Clara a feminine first name meaning 'bright, illustrous' (*Latin*). A variant form is CLARE. A diminutive form is Clarrie.

Clarabel or **Clarabella** or **Clarabelle** a feminine first name formed from a combination of CLARA and BELLA or BELLE, meaning 'bright, shining beauty' (*Latin/French*). A variant form is Claribel.

Clare (1) a feminine variant form of CLARA. St Clare (1194–1253) was an Italian saint who, influenced by St Francis of Assissi, founded the order of Minoresses or Poor Clares. In the twentieth century she was made patron saint of television. (2) a surname, meaning 'bright, shining', used as a masculine or feminine first name (*Latin*). In the novel *Lolita* (1955) by Vladimir Nabokov (1899–1977), Clare Quilty is am important male character.

Clarence a masculine first name meaning 'bright, shining' (*Latin*). A diminutive form is Clarrie.

Claribel a feminine variant form of CLARABEL.

Clarice (1) a feminine first name meaning 'fame' (*Latin*). (2) a variant form of CLARA. A variant form is Clarissa.

Clarinda a feminine first name formed from a combination of CLARA and BELINDA or LUCINDA.

Clarissa a feminine variant form of CLARICE. Sir John Vanbrugh (1664–1726) used the name in his play *The Confederacy* (1705), and Samuel Richardson (1689–1761) used it for the eponymous heroine of his epistolary novel *Clarissa Harlowe*, one of the longest novels in the English language.

Clark or **Clarke** a surname, meaning 'cleric, scholar or clerk' (*Old French*), used as a masculine first name. Clark Gable (1901–60) was a famous American film actor of the 1930s and 1940s). The 'earth' name of Superman is Clark Kent. A variant form is Clerk.

Clarrie (1) a feminine diminutive form of CLARA. (2) a masculine diminutive form of CLARENCE.

Claud the English masculine form of CLAUDIUS.

Claude (1) the French masculine form of CLAUD. (2) the French feminine form of Claudia.

Claudette a feminine diminutive form of CLAUDIA. Claudette Colbert (1903–96) was a French-born American film actress of the 1930s and 1940s.

Claudia feminine form of CLAUD. In the New Testament Claudia was a Christian woman in Rome who was mentioned in one of Paul's epistles. Diminutive forms are Claudette, Claudine.

Claudine a diminutive form of CLAUDIA. The French writer Colette (1873–1954) used the name for the heroine for four semi-autobiographical novels.

Claudio the Italian and Spanish masculine form of CLAUD. Claudio Aquaviva (1543–1615) was a general of the Society of Jesus (Jesuits) under whose leadership the order grew rapidly. William Shakespeare (1564–1616) used the name in two of his plays: for a young lord of Florence in *Much Ado About Nothing* and the brother of the heroine, Isabella, in *Measure for Measure*.

Claudius a masculine first name meaning 'lame' (*Latin*); the Dutch and German forms of CLAUD. William Shakespeare (1564–1616) used the name for Hamlet's uncle and stepfather in *Hamlet*.

Claus a masculine variant form of KLAUS.

Clay (1) a surname, meaning 'a dweller in a place with clay soil' (*Old English*), used as a masculine first name. (2) a diminutive form of CLAI-

BORNE, CLAYBORNE, CLAYTON.

Clayborne a surname, meaning 'a dweller in a place with clay soil by a brook' (*Old English*), used as a masculine first name. A variant form is CLAIBORNE. A diminutive form is Clay.

Clayton a place name and surname, meaning 'place in or with good clay' (*Old English*), used as a masculine first name. A diminutive form is Clay.

Cledwyn a masculine first name from a Denbigh river name, although a derivation from *cledd*, 'sword' (*Welsh*) is perhaps more likely for the personal name. Cledwyn Hughes, later Lord Cledwyn, was a prominent political figure in the 1960s and 70s.

Clem (1) a feminine diminutive form of CLEMATIS, CLEMENCE, CLEMENCY, CLEMENTINE, CLEMENTINA. (2) a masculine diminutive form of CLEMENT.

Clematis a feminine first name meaning 'climbing plant' (*Greek*), the name of a climbing plant with white, blue or purple flowers used as a feminine first name. Diminutive forms are Clem, Clemmie.

Clemence a variant form of CLEMENCY.

Clemency the abstract noun for the quality of tempering justice with mercy used as a feminine first name (*Latin*). A variant form is Clemence. Diminutive forms are Clem, Clemmie.

Clement a masculine first name meaning 'mild-tempered, merciful' (*Latin*). It was the name adopted by several popes. A diminutive form is Clem.

Clementine or **Clementina** feminine forms of CLEMENT. Diminutive forms are Clem, Clemmie.

Clemmie a feminine diminutive form of CLEMATIS, CLEMENCY and CLEMENTINE.

Cleo a short form of CLEOPATRA, used as an independent feminine first name.

Cleopatra a feminine first name meaning 'father's glory' (*Greek*). Cleopatra (*c.*69–30 BC) was an Egyptian queen (51–30 BC) noted for her beauty. She was the mistress of Julius Caesar and later had a love affair with Mark Antony, which was dramatised in the play Antony and Cleopatra by William Shakespeare (1564–1616). She killed herself with an asp rather than be captured by Octavian. A diminutive form is Cleo.

Clerk a masculine variant form of CLARK.

Cleveland a place name, meaning 'land of hills' (*Old English*), used as a masculine first name.

Clia a feminine diminutive form of CLIANTHA.

Cliantha a feminine first name meaning 'glory flower' (*Greek*). A diminutive form is Clia.

Clídna a feminine variant form of CLÍODHNA.

Cliff a masculine diminutive form of CLIFFORD, now used independently.

Clifford a surname, meaning 'ford at a cliff' (*Old English*), used as a masculine first name. Clifford Odets (1906–63) was an American playwright. A diminutive form is Cliff.

Clifton a place name, meaning 'place on a cliff' (*Old English*), used as a masculine first name.

Clint a masculine diminutive form of CLINTON, now used independently. Clint Eastwood is a well-known American film actor and director.

Clinton a place name and surname, meaning 'settlement on a hill', used as a masculine first name. A diminutive form is CLINT.

Clio a feminine first name meaning 'glory' (*Greek*).

Clíodhna (pronounced *klee-ona*) an Irish Gaelic feminine first name the origin of which is unclear. In legend she was one of the three daughters of a prince of the sea kingdom of Mannannan who eloped with CIABHÁN, son of the king of Ulster, and was drowned in punishment by a tidal wave. A variant form is Clídna, and the anglicised form is Cliona.

Cliona the anglicised feminine form of CLÍODHNA.

Clive a surname, meaning 'at the cliff' (*Old English*), used as a masculine first name. Clive James is an Australian-born writer and TV host.

Clodagh (pronounced *kloda*) an Irish Gaelic feminine first name, probably from the river name Clóideach, in County Tipperary.

Clorinda a feminine first name formed from a combination of CHLORIS and BELINDA or LUCINDA.

Cloris a feminine variant form of CHLORIS.

Clothilde or **Clotilde** or **Clotilda** a feminine first name meaning 'famous fighting woman' (*Germanic*).

Clover the name of a flowering plant used as a feminine first name (*English*).

Clovis the Old French form of LEWIS. Clovis I (*c*.466–511) was a king of the Franks (481–511).

Clyde the name of a Scottish river, meaning 'cleansing one', used as a masculine first name. The name was taken up outside Scotland as a first name, especially in the USA, and was reimported to Scotland. In America its most notorious holder was the gangster Clyde Barrow, shot dead in 1934.

Cnut a masculine variant form of Canute.

Cody a surname used as a masculine or feminine first name.

Coel (pronounced *koil*) a masculine first name meaning 'trust' (*Welsh*). Coel was a king in the British kingdom of Strathclyde; in fact probably the origin of 'Old King Cole'.

Cóilín the Irish Gaelic masculine form of Colin.

Col a masculine diminutive form of Colin, Colmán, Columba.

Colby a masculine first name meaning 'from the dark country' (*Norse*).

Cole (1) a diminutive form of Coleman, Colmán, Nicholas. (2) a surname, meaning 'swarthy' or 'coal-black' (*Old English*), used as a masculine first name.

Coleman a surname, meaning 'swarthy man' or 'servant of Nicholas' (*Old English*), used as a masculine first name.

Colette a feminine diminutive form of Nicole, now used independently. St Colette (1381–1447) was a member of the Poor Clares and founder of the Colettine Poor Clares. A variant form is Collette.

Colin (1) a Scottish masculine first name from the Gaelic Cailean, 'youth', which has close associations with the Campbell clan, whose chief has the Gaelic title MacCailein Mór, 'son of Great Colin'. (2) an Irish masculine first name from Col, an abbreviation of Gaelic Cóilín. (3) an English masculine diminutive form of Nicholas, long used independently.

Colla a masculine first name meaning 'lord' (*Irish Gaelic*). It was a frequent name in early Irish legend. The Clan Donald traces its origins back to Colla Uais, an Irish prince of the fifth century.

Colleen a feminine first name meaning 'girl', from *cailin*, 'girl', 'maiden' (*Irish Gaelic*). The generic word for a girl has been taken up as an individual name.

Collette a feminine variant form of Colette.

Collier or **Collyer** a surname, meaning 'charcoal seller or burner' (*Old English*), used as a masculine first name. A variant form is Colyer.

Colm (pronounced *collum*) an Irish Gaelic masculine first name meaning 'dove'. The derivation is from Latin *columba*, 'dove'. The most famous bearer of the name is Columcille, 'dove of the church', the Gaelic name of St Columba, founder of Irish monasteries at Durrow, Kells, and other places, and who, when expelled from Ireland for pride and contumacity, established himself on Iona, where he died in 597, having become the most celebrated missionary saint of Scotland. *See* CALUM.

Colmán (pronounced *collaman*) a masculine first name meaning 'little dove' (*Irish Gaelic*). Many holy men bore this name in Ireland and in Scotland, and it is preserved in many place names. Diminutive forms are Col, Cole.

Colombe the French masculine or feminine form of COLUMBA.

Columba *see* COLM.

Columbanus a masculine first name meaning 'little dove', a Latinised form of COLMÁN. St Columbanus (died AD 615) was one of the missionaries who brought Christianity to central Europe. His hermitage cave near Interlaken in Switzerland can still be visited.

Columbine a feminine first name meaning 'little dove' (*Latin*); the name of a flowering plant used as a feminine first name.

Columcille the Gaelic name, meaning 'dove of the church', of St Columba (*see* COLM). It is the middle name of the American-Australian actor Mel Gibson.

Colyer a masculine variant form of COLLIER.

Comfort the abstract noun for the state of wellbeing or bringer of solace used as a feminine first name, in the Puritan tradition (*Latin/French*).

Comgall or **Comghall** or **Comhghall** (pronounced *cow-al*) an Irish Gaelic masculine first name of uncertain meaning. St Comgall founded the monastery at Bangor, County Down. Cowal in Scotland is named after Comghall, a descendant of the first Dalriadic kings.

Comyn a Scottish masculine surname that may have come from the Old French personal name Comin, used as a first name. The Comyns became a powerful family in medieval Scotland and claimants to the throne. Bruce slew John Comyn in Greyfriars Kirk, Dumfries in 1306.

Con (1) a masculine diminutive form of CONAN, CONNALL, CONNOR, CONRAD. (2) a feminine diminutive form of CONSTANCE, etc.

Conachar a variant masculine form of CONCHOBAR.

Conaire (pronounced *con-yara*) a masculine first name from the root *cú*, 'hound' (*Irish Gaelic*). It was the name of a legendary hero and high king of Ireland.

Conall a masculine first name meaning 'wolfish', from *cú*, which means 'wolf' as well as 'hound' (*Irish Gaelic*). Conall Cearnach, 'victorious', is one of the heroes of the Ulster Cycle of legends. The anglicised form is Connel, or Connell.

Conán (pronounced *con-ann*) or **Conan** a masculine first name from *cú*, 'hound', 'wolf' (*Irish Gaelic*). In the Fenian Cycle of legends, Conán macMorna, one of the Fianna, plays the part of a mischief-maker and boaster.

Concepción a feminine first name meaning 'beginning, conception' (*Spanish*), a reference to the Immaculate Conception of the Virgin Mary. Diminutive forms are Concha, Conchita.

Concepta the Latin feminine form of CONCETTA.

Concetta a feminine first name meaning 'conceptive' (*Italian*), a reference to the Virgin Mary and the Immaculate Conception.

Concha or **Conchita** feminine diminutive forms of CONCEPCIÓN.

Conchobar (pronounced *con-ko-warr*) a masculine first name meaning 'lover of hounds' (*Irish Gaelic*). It was borne most famously by the legendary Conchobar macNessa, king of Ulster and frustrated lover of Deirdre. There are many other stories in which he appears. The name has a variety of forms, including Conchubor, Conchobhar, Conachar, and the anglicised form is Conor or Connor.

Conn a masculine first name the source of which is variously taken as from *cú*, 'hound', 'wolf' (*Irish Gaelic*) or from an Old Gaelic root word implying wisdom. The name is borne by some celebrated figures of antiquity, including Conn Céadcathach, 'of the hundred battles', high king of Ireland and regarded as the progenitor of several noble families in Ireland and Scotland.

Connel or **Connell** the anglicised masculine form of CONALL.

Connla a masculine first name meaning 'little hound' (*Irish Gaelic*). The name of the son of CUCHULAINN and AOIFE, slain in fight by Cuchulainn who did not know who he was.

Connor or **Conor** the anglicised masculine form of Irish Gaelic CONCHOBAR.

Conrad a masculine first name meaning 'able counsellor' (*Germanic*). William Shakespeare (1564–1616) used the name for one of the followers of Don John in his comedy *Much Ado About Nothing*. Lord Byron (1788–1824) used the name for the hero of his poem *The Corsair* (1814). A diminutive form is Con.

Conroy a masculine first name meaning 'wise' (*Gaelic*).

Consolata a feminine first name meaning 'consoling', a reference to the Virgin Mary (*Italian*).

Consolation the abstract noun for the act of consoling or the state of solace used as a feminine first name in the Puritan tradition.

Constance feminine form of CONSTANT. Diminutive forms are Con, Connie. A variant form is Constanta.

Constant a masculine first name meaning 'firm, faithful' (*Latin*). Constant Lambert (1905–51) was an English composer. A diminutive form is Con.

Constanta a feminine variant form of CONSTANCE.

Constantine a masculine first name meaning 'resolute, firm' (*Latin*). Constantine I (280–337) was the first Christian emperor of Rome. Constantinople (modern Istanbul) was founded by him. It was also the name of three Scottish kings.

Constanza the Italian and Spanish feminine forms of CONSTANCE.

Consuela a feminine first name meaning 'consolation' (*Spanish*), a reference to the Virgin Mary.

Consuelo the masculine form of CONSUELA.

Conway the anglicised masculine form of Welsh CONWY.

Conwy (pronounced *konn-wee*) a Welsh masculine first name of modern times from what was originally a river name and later also that of a famous castle. The anglicised form is Conway.

Coop a masculine diminutive form of COOPER.

Cooper a surname, meaning 'barrel maker' (*Old English*), used as a masculine first name. A diminutive form is Coop.

Cora a feminine first name meaning 'maiden' (*Greek*). A variant form is Corinna, Corinne.

Corabella or **Corabelle** a feminine first name meaning 'beautiful maiden', a combination of CORA and BELLA.

Coral the name of the pink marine jewel material used as a feminine first name.

Coralie the French feminine form of CORAL.

Corazón (pronounced *cor-a-thon*) a feminine first name meaning '(sacred) heart' (*Spanish*).

Corbin a surname, meaning 'raven, black-haired' or' raucousness' (*Old French*), used as a masculine first name. Corbin Bernsen is an American actor, one of the stars of the TV series *LA Law*.

Corcoran a surname, meaning 'red- or purple-faced' (*Irish Gaelic*), used as a masculine first name.

Cordelia a feminine first name meaning 'warm-hearted' (*Latin*). Cordelia is the youngest daughter of King Lear in the eponymous play by William Shakespeare (1564–1614).

Corey a surname, meaning 'God peace' (*Irish Gaelic*), used as a masculine first name. A variant form is Cory.

Cori or **Corrie** a feminine form of Corey.

Corin in medieval times a conventional name for a shepherd. William Shakespeare (1564–1616) used the name for that of an old shepherd in his comedy *As You Like It*. Corin Redgrave is an English actor.

Corinna or **Corinne** feminine variant forms of CORA.

Cormac (pronounced *corra-mac*) a masculine first name, probably from *corb*, 'chariot', with *mac*, 'son' (*Irish Gaelic*). A popular name in the Gaelic world. Cormac macAirt was the first high king of Ireland, recorded as having his capital at Tara (third century AD). The hero of many stories, he left a reputation for wisdom and prudence. An anglicised form is Cormack or Cormick.

Cormack or **Cormick** anglicised masculine forms of Irish Gaelic CORMAC.

Cornelia the feminine form of CORNELIUS.

Cornelius a masculine name the origin of which is uncertain, possibly 'horn-like', a Roman family name. St Cornelius (178–253) was pope for two years. William Shakespeare (1564–1616) used the name for characters in *Cymbeline* and *Hamlet*. Cornelius Vanderbilt (1794–1877) was an American financier, and the name has been used for several of his descendants. A variant form is CORNELL.

Cornell (1) a surname, meaning 'Cornwall' or 'a hill where corn is sold', used as a masculine first name. (2) a variant form of CORNELIUS.

Corona a feminine first name meaning 'crown' (*Latin*).

Corrado the Italian masculine form of CONRAD.

Corwin a masculine first name meaning 'friend of the heart' (*Old French*).

Cory a masculine variant form of COREY.

Cosima the feminine form of COSMO.

Cosimo an Italian masculine form of COSMO. Cosimo de' Medici (1389–1464) was the first of the famous Florentine family to exert cultural influence by his patronage of the arts.

Cosmo a masculine first name meaning 'order, beauty' (*Greek*). Cosmo Gordon Lang, Baron Lang of Lambeth (1864–1945), was Archbishop of Canterbury (1928–45).

Cospatrick a masculine first name meaning 'servant of Patrick'. This name is an anglicised version of *gwas* (*Old Welsh*) 'servant', and Padruig, 'Patrick' (*Irish Gaelic*).

Costanza an Italian feminine form of CONSTANCE.

Courtney a surname, meaning 'short nose' (*Old French*), used as a masculine or feminine first name.

Cradoc a masculine variant form of CARADOC.

Craig a surname meaning 'rock', from *carraig*, 'rock, crag' (*Scottish Gaelic*), used as a masculine first name. Craig Ferguson is a Scottish actor who works in the United States and Craig Raine is an English poet.

Cranley a surname, meaning 'crane clearing, spring or meadow' (*Old English*), used as a masculine first name.

Crawford a place name and surname, meaning 'ford of the crows' (*Old English*), used as a masculine first name.

Créd (pronounced *craith*) an Irish Gaelic feminine first name from the name of a daughter of the king of Kerry, who was wooed and won by CÁEL. After his death in the battle of Ventry, she committed suicide.

Creiddlad and **Creiddylad** variant forms of CREUDDYLAD

Creidne (pronounced *craith-nya*) a feminine first name meaning 'loyal' (*Irish Gaelic*). In Irish legend, Creidne was a female member of the Fianna, the troop of warrior-bards who were bodyguards to various kings and high kings. In Celtic legend, female warriors were by no means unusual.

Creighton a surname, meaning 'rock or cliff place (*Old Welsh*, *Old English*) or 'border settlement' (*Scots Gaelic*), used as a masculine first name.

Crépin the French masculine form of CRISPIN.

Cressa a contracted feminine form of CRESSIDA.

Cressida a feminine first name meaning 'gold' (*Greek*). William Shakespeare (1564–1616) used the name for the faithless heroine of his play about the Trojan War, *Troilus and Cressida*, changing if from the Criseyde form used by Geoffrey Chaucer (*c*.1343–1400) in *Troilus and*

Criseyde, his version of the same story. A contracted form is Cressa.

Creuddylad (pronounced *kry-the-lad*) a feminine first name that is the Welsh form of Cordelia. In the story of *Culhwych ac Olwen*, a maiden of this name is described as the most majestic who ever lived. Other forms are Creiddylad, Crieddlad.

Crimthann or **Criomhthann** (pronounced *creev-thann*) a masculine first name meaning 'fox', implying cleverness (*Irish Gaelic*). Crimthann was a name given to Colum Cille before he entered the church.

Crisiant (pronounced *krees-yant*) a feminine first name derived from *crisial* meaning 'crystal' (*Welsh*).

Crispin or **Crispian** a masculine first name meaning 'having curly hair' (*Latin*). St Crispin and St Crispinian were third-century saints who became the patron saints of shoemakers.

Crispus the German masculine form of CRISPIN. In the New Testament, Crispus was the presiding officer of the synagogue at Corinth who was baptised by Paul.

Cristal a feminine variant form of CRYSTAL.

Cristiano the Italian and Spanish masculine form of CHRISTIAN.

Cristina the Italian, Portuguese and Spanish feminine form of CHRISTINA.

Cristóbal the Spanish masculine form of CHRISTOPHER.

Cristoforo the Italian masculine form of CHRISTOPHER.

Cromwell a place name and surname, meaning 'winding spring' (*Old English*), used as a masculine first name.

Crosbie or **Crosby** a place name and surname, meaning 'farm or village with crosses' (*Old Norse*), used as a masculine first name.

Cruithne (pronounced *kroo-eena*) an Old Gaelic masculine or feminine first name. It was the Gaelic name given to the founder of the Picts, whose seven sons represent the seven provinces of Pictland. It was also used as a female name, as in Cruithne, the daughter of the great smith and weapon-maker Lóchan.

Crystal the name of a very clear brilliant glass used as a feminine first name. Variant forms are Cristal, Chrystal.

Crystyn a feminine first name meaning 'follower of Christ', the Welsh form of CHRISTINA.

Cuchulainn (pronounced *koo-hoolin*) a masculine first name meaning 'hound of Culann' (*Irish Gaelic*). In Celtic mythology, when the boy Setanta killed Culann's hound, he promised to play the part of the dog himself, and took this name accordingly: one of many evidences in Celtic lore of shape-changing between people and animals. The boy went on to become the great hero of the Ulster Cycle of legends.

Cuilean (pronounced *cul-yan*) a masculine first name from *cúilean*, 'whelp' (*Scottish Gaelic*) the name of a tenth-century contender for the kingship of the Picts and Scots, killed in battle against King Indulf.

Culann (Irish Gaelic, male) a masculine first name that is probably formed from the Old Irish Gaelic root word *col*, 'chief'. Known from the Cuchulainn story, this name of a legendary smith, maker of the armour of Conchobhar macNessa, king of Ulster. Its anglicised form is Callan or Cullen.

Culhwych (pronounced *kool-hooh*) a masculine first name that may stem from an Old Welsh root-word meaning 'pig-lord'. It was borne by the hero of the old Welsh legend of *Culhwych ac Olwen*. Culhwych, son of Cilydd, bears a curse from before his birth that can only be ended when he wins the love of OLWEN, daughter of the giant Ysbaddaden.

Cullan (1) a surname, meaning 'Cologne' (*Old French*), used as a masculine first name. (2) a place name, meaning 'at the back of the river' (*Scottish Gaelic*), used as a masculine first name. A variant form is Cullen.

Cullen (1) an anglicised masculine form of the Irish Gaelic CULANN. (2) a variant form of CULLAN.

Culley a surname, meaning 'woodland' (*Scottish Gaelic*), used as a masculine first name.

Cunobelinus *see* CYMBELINE.

Curig a Welsh masculine first name and the name of a Welsh saint whose name is preserved in Capel Curig, Caernarvon, Llangurig, Montgomery, and other places.

Curran a surname, of uncertain meaning, possibly 'resolute hero' (*Irish Gaelic*), used as a masculine first name.

Curt (1) a masculine variant form of KURT. (2) a masculine diminutive form of CURTIS.

Curtis a surname, meaning 'courteous, educated' (*Old French*), used as a masculine first name. William Shakespeare (1564–1616) used the name for a character in his comedy *The Taming of the Shrew*. A diminutive form is Curt.

Cuthbert (1) a masculine first name meaning 'famous bright' (*Old English*). St Cuthbert (634–687) was bishop of the Benedictine abbey of Lindisfarne, from which he evangelised Northumbria. (2) the anglicised masculine form of Irish Gaelic CATHBAD.

Cy a masculine diminutive form of CYRIL, CYRUS.

Cymbeline the anglicised masculine form of Cunobelinus, which is a Latinised form of 'hound of Belenus', from *cú*, 'dog', a name borne by a first-century chieftain of south Britain who resisted the Roman invasion. The character of Cymbeline in the eponymous play by William Shakespeare (1564–1616) bears no relation to the historical figure.

Cynan (pronounced *kee-nan*) a masculine first name meaning 'chief' (*Welsh*) and that of a thirteenth-century Welsh prince, Cynan ap Hywel.

Cynddelw (pronounced *keen-dellow*) a Welsh masculine first name and that of a major twelfth-century poet.

Cynddylan (pronounced *keen-thilann*) a Welsh masculine first name and that of a sixth-century prince of Powys.

Cynedda (pronounced *kee-netha*) a Welsh masculine first name and that of a semi-legendary figure of the fifth century: a king of the Britons of Strathclyde, who established their kingdom also in Gwynedd.

Cynfab (pronounced *keen-fab*) a masculine first name meaning 'first son' (*Welsh*).

Cynfael (pronounced *keen-file*) a masculine first name from *cyn*, 'chief'; *mael*, 'armour' or 'prince' (*Welsh*). It was a warrior name.

Cynfrig (pronounced *keen-frec*) a masculine first name from a river name, incorporating Welsh *cyn*, 'head', 'top' (*Welsh*). Anglicised forms are Kendrick, Kendrew.

Cynog (pronounced *kee-noc*) a Welsh masculine first name and that of a sixth-century saint, whose name is preserved in numerous places, including Llangynog and Ystradgynlais.

Cynon a Welsh masculine first name, probably originally a river name, Afon Cynon, and incorporating Welsh *cynnig*, 'offer', suggesting a river that flowed by a chapel or place of offering (like the Scottish river Orrin) but could also derive from *cú*, 'hound', like many other names. Long in use as a personal name and borne by many Old Welsh heroes.

Cynthia a feminine first name meaning 'belonging to Mount Cynthus' (*Greek*). A diminutive form is Cindie or Cindy.

Cyprian a masculine first name meaning 'from Cyprus', the Mediterranean island (*Greek*). St Cyprian (200–258) was an early Christian theologian and bishop of Carthage.

Cyrano a masculine first name meaning 'from Cyrene', an ancient city of North Africa (*Greek*). Cyrano de Bergerac was a French soldier and writer famed as a duellist and for his large nose celebrated in the play by the French writer Edmond Rostand.

Cyrene or **Cyrena** a feminine first name meaning 'from Cyrene' (*Greek*), an ancient city of North Africa. In Greek mythology, Cyrene was a water nymph loved by Apollo. A variant form is Kyrena.

Cyril a masculine first name meaning 'lordly' (*Greek*). St Cyril of Jerusalem (315–386) was bishop of Jerusalem and a Doctor of the Roman Catholic Church. A diminutive form is Cy.

Cyrill the German masculine form of CYRIL.

Cyrille (1) the French masculine form of CYRIL. (2) feminine form of CYRIL (*French*).

Cyrillus the Danish, Dutch and Swedish masculine forms of CYRIL.

Cyrus a masculine first name meaning 'the sun' (*Persian*). Cyrus II (590–529 BC) founded the Persian Empire. A diminutive form is Cy.

Cytherea a feminine first name meaning 'from Cythera', an island off the southern coast of the Peloponnese, in Greek mythology, home of a cult of Aphrodite (*Greek*).

Cythereia a feminine first name, from CYTHEREA. In Greek mythology, it is an alternative name for Aphrodite.

D

Daffodil the name of the spring plant that yields bright yellow flowers used as a feminine first name (*Dutch/Latin*). A diminutive form is Daffy.

Daffy a feminine diminutive form of DAFFODIL.

Dafydd (pronounced *daf-ith*) a masculine first name, the Welsh form of David. Dafydd ap Gwilym (fourteenth century) is one of Wales's greatest poets. The one-time by-name for a Welshman, 'Taffy', comes from this name, because of its frequency in earlier times. Diminute forms are DEWI, Deian and DAI.

Dag a masculine first name meaning 'day' (*Norse*).

Dagan a masculine first name meaning 'earth', the name of an earth god of the Assyrians and Babylonians (*Semitic*).

Dagmar a feminine first name meaning 'bright day' (*Norse*).

Dahlia the name of the plant with brightly coloured flowers, named after the Swedish botanist Anders Dahl ('dale'), used as a feminine first name.

Dai a Welsh masculine diminutive form of DAVID, formerly a name in its own right, meaning 'shining'.

Daibhidh a masculine first name, a Scottish Gaelic form of David and a name borne by two Scottish kings.

Daimíne (pronounced *daa-win*) an Irish Gaelic masculine first name from *daimhín*, 'little fawn' (*Irish Gaelic*). It is anglicised as Damien or Damian.

Dair a Scottish masculine first name that may hark back to *dar*, 'oak' (*Scottish Gaelic*) or may simply be the latter part of ALASDAIR, originally an abbreviation but turned into a separate name by the association with oak.

Dáire (pronounced *darr-ya*) a masculine first name meaning 'fruitful', 'fertile' (*Irish Gaelic*). A popular name in early Ireland. Dáire macFiachna was the owner of the famous Brown Bull of Cooley.

Dairean and **Dáirine** Irish Gaelic feminine forms of DARINA.

Daisy the name of the plant, 'the day's eye' (*Old English*), used as a feminine first name. The American-born writer Henry James (1843–1916) used the name for the pretty but unsophisticated eponymous heroine of his short novel *Daisy Miller* (1878). The American writer F. Scott Fitzgerald (1896–1940) used the name for Daisy Buchanan, the main female character in his novel *The Great Gatsby* (1925).

Dale a surname, meaning 'valley', used as a masculine or feminine first name (*Old English*). Dale Winton is a popular TV game show host.

Daley a masculine and feminine variant of DALY.

Dalilah or **Dalila** feminine variant forms of DELILAH.

Dallas (1) a place name and surname, from *dail*, 'field', *eas*, 'falling stream' (*Scottish Gaelic*), used as a first name. (2) a surname, meaning 'dale house' (*Old English*), used as a masculine first name.

Dalton a surname, meaning 'dale farm' (*Old English*), used as a masculine first name.

Daly a surname, from *dáil*, 'meeting', perhaps with the sense of 'counsellor' (*Irish Gaelic*), used as a masculine or feminine first name. A variant form is Daley.

Dalziel a place name and surname, meaning 'field of the sun gleam' (*Scots Gaelic*), used as a masculine first name.

Damian (1) the French masculine form of DAMON. (2) an anglicised masculine form of Irish Gaelic DAIMÍNE.

Damiano the Italian masculine form of DAMON.

Damien (1) a masculine first name meaning 'taming' (*Greek*). (2) an anglicised masculine form of Irish Gaelic DAIMÍNE.

Damon a masculine first name meaning 'conqueror' (*Greek*).

Dan a masculine diminutive form of DANBY, DANIEL.

Dana (1) (pronounced *daa-na*) an ancient Irish Gaelic feminine first name that comes from a Celtic goddess, originally ANU or Ana, 'the abundant one'. The name later was modified to Danu or Dana. An anglicised form is Don. (2) a surname, of uncertain meaning, possibly 'Danish' (*Old English*), used as a masculine or feminine first name. Dana Andrews (1909–92) was an American film actor who starred in such films as *Laura* (1944) and *The Best Years of Our Lives* (1946). (3) a feminine form of DAN, DANIEL.

Danaë a feminine first name from Greek mythology, that of the mother of

Perseus by Zeus, who came to her as a shower of gold while she was in prison. Diminutive forms are Dannie, Danny.

Danby a place name and surname, meaning 'Danes' settlement', used as a masculine first name (*Old Norse*). A diminutive form is Dan.

Dandie or **Dandy** a Scottish masculine diminutive form of ANDREW.

Daniel a masculine first name meaning 'God is my judge' (*Hebrew*). In the Old Testament it was the name of the second son of David and also of the author of the Book of Daniel, a youth who was taken into the household of Nebuchadnezzar, who was given divine protection when thrown into a den of lions. Daniel Day Lewis is an English actor and the son of C. Day Lewis, poet laureate. Diminutive forms are Dan, Dannie, Danny.

Danielle (1) feminine form of DANIEL. (2) the masculine Italian form of DANIEL.

Dannie or **Danny** (1) a masculine diminutive of DANBY, DANIEL. Danny De Vito is an American film actor and producer. (2) a feminine diminutive of DANAË, DANIELLE.

Dante a masculine first name meaning 'steadfast' (*Latin/Italian*). Dante Alighieri (1265–1321) was an Italian poet, philosopher, soldier and politician whose supreme masterpiece was *La Divina Commedia* (*The Divine Comedy*), an allegorical account of his journey through Hell, Purgatory and Paradise.

Danu *see* DANA.

Daphne a feminine first name meaning 'laurel' (*Greek*). In Greek mythology Daphne was a nymph who was loved by Apollo. She beseeched Zeus to protect her, which he did by turning her into a laurel at the moment Apollo was to about to encircle her in his arms. The laurel is particularly associated with Apollo.

Dara (1) a feminine first name meaning 'oak', from *dar*, 'oak' (*Irish Gaelic*). A variant form is Deri. The oak was a venerated tree in Celtic lore, playing a part in the druidic cult. (2) a feminine first name meaning 'charity' (*Hebrew*).

Darby (1) a variant form of Derby, a surname meaning 'a village where deer are seen' (*Old Norse*), used as a masculine first name. (2) a diminutive form of DERMOT and DIARMAID.

Darcey or **Darci** or **Darcie** a feminine form of DARCY.

Darcy or **D'Arcy** a surname, of Norman French origin, used as a masculine or feminine first name. Its use as a first name in Ireland may be influenced by its assimilation to Gaelic *dorcha*, 'dark'. A feminine variant form is Darcey, Darci or Darcie.

Darell a masculine variant form of DARRELL.

Daria the feminine form of DARIUS.

Darian or **Darien** a masculine variant form of DARREN.

Darina a feminine first name from *dáireann*, 'fruitful' (*Irish Gaelic*). The Gaelic name is Dáirine, with alternative forms Daireann, Doirend, Doirenn. Darina Allen is one of Ireland's best-known cooks.

Dario the Italian masculine form of DARIUS.

Darius a masculine first name meaning 'preserver' (*Persian*). Darius I, 'the Great', (550–486 BC) was king of Persia (522–486 BC) and known for his great building projects.

Darlene or **Darleen** the endearment 'darling' combined with a suffix to form a feminine first name (*Old English*).

Darnell a surname, meaning 'hidden nook' (*Old English*), used as a masculine first name.

Darrell or **Darrel** a surname, meaning 'from Airelle in Normandy', used as a masculine first name. Variant forms are Darell, Darryl, Daryl.

Darrelle feminine form of Darrell.

Darren or **Darin** a surname, of unknown origin, used as a masculine first name. A variant form is Darian, Darien.

Darryl a variant form of DARRELL, also used as a girl's name.

Darshan a masculine first name meaning 'see' (*Sanskrit*).

Darthula an English feminine first name adapted by the Scottish poet James Macpherson (1736–96) from the name DEIRDRE in his Ossian poems.

Darton a surname, meaning 'deer enclosure or forest' (*Old English*), used as a masculine first name.

Daryl a variant form of DARRELL, also used as a girl's name. Daryl Hannah is an American film actress.

Dave a masculine diminutive form of DAVID.

David a masculine first name meaning 'beloved' (*Hebrew*). In the Old Testament, David was the second king of the Hebrews (after Saul), who reigned *c*.1000–960 BC. He united the kingdom of Israel and established the capital at Jerusalem. The Welsh form is DAFYDD and the Scottish Gaelic form DAIBHIDH. Diminutive forms are Dave, Davie, Davy. St

David (*c*.520–600), who was a monk and bishop, is the patron saint of Wales.

Davida a Scottish feminine form of David. A diminutive form is Vida.

Davidde the Italian masculine form of DAVID.

Davide the French masculine form of DAVID.

Davidina a Scottish feminine form of DAVID.

Davie a masculine diminutive form of DAVID.

Davin a masculine variant form of DEVIN.

Davina or **Davinia** a Scottish feminine form of David, but the name could also be linked to *daimhin*, 'fawn' (*Scottish Gaelic*). A diminutive form is Vina.

Davis a surname, meaning 'DAVID's son' (*Old English*), used as a masculine first name.

Davy a masculine diminutive form of DAVID.

Dawn the name of the first part of the day used as a feminine first name.

Deaglán the Irish Gaelic form of DECLAN.

Dean (1) a surname, meaning 'one who lives in a valley' (*Old English*) or 'serving as a dean' (*Old French*), used as a masculine first name. Dean Stockwell is an American film actor. (2) the anglicised form of DINO.

Deana or **Deane** feminine forms of DEAN. Variant forms are Dena, Dene.

Deanna or **Deanne** a feminine variant form of DIANA.

Dearbhail (pronounced *jerval*) a feminine first name meaning 'sincere' (*Irish Gaelic*). The anglicised form is DERVLA.

Dearbhorgaill (pronounced *jer-vor-gil*) an Irish and Scottish Gaelic feminine first name that perhaps stems from the same root as DEARBHAIL. An anglicised form is DEVORGUILLA or DEVORGILLA.

Dearborn a surname, meaning 'deer brook' (*Old English*), used as a masculine first name.

Deasúin the modern Irish Gaelic masculine form of DESMOND.

Deb or **Debbie** or **Debby** feminine diminutive forms of DEBORAH.

Deborah or **Debra** a feminine first name meaning 'bee' (*Hebrew*). In the Old Testament Deborah was a prophet and heroine of Israel who fought the Canaanites. Deborah Kerr is a Scottish-born film actress. Debra Winger is an American film actress. Diminutive forms are Deb, Debbie, Debby.

Dechtire (pronounced *dec-tira*) a feminine first name possibly stemming from *deich*, 'ten' (*Irish Gaelic*). In Celtic mythology, Dechtire, daughter of the druid Cathbad, was the mother of CUCHULLAIN. Variant forms are Deichtine, Deicteir and the anglicised Dectora.

Decima feminine form of DECIMUS.

Decimus a masculine first name meaning 'tenth' (*Latin*).

Declan a masculine first name perhaps stemming from *deagh*, 'good' (*Irish Gaelic*). The Gaelic form is Deaglán. It was the name of a fifth-century Celtic missionary who preceded St Patrick to Ireland.

Dectora the anglicised feminine form of Irish Gaelic DECHTIRE.

Dedrick a masculine first name meaning 'people's ruler' (*Germanic*).

Dedwydd (pronounced *ded-with*) a masculine first name meaning 'blessed one' (*Welsh*).

Dee (1) a feminine first name from a river name in Ireland, Wales, England and Scotland that derives from a root word *dia*, 'goddess' (*Gaelic/Welsh*). (2) or **Deedee** a feminine diminutive form of names beginning with D.

Deepak a masculine first name meaning 'small lamp' (*Sanskrit*). A variant form is Dipak.

Deian a Welsh diminutive form of DAFYDD.

Deichtine and **Deicteir** variant feminine forms of DECHTIRE.

Deiniol a masculine first name possibly meaning 'charming' (*Welsh*). St Deiniol was the founder of abbeys at Bangor, Caernarfon, and Bangor-on-Dee.

Deirdre (pronounced *deer-dra*) an Irish Gaelic feminine first name the source of which is uncertain, but despite its legendary linking with 'sorrows', it is unlikely to be anything to do with grief. It may simply mean 'girl' or 'daughter'. It is the name of the tragic heroine of a great poem from the Ulster Cycle and is widely used in Ireland and Scotland. A variant form is Deirdra.

Delfine a feminine variant form of DELPHINE.

Delia a feminine first name meaning 'woman of Delos' (*Greek*). Delos was one of the sacred places of ancient Greece. Delia Smith is probably Britain's best-known cook.

Delicia a feminine first name meaning 'great delight' (*Latin*).

Delight the abstract noun for great pleasure, satisfaction or joy used as a feminine first name (*Old French*).

Delilah or **Delila** a feminine first name, the meaning of which is uncertain but possibly 'delicate' (*Hebrew*). In the Old Testament Delilah was a

Philistine woman who managed to persuade Samson, who was her lover, to tell her that the secret of his strength was his hair and who betrayed this secret to his enemies. Variant forms are Dalila, Dalilah. A diminutive form is Lila.

Dell (1) a surname, meaning 'one who lives in a hollow', used as a masculine first name. (2) a diminutive form of DELMAR, etc.

Della a diminutive form of ADELA now used independently.

Delma (1) feminine form of DELMAR. (2) a diminutive form of FIDELMA.

Delmar a masculine first name meaning 'of the sea' (*Latin*).

Delores a feminine variant form of DOLORES.

Delphine a feminine first name meaning 'dolphin' (*Latin*). A variant form is Delfine.

Delwyn or **Delwin** a masculine first name meaning 'pretty boy', from *del*, 'pretty' (*Welsh*).

Delyth (pronounced *del-ith*) a feminine first name meaning 'pretty girl', from *del*, 'pretty' (*Welsh*).

Demelza a Cornish place name used as a feminine first name, prompted by the heroine of Winston Graham's *Poldark* novels.

Demetra or **Demetria** a feminine form of DEMETRIUS. A diminutive form is Demi.

Demetrius a masculine first name meaning 'belonging to Demeter, goddess of the harvest, earth mother' (*Greek*). In the New Testament Demetrius was a Christian mentioned by John in a letter. William Shakespeare (1564–1616) used the name for one of the heroes of his comedy *A Midsummer Night's Dream* and for one of the Goth princes in his tragedy *Titus Andronicus*.

Demi a diminutive form of Demetra. Demi Moore is an American film actress.

Dempsey a surname, meaning 'proud descendant' (*Gaelic*), used as a masculine first name.

Dempster a surname, meaning 'judge' (*Old English*), used as a masculine first name, formerly a feminine one.

Den masculine diminutive form of DENIS, DENNIS, DENISON, DENLEY, DENMAN, DENNISON, DENTON, DENVER, DENZEL, DENZELL, DENZIL.

Dena or **Dene** feminine variant forms of DEANA.

Denby a surname, meaning 'Danish settlement' (*Norse*), used as a masculine first name.

89

Denice a feminine variant form of DENISE.

Denis a masculine variant form of DENNIS. St Denis was the third-century first bishop of Paris and is the patron saint of France.

Denise the feminine form of DENIS. A variant form is Denice.

Denison a masculine variant form of DENNISON.

Denley a surname, meaning 'wood or clearing in a valley' (*Old English*), used as a masculine first name.

Denman a surname, meaning 'dweller in a valley' (*Old English*), used as a masculine first name.

Dennis a masculine first name meaning 'belonging to Dionysus, the god of wine' (*Greek*). Dennis Hopper and Dennis Quaid are American film actors. A variant form is DENIS. The Cornish form is DENZIL, the Welsh is DION. Diminutive forms are Den, Denny.

Dennison a masculine first name meaning 'son of DENNIS' (*Old English*). Variant forms are Denison, Tennison, Tennyson.

Denny a diminutive form of DENISE, DENNIS.

Denton a surname, meaning 'valley place' (*Old English*), used as a masculine first name.

Denver a surname, meaning 'Danes' crossing' (*Old English*), used as a masculine first name.

Denzil (1) a Cornish masculine form of the Greek name Dionysius, whose anglicised form is DENNIS. (2) a variant form of DENZEL.

Denzel or **Denzell** a surname, meaning 'stronghold' (*Celtic*), used as a masculine first name. Denzel Washington is an American film actor. A variant form is Denzil.

Deon a masculine variant form of DION.

Deórsa a Scottish Gaelic masculine form of GEORGE. *See also* SEÓRAS.

Derek an English masculine form of THEODORIC. Variant forms are Derrick, Derrik. A diminutive form is DERRY.

Derfel a Welsh masculine first name and a saint's name, preserved at Llandderfel, Merioneth. The is also the name of a prophetic character portrayed in John Cowper Powys's novel *Owen Glendower*.

Deri (1) a masculine first name meaning 'oak-like', from *derw*, 'oak tree' (*Welsh*). The anglicised form is Derry. (2) a feminine variant form of DARA.

Dermot the anglicised masculine form of DIARMAID. A diminutive form is DERRY.

Derrick or **Derrik** masculine variant forms of Derek. A diminutive form is DERRY.

Derry the anglicised masculine form DERI. (2) a diminutive form of DEREK, DERRICK, DERRIK, DERMOT, DIARMID.

Derryth a Welsh feminine form of DERI.

Dervla the anglicised feminine form of Dearbhail. Dervla Murphy is an intrepid and well-known travel writer who usually takes a bicycle on her travels.

Derwent a place name and surname, meaning 'river that flows through oak woods' (*Old English*), used as a masculine first name.

Desdemona a feminine first name meaning 'ill-fated' (*Greek*). The name given by William Shakespeare (1564–1616) to the wife of Othello in his tragedy of that name.

Desirée a feminine first name meaning 'longed for' (*French*).

Desmond (1) a masculine first name from *deas*, 'south', *Mumu*, 'Munster' (*Irish Gaelic*). It is a territorial name associated especially with the Fitzgerald family. The modern Gaelic form is Deasúin. (2) a masculine variant form of ESMOND (*Germanic*).

Deva the Latinised form of the river name DEE, found in England, Ireland, Wales and Scotland, used as a feminine first name.

Deverell or **Deverill** a surname, meaning 'fertile river bank' (*Celtic*), used as a masculine first name.

Devin or **Devinn** a surname, meaning 'poet' (*Irish Gaelic*), used as a masculine first name. A variant form is Davin.

Devlin a masculine first name meaning 'fiercely brave' (*Irish Gaelic*).

Devon the name of the English county, meaning 'deep ones' (*Celtic*), used as a masculine first name.

Devona the feminine form of DEVON.

Devorguilla or **Devorgilla** an anglicised form of Irish and Scottish Gaelic DEARBHORGAILL. In Irish legend Devorguilla was one of the many women to fall in love with CUCHULLAIN. Devorguilla Balliol, mother of King John Balliol of Scotland, founded Balliol College, Oxford, and Sweetheart Abbey in Dumfriesshire.

Dewey a Celtic masculine form of DAVID.

Dewi a Welsh masculine form of DAVID. Dewi Sant, or St David, the patron saint of Wales, died in 588.

De Witt a masculine first name meaning 'fair-haired' (*Flemish*).

Dexter a surname, meaning '(woman) dyer' (*Old English*), used as a masculine first name.

Di a feminine diminutive form of DIANA, DIANE, DIANNE, DINA, DINAH.

Diamond the name of the gem, meaning 'the hardest iron or steel' (*Latin*), used as a masculine first name.

Diana a feminine first name meaning 'goddess' (*Latin*). In Roman mythology Diana was an ancient goddess. In later times she was identified with the Greek Artemis, with whom she had various attributes in common, being the virgin goddess of the moon and of the hunt. The name gained fame in the twentieth century from Diana, Princess of Wales (1961–97), the ex-wife of Charles, Prince of Wales. Diminutive forms are Dee, Di.

Diane or **Dianne** feminine French forms of DIANA. Diane Keaton and Dianne Wiest are American film actresses.

Diarmaid (pronounced *der-mit*) a masculine first name meaning 'he who reverences God', from Gaelic *dia*, 'God' (*Irish/Scottish Gaelic*). The name of many heroes of legend, especially Diarmait úa Duibne, the hero of *The Pursuit of Diarmaid and Gráinne*. The last pagan high king of Ireland was said to be Diarmait macCearbhal (died *c*.568). Variant forms are Diarmuid, Diarmid, Diarmait and Diarmit, and the anglicised form is Dermot. A diminutive form is Derry.

Diarmid, Diarmait, Diarmit and **Diarmuid** variant masculine forms of DIARMAID.

Dick or **Dickie** or **Dickon** masculine diminutive forms of RICHARD.

Dickson a surname, meaning 'son of RICHARD' (*Old English*), used as a masculine first name. A variant form is Dixon.

Dicky a masculine diminutive form of RICHARD.

Dido a feminine first name meaning 'teacher' (*Greek*). In Greek mythology Dido was a princess from Tyre who founded Carthage and became its queen. According to Virgil's *Aeneid*, she fell in love with AENEAS but he left her and she committed suicide. Dido was also known as Elissa.

Diego a Spanish masculine form of JAMES.

Dietrich the German masculine form of DEREK. A diminutive form is Till.

Digby a surname, meaning 'settlement at a ditch' (*Old Norse*), used as a masculine first name.

Dilic (pronounced *dee-lik*) a Cornish feminine first name, perhaps an early saint's name.

Dillon a surname of uncertain meaning, possibly 'destroyer' (*Germanic/Irish Gaelic*), used as a masculine first name.

Dilly a feminine diminutive form of DILYS. Dilly Kean is a writer and performer.

Dilys a feminine first name meaning 'sincere' (*Welsh*). A diminutive form is DILLY.

Dimitri a Russian masculine form of Demetrius.

Dina (1) feminine form of DINO. (2) a variant form of DINAH.

Dinah a feminine first name meaning 'vindicated' (*Hebrew*). In the Old Testament Dinah was the daughter of Jacob and Leah. A variant form is Dina. A diminutive form is Di.

Dino a masculine diminutive ending, indicating 'little' (*Italian*), now used independently as a first name.

Dion (pronounced *dee-on*) a Welsh masculine form of DENNIS, which comes from Greek DIONYSIUS. William Shakespeare (1564–1616) used the name for that of a Sicilian lord in his play *A Winter's Tale*. A variant form is Deon.

Dione or **Dionne** a feminine first name meaning 'daughter of heaven and earth' (*Greek*). In Greek mythology, Dione was the earliest consort of Zeus and mother of Aphrodite.

Dionysius in Greek mythology, the god of wine. Dionysius is the source of the name DENNIS.

Dipak a masculine variant form of DEEPAK.

Dirk (1) the Dutch masculine form of DEREK. Sir Dirk Bogarde (1920–99) was an English film actor. (2) a diminutive form of THEODORIC.

Dixie a feminine diminutive form of BENEDICTA.

Dixon a masculine variant form of DICKSON.

Dmitri a Russian masculine form of Demetrius. Dmitri Shostakovich (1906–75) was a Russian composer.

Dod and **Doddy** Scottish diminutive forms of GEORGE.

Dodie (1) a feminine diminutive form of DOROTHY. Dodie Smith (1896–1900) was an English playwright. (2) a Scottish masculine diminutive form of GEORGE.

Dodo a feminine diminutive form of DOROTHY.

Dogmael (pronounced *dog-mile*) a Welsh masculine first name. St Dogmael is a Welsh saint, contemporary with St David.

Doirend and **Doirenn** Irish Gaelic feminine forms of DARINA.

Dolan a masculine variant form of DOOLAN.

Dolina (pronounced *dol-eena*) a Scottish feminine form of DONALD, common in Gaelic-speaking areas in the nineteenth and early twentieth centuries, and still in use. *See also* DONALDA.

Doll or **Dolly** a feminine diminutive form of DOROTHY. William Shakespeare (1654–1616) used the name for Doll Tearsheet who appears in his play King Henry IV, Part 2. Dolly Parton is an American country and western singer and film actress.

Dolores a feminine first name meaning 'sorrows' (*Spanish*). A variant form is DELORES. Diminutive forms are Lola, Lolita.

Dolph a masculine diminutive form of ADOLPH. Dolph Lundgren is a Swedish-born film actor who appears in action films.

Dom a masculine diminutive form of DOMINIC.

Domenico the Italian masculine form of DOMINIC. Domenico Barberi (1792–1849) was an Italian prelate who worked as a missionary in England.

Domhnall the Scottish Gaelic form of DONALD.

Domingo the Spanish masculine form of DOMINIC.

Dominic a masculine first name meaning 'belonging to the lord' (*Latin*). St Dominic (1170–1221) was the founder of the Dominican order. Dominic Elwes is an English painter and father of the actor Cary Elwes. A variant form is Dominick. A diminutive form is Dom.

Dominica the feminine form of Dominic.

Dominick a masculine variant form of Dominic.

Dominique the French masculine form of DOMINIC, now used in English as a girl's name.

Don (1) a masculine diminutive form of DONAL, DONALD, DONALL. (2) an anglicised feminine form of DANA.

Donal an Irish masculine form of DONALD. A variant form is Donall. Diminutive forms are Don, Donnie, Donny.

Donald a masculine first name from the Gaelic form Domhnall, from a Celtic root *dubno* or *dumno*, 'great ruler'. Nowadays mostly associated with Scotland and once the most popular boys' name in the Highlands and Islands, it was also a frequently used name in old Ireland and is still used there in the form Donal. Donald Sutherland is a Canadian-born film director. Diminutive forms include Don, Donnie, Donny.

Donalda or **Donaldina** a Scottish feminine form of DONALD, usually given to the daughter of a man named Donald. Other feminine forms are Donaldina, Donella, DOLINA.

Donall a masculine variant form of DONAL.

Donata feminine form of DONATO.

Donato a masculine first name meaning 'gift of God' (*Latin*). Donato Bramante (1444–1514) was an Italian architect and painter.

Donella *see* DONALDA.

Donn an Irish and Scottish masculine first name. 'Brown' is the most common meaning attributed to this name, although Old Gaelic *donn* had a number of meanings, including 'lord'.

Donna a feminine first name meaning 'lady' (*Italian*).

Donnchadh the Gaelic masculine form of DUNCAN. In this form the name was popular in Gaelic Ireland as well as in Scotland.

Donnie or **Donny** masculine diminutive forms of DONAL, DONALD, DONALL.

Donovan a surname, meaning 'dark brown' (*Irish Gaelic*) used as a masculine first name.

Doolan a surname, meaning 'black defiance' (*Irish Gaelic*), used as a masculine first name. A variant form is Dolan.

Dora a feminine diminutive form of DOROTHEA, THEODORA, etc, now used independently. Dora Bryan is an English actress. Diminutive forms are Dorrie, Dorry.

Doran a surname, meaning 'stranger' or 'exile' (*Irish Gaelic*), used as a masculine first name.

Dorcas (1) a feminine first name meaning 'a gazelle' (*Greek*). In the New Testament Dorcas was a Christian woman who lived in Joppa. William Shakespeare (1564–1616) used the name for that of a shepherdess in his play *A Winter's Tale*. (2) an anglicised feminine form of the Gaelic *dorchas*, 'dark'.

Doreen an Irish feminine variant form of DORA.

Dorian a masculine first name meaning 'Dorian man' (*Greek*), one of a Hellenic people who invaded Greece in the 2nd century BC. Its use as a first name was probably invented by Oscar Wilde (1854–1900) for his novel, *The Picture of Dorian Gray*.

Dorinda a feminine first name meaning 'lovely gift' (*Greek*). The English comic dramatist George Farquhar (1678–1707) used the name for the daughter of Lady Bountiful in his play *The Beaux Stratagem* (1707). A diminutive form is Dorrie, Dorry.

Doris a feminine first name meaning 'Dorian woman', one of a Hellenic people who invaded Greece in the second century BC (*Greek*). Doris Day is an American film actress and singer. Diminutive forms are Dorrie, Dorry.

Dorothea a German feminine form of DOROTHEA. George Eliot (1819–80) used the name for the heroine of her novel *Middlemarch* (1871–72). A diminutive form is Thea.

Dorothée a French feminine form of DOROTHEA.

Dorothy a feminine first name meaning 'the gift of God' (*Greek*). The American writer L. Frank Baum (1856–1919) used the name for the heroine of his perennially popular *The Wonderful Wizard of Oz* (1900). Diminutive forms are Dodie, Dodo, Doll, Dolly, Dot, Dottie, Dotty.

Dorrie or **Dorry** feminine diminutive forms of DORA, DORINDA, DORIS.

Dorward a masculine variant form of DURWARD.

Dot and **Dottie** or **Dotty** feminine diminutive forms of DOROTHY.

Doug or **Dougie** a masculine diminutive form of DOUGAL, DOUGLAS.

Dougal or **Dougald** or **Dougall** (pronounced *doo-gal*) a masculine first name meaning 'dark stranger', from Gaelic *dubh*, 'dark', and *gall*, 'stranger' (*Scottish Gaelic*). The Gaels differentiated between the Norwegians, 'fair strangers', and the Danes, 'dark strangers'. This name may have been given to a child with one Norse parent. It is often wrongly assumed to be cognate with Douglas, and the diminutive forms Doug and Dougie are the same in both. Variant forms are Dugal, Dugald.

Douglas (pronounced *dugg-las*) a masculine first name meaning 'dark water' (*Scottish Gaelic/Manx*). This was originally a location name from a place in the Scottish Borders, and the surname was adopted by twelfth-century Flemish immigrants. The name achieved great fame with Sir James Douglas, comrade-in-arms of King Robert I. Diminutive forms are Doug, Dougie.

Douglasina a Scottish feminine form of Douglas.

Dow a surname, meaning 'black' or 'black-haired' (*Scottish Gaelic*), used as a masculine first name.

Dowal the anglicised masculine form of DUNGAL. It is the source of the Galloway surname MacDowall.

Doyle an Irish Gaelic masculine form of DOUGAL.

D'Oyley a surname, meaning 'from Ouilly—rich land' (*Old French*), used as a masculine first name. Richard D'Oyley Carte (1844–1901) was the

English impresario who mounted the comic operas of Sir William S. Gilbert and Sir Arthur Sullivan.

Drake a surname, meaning 'dragon or standard bearer' (*Old English*), used as a masculine first name.

Drew (1) a masculine diminutive form of ANDREW. (2) a surname, meaning 'trusty' (*Germanic*) or 'lover' (*Old French*), used as a masculine first name.

Driscoll or **Driscol** a surname, meaning 'interpreter' (*Irish Gaelic*), used as a masculine first name.

Drostan a variant masculine form of DRUST.

Drostán an Irish Gaelic masculine first name from that of a follower of St Columba and founder of the monastery of Deer in Aberdeenshire.

Druce a surname, meaning 'from Eure or Rieux in France' (*Old French*), or 'sturdy lover' (*Celtic*), used as a masculine first name.

Drudwen a feminine first name meaning 'precious' (*Welsh*).

Drummond a surname, meaning 'ridge', used as a masculine first name.

Drury a surname, meaning 'dear one' (*Old French*), used as a masculine first name.

Drusilla a feminine first name meaning 'with dewy eyes' (*Latin*). In the New Testament Drusilla was the youngest daughter of King Herod Agrippa I and sister of Bernice. Her second husband was Felix, the Roman governor of Caesarea.

Drust a Pictish masculine first name and that of several Pictish kings, including the eighth-century Drust, son of Talorcan. Variant forms are Drustan, Drostan, perhaps commemorated in the hill Trostan in County Antrim.

Drustan (1) a Brythonic Celtic masculine first name that is sometimes taken as an older version of TRYSTAN. (2) a variant form of DRUST.

Dryden a surname, meaning 'dry valley' (*Old English*), used as a masculine first name.

Duane a masculine first name meaning 'dark' (*Irish Gaelic*). Variant forms are Dwane, Dwayne.

Dubh (pronounced *doov*) a feminine first name meaning 'dark one', from Gaelic *dubh*, 'black' (*Irish/Scottish Gaelic*).

Dubthach (pronounced *doo-tach*) a masculine or feminine first name, from Gaelic *dubh*, 'black' (*Irish/Scottish Gaelic*). It is the source of the Irish surname O'Duffy.

Dudley a place name, meaning 'Dudda's clearing' (*Old English*), used as a masculine first name. Dudley Moore is an English-born comedian, pianist and film actor.

Duff an ancient surname, from the stem *dubh*, 'dark' (*Scottish Gaelic*), used as a masculine first name.

Dugal or **Dugald** masculine variant forms of DOUGAL. A diminutive form is Duggie.

Duggie a masculine diminutive form of DOUGAL, DOUGALL, DOUGLAS, DUGAL, DUGALD.

Duke (1) the title of an English aristocrat used as a masculine first name. (2) a diminutive form of MARMADUKE.

Dulcibella a feminine first name meaning 'sweet beautiful' (*Latin*). A diminutive form is Dulcie.

Dulcie a feminine diminutive form of DULCIBELLA also used independently as a first name. Dulcie Gray was a Malaysian-born English stage and film actress

Dunc a masculine diminutive form of DUNCAN.

Duncan a masculine first name whose meaning is 'brown warrior', from *donn*, 'brown', and *cath*, 'warrior' (*Scottish Gaelic*). The Gaelic form is Donnchadh, and in this form the name was popular in Gaelic Ireland as well as in Scotland. The first king of all Scotland (1034–40) was Duncan (*c*.1001–1040). Duncan Bán MacIntyre (1724–1812) was a famous Scottish Gaelic poet. Diminutive forms are Dunc, Dunkie.

Dungal (pronounced *dunn-gal* or *dowall*) a masculine first name meaning 'brown stranger', from *donn*, 'brown', and *gall*, 'stranger' (*Scottish Gaelic*). It is anglicised as Dowal, the source of the Galloway surname MacDowall.

Dunkie a masculine diminutive form of DUNCAN.

Dunlop a surname, meaning 'muddy hill' (*Scottish Gaelic*), used as a masculine first name.

Dunn or **Dunne** a surname, meaning 'dark-skinned' (*Old English*), used as a masculine first name.

Dunstan a masculine first name meaning 'brown hill stone' (*Old English*). St Dunstan (c.909–988) was Archbishop of Canterbury (959–988) and an adviser to the kings of Wessex.

Durand or **Durant** a surname, meaning 'enduring or obstinate' (*Old French*), used as a masculine first name.

Durga a feminine first name meaning 'not accessible' (*Sanskrit*).

Durward a surname, meaning 'doorkeeper or gatekeeper' (*Old English*), used as a masculine first name. A variant form is Dorward.

Durwin a masculine first name meaning 'dear friend' *Old English*). A diminutive form is Durwyn.

Dustin a surname, of uncertain meaning, possibly 'of Dionysus', used as a masculine first name. Dustin Hoffman is an American film actor.

Dwane or **Dwayne** masculine variant forms of DUANE.

Dwight a surname, meaning 'THOR's stone' (*Old Norse*), used as a masculine first name.

Dyan a feminine variant form of DIANE.

Dyfan a masculine first name meaning 'ruler' (*Welsh*).

Dyfri (pronounced *dee-fri*) a Welsh masculine first name and that of an early Welsh saint.

Dylan a masculine first name meaning 'son of the waves' (*Welsh*). In the *Mabinogion* poems, it is the name of a son of Arianrod. Appropriately, it was borne by the poet Dylan Thomas (1914–1953).

Dymphna a feminine first name that may stem from *dán*, 'poetry' (*Irish Gaelic*). It was the name of a seventh-century Irish saint.

E

Eachann (pronounced *yach-ann*) the Scottish Gaelic masculine form of the first name HECTOR. It is a translation rather than a sound adaptation. The derivation of Greek Hector is 'horse lord', and this name stems from Gaelic *each*, 'horse'.

Eachna (pronounced *yach-na*) an Irish Gaelic feminine first name, probably a feminine form of EACHANN. A variant form is Echna.

Eada a feminine variant form of ALDA.

Eadaín a feminine variant form of ETAIN.

Ealasaid (pronounced *yalla-suth*) a feminine first name, the Scottish Gaelic form of ELIZABETH.

Ealga (pronounced *yal-ga*) a feminine first name meaning 'noble, brave' (*Irish Gaelic*).

Eamair a feminine variant form of EMER.

Eamonn or **Eamon** (pronounced *ay-mon*) the Irish Gaelic masculine form of EDMUND. Eamonn an Chnuic, 'of the hill', was a famous outlaw of the seventeenth century in County Tipperary. Eamon de Valera (1882–1975) was the first President of the Irish Republic.

Eanraig the Scottish Gaelic masculine form of HENRY.

Earl or **Earle** an English title, meaning 'nobleman' (*Old English*), used as a masculine first name. Variant forms are Erle, Errol.

Earlene or **Earline** feminine form of EARL. A variant form is Erlene, Erline. Diminutive forms are Earlie, Earley.

Earlie or **Earley** feminine diminutive forms of EARLENE.

Eartha a feminine first name meaning 'of the earth' (*Old English*). A variant form is Ertha.

Easter the name of the Christian festival, used as a feminine first name.

Eaton a surname, meaning 'river or island farm' (*Old English*), used as a masculine first name.

Eavan (pronounced *ay-van*) a feminine first name meaning 'radiant' (*Irish Gaelic*). It is a form of AOIBHINN.

Eb a masculine diminutive form of EBEN, EBENEZER.

Ebba (1) a feminine first name meaning 'wild boar' (*Germanic*). (2) an Old English form of EVE.

Eben a masculine first name meaning 'stone' (*Hebrew*). A diminutive form is Eb.

Ebenezer a masculine first name adopted in the seventeenth century by the Puritans from the name of an Old Testament site, meaning 'stone of help' (*Hebrew*), the scene of two defeats of the Israelites by the Philistines. Two writers used the name for that of a miser: Charles Dickens (1812–70) for Ebenezer Scrooge in *A Christmas Carol* (1843), and Robert Louis Stevenson (1850–94) for the name of David Balfour's grasping uncle in *Kidnapped* (1886). Diminutive forms are Eb, Eben.

Eber an Irish and Scottish Gaelic masculine first name the etymology of which is uncertain. It was the name of the supposed founder of the Scots, great-grandson of Scota, a daughter of the Pharaoh Nectanebo. Another, later, Eber was a son of Míl Espáine (*see* MILES).

Eberhard or **Ebert** German masculine forms of EVERARD.

Ebony the name of the dark hard wood used as a feminine first name.

Echna a feminine variant form of EACHNA.

Echo the name for the physical phenomenon of the reflection of sound or other radiation used as a feminine first name. In Greek mythology it is the name of the nymph who pined away for love of Narcissus.

Ed a masculine diminutive form of EDBERT, EDGAR, EDMUND, EDWARD, EDWIN.

Eda a feminine first name meaning 'prosperity, happiness' (*Old English*).

Edaín a feminine variant form of ETAIN.

Edan an anglicised masculine form of AEDÁN.

Edana feminine form of EDAN.

Edbert a masculine first name meaning 'prosperous; bright' (*Old English*).

Eddie or **Eddy** masculine diminutive forms of EDBERT, EDGAR, EDMUND, EDWARD, EDWIN.

Edel a masculine first name meaning 'noble' (*Germanic*).

Edelmar a masculine first name meaning 'noble, famous' (*Old English*).

Eden (1) a masculine first name meaning 'pleasantness' (*Hebrew*), in the Old Testament the name of the paradise where Adam and Eve lived before they sinned. (2) a surname, meaning 'blessed helmet', used as a masculine first name.

Edgar a masculine first name meaning 'prosperity spear' (*Old English*). William Shakespeare (1564–1616) used the name for that of the legitimate son of the Duke of Gloucester in *King Lear*. Diminutive forms are Ed, Eddie, Eddy, Ned, Neddie, Neddy.

Edie a feminine diminutive form of EDINA, EDITH, EDWINA.

Edina a Scottish feminine variant form of EDWINA.

Edith a feminine first name meaning 'prosperity strife' (*Old English*). Variant forms are Edyth, Edythe. Diminutive forms are Edie, Edy.

Edlyn a feminine first name meaning 'noble maid' (*Old English*).

Edmond the French masculine form of EDMUND.

Edmonda feminine form of EDMUND (*Old English*).

Edmund a masculine first name meaning 'prosperity defender' (*Old English*). St Edmund (1175–1240) was Archbishop of Canterbury (1234–40) and a distinguished scholar. William Shakespeare (1564–1616) used the name for that of the natural son of the Duke of Gloucester determined to oust his legitimate brother EDGAR in *King Lear*.

Edna (1) a feminine first name meaning 'pleasure' (*Hebrew*). (2) an anglicised feminine form of Welsh EITHNA.

Ednyfed (pronounced *ed-niffith*) a Welsh masculine first name and that of a thirteenth-century king of Gwynnedd, but referred to in the poem 'The War Song of Dinas Vawr' by the English poet Thomas Love Peacock (1785–1866) as 'Ednyfed, king of Dyfed'.

Edoardo an Italian masculine form of EDWARD.

Édouard the French masculine form of EDWARD.

Edrea feminine form of EDRIC.

Edric a masculine first name meaning 'wealthy ruler' (*Old English*).

Edryd a masculine first name meaning 'restoration' (*Welsh*).

Edsel a masculine first name meaning 'noble' (*Germanic*).

Eduardo the Italian and Spanish masculine form of EDWARD.

Edwald a masculine first name meaning 'prosperous ruler' (*Old English*).

Edward a masculine first name meaning 'guardian of happiness' (*Old English*). It was the name of several kings of England or Britain, including St Edward the Confessor (*c.* 1003–66, ruled 1042–66) whose death was followed by the short reign of Harold before the Norman conquest of England, Diminutive forms are Ed, Eddie, Eddy, Ned, Ted, Teddy.

Edwardina feminine form of EDWARD.

Edwige the French feminine form of HEDWIG.

Edwin a masculine first name meaning 'prosperity friend' (*Old English*).

Edwina feminine form of EDWIN. Edwina Currie is an English politician and novelist. A variant form is Edina.

Edy a feminine diminutive form of EDITH.

Edyth or **Edythe** feminine variant forms of EDITH.

Eevin a feminine anglicised form of AÍBELL.

Efa the Welsh feminine form of EVE.

Effie a feminine diminutive form of EUPHEMIA.

Egan (1) a surname, meaning 'son of HUGH' (*Irish Gaelic*), used as a masculine first name. (2) anglicised form of Irish Gaelic/Manx AODHAGÁN.

Egbert a masculine first name meaning 'sword bright' (*Germanic*).

Egberta feminine form of EGBERT (*Old English*).

Egidio the Italian and Spanish masculine form of GILES.

Eglantine an alternative name for the wild rose, meaning 'sharp, keen' (*Old French*), used as a feminine first name.

Ehren a masculine first name meaning 'honourable one' (*Germanic*).

Eibhlinn (pronounced *aiv-linn*) a feminine first name that is related to *ao-ibhlinn*, 'radiance' (*Irish/Scottish Gaelic*) and is the source of this name. In the course of time it has sometimes been taken as related to other names, including EVE and AVELINE. Its most common anglicised version is EILEEN.

Eigra (pronounced *eye-gra*) a feminine first name meaning 'fair maid' (*Welsh*). Eigra was the reputed name of King ARTHUR's mother, found in Sir Thomas Malory's Arthurian tales as Igraine.

Eileen (1) the Irish feminine form of HELEN. A variant form is AILEEN. (2) an anglicised feminine form of EIBHLINN.

Eilidh (pronounced *ay-lee*) the Irish and Scottish Gaelic form of HELEN. A diminutive form is Ellie.

Eilir a masculine first name meaning 'butterfly' (*Welsh*).

Eilis an Irish Gaelic feminine first name that is probably a Gaelicised form of ALICE.

Eiluned a Welsh feminine variant form of LUNED.

Eilwen (pronounced *isle-wen*) a feminine first name meaning 'white-browed' (*Welsh*).

Eimear and **Eimer** feminine variant forms of EMER.

Eimhair a Scottish feminine form of EMER.

Einar a masculine first name meaning 'single warrior' (*Old Norse*).

Einion (pronounced *ine-yon*) a masculine first name meaning 'anvil' (*Welsh*). It is a name often found in Welsh legend and anglicised into Eynon. *See* BEYNON.

Eira (pronounced *eye-ra*) a feminine first name meaning 'snow' (*Welsh*). A variant form is Eirwen, equivalent to 'Snow-white'.

Eire (pronounced *ay-ra*) an Irish Gaelic feminine first name and that of an old Irish goddess which has become synonymous with the country of Ireland.

Eirian (pronounced *eye-reean*) a masculine or feminine first name meaning 'fair, shining' (*Welsh*). A feminine-only form is Eirianwen.

Eirianwen the Welsh feminine form of EIRIAN.

Eiriol (pronounced *eye-reeol*) a feminine first name meaning 'beseeching' (*Welsh*).

Eirlys (pronounced *ire-lis*) a feminine first name meaning 'snowdrop' (*Welsh*).

Eirwen a variant feminine form of EIRA.

Eirys (pronounced *eye-ris*) a feminine first name, the Welsh form of IRIS.

Eithlenn a feminine variant form of EITHNA.

Eithna or **Eithne** (pronounced *eth-na*) an Irish Gaelic feminine first name that was also held by some early Irish saints. It stems from Gaelic *eithne*, 'kernel', implying both fertility and the heart of things. Variant forms are Eithlenn and Enya. There is a Welsh form, Ethni, and it is anglicised as Edna, Ena and Ethna.

Ekata a feminine first name meaning 'unity' (*Sanskrit*).

Elaine (1) a French feminine form of HELEN. (2) an anglicised feminine form of Welsh ELEN. Elaine is the name of 'the lily maid of Astolat' who fell in love with Sir Lancelot in the English Arthurian legend related by Sir Thomas Malory.

Elan a feminine first name from a Welsh river name.

Elda a feminine variant form of ALDA.

Elder a surname, meaning 'senior, elder' (*Old English*), used as a masculine first name.

Eldon a surname, meaning 'Ella's hill' (*Old English*), used as a masculine first name.

Eldora a shortened form of El Dorado, meaning 'the land of gold' (*Spanish*), used as a feminine first name.

Eldred a masculine first name meaning 'terrible' (*Old English*).

Eldrid or **Eldridge** a masculine first name meaning 'wise adviser' (*Old English*).

Eldrida feminine form of ELDRID.

Eleanor or **Eleanore** a feminine variant form of HELEN. Eleanor of Aquitaine (*c.*1122–1204) was the wife of King Louis VII of France (1137–52) and then wife of Henry II (1154–89), bringing with her as her dowry the lands that she possessed in France. Eleanor of Castile (1246–90) was the Spanish-born wife of Edward I. A variant form is Elinor. Diminutive forms are Ella, Nell, Nora.

Eleanora the Italian feminine form of ELEANOR.

Eleazer a masculine variant form of ELIEZER.

Electra a feminine first name meaning 'brilliant' (*Greek*).

Elen a feminine first name meaning 'angel, nymph' (*Welsh*).

Elen a Welsh feminine form of HELEN. Elen was the virgin princess in the *Dream of Macsen Wledig*, a tale of the Roman governor Magnus Maximus who tried to make himself emperor of Rome. An anglicised form is ELAINE.

Elena the Italian and Spanish feminine form of HELEN.

Eleonora the Italian feminine form of ELEANOR.

Eleonore the German feminine form of ELEANOR.

Eléonore a French feminine form of LEONORA.

Eleri a Welsh feminine first name and also a river name from Ceredigion. Eleri was a daughter of the fifth-century chieftain BRYCHAN.

Elfed a masculine first name meaning 'autumn' (*Welsh*).

Elffin a masculine variant form of ELPHIN.

Elfleda a feminine first name meaning 'noble beauty' (*Old English*).

Elfreda a feminine first name meaning 'elf strength' (*Old English*).

Elfreida or **Elfrida** or **Elfrieda** feminine variant forms of ALFREDA.

Elga (1) a feminine first name meaning 'holy' (*Old Norse*). (2) a variant form of OLGA.

Elgan a masculine first name meaning 'bright circle' (*Welsh*).

Eli a masculine first name meaning 'elevated' (*Hebrew*). In the Old Testament Eli was a high priest of Israel and teacher of Samuel. A variant form is Ely.

Elias a masculine variant form of ELIJAH. A diminutive form is ELI.

Elidir or **Elidor** a Welsh masculine first name and that of a legendary handsome boy, loved by the gods. Elidir was the father of Llywarch Hen (sixth century).

Eliezer a masculine first name meaning 'my God is help' (*Hebrew*). In the Old Testament Eliezer was the heir of Abraham. A variant form is Eleazer.

Elihu a masculine first name meaning 'he is my God' (*Hebrew*).

Elijah a masculine first name meaning 'Jehovah is my God' (*Hebrew*). In the Old Testament Elijah was a ninth-century BC Hebrew prophet who denounced the worship of the goddess Baal that had been introduced by King Ahab of Israel and Queen Jezebel. A diminutive form is Lije.

Elin (1) a Welsh feminine diminutive form of ELINOR. (2) a Welsh variant form of HELEN.

Elinor a Welsh feminine variant form of ELEANOR.

Eliot a masculine variant form of ELLIOT.

Elis a Welsh masculine form of ELIAS.

Elisa an Italian feminine diminutive form of ELISABETTA.

Elisabeth a French and German feminine form of ELIZABETH now used as an English-language form. Elisabeth Shue is an American film actress.

Elisabetta an Italian feminine form of ELIZABETH.

Élise a French diminutive form of ELISABETH.

Elisha a masculine first name meaning 'God is salvation' (*Hebrew*). In the Old Testament Elisha was a Hebrew prophet who succeeded ELIJAH.

Elissa an alternative name of DIDO.

Eliza a feminine diminutive form of ELIZABETH.

Elizabeth a feminine first name meaning 'worshiper of God, consecrated to God' (*Hebrew*). It is the name of several English queens, including Queen Elizabeth (1533–1603), the only child of Henry VIII and Anne Boleyn. She succeeded to the English throne after her half-brother, Edward VI, and her half-sister, Mary. Diminutive forms are Bess, Bet, Beth, Betsy, Betty, Eliza, Elsa, Elsie, Libby, Lisa, Liza, Lisbeth, Liz.

Ella a feminine diminutive form of CINDERELLA, ELEANOR, ISABELLA, now used independently.

Ellen a feminine variant form of HELEN.

Ellice feminine form of ELIAS, ELLIS.

Ellie a feminine diminutive form of ALICE, EILIDH.

Elliot or **Elliott** a surname, from a French diminutive form of Elias, used as a masculine first name.

Ellis a surname, a Middle English form of ELIAS, used as a masculine first name.

Ellison a surname, meaning 'son of ELIAS' (*Old English*), used as a masculine first name.

Elma (1) a feminine diminutive form of WILHELMINA. (2) a contracted form of ELIZABETH MARY.

Elmer a masculine first name meaning 'noble; excellent' (*Germanic*).

Elmo a masculine first name meaning 'amiable' (*Greek*).

Elmore a surname, meaning 'river bank with elms' (*Old English*), used as a masculine first name. Elmore Leonard is an acclaimed American crime writer.

Éloise or **Eloisa** a feminine first name meaning 'sound, whole' (*Germanic*). A variant form is Héloïse.

Elphin a Welsh masculine first name that may be from the same root as *albus*, 'white' (*Latin*). The name of a proverbially unlucky lad whose fortune changes when he rescues and becomes foster father to the baby Taliesin. A variant form is Elffin.

Elroy a masculine variant form of LEROY.

Elsa a feminine diminutive form of ALISON, ALICE, ELIZABETH.

Elsie a feminine diminutive form of ALICE, ALISON, ELIZABETH, ELSPETH.

Elspeth or **Elspet** Scottish feminine forms of ELIZABETH. Elspeth Buchan (1738–99) was a Scottish religious fanatic and founder of a religious sect, the Buchanites. Diminutive forms are Eppie, Elsie, Elspie.

Elspie a feminine diminutive form of ELSPETH.

Elton a surname, meaning 'settlement of Ella' (*Old English*), used as a masculine first name. Sir Elton John is an English songwriter and singer.

Eluned a feminine first name meaning 'idol' (*Welsh*). A diminutive form is LYNETTE.

Elva a feminine first name meaning 'friend of the elf' (*Old English*). A variant form is Elvina.

Elvey a surname, meaning 'elf gift' (*Old English*), used as a masculine first name. A variant form is Elvy.

Elvin a surname, meaning 'elf or noble friend' (*Old English*), used as a masculine first name. A variant form is ELWIN.

Elvina a feminine variant form of ELVA.

Elvira a feminine first name meaning 'white' (*Latin*).

Elvis a masculine first name meaning 'wise one' (*Norse*). It gained worldwide popularity as the name of the American singer Elvis Presley (1935–77).

Elvy a masculine variant form of ELVEY.

Elwin a masculine variant form of ELVIN; 'white brow' (*Welsh*). A variant form is Elwyn.

Elwyn a masculine first name meaning 'kind, fair', from *elus*, 'kind', and *gwyn*, 'fair' (*Welsh*).

Ely a masculine diminutive form of ELIAS.

Elystan a Welsh masculine form of Old English ATHELSTAN.

Emanuel a masculine variant form of EMMANUEL.

Emeline (1) a feminine variant form of AMELIA. (2) a diminutive form of EMMA. A variant form is Emmeline.

Emer (pronounced *ay-mer*) an Irish Gaelic feminine first name and that of the wife of the great legendary hero CUCHULLAIN. Variant forms are Eamair, Eimear, Eimer, and, in Scotland, Eamhair. Emer was said to possess all six gifts of womanhood: beauty, chastity, soft voice, clear speech, skill with the needle, and wisdom.

Emerald the name of the green gemstone that is used as a feminine first name.

Emergaid (pronounced *aymer-gatt*) a Manx feminine first name and that of a legendary princess of Man.

Emery a masculine variant form of AMORY.

Emil a masculine first name, from that of a noble Roman family the origin of whose name, Aemilius, is uncertain.

Émile the French masculine form of EMIL.

Emilia the Italian feminine form of EMILY. William Shakespeare (1564–1616) used the name for the friend of Desdemona and wife of the duplicitous Iago in his tragedy *Othello*.

Emilie the German feminine form of EMILY.

Émilie the French feminine form of EMILY.

Emilio the Italian, Spanish and Portuguese masculine form of EMIL. Emilio Estevez is an American film actor.

Emily a feminine name of a noble Roman family the origin of whose name, *Aemilius*, is uncertain.

Emlyn a masculine name the origin of which is uncertain, possibly from EMIL (*Welsh*).

Emm a feminine diminutive form of EMMA.

Emma a feminine first name meaning 'whole, universal' (*Germanic*). Jane Austen (1775–1817) used the name for the heroine of her eponymous novel *Emma* (1816). Emma Thompson is an English actress. Diminutive forms are Emm, Emmie.

Emmanuel a masculine first name meaning 'God with us' (*Hebrew*). In the Old Testament it was the name of the child whose birth was foretold by Isiah and who is identified by Christians with Jesus. Variant forms are Immanuel. A diminutive form is Manny.

Emmanuelle the feminine form of EMMANUEL.

Emmeline a feminine variant form of EMELINE.

Emmery a masculine variant form of AMORY.

Emmet or **Emmett** or **Emmot** or **Emmott** a surname, from a diminutive form of EMMA, used as a masculine first name. M. Emmet Walsh is an American film actor.

Emmie a feminine diminutive form of EMMA.

Emory a masculine variant form of AMORY.

Emrys (pronounced *em-riss*) the Welsh masculine form of AMBROSE (Latin Ambrosius). Emrys Wledig, 'prince', was the Welsh name of Ambrosius Aurelianus, leader of the Britons against the invading Saxons in the fifth century AD. Emrys Hughes was a fiery twentieth-century Labour MP.

Emyr a Welsh masculine first name, possibly a form of HONORIUS. Emyr Llydaw was a sixth-century saint. Emyr Humphreys was a well-known twentieth-century writer.

Ena (1) an anglicised feminine form of EITHNA. (2) an Irish and Scottish feminine suffix that, like INA, may have taken on a life of its own as a girl's name.

Enda a masculine first name derived perhaps from *éan*, 'bird' (*Irish Gaelic*). It is not uncommon for boys' names in Gaelic to end in -a, and St Enda, or Enna, was a sixth-century holy man, founder of a monastery on the Aran Islands.

Endellion a Cornish feminine first name. The original form of the name was Endelient, preserved in St Endellion, a legendary saint of the fifth century who eschewed all food and lived on milk and water.

Eneas a masculine variant form of AENEAS.

Enée the French masculine form of AENEAS.

Enfys a feminine first name meaning 'rainbow' (*Welsh*).

Engelbert a masculine first name meaning 'bright angel' (*Germanic*).

Engelberta or **Engelbertha** or **Engelberthe** feminine forms of ENGELBERT.

109

Enid a feminine first name from Welsh *enaid*, 'soul' (*Welsh*). It is a name found in the Arthurian legends.

Enna *see* ENDA.

Ennis a masculine first name meaning 'chief one' (*Gaelic*).

Enoch a masculine first name meaning 'dedication' (*Hebrew*). In the Old Testament Enoch was the oldest son of Cain and the father of Methuselah.

Enos a masculine first name meaning 'man' (*Hebrew*).

Enrica the Italian feminine form of HENRIETTA.

Enrichetta the Italian feminine form of HENRIETTA.

Enrico the Italian masculine form of HENRY.

Enrique the Spanish masculine form of HENRY.

Enriqueta the Spanish feminine form of HENRIETTA.

Enya a feminine variant form of EITHNA.

Eocha or **Eochai** or **Eochaid** a variant form of EOCHAIDH.

Eochaidh (pronounced *yoch-ee*) a masculine first name from *each*, 'horse' (*Irish Gaelic*), probably meaning 'horse-master' (*see* EACHANN). A very frequent name in old Irish legends and histories. Eochaidh was the name of an ancient sun-god, said to be the possessor of a single red eye. Eochaidh Airem, 'ploughman', was a legendary high king, earthly lover of the beautiful ETAÍN. The name was also used by the Picts. Variant forms are Eocha, Eochaid, Eochai, Eochy.

Eochy a variant form of EOCHAIDH.

Eoganán (pronounced *yo-hanann*) an Irish and Scottish Gaelic masculine first name stemming from Celtic *eo*, 'yew', so suggestive of tree worship in an earlier period. It was the name of one of the seven sons of Oengus (*see* ANGUS), all of whom were holy men of the sixth century. It is also found as Eogan, Eoghan. Anglicised forms are Eugene and Owen, both unconnected with the Celtic etymology of the name.

Eoghan or **Eogan** a masculine variant form of EOGANÁN.

Eoin (pronounced *yonn*) a masculine first name. An Irish Gaelic form of JOHN. Eoin macSuibhne was a chieftain of Ulster in the early fourteenth century. *See also* IAIN, SEAN.

Eolas (pronounced *yo-las*) a masculine or feminine first name meaning 'knowledge', 'experience' (*Irish Gaelic*).

Eph a masculine diminutive form of EPHRAIM.

Ephraim a masculine first name meaning 'fruitful' (*Hebrew*). In the Old

Testament Ephraim was the younger son of Joseph and grandson of Jacob. He founded one of the Twelve Tribes of Israel. A diminutive form is Eph.

Epiphany the name of the Christian festival celebrated on 6 January, meaning 'revelation' (*Greek*), used as a feminine first name.

Eppie a feminine diminutive form of ELSPETH.

Eranthe a feminine first name meaning 'flower of spring' (*Greek*).

Erasmus a masculine first name meaning 'lovely; worthy of love' (*Greek*). Diminutive forms are Ras, Rasmus.

Erastus a masculine first name meaning 'beloved' (*Greek*). In the New Testament Erastus was a Christian who attended Paul on his third missionary tour. Diminutive forms are Ras, Rastus.

Erc a masculine first name from Old Irish Gaelic *earc*, 'speckled'. Erc was the father of Fergus, Angus and Loarn, first lords of Gaelic Dalriada. Erc macTelt is recorded as the ultimate ancestor of the Clan Cameron.

Ercol a masculine first name perhaps combining Gaelic *earc*, 'speckled', and *col*, 'lord' (*Irish Gaelic*), although its resemblance to Greek Hercules has also been noted. It was the name of a Connacht warrior, humbled by CUCHULAINN.

Ercole the Italian masculine form of HERCULES.

Erda a feminine first name meaning 'of the earth' (*Germanic*).

Eric a masculine first name meaning 'rich; brave; powerful' (*Old English*). Eric Roberts is an American film actor. A variant form is Erik.

Erica feminine form of ERIC. A variant form is Erika.

Erich the German masculine form of ERIC.

Erik a masculine variant form of ERIC.

Erika a feminine variant form of ERICA.

Erin or **Eriu** the Irish Gaelic poetic name for Ireland used as a feminine first name.

Erland a masculine first name meaning 'stranger' (*Old Norse*).

Erle a masculine variant form of EARL.

Erlene a feminine variant form of EARLENE. A diminutive form is Erley, Erlie.

Erley or **Erlie** a feminine diminutive form of ERLENE, ERLINE.

Erline a feminine variant form of EARLENE. A diminutive form is Erley, Erlie.

Erma a feminine first name meaning 'warrior maid' (*Germanic*).

Erminie or **Erminia** feminine variant forms of ARMINA.

Ern a masculine diminutive form of ERNEST.

Erna a feminine diminutive form of ERNESTA, ERNESTINE.

Ernan the anglicised masculine form of IARNAN.

Erne (pronounced *er-na*) an Irish Gaelic feminine first name and that of a legendary princess. It is preserved in Lough Erne.

Ernest a masculine first name meaning 'earnestness' (*Germanic*). Diminutive forms are Ern, Ernie.

Ernesta the feminine form of ERNEST. A diminutive form is Erna.

Ernestine the feminine form of ERNEST. Diminutive forms are Erna, Tina.

Ernesto the Italian and Spanish masculine forms of ERNEST.

Ernie a masculine diminutive form of ERNEST.

Ernst the German masculine form of ERNEST.

Errol a masculine variant form of EARL.

Erskine a place name and surname, meaning 'projecting height' (*Scottish Gaelic*), used as a masculine first name.

Ertha (1) a Cornish feminine first name and that of an early Celtic saint. (2) a feminine variant form of EARTHA.

Erwin (1) a masculine first name meaning 'friend of honour' (*Germanic*). (2) a surname, meaning 'wild-boar friend' (*French*), used as a masculine first name. A variant form is Orwin.

Eryl a masculine first name meaning 'watcher' (*Welsh*).

Esau a masculine first name meaning 'hairy' (*Hebrew*). In the Old Testament Esau was the twin brother of Jacob to whom he sold his birthright.

Esmé a masculine or feminine first name meaning 'beloved' (*French*).

Esmeralda a Spanish feminine form of EMERALD. The French writer Victor Hugo (1802–85) used the name for the heroine of his novel *The Hunchback of Notre Dame* (1831).

Esmond a masculine first name meaning 'divine protection' (*Old English*).

Ess or **Essie** feminine diminutive forms of ESTHER.

Essyllt a feminine variant form of ISEULT.

Esta a feminine variant form of ESTHER.

Este a masculine first name meaning 'man from the East' (*Italian*).

Estéban the Spanish masculine form of STEPHEN.

Estelle or **Estella** feminine variant forms of STELLA. Charles Dickens (1812–72) used the form Estella for the heroine of his novel *Great Expectations* (1860–61).

Ester the Italian and Spanish feminine forms of ESTHER.

Esther a feminine first name from the name of the planet Venus (*Persian*). In the Old Testament Esther was a Jewish woman wh became queen of Persia and saved her people from massacere. A variant form is Esta. Diminutive forms are Ess, Essie, Tess, Tessie.

Estrella the Spanish feminine form of ESTELLE.

Etaín or **Etáin** (pronounced *ithoyne*) an Irish Gaelic feminine first name and found in Irish mythology. Etaín was the second wife of MIDIR but was changed into a fly and swallowed by a woman, who then gave birth to a 'new' Etaín who married King EOCHAIDH but was eventually reclaimed by Midir and brought back to the 'Land of Many Colours'. Her name is synonymous with feminine beauty. Alternative forms are Edaín, Eadain. The name is sometimes anglicised to Aideen.

Ethan a masculine first name meaning 'firm' (*Hebrew*). In the Old Testament Ethan was one of four men whose wisdom, although great, was surpassed by Solomon. Ethan Coen is an American film writer and director and brother of Joel Coen, with whom he works.

Ethel a feminine first name meaning 'noble' or 'of noble birth' (*Old English*).

Ethelbert a masculine first name meaning 'noble, bright' (*Old English*). St Ethelbert (*c.* 552–616) was a king of Kent (560–616) who was converted to Christianity by St Augustine. A variant form is Aethelbert.

Ethna an anglicised feminine form of EITHNA.

Ethni a Welsh feminine variant form of EITHNA.

Etienne the French masculine form of STEPHEN.

Etta or **Ettie** feminine diminutive forms of HENRIETTA.

Ettore the Italian masculine form of HECTOR.

Euan a masculine variant form of EWAN.

Eudora a feminine first name meaning 'good gift' (*Greek*).

Eufemia the Italian and Spanish feminine form of EUPHEMIA.

Eugen the German masculine form of EUGENE.

Eugene (1) a masculine first name meaning 'well-born; noble' (*Greek*). A diminutive form is Gene. (2) an anglicised form of EOGANÁN.

Eugène the French masculine form of EUGENE.

Eugenia feminine form of EUGENE. Diminutive forms are Ena, Gene.

Eugénie the French feminine form of EUGENIA.

Eulalie a feminine first name meaning 'fair speech' (*Greek*).

Eunice a feminine first name meaning 'good victory' (*Greek*). In the New Testament Eunice was a Jewish woman who, with her mother, Lois, converted to Christianity. Eunice was the mother of Timothy, who became a disciple of Paul.

Euphemia a feminine first name meaning 'of good report' (*Greek*). Diminutive forms are Fay, Effie, Phamie, Phemie.

Eurfron (pronounced *ire-fronn*) a feminine first name meaning 'golden-breasted', from *aur*, 'gold' (*Welsh*).

Eurig (pronounced *eye-ric*) a masculine first name meaning 'golden', from *aur*, 'gold' (*Welsh*).

Euron (pronounced *eye-ronn*) a feminine first name meaning 'golden one', from *aur*, 'gold' (*Welsh*). This was the name of the beloved of the bard Iolo Morgannwg.

Eurwen a feminine first name meaning 'fair, golden', from *aur*, 'gold', and *ven*, 'white' (*Welsh*).

Eurwyn (pronounced *ire-win*) a masculine first name meaning 'fair, golden' (*Welsh*), a masculine form of EURWEN.

Eusebio a masculine first name meaning 'pious' (*Greek*).

Eustace a masculine first name meaning 'rich' (*Greek*). Diminutive forms are Stacey, Stacy.

Eustacia feminine form of EUSTACE. Diminutive forms are Stacey, Stacie, Stacy.

Eva the German, Italian and Spanish feminine forms of EVE.

Evadne a feminine first name the origin of which is uncertain but possibly meaning 'high-born' (*Greek*).

Evalina the Latin feminine form of AVELINE.

Evan a Welsh masculine form of JOHN.

Evangeline a feminine first name meaning 'of the Gospel' (*Greek*).

Eve a feminine first name meaning 'life' (*Hebrew*). In the Old Testament Eve is the first woman on earth and the wife of Adam from whose rib God created her. Diminutive forms are Eveleen, Evelina, Eveline, Evie.

Eveleen or **Evelina** feminine diminutive forms of EVE.

Eveline a feminine diminutive form of EVA, EVE.

Evelyn a feminine or masculine first name that evolved from the Norman French first name AVELINE into a surname before returning to use as a first name. The Irish and Scottish form is AIBHLINN. Evelyn Waugh was a noted English novelist.

Everard a masculine first name meaning 'strong boar' (*Germanic*).

Everett an English masculine form of AEBHRIC.

Everley a masculine first name meaning 'field of the wild boar' (*Old English*).

Evita Spanish feminine diminutive form of EVA. The name was made famous outside the Spanish-speaking world by the musical *Evita* by Andrew Lloyd-Webber about the life of Eva Peron, the wife of the Argentine dictator.

Evric an English masculine form of AEBHRIC.

Evodia a feminine first name meaning 'good journey' (*Greek*).

Ewan (pronounced *yoo-wan*) (1) an anglicised Scottish masculine first name meaning 'youth' (*Gaelic*). Variant forms include Euan, Ewen, Evan. (2) Irish and Scots Gaelic masculine forms of OWEN. (3) a Scottish masculine form of EUGENE. Ewan MacGregor is a Scottish actor. A variant form is Euan.

Ewart (1) an Old French variant form of EDWARD. (2) a surname, meaning 'herd of ewes' (*Old English*), used as a masculine first name.

Ewen a masculine variant form of EWAN.

Eynon the anglicised masculine form of EINION.

Ezekiel a masculine first name meaning 'strength of God' (*Hebrew*). In the Old Testament Ezekiel was a sixth-century BC priest and prophet who was exiled to Babylon. His prophecies are recorded in the Book of Ezekiel. A diminutive form is Zeke.

Ezra a masculine first name meaning 'help' (*Hebrew*). In the Old Testament Ezra was a fifth-century BC priest whose writings are recorded in the Book of Ezra.

F

Faber or **Fabre** a surname, meaning 'smith' (*Latin*), used as a masculine first name.

Fabia feminine form of FABIO. A variant form is FABIOLA.

Fabian the anglicised masculine form of the Roman family name Fabianus, derived from Fabius, from *faba*, 'bean' (*Latin*). St Fabian (189–200) was a pope (236–250) and martyr. William Shakespeare (1564–1616) used the name for one of the characters in his comedy *Twelfth Night*.

Fabián the Spanish masculine form of FABIAN.

Fabiano the Italian masculine form of FABIAN.

Fabien the French masculine form of FABIAN.

Fabienne feminine form of FABIEN.

Fabio the Italian masculine form of the Roman family name Fabius, from *faba*, 'bean' (*Latin*).

Fabiola a feminine variant form of FABIA. St Fabiola (*c.* 325–399) is said to have founded the first public hospital in western Europe.

Fabrice the French masculine form of the Roman family *Fabricius*, from *faber*, 'smith'.

Fabrizio the Italian masculine form of FABRICE.

Fahimah a feminine first name meaning 'intelligent' (*Arabic*).

Fairfax the surname, meaning 'lovely hair' (*Old English*), used as a masculine first name.

Fairley or **Fairlie** a surname, meaning 'clearing with ferns' (*Old English*), used as a masculine first name.

Faisal a masculine first name meaning 'judge' (*Arabic*). Variant forms are Faysal, Feisal.

Faith the quality of belief or fidelity used as a feminine first name. A diminutive form is FAY or Faye.

Fanchon a feminine diminutive form of FRANÇOISE.

Fand a feminine first name from *fand*, 'tear' (*Old Irish*). It was the name of a beautiful heroine of legend.

Fane a surname, meaning 'glad or eager' (*Old English*), used as a masculine first name.

Fanny a feminine diminutive form of FRANCES, also used independently.

Faolán a masculine first name meaning 'wolf-like', from *faolán*, 'wolf' (*Irish Gaelic*). This was a term of praise rather than denigration. The name was borne by an Irish missionary to Scotland and is preserved in the village name St Fillans.

Farah a feminine first name meaning 'joy' (*Arabic*). A variant form is FARRAH.

Farnall or **Farnell** a surname, meaning 'fern hill' (*Old English*), used as a masculine first name. Variant forms are Fernald, Fernall.

Farquhar (pronounced *farr-char*) a Scottish masculine first name, the anglicised form of Fearchar, from Old Gaelic *ver-car-os*, 'very dear one' (*Old Gaelic*).

Farr a surname, meaning 'bull' (*Old English*), used as a masculine first name.

Farrah a feminine variant form of FARAH. Farrah Fawcett is an American film actress who appeared in the TV series *Charlie's Angels*.

Farrell a masculine first name meaning 'warrior' (*Irish Gaelic*).

Fatima (1) a feminine first name meaning 'motherly' or 'chaste' (*Arabic*). It was the name of the daughter of Mohammed. (2) a feminine first name meaning 'of Fatima' in Portugal (*Portuguese*), used as a feminine first name.

Faustina or **Faustine** a feminine first name meaning 'lucky' (*Latin*).

Favor or **Favour** an abstract noun, meaning 'good will or an act of good will, from *favere*, to protect', used as a feminine first name (*Latin*).

Fawn the name for a young deer or a light greyish-brown colour used as a feminine first name (*Old French*).

Fay or **Faye** (1) a feminine first name meaning 'faith' (*Irish/Scottish Gaelic*) (2) a feminine first name meaning 'witch' or 'wise woman from *fée* (*Old French*) or *fay* (*Norman French*). (3) a feminine diminutive form of Faith. (4) a feminine diminutive form of EUPHEMIA.

Faysal a masculine variant form of FAISAL.

Fearchar the Gaelic masculine form of FARQUHAR.

Féchin or **Féchine** (pronounced *fay-hin*) a masculine first name from *fia-*

117

ch, 'raven' (*Irish Gaelic*). It was a name borne by numerous early saints. A variant form is Féichin. *See also* FIACHRA.

Fedelm *see* FIDELMA.

Federico an Italian and Spanish masculine form of FREDERICK.

Fedlimid or **Fedelmid** (pronounced *fellimy*) an Irish Gaelic masculine or feminine first name of unclear derivation. It is a name found often in ancient sources, occasionally as a female name. A variant form is Feidhilim or Feidhlimidh. It is anglicised as Felim or Felimy.

Féichin a variant form of FÉCHIN.

Feidhilim or **Feidhlimidh** a feminine variant form of FEDLIMID.

Feisal a masculine variant form of FAISAL.

Felice the Italian masculine form of FELIX.

Felicia feminine form of FELIX.

Felicidad the Spanish feminine form of FELICIA.

Felicie the Italian feminine form of FELICIA.

Felicitas a feminine first name from *felicitas*, 'happiness' (Latin) and also the name of the Roman goddess of good luck.

Felicity a feminine first name meaning 'happiness' (*Latin*).

Felim or **Felimy** the anglicised form of FEDELIMID.

Felipe the Spanish masculine form of PHILIP.

Felix a masculine first name from *felix*, 'happy' (*Latin*). In the New Testament Felix was the Roman governor of Caesarea who kept Paul in prison for two years. His wife was DRUSILLA. The name was adopted by several popes.

Felton a place name and surname, meaning 'place in a field' (*Old English*), used as a masculine first name.

Fenella an anglicised feminine form of FIONNUALA. Sir Walter Scott (1771–1832) used the name for a female character in his novel *Peveril of the Peak* (182). Fenella Fielding is an English actress.

Fenton a place name and surname, meaning 'a place in marshland or fens' (*Old English*), used as a masculine first name.

Ferd a masculine diminutive form of FERDINAND.

Ferdia or **Ferdiad** a masculine first name derived from *fear*, 'man', and *dia*, 'god' (*Irish Gaelic*), but if so it is a pre-Christian god; also from *diad*, 'smoke'. Ferdia or Ferdiad was the brother-in-arms of CUCHULAINN, but Cuchulainn slew him in single combat.

Ferdinand a masculine first name meaning 'peace bold' (*Germanic*).

William Shakespeare (1564–1616) used the name for royal characters in two of his comedies, the king of Navarre in *Love's Labour's Lost* and a prince of Naples in *The Tempest*. Diminutive forms are Ferd, Ferdy.

Ferdinando an Italian masculine form of FERDINAND.

Ferdy a masculine diminutive form of FERDINAND.

Fergal a masculine first name derived from *fearghal*, 'brave' (*Irish Gaelic*). Diminutive forms are Fergie, Fergy.

Fergie (1) a masculine diminutive form of FERGAL, FERGUS, FERGUSON. (2) a feminine diminutive form of FERGUSON as a surname. A variant form is Fergy.

Fergus a masculine first name meaning 'best warrior', from Gaelic *fearr*, 'best', and *gas*, 'warrior' (*Irish Gaelic*), or 'only choice' from an older Celtic root, *ver gustu*; although another possibility is 'virile man'. Fergus was a legendary king of Ulster who was supplanted by CONCHOBHAR and so supported Queen Medb in her famous 'Cattle Raid', and the name was borne by many others, including Fergus Mór macErc, founder of the kingdom of Dalriada in Scotland. Diminutive forms include Fergy, Fergie.

Ferguson or **Fergusson** a surname, meaning 'son of Fergus', used as a masculine first name. Diminutive forms are Fergie, Fergy.

Fergy a masculine variant or feminine form of FERGIE.

Fern the name of the plant used as a feminine first name (*Old English*).

Fernald or **Fernall** masculine variant forms of FARNALL, FARNELL.

Fernand a French masculine form of FERDINAND.

Fernanda feminine form of FERDNAND.

Fernando a Spanish masculine form of FERDINAND.

Ffion a feminine first name from a flower name, 'rose' or 'foxglove finger' (*Welsh*).

Ffraid (pronounced *fryde*) a Welsh feminine form of BRIDE found in numerous place names.

Fiachna a masculine first name from *fiach*, 'raven' (*Irish Gaelic*). This name and FIACHRA are often confused.

Fiachra a masculine first name from *fiach*, 'raven' (*Irish Gaelic*). St Fiachra was a seventh-century Celtic saint whose name is preserved in French in St Fiacre and the *fiacre* or horse-drawn cab.

Fianaid (pronounced *fee-ana*) a feminine first name meaning 'little deer' (*Irish Gaelic*).

Fid a feminine diminutive form of FIDELIA, FIDELIS.

Fidel a Spanish masculine form of FIDELIS.

Fidèle a French masculine form of FIDELIS.

Fidelia a feminine variant form of FIDELIS. A diminutive form is Fid.

Fidelio an Italian masculine form of FIDELIS. The German composer Ludwig von Beethoven (1770–1827) used the name for the title of his only opera, *Fidelio*, in which the heroine, Leonora, pretends to be a boy and calls herself Fidelio in order to rescue her husband from prison.

Fidelis a masculine or feminine first name meaning 'faithful' (*Latin*). A feminine variant form is FIDELIA. A diminutive form is Fid.

Fidelma (1) an Irish feminine first name from Fedelm, the prophetess who warned Queen Medb of the coming rout of her army in the Cattle Raid of Cooley. The name has also been borne by a number of Celtic saints, and athough its origin is obscure, it clearly indicates a person of spiritual force. (2) a feminine first name meaning 'faithful Mary' (*Latin/Irish Gaelic*). Diminutive forms are Fid and Delma.

Fifi a French feminine diminutive form of JOSEPHINE.

Filippo the Italian masculine form of PHILIP.

Filippa the Italian feminine form of PHILIPPA.

Fillan *see* FAOLÁN.

Finán (pronounced *fin-ann*) a Scottish and Irish Gaelic masculine first name and that of several early saints of the Celtic church.

Finbarr or **Finbar** or **Findbarr** a masculine first name whose likely meaning is 'the fair-haired one' from *fionn*, 'white', and *barr*, 'head, crest' (*Irish Gaelic*). St Finbarr of Cork was widely venerated in the Celtic lands. A variant form is Finnbar or Finnbarr. *See* BARRFIND.

Findlay a masculine variant form of FINLAY.

Finegas a masculine variant form of FINNEGAS.

Finegin a masculine variant form of FINGEIN.

Finella an anglicised feminine form of FIONNUALA.

Fingal a masculine first name meaning 'fair stranger', from *fionn*, 'white, fair', and *gall*, 'stranger' (*Scottish Gaelic*). It was a name given to Norsemen by the Celts. In Scotland, however, it is also a name given to FIONN macCumhaill, at least since the fourteenth century, and perpetuated in 'Fingal's Cave' on the Scottish island of Staffa (although this name was not given to the 'cave of music' until the eighteenth century).

Fingein or **Finghean** or **Fingon** a masculine first name meaning 'wine birth' (*Irish Gaelic*), a common name in old Irish sources. A variant form is Finegin. The anglicised form is Finnigan.

Finlay or **Finley** (pronounced *finn-la*) a masculine first name from *fionn*, 'fair', and *laoch*, 'hero', 'warrior' (*Scottish Gaelic*). Finlay Currie (1878–1968) was a Scottish-born film actor, his best-known part probably being that as the convict Magwitch in the film of *Great Expectations* (1946).A variant form, and the surname from it, is Findlay.

Finn (1) a masculine anglicised form of FIONN. (2) In Northern Scotland, a Norse name.

Finnabair (pronounced *finna-warr*) a feminine first name meaning 'fair-browed' (*Irish Gaelic*). In legend it was the name of MEDB's daughter, lover of Fráech (*see* FRAOCH), who died of grief when he was killed by CUCHULAINN. The name is related to Welsh GWENHWYFAR.

Finnán a masculine first name meaning 'little fair one', from *fionn*, 'fair', with the diminutive ending -an (*Irish/Scottish Gaelic*). *See also* FINNIAN.

Finnbar or **Finnbarr** a masculine variant form of FINBARR.

Finnbheara (pronounced *finn-waira*) an Irish Gaelic masculine first name from that of a fairy king of Connaught.

Finnegas a masculine first name from *fionn*, 'fair', and *geas*, 'warrior' (*Irish Gaelic*). It was the name of the tutor of FIONN macCumhaill. Finnegas sought to catch the magic salmon of all knowledge, and did so, but his pupil touched the fish, sucked his finger and acquired the knowledge. A variant form is Finegas.

Finnian an Irish and Scottish Gaelic masculine first name whose derivation is the same as that of FINNÁN, and the two names have often been confused. St Finnian of Clonard (sixth century) is the best-known bearer of the name.

Finnigan the anglicised masculine form of FINGEIN.

Finola a feminine variant form of FIONNUALA.

Fintan a masculine first name and one of the many incorporating *fionn*, 'white, fair', the other element being construed both as 'ancient' and as 'fire' (*Irish Gaelic*). There were many St Fintans in the Celtic church, but it goes back into ancient legend as the name of the salmon of knowledge. In another legend, Fintan macBochra was the only Irishman to survive Noah's flood.

Fiona a feminine first name that is a relatively modern 'artificial' name, athough very popular. It recalls *fionn*, 'white' (*Gaelic*), a constituent of many names.

Fionn (pronounced fin) a masculine first name meaning 'fair-haired' from 'fair, bright' (*Irish/Scottish Gaelic*). This was the name of one of the greatest figures of Celtic legend, the mighty warrior, wise man and bard FIONN macCumhaill, the leader of the Fianna. The anglicised form is Finn. *See also* FINGAL.

Fionnuala or **Fionola** (pronounced *finn-oola*) a feminine first name that stems from *fionn*, 'white', and *ghuala*, 'shoulders' (*Irish Gaelic*). Fionnuala was one of the four children, and only daughter of king Lír and his wife AOBH, all of whom were transformed by enchantment into swans. A variant formis Finola, and the anglicised form is Fenella or Finella. A diminutive form is NUALA.

Fiske a surname, meaning 'fish' (*Old English*), used as a masculine first name.

Fitch a surname, meaning 'point' (*Old English*), used as a masculine first name.

Fitz (1) a masculine first name meaning 'son' (*Old French*). (2) a diminutive form of names beginning with Fitz-.

Fitzgerald a surname, meaning 'son of Gerald' (*Old French*), used as a masculine first name. A diminutive form is Fitz.

Fitzhugh a surname, meaning 'son of HUGH' (*Old French*), used as a masculine first name. A diminutive form is Fitz.

Fitzpatrick a surname, meaning 'son of Patrick' (*Old French*), used as a masculine first name. A diminutive form is Fitz.

Fitzroy a surname, meaning '(illegitimate) son of the king' (*Old French*), used as a masculine first name. A diminutive form is Fitz.

Flann a masculine or feminine first name meaning 'red' or 'red-haired' (*Irish Gaelic*). This ancient name became famous in the later twentieth century as a pen-name of Brian O'Nolan, who wrote as Flann O'Brien.

Flanna feminine form of FLANN.

Flannan a masculine first name meaning 'red-complexioned' (*Irish Gaelic*).

Flavia a feminine first name meaning 'yellow-haired, golden' (*Latin*).

Flavian or **Flavius** masculine forms of FLAVIA. William Shakespeare (1564–1616) used the name for minor characters in several plays, including *Julius Caesar*.

Fleming a surname, meaning 'man from Flanders' (*Old French*), used as a masculine first name.

Fletcher a surname meaning 'arrow-maker' (*Old French*), used as a masculine first name.

Fleur the French word for 'flower' used as a feminine first name.

Fleurette a feminine first name meaning 'little flower' (*French*).

Flinn a masculine variant form of FLYNN.

Flint a masculine first name meaning 'stream, brook' (*Old English*).

Flo a feminine diminutive form of FLORA, FLORENCE.

Flora a feminine first name meaning 'flower' (*Latin*) and that of the Roman goddess of flowers. It became particularly popular in Scotland through Flora MacDonald (1722–90), who aided Prince Charles Edward Stewart in his escape after the failure of the 1745–46 uprising, making her a heroine even among those who opposed the rising. Diminutive forms are Flo, Florrie, Flossie.

Florence (1) a feminine first name meaning 'blooming; flourishing' (*Latin*). Diminutive forms are Flo, Florrie, Flossie, Floy. (2) in Ireland, a masculine name, evidently stemming from an anglicisation of FURSA, which may have been supposed to be linked to Italian Firenze (the city of Florence). A diminutive form is FLURRY.

Florian and **Florent** masculine forms of FLORA.

Florrie or **Flossie** feminine diminutive forms of FLORA, FLORENCE.

Flower the English word for 'bloom' or 'blossom' used as a feminine first name.

Floy a feminine diminutive form of FLORA, FLORENCE.

Floyd an anglicised masculine variant form of the surname Llwyd, or Lloyd, used as a masculine first name. 'Pretty Boy Floyd' is a popular American folk song.

Flurry a masculine diminutive form of FLORENCE. In the *Irish R.M.* stories by Somerville and Ross, the pen names of Edith Somerville (1858–1949) and her second cousin, Violet Martin (1862–1915), Flurry Knox is a 'gentleman among stableboys and a stableboy among gentlemen'.

Flynn a surname, meaning 'son of the red-haired one' (*Scots Gaelic*), used as a masculine first name. A variant form is Flinn.

Fódla (pronounced *foh-la*) an Irish Gaelic land goddess name, synonymous with Ireland, like ERIN and BANBA. In one tradition these three were sisters.

Forbes a place name and surname, meaning 'fields or district', from Old Gaelic *forba*, 'field', used as a masculine first name.

Ford the English word for a crossing place of a river used as a masculine first name.

Forrest or **Forest** a surname, meaning 'forest' (*Old French*), used as a masculine first name. Forest Whitaker is an American actor.

Forrester or **Forster** a surname, meaning 'forester' (*Old French*), used as a masculine first name.

Fortuna a feminine variant form of FORTUNE.

Fortune the word for 'wealth', 'fate' or 'chance' (*Latin*) used as a feminine first name. A variant form is FORTUNA.

Foster a surname, meaning 'forester or cutler' (*Old French*) or 'foster parent' (*Old English*), used as a masculine first name.

Fra a masculine diminutive form of FRANCIS.

Fráech a masculine variant form of FRAOCH.

Fraine a masculine variant form of FRAYN.

Fran a feminine diminutive form of FRANCES.

Franca a feminine diminutive form of FRANCESCA.

Frances the feminine form of FRANCIS. Frances McDormand is an American film actress. Diminutive forms are Fanny, Fran, Francie, Franny.

Francesca the Italian feminine form of FRANCES. A diminutive form is Francheschina.

Francesco the Italian masculine form of FRANCIS. A contracted form is FRANCO.

Francheschina a feminine diminutive form of FRANCESCA.

Francie a feminine diminutive form of FRANCES.

Francine a feminine diminutive form of FRANCES, FRANÇOISE.

Francis a masculine first name meaning 'free' (*Germanic*). It is the name of several saints, most notably St Francis of Assisi (1182–1226), the founder of the Franciscan order. Francis Ford Coppola is an American film director. Diminutive forms are Fra, Frank, Francie.

Francisca the Spanish feminine form of FRANCES.

Francisco the Spanish masculine form of FRANCIS. William Shakespeare (1564–1616) used the name for one of the characters in his comedy *The Tempest*.

Franco a contracted masculine form of FRANCESCO.

François the French masculine form of FRANCIS.

Françoise the French feminine form of FRANCES.

Frank (1) a masculine first name meaning 'Frenchman' (*Old French*). (2) a masculine diminutive form of FRANCIS, FRANKLIN. Diminutive forms are Frankie, Franky.

Frankie a masculine diminutive form of FRANK, FRANKLIN.

Franklin or **Franklen** or **Franklyn** a surname, meaning 'free–holder' (*Old French*), used as a masculine first name. Franklin D. Roosevelt (1882–1945) was the 32nd President of the United States (1933–45). Diminutive forms are Frank, Frankie, Franky.

Franky a masculine diminutive form of FRANK, FRANKLIN.

Frans the Swedish masculine form of FRANCIS.

Franz or **Franziskus** German masculine forms of FRANCIS.

Franziska the German masculine form of FRANCES.

Fraoch (pronounced *fraach*) an Irish and Scottish Gaelic masculine first name meaning 'heath'. Although Heather is today a girls' name, Fraoch was a male warrior. An alternative form is Fráech.

Fraser or **Frasier** a Scottish surname, meaning 'from Frisselle or Fresel in France', possibly from *fraise*, 'strawberry', or *frisel*, 'Frisian' (*Old French*), used as a masculine first name. The American sitcom *Frasier* and the character of Dr Frasier Crane have made the name famous. A variant form is Frazer, Frazier.

Frayn or **Frayne** a surname, meaning 'ash tree' (*Old French*), used as a masculine first name. A variant form is Fraine.

Frazer or **Frazier** masculine variant forms of FRASER.

Frea a feminine variant form of FREYA.

Fred a masculine diminutive and feminine form of FREDERICK, FREDERICA.

Freda (1) a feminine diminutive form of WINIFRED. (2) a variant form of FRIEDA.

Freddie or **Freddy** a masculine diminutive and feminine form of FREDERICK, FREDERICKA.

Frédéric the French masculine form of FREDERICK.

Frederica feminine form of FREDERICK. Diminutive forms are Fred, Freddie, Freddy, Frieda.

Frederick or **Frederic** a masculine first name meaning 'abounding in peace', 'peaceful ruler' (*Germanic*). William Shakespeare (1564–1616) used the name Frederick for the brother of the duke and his usurper in his comedy *As You Like It*. Diminutive forms are Fred, Freddie, Freddy.

Frederika a feminine variant form of FREDERICA. Frederika von Stade is an American opera singer.

Frédérique the French feminine form of FREDERICA.

Fredrik the Swedish masculine form of FREDERICK.

Freeman a surname, meaning 'free man' (*Old English*), used as a masculine first name.

Frewin a surname, meaning 'generous friend' (*Old English*), used as a masculine first name.

Freya or **Freyja** a feminine first name meaning 'lady' (*Norse*) and the name of the Norse goddess of love. Dame Freya Stark (1893–1993) was a British traveller and writer. A varaiant form is Frea.

Frieda (1) a feminine first name meaning 'peace' (*Germanic*). (2) a diminutive form of FREDERICA.

Friede the German feminine form of FRIEDA.

Friederike the German feminine form of FREDERICA. A diminutive form is Fritzi.

Friedrich German masculine forms of FREDERICK. A diminutive form is Fritz.

Fritz a masculine diminutive form of FRIEDRICH, also used independently. Fritz Lang (1890–1976) was an Austrian-born American film director.

Fritzi a feminine diminutive form of FRIEDERIKE.

Fulton a surname, meaning 'muddy place' (*Old English*), used as a masculine first name.

Fulvia a feminine first name meaning 'yellow-haired' (*Latin*).

Fursa an Irish Gaelic masculine first name of uncertain derivation. It was borne by a number of Celtic saints, most notably St Fursa who had ecstatic and terrifying visions, the account of which is said to have inspired Dante to write his *Inferno*. The anglicised form is Fursey. *See* FLORENCE.

Fursey the anglicised masculine form of FURSA.

Fychan (pronounced *fee-han*) the Welsh form of Vaughan.

Fyfe or **Fyffe** a surname, meaning 'from Fife', used as a masculine first name.

G

Gabe masculine diminutive form of GABRIEL.

Gabbie or **Gabby** feminine diminutive forms of GABRIELLE.

Gabrán (pronounced *gaw-ran*) a masculine first name perhaps linked with *gabhar*, 'goat' (*Scottish Gaelic*). It was the name of a Dalriadic king, The name is preserved in the Gowrie district of Angus.

Gabriel a masculine first name meaning 'man of God' (*Hebrew*). In the Bible, Gabriel is one of the archangels who was sent to tell Zachariah of the birth of John the Baptist and Mary of the birth of Jesus. Gabriel Byrne is an Irish actor. A diminutive form is Gabe.

Gabrielle feminine form of GABRIEL. Gabrielle Anwar is an English actress. Diminutive forms are Gabbie, Gabby.

Gaea the Latin feminine form of GAIA.

Gael a feminine first name meaning a Gael; *Gaidheal* is a Gaelic speaker (*Irish/Scottish Gaelic*). This modern name is also seen in the forms Gail, Gayle.

Gaenor a Welsh feminine abbreviated form of GWENHWYFAR. It is also found in the anglicised form of Gaynor.

Gaia a feminine first name meaning 'earth' (*Greek*). In classical mythology, Gaia was the goddess of the earth. The Latin form is GAEA.

Gail a feminine diminutive form of ABIGAIL, now used independently. Variant forms are Gale, Gayle.

Gaius a masculine variant form of CAIUS.

Galatea a feminine first name meaning 'white as milk' (*Greek*). In Roman mythology, Galatea was a statue brought to life by Venus. The story inspired the play *Pygmalion* (1913) by the Irish dramatist George Bernard Shaw (1856–1950).

Gale (1) a feminine variant form of GAIL. (2) a surname, meaning 'jail' (*Old French*), used as a masculine first name.

Galen the anglicised masculine form of the Roman family name Galenus, 'calmer' (*Latin*).

Galia a feminine first name meaning 'wave' (*Hebrew*).

Gallagher a surname, meaning 'foreign helper' (*Irish Gaelic*), used as a masculine first name.

Galloway a place name and surname, meaning 'stranger' (*Scots Gaelic*), used as a masculine first name.

Galton a surname, meaning 'rented farm' (*Old English*), used as a masculine first name.

Galvin (1) a masculine or feminine first name, the source of which has been traced to Gaelic *geal*, 'white', and *fionn*, 'bright' and also to *gealbhan*, 'sparrow' (*Irish Gaelic*). (2) a masculine first name that may be a form of GAWAIN.

Gamaliel a masculine first name meaning 'reward of God' (*Hebrew*). In the Old Testament Gamaliel was one of the chieftains chosen by God to help Moses and Aaron in selecting an army.

Ganesh a masculine first name meaning 'lord of the hosts' (*Sanskrit*) and the name of the Hindu god of prophecy.

Garaidh an Irish masculine form of GARETH.

Gardenia the name of a flowering plant with fragrant flowers, called after Dr Alexander Garden, used as a feminine first name (*New Latin*).

Gareth a Welsh masculine form of GERAINT. In the Arthurian legend of the Round Table, Sir Gareth is the younger brother of Sir Gawaine and Sir Gaheris. His nickname in the English versions was 'Beaumains' or 'fine hands', and the name was once taken to stem from Welsh *gwared*, 'mild, gentle', but this is now not accepted. An Irish form of it is Garaidh and it is now increasingly being used as a feminine form. Diminutive forms are Gary, Garry. A variant masculine form is GARTH.

Garfield a surname, meaning 'triangular piece of open land' (*Old English*), used as a masculine first name. Sir Garfield Sobers is a West Indian cricketer who also uses the diminutive form of GARRY.

Garland (1) the name for a wreath or crown of flowers (*Old French*) used as a feminine first name. (2) a surname, meaning 'a maker of metal garlands' (*Old English*), used as a masculine first name.

Garnaid a masculine variant form of GARTNAIT.

Garnet (1) the name of a deep-red gemstone used as a feminine first name (*Old French*). (2) an anglicised masculine form of GARTNAIT or Garnaid. (3) or **Garnett** a surname, meaning 'pomegranate' (*Old French*), used as a masculine first name.

Garrard a masculine variant form of GERARD.

Garratt a masculine variant form of GERARD.

Garret (1) the anglicised masculine form of Irish Gaelic GEARÓID. (2) or **Garrett** a masculine variant form of GARRARD.

Garrison a surname, meaning 'son of GARRET' (*Old English*), used as a masculine first name. Garrison Keillor is an American writer, speaker and broadcaster.

Garry (1) a Scottish river name and place name, meaning 'rough water', that is sometimes used as a masculine first name. (2) a masculine variant form of GARY.

Garth (1) a surname, meaning 'garden or paddock' (*Old Norse*), used as a masculine first name. (2) a variant form of GARETH.

Gartnait a masculine first name of uncertain derivation. It was a common name in the Pictish kingdom and was preserved in the family of the earls of Huntly. A variant form is Garnaid, and although it could be anglicised as Garnet, there is no etymological connection.

Garton a surname, meaning 'fenced farm' (*Old Norse*), used as a masculine first name.

Garve a place name, meaning 'rough place' (*Scots Gaelic*), used as a masculine first name.

Gary (1) a masculine first name meaning 'spear carrier' (*Germanic*). (2) a diminutive form of GARETH. A variant form is GARRY.

Gaspard the French masculine form of JASPER.

Gaston a masculine first name meaning 'stranger, guest' (*Germanic*); from Gascony (*Old French*).

Gauri a feminine first name meaning 'white' (*Sanskrit*).

Gautier or **Gauthier** French masculine forms of WALTER.

Gavan or **Gavin** an anglicised masculine form of GAWAIN.

Gawain a masculine first name meaning 'white hawk', from *gwalch*, 'falcon', *gwyn*, 'white' (*Welsh*). The Welsh form is Gwalchgwyn, and it is taken to be the same name as GWALCHMAI. Sir Gawain of Malory's Arthurian romance is known in Welsh as *Gwalchmai fab Gwyar*. As the principal knight of King ARTHUR he had great prestige, and the name was adopted in Ireland and Scotland as Gavan, Gavin. His parents, Lot and Morgause, were said to be from Lothian and Orkney (the latter being part of the Pictish kingdom until the ninth-century Viking conquest).

Gay (1) or **Gaye** an English adjective, meaning 'being joyous', used as a feminine first name (*Old French*). (2) a masculine first name meaning 'spear', from Gaelic *gáe*, 'spear' (*Irish Gaelic*). Spears were highly significant weapons among the Celts. (3) an Irish masculine diminutive form of GABRIEL. Gay Byrne is a popular Irish TV chat show host.

Gayle a feminine variant form of GAIL.

Gaylord a surname, meaning 'brisk noble man' (*Old French*), used as a masculine first name.

Gaynor the feminine anglicised form of GAENOR. *See also* GWENHWYFAR.

Gearóid (pronounced *garr-rode*) a masculine first name, the Irish Gaelic form of GERALD. The anglicised form is Garret. The name is closely linked to the Fitzgerald family, notably in the person of the fourteenth century third earl of Desmond, the magic-working Gearóid Iarla, 'Earl Gerald', and in the twentieth century by the Irish statesman Garret Fitzgerald.

Gearóidin (pronounced *garr-roh-din*) an Irish feminine first name, the Gaelic form of GERALDINE, a Norman name familiar in Ireland.

Geena a variant form of GINA. Geena Davis is an American film actress.

Gemma the Italian word for 'gem' used as a feminine first name. A variant form is Jemma.

Gene a masculine diminutive form of EUGENE, now used independently. Gene Hackman is an American film actor.

Geneva a feminine variant form of GENEVIEVE; the name of a Swiss city used as a feminine first name.

Genevieve a feminine first name the meaning of which is uncertain but possibly 'tribe woman' (*Celtic*).

Geneviève the French feminine form of GENEVIEVE.

Geoff a masculine diminutive form of GEOFFREY.

Geoffrey a masculine variant form of JEFFREY. Sir Geoffrey Johnson-Smith is an English politician. A diminutive form is Geoff.

Geordie a Scottish masculine diminutive form of GEORGE.

Georg the German masculine form of GEORGE.

George a masculine first name meaning 'a landholder, husbandman' (*Greek*). St George (died *c*.303) was a Christian martyr who became patron saint of England. The Scottish Gaelic form is Deórsa. Diminutive forms are Dod, Geordie, Georgie, Georgy.

Georges the French masculine form of GEORGE.

Georgia or **Georgiana** a feminine form of GEORGE. A diminutive form is Georgie.

Georgie (1) a masculine diminutive form of GEORGE. (2) a feminine diminutive form of GEORGIA, GEORGIANA, GEORGINA, GEORGINE.

Georgina or **Georgine** a feminine form of GEORGE. A diminutive form is Georgie.

Georgy a masculine diminutive form of GEORGE.

Geraint a Welsh masculine form of the Latin name Gerontius. It was the name of the warlike hero of the Welsh Arthurian tale *Geraint and ENID*. Sir Geraint Evans (1922–92) was a noted Welsh opera baritone.

Gerald a masculine first name meaning 'strong with the spear' (*Germanic*). Diminutive forms are Gerrie, Gerry, Jerry. The Irish form is GEARÓID, anglicised as GARRET. *See also* GIRALDUS.

Geraldine the feminine form of GERALD. The Irish form is GEARÓDIN.

Gerallt the Welsh masculine form of GERALD.

Gerard a masculine first name meaning 'firm spear' (*Old German*). Variant forms are Garrard, Garratt, Gerrard. Diminutive forms are Gerrie, Gerry, Jerry.

Gérard the French masculine form of GERARD. Gérard Depardieu is a French film actor.

Gerardo the Italian masculine form of GERARD.

Géraud a French masculine form of GERALD.

Gerhard the German masculine form of GERARD.

Gerhold a German masculine form of GERALD.

Germain a masculine first name meaning 'brother' (*Latin*). Diminutive forms are Gerrie, Gerry.

Germaine the feminine form of GERMAIN. Germaine Greer is an Australian writer and feminist. A variant form is Jermaine.

Geronimo or **Gerolamo** Italian masculine forms of JEROME.

Gerrard a masculine variant form of GERARD.

Gerrie or **Gerry** masculine diminutive forms of GERALD, GERARD. A feminine diminutive form of GERALDINE.

Gershom or **Gershon** a masculine first name meaning 'a stranger there' (*Hebrew*). In the Old Testament Gershon was one of the three sons of Levi.

Gert or **Gertie** feminine diminutive forms of GERTRUDE.

Gertrude a feminine first name meaning 'spear maiden' (*Germanic*).

William Shakespeare (1564–1616) used the name for the queen of Denmark, Hamlet's mother, in his tragedy *Hamlet*. Diminutive forms are Gert, Gertie, Trudi, Trudy.

Gervais the French masculine form of GERVASE.

Gervaise a masculine variant form of GERVASE.

Gervas the German masculine form of GERVASE.

Gervase or **Gervaise** a masculine first name meaning 'spearman' (*Germanic*). Variant forms are Jarvis, Jervis.

Gervasio the Italian, Portuguese and Spanish masculine form of GERVASE.

Gethin a masculine first name meaning 'dark', from *cethin*, 'dusky, dark' (*Welsh*).

Ghislaine an Old French form of GISELLE.

Giacomo an Italian masculine form of JAMES.

Gian or **Gianni** masculine diminutive forms of GIOVANNI.

Gibson a surname, meaning 'son of GILBERT' (*Old English*), used as a masculine first name.

Gideon a masculine first name meaning 'of a hill' (*Hebrew*). In the Old Testament Gideon was one of the great judges of Israel who also led the Israelites to victory over the Midianites.

Giffard or **Gifford** a surname, meaning 'bloated' (*Old French*) or 'gift' (*Germanic*), used as a masculine first name.

Gigi a French feminine diminutive form of GEORGINE, GILBERTE, VIRGINIE.

Gil (1) a masculine diminutive form of GILBERT, GILCHRIST, GILES. (2) a Spanish form of GILES.

Gilbert a masculine first name meaning 'yellow-bright; famous' (*Germanic*). A diminutive form is Gil.

Gilberta a feminine form of GILBERT. Diminutive forms are Gill, Gillie, Gilly.

Gilberte the French feminine form of GILBERT. A diminutive form is GIGI.

Gilchrist a masculine first name meaning 'servant or follower of Christ', from *gille*, 'follower' (*Scottish Gaelic*). A diminutive form is Gil.

Gilda a feminine first name meaning 'sacrifice' (*Germanic*).

Gildas a Welsh masculine first name and that of an ecclesiastic and historian, a contemporary of St David, said to have been born in the kingdom of Strathclyde, and author of *De Excidio Britanniae*, a description of the Saxon conquest of Britain. The name is found in Brittany as Gueltaz.

Giles a masculine first name that comes from *aigidion*, 'young goat'

(*Greek*), referring to the goatskin mantle of the saint. As the name of the patron of Edinburgh's high kirk, the name has some following in Scotland, where it also gains a Gaelic resonance from its resemblance to Gaelic *gille*, 'boy'. A variant form is Gyles.

Gill a feminine diminutive form of GILBERTA, GILBERTE, GILLIAN.

Gilleasbuig (pronounced *gheel-espic*) a masculine first name meaning 'servant of the bishop', from Gaelic *gille*, 'servant' (*Scottish Gaelic*). In the past it was assumed erroneously to be a Gaelic version of Archibald ('bald' implying a clerical tonsure), resulting in numerous Gilleasbuigs anglicising their names to this instead of the more usual Gillespie.

Gilles the French masculine form of GILES.

Gillespie the anglicised form of GILLEASBUIG.

Gillie a feminine diminutive form of GILBERTA, GILBERTE, GILLIAN.

Gillian feminine form of JULIAN. Diminutive forms are Gill, Gillie, Gilly.

Gillmore a masculine variant form of GILMORE.

Gilly a feminine diminutive form of GILBERTA, GILBERTE, GILLIAN.

Gilmore or **Gilmour** a surname, meaning 'follower of Mary', from *gille*, 'follower', *Mhuire*, 'of Mary' (*Scottish Gaelic*), used as a masculine first name. The name of a priest originally. A variant form is GILLMORE.

Gilroy a surname, meaning 'servant of the red haired one' (*Gaelic*), used as a masculine first name.

Gina a feminine diminutive form of GEORGINA, also used independently. Geena is a variant form.

Ginnie or **Ginny** a feminine diminutive form of VIRGINIA.

Gioacchino the Italian masculine form of JOACHIM.

Giorgio the Italian masculine form of GEORGE.

Giorsail (pronounced *ghee-orrsal*) a feminine first name meaning 'grace' (*Scottish Gaelic*).

Giovanna the Italian feminine form of JANE.

Giovanni the Italian masculine form of JOHN. Giovanni Lorenzo Bernini was a great Italian sculptor and architect of St Peter's Basilica in Rome. Diminutive forms are Gian, Gianni.

Gipsy a feminine variant form of GYPSY.

Giraldo the Italian masculine form of GERALD.

Giraldus the masculine Latin form of GERALD. The ecclesiastic Giraldus Cambrensis (Gerald the Welshman) (*c*.1146–*c*.1223) wrote extensively about life in the Celtic world in his own era and its earlier history.

Giraud or **Girauld** French masculine forms of GERALD.

Girolamo an Italian masculine form of JEROME.

Girvan a place name, meaning 'short river' (*Scots Gaelic*), used as a masculine first name.

Gisela the Dutch and German feminine form of GISELLE.

Gisèle the French feminine form of GISELLE.

Giselle a feminine first name meaning 'promise, pledge' (*Germanic*).

Gita a feminine first name meaning 'song' (*Sanskrit*).

Gitana a feminine first name meaning 'gipsy' (*Spanish*).

Giulio the Italian masculine form of JULIUS.

Giuseppe the Italian masculine form of JOSEPH. A diminutive form is Beppe, Beppo.

Gladwin a surname, meaning 'glad friend' (*Old English*), used as a masculine first name.

Gladys the feminine anglicised Welsh form of GWLADYS.

Glanmor a masculine first name from 'clean or bright', and 'great' (*Welsh*).

Glanvil a masculine diminutive form of GLANVILLE.

Glanville a masculine first name meaning 'dweller on the oak tree estate' (*French*). A diminutive form is Glanvil.

Gleda Old English feminine version of GLADYS.

Glen the surname, from *gleann*, 'mountain valley' (*Scottish Gaelic*), used as a masculine first name. A variant form is GLENN.

Glenda a feminine first name meaning 'good, holy' (*Welsh*). Glenda Jackson is an English actress and MP.

Glendon a masculine first name meaning 'from the fortress in the glen' (*Celtic*).

Glenn a masculine variant form of GLEN, now also used as a feminine first name. Glenn Close is an American actress.

Glenna or **Glenne** a feminine form of GLEN.

Glenys a feminine first name meaning 'holy, fair one', from *glân*, 'pure, holy and fair' (*Welsh*). Glenys Kinnock is an MEP.

Gloria a feminine first name meaning 'glory' (*Latin*).

Glyn a masculine first name meaning 'valley' (*Welsh*). A variant form is GLYNN.

Glynis a Welsh feminine first name, the stem of which may be *glân,* as in GLENYS, or it may be *glyn*, 'valley', indicating 'girl of the valley', and the female form of Glyn.

Glynn a masculine variant form of GLYN.

Goddard a masculine first name meaning 'God strong' (*Old German*).

Godfrey a masculine first name meaning 'God peace' (*Germanic*).

Godiva a feminine first name meaning 'God gift' (*Old English*).

Godwin a masculine first name meaning 'God friend' (*Old English*).

Gofannon a masculine first name meaning 'smith', from *gofan*, 'smith' (*Welsh*). It is the name of a legendary blacksmith.

Golda or **Golde** a feminine first name meaning 'gold' (*Yiddish*).

Goldie an anglised feminine form of GOLDA; 'fair-haired' (*English*). Goldie Hawn is an American film actress and comedienne.

Golding a surname, meaning 'son of gold' (*Old English*), used as a masculine first name.

Goldwin a masculine first name meaning 'gold friend' (*Old English*).

Goll a masculine first name meaning 'one-eyed' (*Irish Gaelic*). The best known bearer of this name in Irish legend is Goll macMorna, opponent of FIONN macCumhaill in his bid to lead the Fianna.

Gomer a masculine first name from the Old Testament. He was grandson of Noah and, in Welsh legend, the progenitor of the Welsh people.

Goodwin a surname, meaning 'good friend' (*Old English*), used as a masculine first name.

Gopal a masculine first name meaning 'protector of cows' (*Sanskrit*).

Gordon a masculine first name that was originally a location name, from *gor dun*, 'hill fort' (*Old Gaelic*), of the Scottish Borders, it became a family name and transferred with the family to Strathbogie in northeast Scotland. Diminutive forms are Gord, Gordie.

Gormflath (pronounced *gorrum-la*) a feminine first name meaning 'illustrious ruler', from Gaelic *gorm*, 'illustrious' (and also 'blue') and *flaith*, 'sovereignty' (*Irish Gaelic*). In legend it is the name of numerous princesses and holy women; the best known is the wife of BrianBorú, a powerful dynastic figure in her own right.

Goronwy a masculine first name that was popularised by Goronwy Owen, the Anglesey bard (1723–1769).

Gottfried the German masculine form of GODFREY. A diminutive form is Götz.

Götz a masculine diminutive form of GOTTFRIED.

Grace a feminine first name meaning 'grace' (*Latin*). A diminutive form is Gracie.

Gracie a feminine diminutive form of GRACE. Dame Gracie Fields (1898–1979) was a popular English singer and entertainer.

Grady a surname, meaning 'noble' (*Irish Gaelic*), used as a masculine first name.

Graeme or **Graham** or **Grahame** (pronounced *graym*) a masculine first name that was originally a place name, either from Grantham in England or from Scots *gray hame*, 'grey house', and then became a surname.

Gráinne (pronounced *grawn-ya*) a feminine first name that may come from *grán*, 'grain' (*Irish Gaelic*), suggesting an ancient fertility goddess; it has also been construed as 'she who terrifies'. A name from Irish legend; its most famous bearer was the Gráinne who was intended for marriage to the elderly FIONN macCumhaill but rebelled and eloped with Diarmaid, his nephew, as told in *The Pursuit of Diairmaid and Gráinne*. It is anglicised as Grania.

Granger a surname, meaning 'farmer or bailiff' (*Old English*), used as a masculine first name.

Grania a feminine anglicised form of GRÁINNE.

Grant a surname, from Old French *grand*, 'tall', of twelfth-century Norman-French immigrants to the Badenoch district of Scotland, now often used as a masculine first name.

Granuaile (pronounced *grawn-walya*) an Irish Gaelic feminine first name from that of Granuaile Mhaol, 'of the cropped hair', the sixteenth-century 'pirate queen' of Connaught, also known as GRÁINNE, or in English form Grace O' Malley.

Granville a masculine first name meaning 'large town' (*Old French*).

Gray a surname, meaning 'grey-haired' (*Old English*), used as a masculine first name. A variant form is Grey.

Greeley a surname, meaning 'pitted' (*Old English*), used as a masculine first name.

Greer a Scottish feminine first name, a shortened form of GRIGOR. Greer Garson is a Northern Irish-born American film star.

Greg a masculine diminutive form of GREGOR, GREGORY.

Grégoire the French masculine form of GREGORY.

Gregor a Scots masculine form of GREGORY. A diminutive form is Greg.

Gregorio the Italian and Spanish masculine form of GREGORY.

Gregory a masculine first name meaning 'watchman', from *gregorius*

(*Latin*). It is a name given prestige by its links with saints and popes. Two of the Doctors of the Roman Catholic Church were called Gregory, St Gregory of Nazianzus (*c*.329–*c*.389) and Pope Gregory I, 'the Great' (*c*.540–604). William Shakespeare (1564–1616) used the name for those of servants in two of his plays, *The Taming of the Shrew* and *Romeo and Juliet*. A diminutive form is Greg.

Gresham a surname, meaning 'grazing meadow' (*Old English*), used as a masculine first name.

Greta a feminine diminutive form of MARGARET. Greta Scacchi is an Anglo-Italian actress.

Gretchen a feminine diminutive form of MARGARET, MARGARETE.

Grete a feminine diminutive form of MARGARETE.

Greville a surname, meaning 'from Gréville in France', used as a masculine first name.

Grey a masculine variant form of GRAY.

Grier a surname, a contracted form of GREGOR, used as a masculine or feminine first name. A variant feminine form is GREER.

Griff a masculine diminutive form of GRIFFIN, GRIFFITH.

Griffin a Latinised masculine form of GRIFFITH. Griffin Richardes was an officer in the household of Catherine of Aragon, queen of Henry VIII. In his play Henry VIII William Shakespeare (1564–1616) calls him Griffith. A diminutive form is Griff.

Griffith an anglicised masculine form of GRUFFYDD. A diminutive form is Griff.

Grigor (1) a masculine first name that stems from Old Gaelic *giric*, 'king's crest' (*Pictish/Scottish Gaelic*). Girig was the name of more than one Pictish king. (2) or **Gregor** a Scottish masculine form of GREGORY. (3) the Welsh masculine form of GREGORY.

Grisel a feminine diminutive form of GRISELDA.

Griselda a feminine first name meaning 'stone heroine' (*Germanic*). A variant form is Grizelda. A diminutive form is Grisel, Grissel.

Grissel a feminine diminutive form of GRISELDA.

Grizel a feminine diminutive form of GRIZELDA.

Grizelda a feminine variant form of Griselda. Diminutive forms are Grizel, Grizzel, ZELDA.

Grizzel a feminine diminutive form of GRIZELDA.

Grover a surname, meaning 'from a grove of trees' (*Old English*), used as a masculine first name. Grover Cleveland (1837–1908) was a Democratic politician and the 22nd and 24th President of the United States.

Gruffydd or **Gruffudd** (pronounced *griffith*) a masculine first name meaning 'powerful chief' (*Welsh*) and a great name from Welsh history. Gruffydd ap Llewellyn was an eleventh-century ruler of Wales. The anglicised form is Griffith.

Gruoch (Pictish, female) a Pictish feminine first name the derivation of which is uncertain. This was the name of Macbeth's queen, herself a woman of royal descent.

Guaire (pronounced *gwarr-ya*) a masculine first name from *guaire*, 'noble', 'proud' (*Irish Gaelic*). Guaire Aidne was a seventh-century king of Connacht.

Gualterio the Spanish masculine form of WALTER.

Gualtier the French masculine form of WALTER.

Gualtieri the Italian masculine form of WALTER.

Gudrun a feminine first name meaning 'war spell, rune' (*Old Norse*).

Gueltaz a Breton masculine form of GILDAS.

Guglielmo the Italian masculine form of WILLIAM.

Guido the German, Italian and Spanish masculine forms of GUY.

Guilbert a French masculine form of GILBERT.

Guillaume the French masculine form of WILLIAM. Guillaume de l'Estoc was one of the legendary twelve paladins who attended on Charlemagne.

Guillermo or **Guillelmo** Spanish masculine forms of WILLIAM.

Guin a masculine diminutive form of GWYN.

Guinevere the earliest feminine anglicised form of GWENHWYFAR.

Gulab A FEMININE FIRST NAME MEANING 'ROSE' (*SANSKRIT*).

Gunhilda or **Gunhilde** a feminine first name meaning 'strife war' (*Old Norse*).

Gunnar the Scandinavian masculine form of GUNTER.

Gunter a masculine first name meaning 'battle warrior' (*Germanic*).

Günther the German masculine form of GUNTER.

Gus a masculine diminutive form of ANGUS, AUGUSTUS, GUSTAV.

Gussie or **Gusta** feminine diminutive forms of AUGUSTA.

Gustav the German and Swedish form of Gustavus.

Gustavus a masculine first name meaning 'staff of the Goths' (*Old Norse*). A diminutive form is Gus.

Gustave the French masculine form of GUSTAVUS.

Guthrie a surname, meaning 'windy' (*Scottish Gaelic*), used as a masculine first name.

Guy a masculine first name meaning 'a leader' (*German-French*). Guy de Bourgogne was one of the legendary twelve paladins who attended on Charlemagne. Sir Walter Scott (1771–1832) used the name for the eponymous hero of his novel *Guy Mannering* (1815).

Guyon a French masculine form of Guy.

Gwalchgwyn a Welsh masculine form of Gawain.

Gwalchmai a masculine first name meaning 'falcon of May', from *gwalch*, 'falcon', *mai*, 'May' (*Welsh*). The latter part may alternatively mean 'of the plain', from Gaelic *maigh*. Gwalchmai fab Meilir was a poet of the twelfth century. *See* Gawain.

Gwatcyn a Welsh masculine first name, a form of Watkin, 'Little Walter'.

Gwaun a masculine first name meaning 'heath' (Welsh).

Gwen a feminine diminutive form of either Gwenhwyfar or of other names beginning in Gwen-, but also found on its own. From *wen*, 'white, fair' (*Welsh*).

Gwenda a feminine first name meaning 'fair, good' (*Welsh*).

Gwendolen or **Gwendolin** a feminine first name meaning 'blessed, fair' (*Welsh*). Diminutive forms are Gwen, Gwenda, Gwennie. It is often anglicised as Gwendoline.

Gwendoline the anglicised feminine form of Gwendolen.

Gwendolyn a feminine variant form of Gwendolen.

Gwenfron a feminine first name meaning 'fair-breasted' (*Welsh*).

Gwenhwyfar (pronounced *gwen iff-ar*) a feminine first name that stems from *gwyn*, 'white', and *hwyfar*, 'smooth' (*Welsh*). It was the name of Arthur's queen and is found in many legends. Its earliest anglicised form was Guinevere, but it is much more frequently found as Jennifer. Other forms include Gaynor and the abbreviated Gwen.

Gwenllian (pronounced *gwen-hleean*) a feminine first name meaning 'fair, flaxen-haired' (*Welsh*).

Gwennan a feminine first name meaning 'fair, blessed' (*Welsh*).

Gwennie a feminine diminutive form of either Gwenhwyfar or of other names beginning in Gwen-.

Gwenonwyn a feminine first name meaning 'lily of the valley' (*Welsh*).

Gwenydd (pronounced *gwen-ith*) a feminine first name meaning 'Morning Star' (*Welsh*).

Gwili (1) a Welsh river name from Carmarthen used as a masculine first name. (2) a shortened form of Gwilym.

Gwilym or **Gwillym** Welsh masculine forms of William.

Gwion a masculine first name from the boyhood name of Taliesin the minstrel; also subject of the poem 'Gwion Bach'.

Gwladys or **Gwladus** (pronounced *glad-iss*) a feminine first name meaning 'ruler' (*Welsh*). Gwladus Ddu was the daughter of Llywelyn the Great. The anglicised form is Gladys.

Gwydion a Welsh masculine first name from that of a powerful sorcerer, from the *Mabinogion* cycle of legends.

Gwylan a feminine first name meaning 'seagull' (*Welsh*).

Gwyn a masculine first name meaning 'white, blessed' (*Welsh*). Gwyn ap Nudd was a legendary Welsh god, king of the 'Otherworld', Annwn.

Gwyneth a Welsh feminine first name from the name of the old province and modern county of Gwynedd. Gwyneth Paltrow is an American film actress. A variant form is Gwynneth. Diminutive forms are Gwyn, Guin.

Gwynfor a masculine first name meaning 'bright lord', from *gwyn*, 'white', and *ior*, 'lord' (*Welsh*). Gwynfor Evans was for many years leader of Plaid Cymru, the Welsh National Party.

Gwynneth a feminine variant form of Gwyneth.

Gyles a masculine variant form of Giles.

Gypsy the name for a member of a people who live a nomadic life used as a feminine first name. A variant form is Gipsy.

H

Haakon a masculine variant form of HAKON.

Habil the Arabic form of ABEL.

Hackett a surname, meaning 'little woodcutter' (*Old Norse*), used as a masculine first name.

Haddan or **Hadden** or **Haddon** a surname, meaning 'heathery hill' (*Old English*), used as a masculine first name.

Hadley a surname, meaning 'heathery hill or heathery meadow' (*Old English*), used as a masculine first name.

Hadrian a masculine variant form of ADRIAN.

Hafwen a feminine first name meaning 'bright summer', from *haf*, 'summer', and *wen*, 'fair' (*Welsh*).

Hagan or **Hagan** a masculine first name meaning 'young HUGH' (*Irish Gaelic*) or 'thorn bush' or 'thorn fence' (*Germanic*).

Hagar a feminine first name meaning 'flight' (*Hebrew*). In the Old Testament Hagar was the secondary wife of Abraham and the mother of his son Ishmael.

Hagley a surname, meaning 'haw wood or clearing' (*Old English*), used as a masculine first name.

Haidee (1) a feminine first name meaning 'modest', 'honoured' (*Greek*). (2) a variant form of HEIDI.

Haig a surname, meaning 'one who lives in an enclosure' (*Old English*), used as a masculine first name.

Hako a masculine diminutive form of HAKON.

Hakon a masculine first name meaning 'from the exalted race' (*Old Norse*). A variant form is Haakon. A diminutive form is Hako.

Hal a masculine diminutive form of HALBERT, HENRY. In his plays *King Henry IV, Parts 1* and *2*, William Shakespeare (1564–1616) has Sir John Falstaff invariably addressing Prince Henry as Hal.

Halbert a masculine first name meaning 'brilliant hero' (*Old English*). A diminutive form is Hal.

Halcyon or **Halcyone** feminine variant forms of ALCYONE.

Haldan or **Haldane** or **Halden** or **Haldin** a surname, meaning 'half Dane', used as a feminine first name (*Old English*).

Hale a surname, meaning 'from the hall' (*Old English*), used as a masculine first name.

Haley a masculine or feminine variant form of HAYLEY.

Halford a surname, meaning 'from a ford in a hollow' (*Old English*), used as a masculine first name.

Haliwell a masculine variant form of HALLIWELL.

Hall a surname, meaning 'one who lives at a manor house' (*Old English*), used as a masculine first name.

Hallam a surname, meaning 'at the hollow' (*Old English*), or a place name, meaning 'at the rocky place' (*Old Norse*), used as a masculine first name.

Halliwell a surname, meaning 'one who lives by the holy well' (*Old English*), used as a masculine first name. A variant form is Haliwell.

Halstead or **Halsted** a surname, meaning 'from the stronghold' (*Old English*), used as a masculine first name.

Halton a surname, meaning 'from the lookout hill' (*Old English*), used as a masculine first name.

Ham a masculine diminutive form of ABRAHAM.

Hamar a masculine first name meaning 'strong man' (*Old Norse*).

Hamilton a surname, meaning 'farm in broken country' (*Old English*), used as a masculine first name.

Hamish an anglicised masculine form of Gaelic Seumas, JAMES, in its vocative form, A Seamuis.

Hamlet or **Hamlett** a surname, meaning 'little home' (*Germanic*), used as a masculine first name. William Shakespeare (1564–1616) used it as the name of the main protagonist of *Hamlet, Prince of Denmark*.

Hammond a surname, meaning 'belonging to Hamon' (*Old English*), used as a masculine first name.

Hamon a masculine first name meaning 'great protection' (*Old English*).

Hamza or **Hamzah** a masculine first name meaning 'lion' (*Arabic*).

Hana a feminine first name meaning 'happiness' (*Arabic*).

Hanford a surname, meaning 'rocky ford' or 'ford with cocks' (*Old English*), used as a masculine first name.

Hani a masculine first name meaning 'joyful' (*Arabic*).

Hank a masculine diminutive form of HENRY.

Hanley a surname, meaning 'from the high meadow or hill' (*Old English*), used as a masculine first name.

Hannah a feminine first name meaning 'grace' (*Hebrew*). In the Old Testament Hannah was a childless wife of Elkanah who prayed for a son. God answered her prayers and she gave birth to Samuel. A variant form is ANN. A diminutive form is Nana.

Hannibal a masculine first name meaning 'grace of Baal' (*Punic*). Hannibal (247–182 BC) was a Carthaginian general in the Second Punic War. The American writer Thomas Harris used the name for a serial killer, Hannibal Lecter, in a series of novels.

Hans a masculine diminutive form of JOHANN.

Hansel a masculine first name meaning 'gift from God' (*Scandinavian*).

Happy an English adjective, meaning 'feeling, showing or expressing joy', now used as a feminine first name (*Old English*).

Harald a masculine variant form of HAROLD. A diminutive form is Harry.

Haralda a feminine form of HAROLD.

Harbert a masculine variant form of HERBERT.

Harcourt a surname, meaning 'from a fortified court' (*Old French*), or 'falconer's cottage' (*Old English*), used as a masculine first name.

Harden a surname, meaning 'the valley of the hare' (*Old English*), used as a masculine first name.

Hardey or **Hardie** masculine variant forms of HARDY.

Harding a surname, meaning 'brave warrior' (*Old English*), used as a masculine first name.

Hardy a surname, meaning 'bold and daring' (*Germanic*), used as a masculine first name. Variant forms are Hardey, Hardie.

Harford a surname, meaning 'stags' ford' (*Old English*), used as a masculine first name.

Hargrave or **Hargreave** or **Hargreaves** a surname, meaning 'from the hare grove' (*Old English*), used as a masculine first name.

Hari a masculine first name meaning 'yellowish brown' (*Sanskrit*).

Harlan or **Harland** a surname, meaning 'rocky land' (*Old English*), used as a masculine first name.

Harley a surname, meaning 'from the hare meadow or hill' (*Old English*), used as a masculine first name.

Harlow a place name and surname, meaning 'fortified hill' (*Old English*), used as a masculine first name.

Harmony the word for the quality of concord used as a feminine first name.

Harold a masculine first name meaning 'a champion; general of an army' (*Old English*). A variant form is Harald. A diminutive form is Harry.

Haroun an Arabic form of AARON.

Harper a surname, meaning 'harp player or maker' (*Old English*), used as a masculine first name.

Harriet or **Harriot** feminine forms of HARRY. Diminutive forms are Hattie, Hatty.

Harris or **Harrison** a surname, meaning 'son of HAROLD or HARRY', used as a first name (*Old English*). Harrison Ford is an American film actor.

Harry a masculine diminutive form of HARALD, HAROLD, HENRY, also used independently.

Harsha a feminine first name meaning 'happiness' (*Sanskrit*).

Hart a surname, meaning 'hart deer' (*Old English*), used as a masculine first name.

Hartford a place name and surname, meaning 'ford of the deer, or army ford' (*Old English*), used as a masculine first name. A variant form is Hertford.

Hartley a surname, meaning 'clearing with stags' (*Old English*), used as a masculine first name.

Hartmann or **Hartman** a masculine first name meaning 'strong and brave' (*Germanic*).

Hartwell a surname, meaning 'stags' stream' (*Old English*), used as a masculine first name.

Harun an Arabic form of AARON.

Harvey or **Harvie** a surname, meaning 'battle-worthy' (*Breton Gaelic*), used as a masculine first name. Harvey Keitel is an American film actor best known for the film *Reservoir Dogs*. A variant form is Hervey and the French form is Hervé.

Hasan a masculine first name meaning 'fair' or 'good' (*Arabic*). Variant forms are Hassan, Hussain, Hussein.

Haslett a masculine variant form of HAZLETT.

Hassan a masculine variant form of HASAN.

Hastings a place name and surname, meaning 'territory of the violent ones' (*Old English*), used as a masculine first name.

Hattie or **Hatty** a feminine diminutive form of HARRIET.

Havelock a surname, meaning 'sea battle' (*Old Norse*), used as a masculine first name.

Hawley a surname, meaning 'from a hedged meadow' (*Old English*), used as a masculine first name.

Hayden or **Haydon** a surname, meaning 'heather hill or hay hill' (*Old English*), used as a masculine first name.

Hayley a surname, meaning 'hay clearing' (*Old English*), used as a masculine or feminine first name. A variant form is Haley.

Hayward a surname, meaning 'supervisor of enclosures' (*Old English*), used as a masculine first name. A variant form is Heyward.

Haywood a surname, meaning 'fenced forest' (*Old English*), used as a masculine first name. A variant form is Heywood.

Hazel the name of the tree, from *haesel* (*Old English*) used as a feminine first name. The hazel tree is important in Celtic lore and tradition. Its twigs are used as divining rods and it was considered a fairy tree in Ireland and Wales.

Hazlett or **Hazlitt** a surname, meaning 'hazel tree' (*Old English*), used as a masculine first name. A variant form is Haslett.

Heath a surname, meaning 'heathland' (*Old English*), used as a masculine first name.

Heathcliff or **Heathcliffe** a masculine first name meaning 'dweller by the heather cliff' (*Old English*).

Heather the name of a purple or white-flowered plant of the heath family used as a feminine first name. It was first used as a girl's name in the nineteenth century, at a time when plant and flower names were very much in vogue.

Hebe a feminine first name meaning 'young' (*Greek*). In Greek mythology, Hebe was the daughter of Zeus and goddess of youth and spring.

Hector a masculine first name meaning 'holding fast' (*Greek*). In Greek mythology Hector was the eldest son of King Priam of Troy and his wife, Hecuba, and the bravest of the Trojans whose forces he commanded. His exploits are celebrated in the Greek epic poem the *Iliad*, attributed to Homer. He was slain in the Trojan War by the Greek hero Achilles.

Hedda a feminine first name meaning 'war, strife' (*Germanic*).

Hedvig or **Hedwig** a feminine first name meaning 'strife' (*Germanic*).

Hefin a masculine first name meaning 'summery' (*Welsh*).

145

Heidi a feminine diminutive of ADELHEID. A variant form is Haidee.

Heilyn (pronounced *hye-lin*) a masculine first name meaning 'cup-bearer' (*Welsh*).

Heinrich the German masculine form of HENRY. Diminutive forms are Heinz, Heinze.

Heinz or **Heinze** masculine diminutive forms of HEINRICH.

Helen or **Helena** a feminine first name meaning 'bright one' (*Greek*). In Greek mythology, Helen was the most beuatiful woman of her age and the wife of Menelaus. She eloped to Troy with Paris, an event that brought about the Trojan War. Helen Mirren is a well-known English actress. William Shakespeare (1564–1616) used the form Helena for heroines in two of his plays, *A Midsummer Night's Dream* and *All's Well that Ends Well*. Helena Kennedy is a prominent British barrister and a life peer. The Irish and Scottish Gaelic form is Eilidah. Diminutive forms are Lena, Nell.

Helene the German feminine form of HELEN.

Hélène the French feminine form of HELEN.

Helga a feminine first name meaning 'healthy, happy, holy' (*Old Norse*).

Helge masculine form of HELGA.

Helma a feminine first name meaning 'protection' (*Germanic*).

Héloïse a French feminine variant form of ÉLOISE. Héloïse (c.1101–1164) was the pupil, mistress and wife of the French philosopher and theologian Peter Abelard.

Hema a feminine first name meaning 'golden' (*Sanskrit*).

Hendrik the Dutch masculine form of HENRY.

Henri the French masculine form of HENRY.

Henrietta the feminine form of HENRY. Diminutive forms are Hettie, Hetty, Netta, Nettie.

Henriette the French feminine form of HENRIETTA.

Henry a masculine first name meaning 'the head or chief of a house '(*Germanic*). Diminutive forms are Harry, Hal, Hank.

Hephzibah a feminine first name meaning 'my delight is in her' (*Hebrew*). A diminutive form is Hepsy.

Hepsy a feminine diminutive form of HEPHZIBAH.

Hera a feminine first name meaning 'queen of heaven' (*Greek*). In Greek mythology, Hera was the sister and wife of Zeus. Her counterpart in Roman mythology is JUNO.

Herakles the Greek counterpart of HERCULES.

Herb a masculine diminutive form of HERBERT.

Herbert a masculine first name meaning 'army bright' (*Old English*). A variant form is Harbert. Diminutive forms are Herb, Herbie.

Herbie a masculine diminutive form of HERBERT.

Hercule the French masculine form of HERCULES.

Hercules a masculine first name meaning 'glory of HERA' (the Latin form of the name of Herakles, the Greek hero, son of Zeus and stepson of HERA).

Hergest a Welsh masculine first name from the Radnor place name. *The Red Book of Hergest* is an early (sixth century) source of Welsh verse.

Heribert the German masculine form of HERBERT.

Herman a masculine first name meaning 'warrior' (*Germanic*).

Hermann the German masculine form of HERMAN.

Hermes a masculine name from that of a god in Greek mythology, the messenger of the gods, with winged feet. His counterpart in Roman mythology is MERCURY.

Hermia a feminine first name probably invented by William Shakespeare (1564–1616) who used the name for one of the heroines of his comedy *A Midsummer Night's Dream*.

Hermione a feminine first name derived from that of HERMES. In Greek mythology Hermione was the daughter of the Greek Menelaus and his wife Helen who was nine years old when Helen went to Troy with Paris. William Shakespeare (1564–1616) used the name for the queen of Sicily in his play *The Winter's Tale*. Hermione Gingold (1897–1987) was an English actress.

Hermosa a feminine first name meaning 'beautiful' (*Spanish*).

Hernando a Spanish masculine form of FERDINAND.

Hero a feminine first name of unknown meaning, possibly connected with the name of the Greek goddess Hera and not connected to the noun 'hero'. In Greek mythology Hero was a priestess of Aphrodite who killed herself when her lover, Leander, was drowned swimming the Hellespont to visit her. William Shakespeare (1564–1616) used the name for the wronged cousin of Beatrice in his comedy *Much Ado About Nothing*.

Herrick a surname, meaning 'powerful army' (*Old Norse*), used as a masculine first name.

Herta a feminine first name meaning 'of the earth' (*Old English*). A variant form is Hertha.

Hertford a masculine variant form of HARTFORD.

Hertha a feminine variant form of HERTA.

Hervé a French masculine form of HARVEY.

Hervey a masculine variant form of HARVEY.

Hesketh a surname, meaning 'horse track' (*Old Norse*), used as a masculine first name.

Hester or **Hesther** feminine variant forms of ESTHER.

Hestia a feminine first name meaning 'hearth' (*Greek*). In Greek mythology Hestia was the goddess of family peace.

Hettie or **Hetty** feminine diminutive forms of HENRIETTA.

Heulwen a feminine first name meaning 'sunshine' (*Welsh*).

Hew a Welsh masculine form of HUGH.

Hewett or **Hewit** a surname, meaning 'little HUGH or cleared place' (*Old English*), used as a masculine first name.

Heyward a masculine variant form of HAYWARD.

Heywood a masculine variant form of HAYWOOD.

Hezekiah a masculine first name meaning 'strength of the Lord' (*Hebrew*). In the Old Testament was a king of Judah who undertook reforms.

Hi a masculine diminutive form of HIRAM, HYRAM.

Hibernia the Latin name for Ireland used as a feminine first name.

Hibiscus the marshmallow, the Greek/Latin) name of a brightly flowering plant used as a feminine first name.

Hieronymus the Latin and German masculine forms of JEROME. Hieronymus Bosch (*c*.1450–1516) was a Dutch painter noted for his macabre allegorical paintings of Biblical subjects.

Hilaire the French masculine form of HILARY.

Hilario the Spanish masculine form of HILARY.

Hilary now principally a feminine first name meaning 'cheerful; merry' (*Latin*) but formerly used as a masculine first name. St Hilary of Arles (315–367) was one of the Doctors of the Roman Catholic Church. A variant form is Hillary.

Hilda a feminine first name meaning 'battle maid' (*Germanic*). St Hilda (614–680) was an English nun who founded the abbey of Whitby of which she became the abbess. A variant form is Hylda.

Hildebrand a masculine first name meaning 'battle sword' (*Germanic*).

Hildegard or **Hildegarde** a feminine first name meaning 'strong in battle' (*Germanic*). St Hildegard of Bingen was a composer, poet and mystic.

Hillary a variant form of HILARY.

Hilton a surname, meaning 'from the hill farm' (*Old English*), used as a masculine first name. A variant form is Hylton.

Hippolyta the feminine form of HIPPOLYTUS. In Greek mythology Hippolyta was an alternative name for the queen of the Amazons. William Shakespeare (1564–1616) used the names Theseus and Hippolyta for the Duke and Duchess of Athens in his comedy *A Midsummer Night's Dream.*

Hippolyte the French masculine form of HIPPOLYTUS.

Hippolytus a masculine first name meaning 'allowing horses loose' (*Greek*). In Greek mythology Hippolytus was a son of Theseus and Hippolyta whose stepmother, Phaedra, fell in love with him and made accusations about him to revenge herself for his indifference. After Theseus arranged for Hippolytus's death, Phaedra killed herself. The story forms the basis of the tragedy *Phèdre* (1677) by the French dramatist Jean Racine (1639–99).

Hiram a masculine first name meaning 'brother of the exalted one' (*Hebrew*). In the Old Testament Hiram was a king of Tyre (970–936 BC) who was an ally of David and Solomon. A variant form is Hyram. A diminutive form is Hi.

Hobart a masculine variant form of HUBERT.

Hogan a masculine first name meaning 'youthful' (*Irish Gaelic*).

Holbert or **Holbird** masculine variant forms of HULBERT.

Holbrook a surname, meaning 'brook in the valley', used as a masculine hero of the Napoleonic Wars, Captain Horatio Hornblower, in a series of novels.

Hortensia or **Hortense** a feminine first name meaning 'of the garden' (*Latin*).

Hortensio the masculine form of Hortensia. The name was used by William Shakespeare (1564–1616) for a suitor of BIANCA in *The Taming of the Shrew.*

Horton a surname, meaning 'muddy place' (*Old English*), used as a masculine first name.

Hosea a masculine first name meaning 'salvation' (*Hebrew*). In the Old

Testament it was the name of the Hebrew prophet who wrote the Book of Hosea.

Houghton a surname, meaning 'place in an enclosure' (*Old English*), used as a masculine first name. A variant form is HUTTON.

Houston or **Houstun** a surname, meaning 'HUGH's place' (*Old English*), used as a masculine first name.

Howard a surname, meaning 'mind strong' (*Germanic*), used as a masculine first name. Howard Keel is an American singer and film actor. A diminutive form is Howie.

Howe a surname, meaning 'high one (*Germanic*) or hill (*Old English*) used as a masculine first name.

Howel or **Howell** anglicised masculine forms of HYWEL.

Howie a masculine diminutive form of HOWARD.

Hubert a masculine first name meaning 'mind bright' (*Germanic*). A variant surname form is Hobart. A diminutive form is Bert.

Huberta the feminine form of HUBERT.

Hudson a surname, meaning 'son of little HUGH' (*Old English*), used as a masculine first name.

Hugh (1) a masculine first name meaning 'mind; spirit; soul' (*Danish*). (2) an anglicised form of AED.

Hughina a Scottish feminine first name, a typically Highland name, for a daughter of HUGH.

Hugo the Latin, German, and Spanish masculine form of HUGH.

Hugues the French masculine form of HUGH.

Hulbert or **Hulburd** or **Hulburt** a surname, meaning 'brilliant, gracious' (*Germanic*), used as a masculine first name. Variant forms are Holbert, Holbird.

Hulda or **Huldah** a feminine first name meaning 'weasel' (*Hebrew*). In the Old Testament Huldah was a prophetess who interpreted a message from God for Josiah.

Humbert a masculine first name meaning 'bright warrior' (*Germanic*).

Hump or **Humph** masculine diminutive forms of HUMPHREY.

Humphrey or **Humphry** a masculine first name meaning 'giant peace' (*Old English*). Humphrey Lyttleton is an English jazz musician and radio show host. Diminutive forms are Hump, Humph.

Hunt or **Hunter** a surname, meaning 'hunter' (*Old English*), used as a masculine first name.

Huntingdon a place name and surname, meaning 'hunter's hill' (*Old English*), used as a masculine first name.

Huntington a surname, meaning 'hunter's farm' (*Old English*), used as a masculine first name.

Huntley or **Huntly** a surname, meaning 'hunter's meadow' (*Old English*), used as a masculine first name.

Hurley a masculine first name meaning 'sea tide' (*Gaelic*).

Hurst a surname, meaning 'wooded hill' (*Old English*), used as a masculine first name.

Hussain or **Hussein** a masculine variant form of HASAN.

Hutton a masculine variant form of HOUGHTON.

Huw (pronounced *hyoo*) a Welsh masculine form of HUGH.

Huxley a surname, meaning 'HUGH's meadow' (*Old English*), used as a masculine first name.

Hy a masculine diminutive form of HYAM.

Hyacinth the name of the flower adapted from the name of the hero of Greek mythology whose blood after his killing by Apollo caused a flower to spring up, used as a feminine first name.

Hyam a masculine first name meaning 'man of life' (*Hebrew*). A variant form is Hyman. Diminutive forms are Hi, Hy.

Hyde a surname, meaning 'a hide (a measurement unit) of land' (*Old English*), used as a masculine first name.

Hylda a feminine variant form of HILDA.

Hylton a masculine variant form of HILTON.

Hyman a masculine variant form of HYAM.

Hypatia a feminine first name meaning 'highest' (*Greek*).

Hyram a masculine variant form of HIRAM. Diminutive forms are Hi, Hy.

Hywel (pronounced *how-el*) a masculine first name meaning 'outstanding, eminent' (*Welsh*). Hywel Dda, 'the good', was a tenth-century Welsh king, famous for setting up a system of laws. Anglicised forms are Howel, Howell.

I

Iachimo an Italian masculine form of JAMES. William Shakespeare (1564–1616) used the name for one of the characters in his play *Cymbeline*.

Iacovo an Italian masculine form of JACOB.

Iago a Welsh masculine form of JAMES, from Latin Jacobus. William Shakespeare (1564–1616) used the name for Othello's duplicitous lieutenant in his tragedy *Othello*.

Iain (pronounced *ee-yann*) the Scottish Gaelic masculine form of JOHN. The anglicised version Ian is also very popular.

Ian an anglicised masculine form of IAIN. A variant form is Ion.

Ianthe a feminine first name meaning 'violet flower' (*Greek*). The English poet Walter Savage Landor (1775–1864) used it as a poetic name for his early sweetheart, Sophia Jane Swift, thus setting a fashion that was followed by other poets, including Lord Byron (1788–1824) and Percy Bysshe Shelley (1792–1822).

Ianto a Welsh masculine diminutive form of IFAN.

Iarlaith (pronounced *yarr-la*) a masculine first name from *iarl*, 'knight' (*Irish Gaelic*). It was the name of a fifth-century Irish saint. The anglicised form is Jarlath.

Iarnan (pronounced *yarr-nan*) a masculine first name meaning 'iron man', from *iarann*, 'iron' (*Irish/Scottish Gaelic*), indicating strength and fixity of purpose. St Iarnan was an uncle of St Columba. His name is preserved in Killearnan, on the Black Isle in Scotland. An anglicised form is Ernan.

Ibby a feminine diminutive form of ISABEL.

Ibrahim the Arabic masculine form of ABRAHAM.

Ichabod a masculine first name meaning 'inglorious' (*Hebrew*). In the Old Testament Ichabod was the posthumous son of Phinehas and grandson of Eli.

Ida (1) a feminine first name meaning 'god-like' (*Germanic*). (2) the anglicised feminine form of IDE.

Idabell a feminine first name meaning 'god-like and fair'.

Ide (pronounced *ee-ja*) a feminine first name from *íde*, 'thirst' (*Old Irish Gaelic*), meaning in this case thirst for virtue and knowledge. It was was the name of St Ide. It is anglicised to Ida, though in this form it can also derive from other sources including Greek.

Idonia a feminine first name meaning 'sufficient' (*Latin*).

Idony or **Idonie** a feminine first name from Norse mythology, the name of the keeper of the golden apples of youth.

Idris a masculine first name meaning 'fiery lord' (*Welsh*). Idris Gawr was a legendary figure from around the seventh century, who has given his name to Cader Idris (Idris's Fort), a mountain in Merioneth.

Idwal a masculine first name meaning 'lord of the ramparts', from *iud*, 'lord' (*Welsh*).

Iestyn the Welsh masculine form of JUSTIN.

Ieuan a Welsh masculine form of JOHN. A variant form is Iwan.

Ifan (pronounced *ee-fan*) a Welsh masculine form of John.

Ifor a Welsh masculine form of IVOR.

Igerna a feminine variant form of IGRAINE.

Ignace the French masculine form of IGNATIUS.

Ignacio a Spanish masculine form of IGNATIUS.

Ignatia feminine form of IGNATIUS.

Ignatius a masculine first name, from *ignis*, 'fire' (*Greek*). St Ignatius of Antioch (died *c*.110), on his way to martyrdom in Rome, wrote seven letters that cast light on the early Christian church. St Ignatius of Loyola (1491–1556) was the Spanish founder of the Society of Jesus (Jesuits).

Ignatz or **Ignaz** German masculine forms of IGNATIUS.

Ignazio the Italian masculine form of IGNATIUS.

Igor the Russian masculine form of IVOR.

Igraine a Cornish feminine first name. This was the name of the mother of King ARTHUR. Wife of Gorlois, duke of Cornwall, she conceived Arthur by UTHER Pendragon, whom she married after Gorlois's death in battle. Variants are Igerna, Ygraine, Yguerne. *See* EIGRA.

Ike a masculine diminutive form of ISAAC.

Ilario the Italian masculine form of HILARY.

Ilka a feminine diminutive form of HELEN.

Illtyd (pronounced *il-tood*) a masculine first name from *iud*, 'lord', probably meaning 'lord of all' (*Welsh*) (*see* DONALD). He was a Welsh saint of the fifth century whose name is preserved in Llantwit Major, in Glamorgan.

Ilona a Hungarian feminine form of HELEN. A diminutive form is Ilka.

Ilse a feminine diminutive form of ELISABETH.

Imelda an Italian feminine form of a Germanic name meaning 'universal battle'. Imelda Staunton is an English actress.

Immanuel a masculine variant form of EMMANUEL. A diminutive form is Manny.

Imogen (pronounced *immo-genn*) a feminine first name from *innogen*, 'girl, maiden' (*Celtic*), which probably has the same source as Gaelic *nighean*, 'daughter, girl'. It was used by William Shakespeare (1564–1616) for one of his characters in *Cymbeline* and misspelled by him or his printer. Imogen Stubbs is an English actress.

Imperial a feminine first name meaning 'relating to an emperor' (*Latin*).

Imran a masculine first name meaning 'the family of Imran' (*Arabic*). Imran Khan is a Pakistani cricketer and politician.

Ina a feminine diminutive form of names ending in *-ina*, e.g. GEORGINA, WILHELMINA.

Inderjit a masculine first name meaning 'conqueror of Indra' (*Sanskrit*).

India the name of the South Asian country used as a first name.

Indra a masculine first name of uncertain meaning and that of a Hindu god.

Indulf an ancient Pictish masculine first name and that of more than one Pictish king.

Ineda (pronounced *inn-ida*) a Cornish feminine first name and that of a Celtic saint, possibly confused with St ENDA. The derivation seems to be the same as that of Enda.

Inés or **Inez** Spanish feminine forms of AGNES.

Inga a feminine diminutive form of INGEBORG, INGRID.

Inge (1) a masculine diminutive form of INGEMAR. (2) a feminine diminutive form of INGEBORG, INGRID.

Ingeborg a feminine first name meaning 'fortification of Ing', the god of fertility (Frey) (*Old Norse*). Diminutive forms are Inga, Inge.

Ingemar a masculine first name meaning 'famous son of Ing' (*Old Norse*). A variant form is Ingmar. A diminutive form is Inge.

Inger a feminine variant form of INGRID.

Ingmar a masculine variant form of INGEMAR. Ingmar Bergman is a Swedish film and stage director.

Ingram a surname, meaning 'raven angel' (*Germanic*) or 'river meadow' (*Old English*), used as a masculine first name.

Ingrid a feminine first name meaning 'maiden of Ing', the god of fertility (Frey) (*Old Norse*). Ingrid Bergman (1915–82) was a famous Swedish film star. A variant form is Inger. A diminutive form is Inga, Inge.

Inigo a Spanish masculine form of IGNATIUS, now used as an English-language form. Inigo Jones (1573–1862) was an English architect and designer who introduced Palladianism into England.

Innes or **Inness** a surname, meaning 'island or meadow-dweller', from Gaelic *inis*, 'island, water-meadow' (*Scottish Gaelic*), occasionally used as a masculine or feminine first name.

Innogen *see* IMOGEN.

Ioan one of the Welsh masculine forms of JOHN.

Iola a feminine variant form of IOLE.

Iolanthe a feminine first name meaning 'violet flower' (*Greek*). The name was used by Sir William S. Gilbert (1836–1911) and Sir Arthur Sullivan (1842–1900) for the name of a fairy who married a mortal in their comic opera satirising the House of Lords and Courts of Chancery.

Iole a feminine first name meaning 'violet' (*Greek*). In Greek mythology Iole was a princess who was promised by her father to anyone who could defeat him in an archery competition. When he was defeated by Hercules, he refused to honour his promise. A variant form is Iola.

Iolo or **Iolyn** a Welsh masculine diminutive form of IORWERTH. Iolo Goch, the bard, was an associate of Owain Glyndwr. Another bard, Iolo Morgannwg (1747–1826) created the *Gorsedd of Bards*.

Ion (1) a masculine variant form of Ian. (2) in Greek mythology the name of the founder of the Ionian race and the eponymous subject of drama by Euripides (418 BC).

Iona a feminine first name from that of the name of the Scottish Hebridean island. It is actually a medieval misreading of the original name, Ioua, perhaps meaning 'island of yews'. Iona Brown is a noted English violinist and conductor.

Ione a feminine first name meaning 'a violet' (*Greek*).

Iorweth a masculine first name meaning 'worthy lord' (*Welsh*). An alternative, usually found as a surname, is Yorath. A diminutive form is IOLO or Iolyn.

Iphigenia a feminine first name meaning 'strong' (*Greek*). In Greek mythology Iphigenia was the daughter of Agamemnon and Clytemnestra who was taken by her father to be sacrificed to the goddess Artemis who saved her and made her a priestess. The story has inspired tragedies by the Greek dramatist Euripides (*c*.480–406 BC), the French dramatist Jean Racine (1639–99) and the German dramatist Johann Wolfgang von Goethe (1749–1832).

Ira a masculine first name meaning 'watchful' (*Hebrew*). In the Old Testament Ira was one of King David's leading officers.

Irene a feminine first name meaning 'peace' (*Greek*). Irene (752–803) was the wife of the Byzantine emperor Leo IV and ruled as guardian of her son, Constantine VI, and later co-emperor with him. She became a saint of the Greek Orthodox Church. A diminutive form is Renie.

Iris a feminine first name meaning 'rainbow' (*Greek*). In Greek mythology Iris was the swift golden-winged messenger of the gods and the personification of the rainbow. Dame Iris Murdoch (1919–99) was an English novelist and philosopher.

Irma a feminine first name meaning 'noble one' (*Germanic*).

Irvine or **Irving** a surname, meaning 'fresh or green river' (*Celtic*), used as a masculine first name.

Irwin a surname, meaning 'friend of boars' (*Old English*), used as a masculine first name. Irwin Shaw (1913–84) was a prolific American playwright and novelist.

Isa (1) a feminine diminutive form of ISABEL. (2) the Arabic name for Jesus.

Isaac a masculine first name meaning 'laughter' (*Hebrew*). In the Old Testament was the only son of Abraham and Sarah and father of Esau and Jacob who became second of the patriarchs of Israel. A variant form is IZAAK. A diminutive form is Ike.

Isabel or **Isabella** Spanish feminine forms of ELIZABETH, now used as separate English-language names. William Shakespeare (1564–1616) used the form Isabella for the heroine of his play *Measure for Measure*. A variant form is Isobel. Diminutive forms are Ibby, Isa, Izzie, Izzy, Tib, Tibbie.

Isabelle the French feminine form of ISABEL.

Isadora a feminine variant form of ISIDORA. Isadora Duncan (1878–1927) was an innovative American dancer and choreographer.

Isaiah a masculine first name meaning 'salvation of Jehovah' (*Hebrew*).

In the Old Testament he was the Hebrew prophet after whom the Book of Isaiah is named.

Iseabail (pronounced *ish-bel*) the Scottish Gaelic feminine form of ISA-BEL. It is anglicised as Ishbell.

Iseabeal (pronounced *eesh-aval*) the Irish Gaelic feminine form of Isabel, itself a Spanish form of Elizabeth.

Iseult a feminine first name meaning 'fair to look on' (*Cornish/Welsh*). There are two famous Iseults in the Arthurian legends, Iseult of Ireland, the true lover of TRISTAN, and Iseult 'of the White Hands' of Brittany, who deceives him into thinking she is the other. Variant forms are ISOL-DE, Isoult, Yseult, Essyllt.

Isham a surname, meaning 'home on the water' (*Old English*), used as a masculine first name.

Ishbel the anglicised feminine form of ISEABAIL.

Ishmael the name in the Old Testament of the first-born son of Abraham, borne by Hagar, his wife Sarah's Egyptian slave whom Sarah gave to him as she thought she was too old to give birth. When Sarah did give birth to Isaac, Hagar and Ishmael were driven into the desert but were saved by God who miraculously created a spring. Ishmael became a notable warrior and the father of twelve sons. The Arabic form is IS-MAIL.

Isidor the German masculine form of ISIDORE.

Isidora feminine form of ISIDORE. A variant form is ISADORA.

Isidore a masculine first name meaning 'gift of Isis' (*Greek*). St Isidore of Seville (*c*.560–636) was a Spanish theologian and Father of the Church.

Isidoro an Italian masculine form of ISIDORE.

Isidro Spanish masculine forms of ISIDORE.

Isla (pronounced *eye-la*) a Scottish river name from Perthshire, in use as a feminine first name since the nineteenth century.

Islay (pronounced *eye-la*) the name of an island of the Inner Hebrides. As a Scottish masculine first name it is almost exclusively associated with Clan Campbell.

Ismail the Arabic masculine form of ISHMAEL, son of IBRAHIM. Ismail was a major Muslim prophet.

Isobel a feminine variant form of ISABEL.

Isola a feminine first name meaning 'isolated, alone' (*Latin*).

Isolde or **Isolda** or **Isold** or **Isoult** a feminine variant form of ISEULT. The

German composer Richard Wagner (1813–83) used the form Isolde for the heroine of this opera *Tristan und Isolde*.

Israel a masculine first name meaning 'a soldier of God ruling with the Lord' (*Hebrew*). In the Old Testament it was the name given to Jacob after he wrestled with the angel of the Lord, thus becoming the name given to the Jewish nation descended from him. A diminutive form is Izzy.

Istvan the Hungarian masculine form of STEPHEN.

Ita or **Ite** a feminine first name meaning 'thirst (for truth)' (*Irish Gaelic*).

Ivan the Russian masculine form of JOHN. It was the name of several tsars.

Ivana a feminine form of IVAN.

Ivar a Scottish masculine variant form of IVOR.

Ives a surname, meaning 'son of Ive (yew) (*Germanic*)', used as a masculine first name. Yves St Laurent is a French couturier who popularised the wearing of trousers for women.

Ivo the Old French and Welsh masculine form of YVES. St Ivo of Chartres (1040–1116) was bishop of Chartres.

Ivor a masculine first name from an Old Norse personal name, Ivar, possibly meaning 'yew army' (Old Norse) adopted into Gaelic as Iomhar. A variant Scottish form is Ivar. A Welsh form is Ifor.

Ivy the name of the plant used as a feminine first name (*English*). Dame Ivy Compton-Burnett (1884–1969) was an English novelist.

Iwan a masculine variant form of IEUAN.

Izaak a masculine variant form of ISAAC.

Izzie or **Izzy** masculine and feminine diminutive forms of ISABEL, ISRAEL.

J

Jabal a masculine first name meaning 'guide' (*Hebrew*). In the Old Testament he was a descendant of CAIN.

Jabez a masculine first name meaning 'causing pain' (*Hebrew*).

Jacinta the Spanish feminine form of HYACINTH.

Jacinth a feminine variant form of HYACINTH.

Jack a masculine diminutive form of JOHN, now used independently. Diminutive forms are Jackie, Jacky.

Jackie or **Jacky** (1) a masculine diminutive form of JACK, JOHN. (2) a feminine diminutive form of JACQUELINE.

Jackson a surname, meaning 'son of Jack', used as a masculine first name. Jackson Pollock (1912–56) was an American abstract expressionist painter.

Jacob a masculine first name meaning 'supplanter' (*Hebrew*). In the Old Testament Jacob was the son of Isaac and Rebecca and ancestor of the Israelites. A diminutive form is Jake. *See also* ISRAEL, JAQUES.

Jacoba the feminine form of JACOB.

Jacobo the Spanish masculine form of JACOB.

Jacqueline a feminine diminutive form of JACQUES. Jacqueline du Pre (1945–87) was an English cellist whose career was brought to an end by mutiple sclerosis. A variant form is Jaqueline. A diminutive form is Jackie.

Jacques the French masculine form of JACOB, JAMES.

Jacquetta or **Jacquenetta** a feminine form of JAMES. William Shakespeare (1564–1616) used Jacquenetta for a character in *Love's Labour's Lost*. Jacquetta Hawkes (1910–96) was an eminent English archaeologist.

Jade the name of the light-green semiprecious stone used as a feminine first name.

Jael a feminine first name meaning 'wild she-goat' (*Hebrew*). In the Old Testament Jael was the woman who killed the Canaanite army chief Sisera when he hid in her tent.

Jagger a surname, meaning 'a carter' (*Middle English*), used as a masculine first name.

Jago a Cornish masculine form of JAMES.

Jaikie a Scottish masculine diminutive form of JAMES.

Jaime (1) a Spanish masculine form of JAMES. (2) a feminine variant form of JAMIE.

Jairus a masculine first name meaning 'he will enlighten' (*Hebrew*). In the New Testament Jairus was an officer of the synagogue whose daughter was resurrected by Jesus.

Jake a masculine diminutive form of JACOB, now used independently.

Jakob the German masculine form of JACOB, JAMES.

Jalal a masculine first name meaning 'glory' (*Arabic*).

Jalil a masculine first name meaning 'honoured' (*Arabic*).

Jalila the feminine form of JALAL, JALIL.

Jamal a masculine or feminine first name meaning 'beauty' (*Arabic*).

James a masculine first name from Jacobus, the Latin form of JACOB. It was the name of two of Christ's apostles, James the Great, son of ZEBEDEE, who was beheaded in Palestine in AD 44, and James the Less, son of ALPHAEUS. It has strong Scottish associations, with six Scottish kings bearing the name. Diminutive forms are Jaikie, JAMIE, Jem, Jemmie, Jemmy, Jim, Jimmie and Jimmy. *See also* JAQUES.

Jamesina a Scottish feminine first name and another example of the once common practice of tacking -ina on to a father's name. A diminutive form is INA.

Jamie a Scottish diminutive form of JAMES that has taken off as a masculine or feminine name in its own right. Jamie Lee Curtis is an American actress.

Jan (1) a masculine diminutive form of JOHN. (2) the Dutch form of JOHN. (3) a feminine diminutive form of JANCIS, JANE, JANET, now used independently.

Jancis a feminine first name formed from a combination of JAN and FRANCES. A diminutive form is Jan.

Jane feminine form of JOHN. Variant forms are Janet, Janeta, Janette, Janice, Janine, Jayne, Jean, Joan. Diminutive forms are Jan, Janey, Janie.

Janet or **Janeta** or **Janette** feminine variant forms of JANE. A diminutive form is Jan.

Janey a feminine diminutive form of JANE.

Janice a feminine variant form of JANE.

Janie a feminine diminutive form of JANE.

Janine a feminine variant form of JANEY.

Japheth a masculine first name meaning 'extension' (*Hebrew*). In the Old Testament Japheth was a son of Noah and brother of Shem and Ham who, with his wife, was among the occupants of the ark.

Jaqueline a feminine variant form of JACQUELINE. A diminutive form is Jaqui.

Jaques a form of Jacob or James adopted by William Shakespeare (1564–1616) for a character in his comedy *As You Like It*.

Jaqui a feminine diminutive form of JACQUELINE.

Jared a masculine first name meaning 'servant' (*Hebrew*). In the Old Testament Jared was the father of Enoch and an ancestor of Jesus.

Jarlath the anglicised masculine form of IARLAITH.

Jarvis a surname form of GERVASE used as a masculine first name. A variant form is Jervis.

Jasmine or **Jasmin** the name of the flower used as a feminine first name. Variant forms are Jessamine, Jessamyn, Yasmin, Yasmine.

Jason a masculine first name meaning 'healer' (*Greek*). In Greek mythology, Jason was the hero who led the Argonauts and had many adventures. In the New Testament Jason was a prominent early Christian in Thessalonica.

Jasper a masculine first name meaning 'treasure master' (*Persian*). *See also* CASPAR.

Javan a masculine first name meaning 'clay' (*Hebrew*). In the Old Testament was a son of JAPHETH and grandson of NOAH whose descendants settled the earth after the flood.

Javier a Portuguese and Spanish masculine form of XAVIER.

Jay (1) a surname, meaning 'jay', the bird (*Old French*), used as a masculine first name. The American writer F. Scott Fitzgerald (1896–1940) used the name for Jay Gatsby, the main male character in his novel *The Great Gatsby* (1925). Jay Presson Allen was an American playwright, screen writer and film producer. (2) a masculine and feminine diminutive form for names beginning with J.

Jayne a feminine variant form of JANE.

Jean (1) the French masculine form of JOHN. (2) a Scottish feminine form of JOHN, from Old French Jehane. This was once one of the most frequent girls' names in Scotland. Robert Burns wrote many love poems to his wife, Jean Armour. The diminutive form is Jeanie or Jeannie.

Jeanette or **Jeannette** a feminine diminutive form of JEANNE, now used independently. Jeannette is a variant form.

Jeanie or **Jeannie** a feminine diminutive form of JEAN.

Jeanne the French feminine form of JANE. A diminutive form is Jeanette.

Jeannette a feminine variant form of JEANNETTE.

Jed a masculine diminutive form of JEDIDIAH.

Jedidiah a masculine first name meaning 'beloved of the Lord' (*Hebrew*). In the Old Testament Jedidiah was the second son of David and Bathsheba. A diminutive form is Jed.

Jeff a masculine diminutive form of JEFFREY. Jeff Bridges is an American actor and son of Lloyd Bridges.

Jefferson a surname, meaning 'son of JEFFREY or Geffrey' (*Old English*), used as a masculine first name.

Jeffrey or **Jeffery** a masculine first name meaning 'district or traveller peace' (*Germanic*). Jeffrey Jones is an American film actor. A variant form is GEOFFREY. A diminutive form is Jeff.

Jehuda feminine form of JEHUDI. A variant form is YEHUDA.

Jehudi a masculine first name meaning 'Jewish' (*Hebrew*). A variant form is YEHUDI.

Jem or **Jemmie** or **Jemmy** a masculine diminutive form of JAMES.

Jemima or **Jemimah** a feminine first name meaning 'dove' (*Hebrew*). Diminutive forms are Mima, Mina.

Jemma a feminine variant form of GEMMA.

Jen a feminine diminutive form of JENNIFER.

Jenifer a feminine variant form of JENNIFER.

Jenkin a masculine diminutive form of JOHN, literally 'little John'.

Jenna or **Jenni** or **Jennie** feminine diminutive forms of JANE, JENNIFER, now used independently. A variant form is Jenny.

Jennifer a Cornish feminine form of GWENHWYFAR. Jennifer Jason Leigh is an American film actress. A variant form is Jenifer. Diminutive forms of Jenna, Jennie, Jennie and Jenny.

Jenny a feminine diminutive form of JANE, JENNIFER, now used independently.

Jeremia feminine form of JEREMIAH.

Jeremiah or **Jeremy** a masculine first name meaning 'Jehovah has appointed' (*Hebrew*). In the Old Testament Jeremiah was a prophet who foretold the fall of Judah to Babylon. His prophecies were recorded in the Book of Jeremiah. Jeremy Irons is an English actor. A diminutive form is Jerry.

Jeremias a Spanish masculine form of JEREMY. Jeremias II (1530–95) was a theologian and patriarch of Constantinople (modern Istanbul).

Jermaine a feminine variant form of GERMAINE.

Jerome a masculine first name meaning 'holy name' (*Greek*). St Jerome (*c*.340–420) was one of the Doctors of the Roman Catholic Church. A diminutive form is Jerry.

Jérôme the French masculine form of JEROME.

Jerónimo the Spanish masculine form of JEROME.

Jerry a masculine diminutive form of GERALD, GERARD, JEREMY, JEROME, now used independently.

Jerusha a feminine first name meaning 'possessed; married' (*Hebrew*).

Jervis a masculine variant form of JARVIS.

Jess a feminine diminutive form of JESSICA, JESSIE.

Jessamine or **Jessamyn** feminine variant forms of JASMINE.

Jesse a masculine first name meaning 'wealth' (*Hebrew*). In the Old Testament Jesse was the grandson of Ruth and Boaz and father of King David.

Jessica a feminine first name meaning 'God is looking' (*Hebrew*). William Shakespeare (1564–1616) used the name for Shylock's daughter in *The Merchant of Venice*. Jessica Lange is an American film actress. A diminutive form is Jess.

Jessie or **Jessy** feminine diminutive forms of JANET, now used as names in their own right.

Jesus the Greek masculine form of Joshua. In the New Testament Jesus is the son of God who was born in Bethlehem and grew up in Nazareth and founded Christianity.

Jethro a masculine first name meaning 'superiority' (*Hebrew*). In the Old Testament Jethro was a priest who gave sanctuary to Moses and whose daughter married Moses. Jethro Tull (1674–1741) was an English agriculturalist who invented the seed drill and whose name was adopted by a twentieth-century pop group.

Jewel the name for a precious stone or valuable ornament used as a feminine first name.

Jezebel a feminine first name meaning 'domination' (*Hebrew*). In the Old Testament Jezebel was the wife of AHAB, king of Israel. She encouraged idolatry and disregarded ELIJAH and ELISHA, provoking civil strife.

Jill a feminine diminutive form of GILLIAN, JILLIAN, now used independently.

Jillian feminine form of JULIAN. Diminutive forms are Jill, Jilly.

Jilly a feminine diminutive form of JILLIAN.

Jim or **Jimmie** or **Jimmy** a masculine diminutive form of JAMES.

Jo (1) a masculine diminutive form of JOAB, JOACHIM, JOSEPH. (2) a feminine diminutive form of JOANNA, JOSEPHA, JOSEPHINE. It was used by the American writer Louisa May Alcott (1832–88) for the young tomboyish heroine, Jo March, of her popular novels *Little Women* (1869), *Good Wives* (1871), *Little Men* (1871) and *Jo's Boys* (1886).

Joab a masculine first name meaning 'Jehovah is Father' (*Hebrew*). In the Old Testament Joab was a nephew of DAVID and his military commander. He defeated the rebellion of ABSALOM, David's son and slew Absalom.

Joachim a masculine first name meaning 'God has established' (*Hebrew*). Joachim of Fiore (*c*.1132–1202) was an Italian mystic and philosopher.

Joan a feminine form of JOHN. St Joan of Arc (1412–31) was a French heroine of the Hundred Years' War. Variant forms are Joann, Joanna, Joanne. Diminutive forms are Joanie, Joni.

Joanie a feminine diminutive form of JOAN.

Joan or **Joann** or **Joanna** or **Joanne** feminine variant forms of JOAN. Joanna Trollope is a popular English novelist. Joanne Woodward is an American film actor and wife of Paul Newman. Diminutive forms are Joanie, Joni.

Joaquin the Spanish masculine form of JOACHIM.

Job a masculine first name meaning 'one persecuted' (*Hebrew*). In the Old Testament Job was a patriarch who was tested by God. The story of his suffering is recorded in the Book of Job.

JoBeth a feminine first name formed by a combination of the diminutives of JOSEPHINE and ELIZABETH. JoBeth Williams is an American film actress.

Jobina feminine form of JOB.

Jocasta the name in Greek mythology of a queen of Thebes who unknowingly married her son. Jocasta Innes is an English interior designer.

Jocelyn or **Jocelin** a masculine or feminine first name meaning 'little Goth' (*Germanic*). Diminutive forms are Jos, Joss.

Jock a masculine diminutive form of JOHN. When John was the most popular boys' name, Jock became synonymous with 'Scotsman'. It has a diminutive form of its own, Jockie or Jocky.

Jockie or **Jocky** a masculine diminutive form of JOCK.

Jodie or **Jody** feminine diminutive forms of JUDITH, now used independently. Jodie Foster is an American film actress and director.

Joe a masculine diminutive form of JOSEPH.

Joel a masculine first name meaning 'Jehovah is God' (*Hebrew*). In the Old Testament Joel was a Hebrew prophet whose oracles are recorded in the Book of Joel. Joel Coen is an American film writer and director and brother of Ethan Coen with whom he works.

Joey a masculine diminutive form of JOSEPH.

Johan a Swedish masculine form of JOHN.

Johann a German masculine form of JOHN. A diminutive form is HANS.

Johanna the Latin and German feminine form of JANE.

Johannes a Latin and German masculine form of JOHN.

John a masculine first name meaning 'Jehovah has been gracious' (*Hebrew*). In the New Testament John was the name of one of Christ's Apostles. Three of the Doctors of the Roman Catholic Church are named John – St John Chrysostom of Constantinople (*c*.329–407), St John Bonaventura (*c*.1217–1274) and St John of the Cross (1542–91) – and many popes adopted the name. John (1167–1216) was king of England (1199–1216). John of Gaunt (1340–99), 'the kingmaker', was a son of Edward III and virtual ruler during the latter years of his father's reign and during Richard II's minority. William Shakespeare (1564–1616) used the name for the double-dealing Don John in *Much Ado About Nothing*. Diminutive forms are Jack, Jackie, Jan, Jock, Johnnie, Johnny.

Johnnie or **Johnny** masculine diminutive forms of JOHN. Johnny Depp is an American film actor.

Jolyon a masculine variant form of JULIAN. This form was used by the English playwright and novelist John Galsworthy (1867–1933) for a character in his Forsyte Saga series of novels.

Jon (1) a masculine variant form of JOHN. (2) a diminutive form of JONATHAN. Jon Lovitz is an American film actor.

Jonah or **Jonas** a masculine first name meaning 'dove' (*Hebrew*). In the Old Testament was a Hebrew prophet who was shipwrecked and swallowed by a 'great fish'. The story is recorded in the Book of Jonah.

Jonathan or **Jonathon** a masculine first name meaning 'Jehovah gave' (*Hebrew*). In the Old Testament Jonathan was the eldest son of SAUL and the great friend of DAVID. A diminutive form is Jon.

Joni a feminine diminutive form of JOAN. Joni Mitchell is a Canadian singer.

Jordan a masculine first name meaning 'flowing down' (*Hebrew*) and the name of an important river in the Middle East. Diminutive forms are Jud, Judd.

Jordana feminine form of JORDAN.

Jorge the Spanish masculine form of GEORGE.

Jos (1) a masculine diminutive form of JOSEPH, JOSHUA. (2) a masculine or feminine diminutive form of JOCELYN, JOCELIN.

Joscelin a French masculine or feminine form of JOCELYN.

Josceline feminine form of JOCELYN.

José the Spanish masculine form of JOSEPH. Diminutive forms are Pepe, Pepillo, Pepito.

Josef a German masculine form of JOSEPH.

Josefa feminine form of JOSEF.

Joseph a masculine first name meaning 'God shall add' (*Hebrew*). In the Old Testament Joseph was the eleventh son of Jacob and one of the twelve patriarchs of Israel. In the New Testament Joseph was the husband of Mary, mother of Jesus. Diminutive forms are Jo, Joe, Joey, Jos.

Josepha feminine form of JOSEPH.

Josephine feminine form of JOSEPH. Diminutive forms are Jo, Josie, Phenie.

Josette a French feminine diminutive form of JOSEPHINE, now used independently.

Josh a masculine diminutive form of JOSHUA, now used independently.

Joshua a masculine first name meaning 'Jehovah is salvation' (*Hebrew*). In the Old Testament Joshua was the successor of Moses who defeated the Canaanites, his story being told in the Book of Joshua. A diminutive form is Josh.

Josiah or **Josias** a masculine first name meaning 'Jehovah supports' (*Hebrew*). In the Old Testament Josiah was a king of Judah who initiated reform and the abandonment of idolatry.

Josie a feminine diminutive form of JOSEPHINE.

Joss a masculine or feminine diminutive form of JOCELYN, JOCELIN, JOSCELIN.

Joy the name of the feeling of intense happiness used as a feminine first name (*English*).

Joyce a feminine first name meaning 'sportive' (*Latin*).

Juan the Spanish masculine form of JOHN, now used as an English-language form.

Juana the Spanish feminine form of JANE. A diminutive form is Juanita.

Juanita a feminine diminutive form of JUANA.

Jud or **Judd** masculine diminutive forms of JORDAN, also used independently.

Judah a masculine first name meaning 'confession' (*Hebrew*). In the Old Testament Judah was the fourth son of Jacob and Leah one of whose descendants was to be the Messiah. His descendants settled in the area south of Jerusalem, which was named Judah. A diminutive form is JUDE.

Jude a masculine diminutive form of JUDAH. In the New Testament Jude was a follower of Jesus and brother of James. Jude Law is an English actor.

Judie or **Judi** feminine diminutive forms of JUDITH, now used independently.

Judith a feminine first name meaning 'of Judah' (*Hebrew*). In the Old Testament Judith was a Jewish widow who beheaded the Assyrian general Holofernes in order to save her native town. The story is told in the Book of Judith. Diminutive forms are Jodie, Judie, Judy.

Judy a feminine diminutive form of JUDITH, now used independently. Judy Davis is an Australian film actress.

Jules (1) the French masculine form of JULIUS. (2) a diminutive form of JULIAN, JULIUS. (3) a feminine diminutive form of JULIA, JULIANA.

Julia a feminine form of JULIUS. William Shakespeare (1564–1616) used the name for one of the heroines in his comedy *Two Gentlemen of Verona*. Julia Roberts is an American film actress. A variant form is JULIANA. A diminutive form is Julie.

Julian a masculine first name meaning 'sprung from or belonging to Julius' (*Latin*). Julian the Apostate (331–363) was the last Roman emperor (361–363) to oppose Christianity although brought up as a Christian himself. Julian Sands is an English film actor. A variant form is Jolyon.

Juliana a feminine form of JULIUS.

Julie or **Juliet** feminine diminutive forms of JULIA, now used independently. William Shakespeare (1654–1616) used the name for the young daughter of the Capulets who falls in love with Romeo, the young heir of the Montagues, the enemies of the Capulets, in his tragedy *Romeo and Juliet*, which is probably the world's best-known love story. Julie Walters is an English actress.

Julien the French masculine form of JULIAN.

Julienne feminine form of JULIEN.

Julieta a Spanish feminine form of JULIA.

Juliette the French feminine form of JULIA, now used as an English-language form. Juliette Lewis is an American film actress.

Julio a Spanish masculine form of JULIUS.

Julius a masculine first name meaning 'downy-bearded' (*Greek*). The name was adopted by several popes.

Junaid or **Junayd** a masculine first name meaning 'warrior' (*Arabic*).

June the name of the month used as a feminine first name (*Latin*).

Juno a feminine first name meaning 'queen of heaven' (Latin). In Roman mythology Juno was the equivalent of THE GREEK HERA.

Justin the English masculine form of Justinus, a Roman family name from JUSTUS (*Latin*). A variant form is Justinian.

Justina or **Justine** feminine forms of JUSTIN.

Justinian or **Justus** masculine variant forms of JUSTIN.

Justus a masculine first name meaning 'fair, just' (*Latin*).

K

Kady an Irish feminine first name perhaps influenced by Katie, but the name could stem from *céadach*, 'first' (*Irish Gaelic*).

Kamal (1) a masculine first name meaning 'pale red' (*Sanskrit*). (2) a masculine first name meaning 'complete' (*Arabic*). A variant form is Kamil.

Kamala the feminine form of Sanskrit KAMAL.

Kamil a variant form of Arabic KAMAL.

Kamila or **Kamilah** the feminine form of Kamil.

Kalantha or **Kalanthe** feminine variant forms of CALANTHA.

Kalypso a feminine variant form of CALYPSO.

Kane a surname, meaning 'warrior' (*Irish Gaelic*), used as a masculine first name.

Kara a feminine variant form of CARA.

Karadoc a Breton masculine form of CARADOG.

Karel (1) the Czech and Dutch masculine form of CHARLES. (2) a Breton feminine form of CAROL.

Karen (1) a Dutch and Scandinavian feminine form of KATHERINE. Variant forms are Caron, Caryn. (2) an anglicised feminine form of CAIRENN.

Kari a feminine variant form of CERI.

Karin a Scandinavian feminine form of KATHERINE.

Karina an anglicised feminine form of CAIRENN.

Karl a German masculine form of CHARLES.

Karla a feminine form of KARL.

Karlotte a German feminine form of CHARLOTTE.

Karol the Polish masculine form of CHARLES.

Karoline a German feminine form of CAROLINE.

Karr a masculine variant form of KERR.

Kashif a masculine first name meaning 'discoverer' (*Arabic*).

Kasia a feminine variant form of KEZIA.

Kasimir a masculine first name meaning 'peace' (*Polish*).

Kaspar the German masculine form of JASPER.

Kate a feminine diminutive form of KATHERINE, also used independently. William Shakespeare (1564–1616) used this diminutive for KATHARINA in *The Taming of the Shrew*.

Katerina a feminine variant form of KATHERINE.

Kath or **Kathie** or **Kathy** feminine diminutive forms of KATHERINE.

Katharina or **Katharine** German feminine forms of KATHERINE. William Shakespeare (1564–1616) used the form Katharina for the heroine of his comedy *The Taming of the Shrew* and Katharine for a character in *Love's Labour's Lost*. A diminutive form is KATRINE.

Katherine a feminine first name meaning 'pure' (*Greek*). Diminutive forms are Kate, Kath, Katie, Katy, Kay, Kit, Kittie.

Kathleen an anglicised feminine form of CAITLÍN. Kathleen Turner is an American actress.

Kathryn an American feminine form of KATHERINE.

Katie a feminine diminutive form of KATHERINE, now independent.

Katinka a Russian feminine form of KATHERINE.

Katrina a feminine variant form of CATRIONA.

Katrine (1) a feminine diminutive form of KATHARINA. (2) a variant form of CATRIONA. (3) the name of a Scottish loch, meaning 'wood of Eriu', used as a feminine first name.

Katriona a feminine variant form of CATRIONA. A variant form is KATRINE.

Katy a feminine diminutive form of KATHERINE, now used independently.

Kavan a masculine variant form of CAVAN.

Kay (1) a masculine first name meaning 'giant' (*Scots Gaelic*). (2) a feminine diminutive form of KATHERINE, or Catherine, now used independently. A variant form is Kaye. (3) an anglicised masculine form of CEI. Sir Kay was the foster-brother and seneschal of King ARTHUR in the English Arthurian legends.

Kaye a feminine variant form of KAY.

Kayleigh or **Kayla** or **Kayley** (1) a feminine first name the derivation of which is uncertain but possibly 'slender' (*Irish Gaelic*). (2) a feminine first named formed from a combination of KAY and LEIGH, or a variant form of KELLY.

Kaylin or **Kayline** an anglicised feminine form of CAOILFHINN.

Kean or **Keane** anglicised masculine forms of CIAN.

Kedar a masculine first name meaning 'powerful' (*Arabic*). In the Old

Testament Kedar was one of the twelve sons of ISHMAEL (ISMAIL) whose descendants formed a tribe in the Arabian Desert.

Keefe a masculine first name meaning 'noble, admirable' (*Irish Gaelic*).

Keegan a surname, meaning 'son of EGAN' (*Irish Gaelic*), used as a masculine first name.

Keelan or **Keelin** an anglicised feminine form of CAOILFHINN.

Keenan a surname, meaning 'little ancient one' (*Irish Gaelic*), used as a masculine first name.

Keera an anglicised feminine form of Irish Gaelic CIARA.

Keeva a feminine variant form of KEVA.

Keevan the anglicised form of Irish Gaelic CIABHÁN.

Keir a surname, meaning 'dark', from *ciar* (*Scottish Gaelic*), used as a masculine first name. A variant form is Kerr. See also CIARÁN, KIERAN.

Keira an anglicised feminine form of Irish Gaelic CIARA.

Keith (pronounced *keeth*) a place name and surname, probably from *coit*, 'wood' (*Scottish Gaelic*), used as a masculine first name, although it has also been associated with Cait, one of the seven sons of CRUITHNE, father of the Picts.

Keld a Danish masculine form of KEITH.

Kelly (1) a surname, the source of which is *cill*, 'church' (*Irish Gaelic*), indicating a special supporter of the church, used as a feminine or masculine first name. (2) the anglicised masculine or feminine form of CEALLACH. Kelly Lynch and Kelly McGillis are American film actresses.

Kelsey a surname, meaning 'victory' (*Old English*), used as a masculine and feminine first name. Kelsey Grammer is an American actor and star of *Frasier*.

Kelvin the name of a Scottish river, whose name stems from Gaelic *caol*, 'narrow', and *abhainn*, 'stream' (*Scottish Gaelic*), used as a masculine first name.

Kemp a surname, meaning 'warrior' (*Old English*) or 'athlete' (*Middle English*), used as a masculine first name.

Ken a masculine diminutive form of KENDAL, KENDALL, KENDELL, KENDRICK, KENELM, KENNARD, KENNEDY, KENNETH.

Kendall or **Kendal** or **Kendell** a surname, meaning 'valley of the holy river' (*Celtic/Old English*), used as a masculine first name. A diminutive form is Ken.

Kendra feminine form of KENDRICK.

Kendrew and **Kendrick** anglicised forms of Welsh CYNFRIG. A variant form is Kenrick. A diminutive form is Ken.

Kenelm a masculine first name meaning 'royal helmet' (*Germanic*). A diminutive form is Ken.

Kennard a surname, meaning 'strong royal' (*Germanic*), used as a masculine first name. A diminutive form is Ken.

Kennedy a surname, originally a nickname, from *ceann*, 'head', *eidhigh*, 'ugly' (*Scottish/Irish Gaelic*), used as a first name. This name is associated with southwest Scotland and Ireland. A diminutive form is Ken.

Kennet a Scandinavian masculine form of KENNETH. Diminutive forms are Ken, Kent.

Kenneth a masculine first name meaning 'handsome', from *coinneach*, 'handsome' (*Scottish Gaelic*). As the name of a Celtic saint, St Kenneth (515–599), and of the first king of the united Picts and Scots, Kenneth MacAlpin (died 858), it had great prestige. Diminutive forms are Ken, Kennie, Kenny.

Kennie or **Kenny** masculine diminutive forms of KENNETH and other names beginning with Ken-.

Kenrick a masculine variant form of KENDRICK.

Kent (1) a surname, meaning 'from the county of Kent' (meaning border), used as a masculine first name. (2) a diminutive form of KENNET, KENTON.

Kentigern a Brythonic masculine first name probably meaning 'of royal descent', from *teyrn*, 'king' (*Welsh*). This was the name of the Celtic missionary who became Glasgow's patron saint. *See also* MUNGO.

Kenton a surname, meaning 'settlement on the river Kenn', or 'royal place' (*Old English*), used as a masculine first name. It features in the long-running radio soap opera, *The Archers*, as the name of one of Phil and Jill's sons, Kenton Archer. Diminutive forms are Ken, Kent.

Kenyon (1) a masculine first name meaning 'white-haired' (*Gaelic*). (2) a surname, meaning 'mound of Ennion' (*Welsh*), used as a masculine first name.

Kermit a masculine first name meaning 'son of DIARMID' (*Irish Gaelic*).

Kern a masculine first name meaning 'dark one' (*Gaelic*).

Kerr (1) a Scottish masculine form of the surname CARR, used as a masculine first name. A variant form is Karr. (2) a variant masculine form of KEIR.

Kerry the name of the Irish county, probably stemming from *ciar*, 'dark', suggesting 'land of the dark (haired) people' (*Irish Gaelic*), now widely used without any direct connection to the area as a feminine or masculine first name.

Kester a masculine diminutive form of CHRISTOPHER.

Keturah a feminine first name meaning 'incense' (*Hebrew*). In the Old Testament Keturah was a wife of Abraham and mother of six sons.

Kev a masculine diminutive form of KEVIN, KEVAN.

Keva an anglicised feminine form of Caoimhe, an old name indicating 'beauty', 'grace' (*Irish Gaelic*). Keeva is an alternative form.

Kevan a masculine variant form of KEVIN.

Keverne an anglicised masculine version of a Cornish form of KEVIN.

Kevin a masculine first name, from Caomhin, 'born handsome' (*Irish Gaelic*), made popular by the story of St Kevin of Glendalough (died around AD 620), celebrated for his chastity and devotion. This name spread from Ireland in the twentieth century to become a popular one throughout the English-speaking world. Kevin Costner and Kevin Kline are American actors. A variant form is Kevan. A diminutive form is Kev.

Kezia or **Keziah** a feminine first name meaning 'the cassia tree' (*Hebrew*). In the Old Testament Keziah was the second of the three daughters of JOB, born after his period of tribulation. Variant forms are Cassia, Kasia. Diminutive forms are Kizzie, Kizzy.

Kiaran a masculine variant form of KIERAN.

Kiera (pronounced *kee-ra*) an Irish feminine first name, a feminine version of KIERAN. *See also* CIARA.

Kieran an anglicised masculine form of CIARÁN, a saint's name, from *ciar*, 'dark', and the diminutive ending -an (*Irish Gaelic*). Other forms are Kiaran, Kiernan, Kieron.

Kiernan a masculine variant form of KIERNAN.

Kieron a masculine variant form of KIERAN.

Kim a feminine diminutive form of KIMBERLEY, also used independently. Kim Bassinger is an American actress.

Kimberley a surname, meaning 'wood clearing', used as a feminine first name (*Old English*). A diminutive form is Kim.

King (1) the title of a monarch or a surname, meaning 'appearance, or serving in a royal household' (*Old English*), used as a masculine first name. (2) a diminutive form of names beginning with King-.

Kingsley a surname, meaning 'king's meadow' (*Old English*), used as a masculine first name. Sir Kingsley Amis (1922–95) was an English novelist.

Kingston a place name and surname, meaning 'king's farm' (*Old English*), used as a masculine first name.

Kinsey a surname, meaning 'royal victor' (*Old English*), used as a masculine first name.

Kira an anglicised feminine form of Irish Gaelic CIARA.

Kirby a surname, meaning 'church village or farm' (*Old Norse*), used as a masculine first name.

Kirk a surname, meaning 'one who lives near a church' (*Old Norse*), used as a masculine first name. The name was adopted by the American actor Kirk Douglas (born Issur Danielovitch).

Kirkwood a surname, meaning 'church wood' (*Old Norse/Old English*), used as a masculine first name.

Kirsten a Scandinavian feminine form of CHRISTINE.

Kirstie a feminine variant form of KIRSTY. Kirstie Alley is an American actress who appeared in the TV sitcom *Cheers*.

Kirstin a Scottish feminine form of CHRISTINE. A diminutive form is Kirstie.

Kirsty a Scottish feminine first name that was originally an abbreviation of CHRISTINA or KIRSTIN but is often now used on its own. Kirsty Wark is a well-known Scottish television presenter. A variant form is Kirstie.

Kish a masculine first name meaning 'a gift' (*Hebrew*). In the Old Testament Kish was (1) a man whose sons married the daughters of his brother, Eleazar, and (2) the great-uncle of Saul.

Kismet the Turkish form of Arabic *qismah* or *qismat*, meaning 'destiny, fate', used as a feminine first name.

Kit (1) a masculine diminutive form of CHRISTOPHER, KRISTOPHER. (2) a feminine diminutive form of KATHERINE.

Kittie or **Kitty** feminine diminutive forms of KATHERINE.

Kizzie or **Kizzy** feminine diminutive forms of KEZIA.

Klara the German feminine form of CLARA.

Klaus a masculine variant form of CLAUS.

Klemens a German masculine form of CLEMENT.

Knight a surname, meaning 'bound to serve a feudal lord as a mounted soldier' (*Old English*), used as a masculine first name.

Knut a masculine variant form of CANUTE.

Konrad a German and Swedish masculine form of CONRAD.

Konstanz the German masculine form of CONSTANT.

Konstanze the German feminine form of CONSTANCE.

Kora a feminine variant form of CORA.

Korah a masculine first name meaning 'baldness' (*Hebrew*). In the Old Testament Korah was (1) a son of Esau and (2) a rebel against the authority of Moses and Aaron.

Kris a masculine diminutive form of KRISTOFFER, KRISTOPHER.

Kristeen a feminine variant form of CHRISTINE.

Kirstel a German feminine form of CHRISTINE.

Kristen the Danish masculine form of CHRISTIAN, now also used in English as a girl's name. A variant form is Kristin.

Kristian a Swedish masculine form of CHRISTIAN.

Kristin a feminine variant form of KRISTEN. Kristin Scott Thomas is an English actress.

Kristina the Swedish feminine form of CHRISTINA.

Kristoffer a Scandinavian masculine form of CHRISTOPHER.

Kristopher a masculine variant form of CHRISTOPHER. Diminutive forms are Kit, Kris.

Kumar a masculine first name meaning 'boy' (*Sanskrit*).

Kumari a feminine first name meaning 'girl' (*Sanskrit*).

Kurt a masculine diminutive form of CONRAD, now used independently. Kurt Russell is an American film actor. A variant form is CURT.

Kyle a masculine or feminine first name from Gaelic *caol*, 'strait' (*Scottish Gaelic*). It is an increasingly popular name, perhaps in modern times seen as a masculine version of Kylie (*see also* GAEL) or Kayleigh. Kyle MacLachlan is an American film actor.

Kylie a feminine first name formed from a combination of KYLE and KELLY. The name was popular in the early 1990s probably because of the success of pop singer and actress Kylie Minogue.

Kyrena a feminine variant form of CYRENA.

L

Laban a masculine first name meaning 'white' (*Hebrew*). In the Old Testament Laban was the father of Leah and Rachel and father-in-law as well as uncle of Jacob.

Labhra or **Labraid** or **Labraidh** (pronounced *lab-rad*) a masculine first name meaning 'speaker' (*Irish Gaelic*). This might indicate one who speaks in assemblies, or a story-teller. Labraid Loingseach, 'seafarer', 'shipman', is a legendary leader and progenitor of the men of Leinster. It is anglicised into Lowry.

Lacey a surname, meaning 'from Lassy in the Calvados region of Normandy', used as a masculine or feminine first name (*Old French*).

Lachlan a masculine first name that originally meant 'man from Scandinavia', Lochlann being the Scottish Gaelic for 'the land of fjords'. The diminutive form is Lachie.

Ladislas a masculine first name meaning 'rule of glory' (*Polish/Latin*).

Láeg an Irish Gaelic masculine first name from Irish legend, Láeg being the name of Cuchulainn's charioteer and friend.

Laetitia a feminine first name meaning 'happiness' (*Latin*). Variant forms are Latisha, Letitia.

Laing a masculine variant form of LANG.

Laird a Scots masculine form of the surname Lord, meaning 'master, landowner' (*Old English*), used as a masculine first name.

Lalage a feminine first name meaning 'chattering' (*Greek-Latin*). Diminutive forms are Lallie, Lally.

Lallie or **Lally** feminine diminutive forms of LALAGE.

Lambert a masculine first name meaning 'illustrious with landed possessions' (*Germanic*). Lambert, Prince de Bruxelles, was one of the legendary twelve paladins who attended on Charlemagne.

Lamberto the Italian masculine form of LAMBERT.

Lamond or **Lamont** a surname, meaning 'law giver' (*Old Norse/Scots Gaelic*), used as a masculine first name.

Lana a feminine variant form of ALANA.

Lance (1) a masculine first name meaning 'land' (*Germanic*). (2) a diminutive form of LANCELOT.

Lancelot a masculine first name meaning 'a little lance' or 'warrior'; or 'a servant' (*French*). Lancelot Andrewes (1555–1626) was an English Anglican theologian and preacher. A variant form is LAUNCELOT. A diminutive form is Lance.

Lander or **Landor** masculine variant forms of the surname LAVENDER.

Lane a surname, meaning 'narrow road, lane' (*Old English*), used as a masculine first name.

Lang a Scottish masculine form of the surname Long, meaning 'tall or long' (*Old English*), used as a masculine first name. A variant form is LAING.

Langford a surname, meaning 'long ford' (*Old English*), used as a masculine first name.

Langley a surname, meaning 'long meadow' (*Old English*), used as a masculine first name.

Lara a feminine diminutive form of LARISSA (*Latin*). Lara Flynn Boyle is an American actress.

Laraine a feminine variant form of LORRAINE, 'the queen' (*Old French*).

Larissa or **Larisa** a feminine first name the meaning of which is uncertain but possibly 'happy as a lark' (*Greek/Russian*). Diminutive forms are Lara, Lissa.

Lark the English word for a bird famed for rising early and for its song Used as a feminine first name.

Larry a masculine diminutive form of LAURENCE, LAWRENCE.

Lars a Scandinavian masculine form of LAURENCE.

Larsen or **Larson** a masculine first name meaning 'son of LARS' (*Scandinavian*).

Lasair a feminine first name meaning 'flame, blaze' (*Irish Gaelic*).

Lascelles a surname, meaning 'hermitage or cell' (*Old French*), used as a masculine first name.

Laszlo the Hungarian masculine form of LADISLAS.

Latham or **Lathom** a surname, meaning 'barns' (*Old Norse*), used as a masculine first name.

Latimer a surname, meaning 'interpreter' (*Old French*), used as a masculine first name.

Latisha a feminine variant form of LAETITIA.

Launcelot a masculine variant form of Lancelot and the one found in Arthurian legend for the name of the most famous of the knights of the Round Table. He is a major figure in *Idylls of the King* by Lord Tennyson (1809–92).

Laura a feminine first name meaning 'laurel, bay tree' (*Latin*). It was the name of a young woman whom the Italian poet Petrarch (1304–74) met in Avignon in 1327 and with whom he fell in love. She became the inspiration for his poetry, and the name has been popular with poets ever since. A diminutive form is Laurie.

Laurabel a feminine first name formed from a combination of LAURA and MABEL.

Laurel a name for the evergreen bay tree used as a feminine first name.

Lauren feminine form of LAURENCE. Lauren Bacall is an American film actress. A variant form is LOREN. A diminutive form is Laurie.

Laurence (1) a masculine first name meaning 'from Laurentium in Italy, place of laurels' (*Latin*). Sir Laurence Olivier (later Lord Olivier) (1907–89) was an eminent English actor and director. A variant form is LAWRENCE. Diminutive forms are Larry, Laurie. (2) a masculine anglicised form of the Irish LORCAN.

Laurens a Dutch masculine form of LAURENCE.

Laurent the French masculine form of LAURENCE.

Lauretta or **Laurette** a French feminine form of LAURA.

Laurie (1) a masculine diminutive form of LAURENCE. It was used by the American writer Louisa May Alcott (1832–88) for the young, rich neighbour of the March family in her popular novels *Little Women* (1869), *Good Wives* (1871), *Little Men* (1871) and *Jo's Boys* (1886). Laurie Lee (1914–97) was an English poet best known for his autobiography, *Cider with Rosie* (1959). (2) a surname form of this used as a masculine first name. Variant forms are LAWRIE, LAWRY. (3) a feminine dimuntive form of LAURA, LAUREN.

Lavender (1) the English name of the plant that bears blue or mauve flowers used as a feminine first name. (2) a surname, meaning 'launderer', used as a feminine first name (*Old French*). A variant form is LANDER.

Laverne a feminine first name meaning 'the alder tree' (*Old French*). Diminutive forms are Verna, Verne.

Lavinia or **Lavina** a feminine first name meaning 'of Latium' in Italy

(*Latin*). William Shakespeare (1564–1616) used the name for the daughter of Titus in his play *Titus Andronicus*.

Lawrence a masculine variant form of LAURENCE. St Lawrence (died 258) was an early Christian martyr. Lawrence Kasdan is an American screen-writer and film director best known for writing the scripts for two of the *Star Wars* films. Diminutive forms are Larry, Lawrie, Lawry.

Lawrie or **Lawry** (1) a masculine diminutive forms of LAWRENCE. (2) a variant form of LAURIE.

Lawson a surname, meaning 'son of LAWRENCE' (*Old English*), used as a masculine first name.

Lawton a surname, meaning 'from the place on the hill' (*Old English*), used as a masculine first name.

Layton a masculine variant form of LEIGHTON.

Lazarus a masculine first name meaning 'destitute of help' (*Hebrew*). In the New Testament was the brother of Martha and Mary and who was raised from the dead by Jesus.

Lea a feminine variant form of LEAH, LEE.

Leah a feminine first name meaning 'languid', or 'wild cow' (*Hebrew*). In the Old Testament Leah was the first wife of Jacob and the elder sister of Rachel, his second wife. Variant forms are Lea, Lee.

Leal or **Leale** a surname, meaning 'loyal, true' (*Old French*), used as a masculine first name.

Leana a feminine variant form of LIANA.

Leander a masculine first name meaning 'lion man' (*Greek*). In Greek mythology it was the name of HERO's lover who drowned in the Hellespont.

Leandre a French masculine form of LEANDER.

Leandro an Italian masculine form of LEANDER.

Leane a feminine variant form of LEANNE, LIANE.

Leanna a feminine variant form of LIANA.

Leanne a feminine first name formed by a combination of LEE and ANNE. A variant form is Leane.

Leanora or **Leanore** German feminine variant forms of ELEANOR.

Leda a feminine first name meaning 'mother of beauty' (*Greek*). In Greek mythology, Leda was a queen of Sparta who was visited by Zeus (who appeared to her in the form of a swan) and gave birth to Helen.

Lee (1) a surname, meaning 'field or meadow', used as a masculine or feminine first name (*Old English*). Lee Marvin (1924–87) was a noted American film actor. A variant form is Leigh. (2) a feminine variant form of LEAH.

Leif a masculine first name meaning 'beloved one' (*Old Norse*).

Leigh a masculine variant form of LEE.

Leighton a surname, meaning 'herb garden' (*Old English*), used as a masculine first name. A variant form is Layton.

Leila a feminine first name meaning 'night, dark' (*Arabic*). Variant forms are Lela, Lila, Lilah.

Leith a place name, meaning 'moist place' (*Celtic*) or 'grey' (*Scots Gaelic*), used as a masculine first name.

Lela a feminine variant form of LEILA.

Leland a masculine variant form of LEYLAND.

Lem a masculine diminutive form of LEMUEL.

Lemuel a masculine first name meaning 'devoted to God' (*Hebrew*). In the Old Testament Lemuel was a king of ancient times mentioned in the Book of Proverbs. The Anglo-Irish clergyman and writer Jonathan Swift (1667–1745) used the name for the hero of his novel *Gulliver's Travels* (1726). A diminutive form is Lem.

Len a masculine diminutive form of LEONARD, LENNOX, LIONEL.

Lena a feminine diminutive form of HELENA, etc, also used independently.

Lennard a masculine variant form of LEONARD.

Lennie a masculine diminutive form of LEONARD, LENNOX, LIONEL.

Lennox a place name and surname, meaning 'abounding in elm trees' (*Scots Gaelic*), used as a masculine first name.

Lenny a masculine diminutive form of LEONARD, LENNOX, LIONEL. A variant form is Lonnie.

Lenora a feminine variant form of LEONORA.

Leo a masculine first name meaning 'lion' (*Latin*). The name was adopted by several popes. A variant form is LEON.

Leon a masculine variant form of LEO.

Leona a feminine variant form of LEONIE.

Leonard a masculine first name meaning 'lion strong' (*Germanic*). A variant form is Lennard. Diminutive forms are Len, Lennie, Lenny.

Leonarda feminine form of LEONARD.

Leonardo an Italian masculine form of LEONARD. Leonardo da Vinci (1452–1519) was an Italian painter, sculptor, architect and engineer, and the greatest artist of his age. Leonardo di Caprio is a popular American film actor.

Leonhard a German masculine form of LEONARD.

Leonidas a masculine first name meaning 'of a lion' (*Greek*).

Leonie feminine form of LEO, LEON. A variant form is Leona.

Leonora an Italian feminine form of ELEANOR. The German composer Ludwig van Beethoven (1770–1827) used the name for the heroine of his only opera, *Fidelio* (1805). A variant form is Lenora. A diminutive form is Nora.

Leontine or **Leontina** feminine form of LEONTIUS.

Leontius a masculine first name meaning 'of the lion' (*Latin*).

Leontyne a feminine variant form of LEONTINE. Leontyne Price is an eminent American opera singer.

Leopold a masculine first name meaning 'bold for the people' (*Germanic*).

Leopoldina or **Leopoldine** feminine forms of LEOPOLD.

Leopoldo an Italian and Spanish masculine form of LEOPOLD.

Leroy a masculine first name meaning 'the king' (*Old French*). A variant form is Elroy. Diminutive forms are Lee, Roy.

Lesley the usual feminine form of LESLIE.

Leslie a location name and surname from Aberdeenshire, from *lios*, 'enclosure', and *liath*, 'grey' (*Scottish Gaelic*), often used as a first name. Leslie Nielson is a Canadian-born film actor. This is the usual masculine form, but it is acquiring popularity, particularly in North America, as a feminine form. Leslie Caron is a French-born dancer and film actress.

Lester a surname, meaning 'from the Roman site' (*Old English*) (i.e. the present city of Leicester), used as a masculine first name.

Leticia or **Letitia** feminine variant forms of LAETITIA.

Letizia an Italian feminine form of LAETITIA.

Lettice a feminine variant form of LAETITIA. Diminutive forms are Lettie, Letty.

Lettie or **Letty** feminine diminutive forms of LETTICE.

Lev a Russian masculine form of LEO.

Levi a masculine first name meaning 'joined' (*Hebrew*). In the Old Testament Levi was the third son of Jacob and Leah and ancestor of one of the Twelve Tribes of Israel. In the New Testament it was the original name of Matthew, the tax collector who became one of Christ's Apostles.

Lew or **Lewie** masculine diminutive forms of LEWIS.

Lewis (1) a masculine first name meaning 'bold warrior' (*Germanic*). (2) a Scottish masculine first name probably from French 'Louis', although it could be influenced by the name of the Isle of Lewis, which has been derived from Old Norse as *ljoth*, 'people', *hus* 'houses'. On the other hand, no other old personal names come from island names: Barra, for example, received its name from the personal name Barr, and not vice versa. (3) a Welsh masculine form of French Louis. Diminutive forms are Lew, Lewie.

Lex a masculine diminutive form of ALEXANDER.

Lexie or **Lexy** feminine diminutive forms of ALEXANDRA.

Leyland a surname, meaning 'fallow or untilled land' (*Old English*), used as a masculine first name. A variant form is Leland.

Liadain or **Líadan** or **Liadhain** (pronounced *leea-dan*) a feminine first name, probably from *liath*, 'grey' (*Irish Gaelic*). The story of Liadain and her tragic love for the poet Cuírithir foreshadows the later one of Abelard and Héloise.

Liam (pronounced *lee-am*) a masculine shortened form of William and the most usual Irish Gaelic form of William. Liam Neeson is an Irish-born film actor best known for the film *Schindler's List*.

Liana or **Liane** or **Lianna** or **Lianne** a feminine first name meaning 'sun' (*Greek*). Variant forms are Leane, Leana, Leanna.

Libby a feminine diminutive form of ELIZABETH.

Lidia an Italian and Spanish feminine form of LYDIA.

Liese a feminine diminutive form of ELISABETH, now used independently.

Lije a masculine diminutive form of ELIJAH.

Lil a feminine diminutive form of LILIAN, LILY.

Lila (1) a feminine variant form of LEILA. (2) a diminutive form of DELILAH.

Lilac a feminine first name meaning 'bluish' (*Persian*), the English name of the syringa plant with fragrant purple or white flowers used as a feminine first name.

Lilah (1) a feminine variant form of LEILA. (2) a diminutive form of DELILAH.

Lili a feminine variant form of LILIE.

Lilian (1) a feminine diminutive form of ELIZABETH. (2) a variant form of LILY. A variant form is Lillian.

Lilias or **Lillias** Scottish feminine forms of LILIAN.

Lilibet a feminine diminutive form of ELIZABETH.

Lilie a German feminine form of LILY. A variant form is Lili.

Lilith a feminine first name meaning 'of the night' (*Hebrew*).

Lilli a feminine variant form of LILY.

Lillian a feminine variant form of LILIAN.

Lily the name of the flowering plant with showy blossoms used as a feminine first name. A variant form is Lilli. A diminutive form is Lil.

Lin a feminine diminutive form of LINDA.

Lina a feminine diminutive form of SELINA and names ending in -lina, -line.

Lincoln a place name and surname, meaning 'the place by the pool' (*Celtic/Latin*), used as a masculine first name.

Linda a feminine diminutive form of BELINDA, ROSALIND, etc, now used independently. A variant form is Lynda. Diminutive forms are Lin, Lindie, Lindy.

Lindall or **Lindell** a surname, meaning 'valley of lime trees' (*Old English*), used as a masculine first name.

Lindie a feminine diminutive form of LINDA.

Lindley a place name and surname, meaning 'lime tree meadow or flax field' (*Old English*), used as a masculine first name. A variant form is Linley.

Lindsay or **Lindsey** a surname, meaning 'island of Lincoln', perhaps from Lindsey in England, used as a masculine or feminine first name. Lindsay Duncan is an English actress. Lindsay Anderson (1923–94) was a British stage and film director and occasionally an actor. Variant forms are Linsay, Linsey, Linzi, Lyndsay, Lynsay, Lynsey.

Lindy a feminine diminutive form of LINDA.

Linet a Welsh feminine variant form of LUNED.

Linford a surname, meaning 'from the ford of the lime tree or flax field' (*Old English*), used as a masculine first name. Linford Christie is a famous English athlete.

Linley a masculine variant form of LINDLEY.

Linnette a feminine variant form of LYNETTE.

Linsay or **Linsey** a masculine or feminine variant forms of LINDSAY.

Linton a surname, meaning 'flax place' (*Old English*), used as a masculine first name.

Linus a masculine first name meaning 'flaxen-haired' (*Greek*). In the New Testament Linus was a Roman Christian mentioned by Paul in one of his epistles.

Linzi a feminine variant form of LINDSAY.

Lionel a masculine first name meaning 'young lion' (*Latin*). A diminutive form is Len.

Lis a feminine diminutive form of ELISABETH.

Lisa a feminine diminutive form of ELIZABETH, now used independently. A variant form is Liza.

Lisbeth a feminine diminutive form of ELISABETH.

Lisette a feminine diminutive form of LOUISE.

Lisle a surname, meaning 'island' or 'from Lisle in Normandy' (*Old French*), used as a masculine first name. Variant forms are Lyall, Lyle.

Lissa a feminine diminutive form of LARISSA, MELISSA.

Lister a surname, meaning 'dyer' (*Old English*), used as a masculine first name.

Lita a feminine diminutive form of ALIDA.

Litton a place name and surname, meaning 'loud torrent' (*Old English*), used as a masculine first name. A variant form is Lytton.

Livia a feminine variant form of OLIVIA.

Liz a feminine diminutive form of ELIZABETH.

Liza a feminine variant form of LISA.

Lizbeth a feminine diminutive form of ELIZABETH.

Lizzie or **Lizzy** feminine diminutive forms of ELIZABETH.

Llew (pronounced *hloo*) (1) a masculine first name from *lleu*, 'light', 'fair' (*Welsh*). Lleu Llawgyffes, 'of the steady hand', son of ARIANRHOD, is a principal figure in one of the *Mabinogion* tales. (2) the name may nowadays also be seen as a shortened form of LLYWELLYN.

Llewelyn a masculine variant form of LLYWELYN.

Llian a feminine first name meaning 'flaxen' (*Welsh*).

Lloyd the anglicised masculine form of LLWYD. Lloyd Bridges was an American actor and the father of Beau and Jeff Bridges.

Llud (pronounced *hlood*) a Welsh masculine first name and that of a legendary king of the ancient Britons. It is anglicised as Lud.

Llwyd (pronounced *hloowid*) a masculine first name from the Welsh root word meaning 'grey,' or 'holy'. It was a name for a priest. The anglicised form is Lloyd.

Llywarch a Welsh masculine first name and that of a sixth-century king. Llywarch Hen, 'the old', is the subject of an old Welsh poem, 'The Song of Llywarch the Old', lamenting the ills of old age.

Llywelyn (pronounced *hloo-ell-in*) a masculine first name meaning 'leader', from *llyw*, 'lead' (*Welsh*). Llywelyn Fawr, 'the great', Prince of Wales, died in 1240. The name is sometimes found spelt Llewellyn. Diminutive forms are Lyn, Lynn.

Loarn *see* LORN.

Locke a surname, meaning 'enclosure, stronghold' (*Old English*), used as a masculine first name.

Logan a surname, meaning 'little hollow' (*Scottish Gaelic*), used as a masculine first name.

Lois a feminine first name the meaning of which is uncertain but possibly 'good, desirable' (*Greek*). In the New Testament Lois and her daughter, EUNICE, were Jewish women who were converted to Christianity.

Lola a feminine diminutive form of DOLORES, CARLOTTA, now used independently.

Lolita a feminine diminutive of DOLORES. Lolita Davidovich is an American film actress.

Lombard a surname, meaning 'long beard' (*Germanic*), used as a masculine first name.

Lona a feminine diminutive form of MAELONA.

Lonán a masculine first name meaning 'little blackbird', from *lon*, 'blackbird', with the diminutive suffix -an (*Irish Gaelic*).

Lonnie a masculine variant form of LENNY. A diminutive form of ALONSO.

Lonny a masculine diminutive form of ZEBULON.

Lora a Welsh feminine form of LAURA.

Lorcan or **Lorcán** a masculine first name meaning 'fierce in battle', from *lorc*, 'fierce' (*Irish Gaelic*). It is anglicised to Laurence, with which it has no etymological connection; hence the twelfth-century St 'Laurence' O'Toole should properly be St Lorcan.

Lorelei the name of a rock in the River Rhine from where, in German legend, a siren lured boatmen, used as a feminine first name.

Loren a feminine variant form of LAUREN.

Lorenz the German masculine form of LAURENCE.

Lorenzo the Italian and Spanish masculine form of LAURENCE. In *The Merchant of Venice* by William Shakespeare (1564–1616) Lorenzo is the Italian man in love with Jessica, the daughter of Shylock.

Loretta a feminine variant form of LAURETTA.

Loring a surname, meaning 'man from Lorraine' (bold and famous) (*Germanic/Old French*), used as a masculine first name.

Lorn a Scottish Gaelic masculine first name from Loarn, one of the early rulers of the Dalriada Scots, one of the three sons of Erc, whose name is preserved in the Lorn district of Argyll. An alternative form is Lorne.

Lorna a feminine form of Lorn. The name was invented by the English novelist R. D. Blackmore (1825–1900) for the eponymous heroine of his novel *Lorna Doone* (1869).

Lorne a masculine variant form of LORN.

Lorraine a surname meaning 'man from Lorraine' (bold and famous) used as a feminine first name (*Old French*). Lorraine Bracco is an American actress. A variant form is Laraine.

Lot a masculine first name meaning 'a veil, a covering' (*Hebrew*). In the Old Testament Lot was the nephew of Abraham who lived in Sodom. He and his wife and daughters escaped from the city before its destruction but Lot's wife was turned into a pillar of salt for looking back at the city as they fled. The Arabic form is Lut.

Lotario the Italian masculine form of LUTHER.

Lothaire the French masculine form of LUTHER.

Lottie or **Lotty** feminine diminutive forms of CHARLOTTE.

Lotus the English name of a fruit that in Greek mythology was said to induce langour and forgetfulness, used as a feminine first name. The lotus is a Buddhist symbol.

Lou (1) a masculine diminutive form of LOUIS. (2) a feminine diminutive form of LOUISA, LOUISE.

Louella a feminine first name formed by a combination of LOUISE and ELLA.

Louie a masculine diminutive form of LOUIS.

Louis the French masculine form of LEWIS. Diminutive forms are Lou, Louie.

Louisa feminine form of LOUIS.

Louise the French feminine form of LOUISA, now used widely as an English-language form. Diminutive forms are Lisette, Lou.

Lovel or **Lovell** a surname, meaning 'little wolf' (*Old French*), used as a masculine first name. A variant form is Lowell.

Lowell a masculine variant form of LOVEL.

Lowri a Welsh feminine form of LAURA. Lowri Turner is an English TV presenter.

Lowry an anglicised masculine form of Irish Gaelic LABHRA.

Luc the French masculine form of LUKE.

Luca the Italian masculine form of LUKE.

Lucan a place name, meaning 'place of elms' (*Irish Gaelic*), used as a masculine first name.

Lucas a masculine variant form of LUKE.

Luce a feminine diminutive form of LUCY.

Lucia feminine form of LUCIAN.

Lucian a masculine first name meaning 'belonging to or sprung from LUCIUS' (*Latin*). Lucian Freud (b.1922) is an artist best known for his portraits of nudes.

Luciano an Italian masculine form of LUCIAN.

Lucien a French masculine form of LUCIAN.

Lucienne feminine form of LUCIEN.

Lucifer a masculine first name meaning 'light bringer' (*Latin*). In the Old Testament Lucifer was the angel, usually identified with Satan, who led a rebellion against God. It is also the name applied to the planet Venus when it rises in the morning.

Lucilla a feminine diminutive form of LUCIA.

Lucille or **Lucile** French feminine forms of LUCIA, now used as English-language forms.

Lucinda a feminine variant form of LUCIA. A diminutive form is Cindy.

Lucio a Spanish masculine form of LUKE.

Lucius a masculine first name from *lux*, 'light' (*Latin*). In the New Testament Lucius was a man who was with Paul in Corinth. William Shakespeare (1564–1616) used the name in several of his plays.

Lucrèce a French feminine form of LUCRETIA.

Lucretia or **Lucrece** a feminine first name from *lucrum*, 'gain' (*Latin*). In Roman legend Lucretia was the daughter of a prefect of Rome and wife of Tarquinius Collatinus. Her rape by Sextus Tarquinius and her subsequent suicide were said to have led to the establishment of the Roman republic. The story was the subject of his second poem, *The Rape of Lucrece* (1594), by William Shakespeare (1564–1616).

Lucretius the masculine form of LUCRETIA.

Lucrezia the Italian feminine form of Lucretia. Lucrezia Borgia (1480–1519) was an Italian noblewoman and a patron of science and the arts.

Lucy a popular feminine form of Lucia. St Lucy (died *c*.303) was a Sicilian martyr. A diminutive form is Luce.

Lud a masculine anglicised form of Welsh Llud. Lud was a mythical king of Britain whose name may survive in 'Ludgate', London.

Ludlow a place name, meaning 'hill by the rapid river' (*Old English*), used as a masculine first name.

Ludmila or **Ludmilla** a feminine first name meaning 'of the people' (*Russian*). St Ludmilla (860–921) established Christianity in Bohemia and was martyred.

Ludo a masculine diminutive form of Ludovic.

Ludovic or **Ludovick** masculine variant forms of Lewis. Ludovic Kennedy is a Scottish journalist. A diminutive form is Ludo.

Ludvig a Swedish masculine form of Lewis.

Ludwig the German masculine form of Lewis. Ludwig van Beethoven (1770–1827) was a German composer whose works express great emotional intensity and bridge the classical and romantic traditions.

Luella a feminine variant form of Louella.

Lugaid (pronounced *loo-gad*) an Irish masculine first name from Old Gaelic *lug*, 'light', a frequent warrior name in Old Irish sources and going back to the name of a major Celtic god, Lug.

Luigi an Italian masculine form of Lewis.

Luis a Spanish masculine form of Lewis.

Luisa an Italian and Spanish feminine form of Louisa.

Luise the German feminine form of Louisa. A diminutive form is Lulu.

Lukas a Swedish masculine form of Luke, Lucas.

Luke a masculine first name meaning 'of Lucania' in Italy (*Latin*). In the New Testament Luke was a gentile and a doctor and a friend of Paul who is considered to have been the author of the third gospel.

Lulu a feminine diminutive form of Luise.

Lundy a place name, meaning 'puffin island' (*Old Norse*), used as a masculine first name.

Luned or **Lunet** a feminine first name probably linked to *eilun*, 'idol', 'image' (*Welsh*). The heroine of a medieval Welsh legend, *Owain and Luned*; daughter of the Lord of the Fountain, she assists Owain to defeat him. Also spelt as Eiluned. Other forms are Linet, Lynette.

Lut the Arabic form of LOT.

Lutero a Spanish masculine form of LUTHER.

Luther a masculine first name meaning 'illustrious warrior' (*Germanic*).

Lyall a masculine variant form of LISLE.

Lycurgus a masculine first name meaning 'wolf driver' (*Greek*).

Lydia a feminine first name meaning 'of Lydia' in Asia Minor (*Greek*). In the New Testament Lydia was one of the first people to be converted to Christianity by Paul.

Lyle a masculine variant form of LISLE.

Lyn (1) a feminine diminutive form of LYNETTE, LYNSAY. (2) a masculine diminutive form of LLYWELYN.

Lynda a feminine variant form of LINDA. Diminutive forms are Lyn, Lynn, Lynne.

Lynden or **Lyndon** a surname, meaning 'dweller by lime trees', used as a masculine first name. A diminutive form is Lyn.

Lynette an English feminine form of ELUNED or LUNED. (2) a feminine first name formed from a double diminutive, with the French -ette suffix, 'little', ending added to Lyn. Variant forms are Lynnette, Linnette.

Lynn (1) a feminine diminutive form of LYNDA, now used independently. (2) a masculine diminutive form of LLYWELYN.

Lynne a feminine diminutive form of LYNETTE, LYNSAY.

Lynn a surname, meaning 'pool or waterfall' (*Celtic*), used as a masculine first name. Diminutive forms are Lyn, Lin, Linn.

Lynne a feminine diminutive form of LYNDA.

Lynnette a feminine variant form of LYNETTE.

Lyndsay or **Lynsay** or **Lynsey** a masculine or feminine variant form of LINDSAY.

Lyris a feminine first name meaning 'she who plays the harp' (*Greek*).

Lysander a masculine first name meaning 'liberator' (*Greek*). William Shakespeare (1564–1616) used the name for one of the heroes of his comedy *A Midsummer Night's Dream*. A diminutive form is Sandy.

Lysandra feminine form of LYSANDER.

Lyss a masculine diminutive form of ULYSSES.

Lytton a masculine variant form of LITTON. Lytton Strachey (1880–1932) was an English critic and biographer.

M

Maarten a Dutch masculine form of MARTIN.

Mab an Irish Gaelic and Welsh feminine abbreviated form of MEDB or Maeve. It is not connected with Mabel, which is from Old French Amabel.

Mabel feminine diminutive forms of AMABEL, also used independently. A variant form is Maybelle.

Mabelle a French feminine form of MABEL.

Mabon a masculine first name and that of a Celtic god of youth; *maban* is Welsh for 'child'.

Macbeth *see* BETHAN.

Macha (pronounced *ma-ha*) a feminine first name, perhaps from *magh*, 'plain', referring to land (*Irish Gaelic*). It was the name of a goddess and legendary queen.

Mackenzie a surname meaning 'son of Kenneth' (*Scottish Gaelic*), used as a masculine or feminine first name. Perhaps because of the Mackenzie River, it has become a popular first name for girls in Canada.

Madalena the Spanish feminine form of MADELEINE.

Maddalena the Italian feminine form of MADELEINE.

Maddie or **Maddy** feminine diminutive forms of MADELEINE.

Madeleine or **Madeline** a feminine first name meaning from Magdala on the Sea of Galilee (*French*). Madeleine Stone is an American film actress. A variant form is MAGDALENE. Diminutive forms are Maddie, Maddy, Mala. *See also* MARY.

Madge feminine diminutive forms of MARGARET, MARJORY.

Madhbh a variant form of MEDB.

Madison a surname, meaning 'son of MATTHEW or MAUD' (*Old English*), used as a masculine first name.

Madog or **Madoc** a masculine first name from a Welsh root word, *maddeugar*, indicating 'generous', 'forgiving'. Madog was a renowned holy man of the seventh century. Madog ab Owain Gwynedd, a twelfth-century Welsh prince, is reputed to have sailed as far as America. His name is preserved in that of Portmadoc.

Madonna a feminine first name meaning 'my lady', from the title of the Virgin Mary (*Italian*). *See also* DONNA.

Mae a feminine variant form of MAY.

Maebh a variant form of MEDB.

Mael (pronounced *myle*) a masculine first name from *mael*, 'prince' (*Welsh*).

Maelgwyn or **Maelgwn** a masculine first name meaning 'bright prince', from *mael*, 'prince', and *gwyn*, 'bright', 'fair' (*Welsh*). Maelgwyn or Maelgwn Gwynedd was a king who lived during the sixth century.

Maelona a feminine first name meaning 'princess' (*Welsh*). A diminutive form is Lona.

Maeve the anglicised feminine form of MEDB. Maeve Binchy is a popular Irish writer.

Magda German and Scandinavian feminine form of MAGDALENE.

Magdalene or **Magdalen** feminine variant forms of MADELEINE. *See also* MARY.

Magee a surname, meaning 'son of HUGH' (*Irish Gaelic*), used as a masculine first name. A variant form is MCGEE.

Maggie feminine diminutive forms of MARGARET.

Magnolia the name of a tree with showy flowers, named after French botanist Pierre Magnol, used as a feminine first name.

Magnus a masculine first name meaning 'great' (*Latin*). It became a popular name with the Norsemen. Magnus Magnusson is an Icelandic-Scottish journalist and television presenter.

Mahalia a feminine first name meaning 'tenderness' (*Hebrew*). Mahalia Jackson was an American gospel and jazz singer.

Mahomet a masculine variant form of MOHAMMED.

Mai a Welsh feminine form of MAY or Mary.

Maida the name of a place in Calabria in Spain, where a battle was fought in 1806, used as a feminine first name. A diminutive form is Maidie.

Maidie a feminine diminutive form of MAIDA.

Mailli a Cornish and Scottish Gaelic feminine form of MARY. The Scots form is Mallie.

Mair a Welsh feminine forms of MARY.

Máire (pronounced *maur-ya*) an Irish Gaelic feminine form of MARY.

Máiread (pronounced *my-ratt*) an Irish and Scottish Gaelic feminine form of MARGARET.

Mairi (pronounced *mah-ri*) a Scottish Gaelic feminine form of MARY.

Máirin the Irish Gaelic feminine form of MAUREEN.

Máirtín a Scottish and Irish Gaelic form of MARTIN, after St Martin of Tours, who was the teacher of St Ninian and was much esteemed by the Celts.

Mairwen a feminine first name meaning 'fair Mary', from *gwen*, 'bright' (*Welsh*).

Maisie a Scottish diminutive form of either MARJORY or MARY, also found as a name in its own right.

Maitland a surname, meaning 'unproductive land' (*Old French*), used as a masculine first name.

Makepeace a surname, meaning 'peacemaker' (*Old English*), used as a masculine first name.

Mal a masculine diminutive form of MALCOLM.

Mala a feminine diminutive form of MADELEINE.

Malachi a masculine first name meaning 'messenger of Jehovah' (*Hebrew*). In the Old Testament prophet who wrote the Book of Malachi.

Malachy a masculine first name meaning 'follower of St Seachlainn', from Gaelic *maol*, 'follower', 'disciple', and the personal name Seachlainn (*Irish Gaelic*). It has also been suggested the name can be interpreted as 'follower of MADOG'. St Malachy (1094–1148) was archbishop of Armagh and prominent in Gregorian reform in Ireland. The name has a close resemblance to the Hebrew MALACHI.

Malcolm a masculine first name meaning 'servant of Columba', from Gaelic *maol*, 'servant', and Calluim, 'of Columba' (*Scottish Gaelic*). St Columba was venerated throughout Gaeldom, and this name was borne by four Scottish kings. Diminutive forms are CALUM, Mal, Malc, Malkie.

Malise a masculine or feminine first name meaning 'servant of Jesus', from *maol*, 'servant', and *Iosa*, 'of Jesus' (*Scottish Gaelic*). This name is particularly associated with the Ruthven and Graham families. A variant form is Maylise.

Mallie the Scots feminine form of MAILLI.

Mallory a surname, meaning 'unfortunate, luckless' (*Old French*), used as a masculine first name.

Malone a surname, meaning 'follower of St John' (*Irish Gaelic*), used as a masculine first name.

Malvina an invented Gaelic-sounding name from the eighteenth-century *Ossian* poems by the Scottish poet James Macpherson (1736–96)

Malvina a feminine first name meaning 'smooth brow' (*Scots Gaelic*).

Mame or **Mamie** feminine diminutive forms of MARY, now used independently.

Manasseh a masculine first name meaning 'one who causes to forget' (*Hebrew*). In the Old Testament Manasseh was the first-born son of Joseph and grandson of Jacob and progenitor of one of the twelve tribes of Israel.

Manda a feminine diminutive form of AMANDA.

Mandy (1) a feminine diminutive form of AMANDA, MIRANDA, now used as an independent name. (2) a masculine name meaning 'little man' (*German*).

Manette a French feminine form of MARY.

Manfred a masculine first name meaning 'man of peace' (*Germanic*). A diminutive form is Manny.

Manfredi the Italian masculine form of MANFRED.

Manfried a German masculine form of MANFRED.

Manley a surname, meaning 'brave, upright' (*Middle English*), used as a masculine first name.

Manny masculine diminutive forms of EMMANUEL, IMMANUEL, MANFRED.

Manuel the Spanish masculine form of EMMANUEL.

Manuela a feminine first name meaning 'God with us' (*Spanish*).

Manus an Irish Gaelic form of MAGNUS.

Marc (1) a French masculine form of MARK. (2) a variant form of MARCUS.

Marcán a masculine first name from Gaelic *marc*, 'steed' (*Irish Gaelic*). It was a common name in early Irish literature and is anglicised as Mark.

Marcel a French masculine form of MARCELLUS.

Marcela a Spanish feminine form of MARCELLA.

Marcella feminine form of MARCELLUS.

Marcelle a French feminine form of MARCELLA.

Marcello the Italian masculine form of MARCEL.

Marcellus the Latin and Scots Gaelic masculine form of MARK. St Marcellus (died 309) was pope from 308 but he became unpopular for enforcing penances and was banished before his death. William Shakespeare (1564–1616) used the name for a character in *Hamlet*, and it was the middle name of the American boxer Cassius Clay before he changed his name to Muhammad Ali.

Marcelo a Spanish masculine form of MARCEL.

Marcia feminine form of MARCIUS. A variant form is Marsha. Diminutive forms are Marcie, Marcy.

Marcie a feminine diminutive form of MARCIA.

Marcius a masculine variant form of MARK.

Marco the Italian masculine form of MARK.

Marcos the Spanish masculine form of MARK.

Marcus the Latin masculine form of MARK, now used as an English-language form. A variant form is Marc.

Marcy a feminine diminutive form of MARCIA.

Mared a Welsh feminine form of MARGARET.

Mareddyd a Welsh variant form of MEREDUDD. Maredydd ab Hywel Dda was a tenth-century king.

Margaret a feminine first name meaning 'a pearl' (*Greek*). It became a popular name in Scotland. St Margaret of Scotland (*c*.1046–93) was a religiously minded English princess who in 1070 married Malcolm III, 'Canmore', (*c*.1031–93), king of Scotland (1040–93). She introduced English ways into Scotland and in 1072 founded Dunfermline Abbey. She was canonised in 1250. Margaret of Anjou (1430–82) was a French princess and queen of Henry VI of England. She became the leader of the Lancastrians in the Wars of the Roses and was defeated at Tewkesbury by Edward IV in 1471. Diminutive forms are Greta, Madge, Maggie, Margie, May, Meg, Meggie, Meta, Peg.

Margarete the Danish and German feminine form of MARGARET. Diminutive forms are Grete, Gretchen.

Margaretha a Dutch feminine form of MARGARET.

Margarita the Spanish feminine form of MARGARET. A diminutive form is Rita.

Margaux a feminine variant form of MARGOT.

Marge a feminine diminutive form of MARGERY.

Marged a Welsh feminine diminutive form of Margaret.

Margery in the Middle Ages a feminine diminutive form of MARGARET, but is now a name in its own right. A variant form is MARJORIE. A diminutive form is Madge or Marge.

Margherita the Italian feminine form of MARGARET. A diminutive form is Rita.

Margiad a Welsh feminine diminutive form of Margaret.

Margie a feminine diminutive form of MARGARET.

Margo or **Margot** feminine diminutive forms of MARGARET, MARGUERITE, now used independently. A variant form is MARGAUX.

Marguerite the French feminine form of MARGARET. Diminutive forms are Margo, Margot.

Mari an Irish and Welsh feminine form of MARY.

Maria the Latin, Italian, German, and Spanish feminine forms of MARY. William Shakespeare (1564–1616) used the name for characters in *Love's Labour's Lost* and *Twelfth Night*. A diminutive form is Ria.

Mariam the Greek feminine form of MARY.

Marian a French feminine form of MARION.

Mariana or **Marianna** an Italian feminine form of MARIANNE, MARION. William Shakespeare (1564–1616) used the name for the woman spurned by Antonio in his play *Measure for Measure*.

Marianne (1) a French and German feminine form of MARION. (2) a compound of MARY and ANN.

Maribella a feminine first name formed from a combination of MARY and BELLA.

Marie French feminine form of MARY. A diminutive form is Marion.

Marietta feminine diminutive form of MARIA, also used independently.

Marigold the name of the golden flower used as a feminine first name.

Marilyn feminine diminutive form of MARY, also used independently.

Marina a feminine first name meaning 'of the sea' (*Latin*). William Shakespeare (1564–1616) used the name for the daughter of Pericles in his play *Pericles* because she was born at sea.

Mario an Italian form of MARIUS.

Marion (1) a feminine variant form of MARY. (2) a French masculine form of MARY, in compliment to the Virgin Mary.

Marisa a feminine first name meaning 'summit' (*Hebrew*). Marisa Tomei is an American film actress.

Marius a masculine first name meaning 'martial' (*Latin*).

Marjorie or **Marjory** feminine variant forms of MARGERY.

Mark (1) a masculine first name meaning 'a hammer'; 'a male'; 'sprung from Mars' (*Latin*). In the New Testament Mark accompanied Paul on his missionary journeys and was author of the second gospel. A variant form is MARCUS. (2) an anglicised masculine form of Irish MARCÁN.

Markus the German and Swedish masculine form of MARK.

Marland a surname, meaning 'lake land' (*Old English*), used as a masculine first name.

Marlene a feminine first name formed from a contraction of Maria Magdalena (*German*).

Marlo a masculine variant form of MARLOW.

Marlon a masculine name of uncertain meaning, possibly 'hawk-like' (*French*).

Marlow a place name and surname, meaning 'land of the former pool' (*Old English*), used as a masculine first name. Variant forms are Marlo, Marlowe.

Marlowe a masculine variant form of MARLOW.

Marmaduke a masculine first name meaning 'follower of MADOG', from *mael*, 'follower' (*Welsh*). A diminutive form is DUKE.

Marmion a surname, meaning 'brat, monkey' (*Old French*), used as a masculine first name.

Marsaili (pronounced *mar-sally*) a Scottish Gaelic feminine form of MARGERY.

Marsden a surname, meaning 'boundary valley' (*Old English*), used as a masculine first name.

Marsh a surname, meaning 'marsh' (*Old English*), used as a masculine first name.

Marsha a feminine variant form of MARCIA.

Marshall a surname, meaning 'horse servant' (*Germanic*), used as a masculine first name. Marshall McLuhan (1911–80) was a Canadian media analyst and author of *The Medium is the Message* (1967).

Marston a surname, meaning 'place by a marsh' (*Old English*), used as a masculine first name.

Marta the Italian, Spanish and Swedish feminine form of MARTHA, now used as an English-language form. A variant form is Martita.

Martha a feminine first name meaning 'lady' (*Hebrew*). In the New Testament was a friend of Jesus and the sister of LAZARUS and MARY. Diminutive forms are Mat, Mattie.

Marthe the French and German feminine form of MARTHA.

Marti a feminine diminutive form of MARTINA, MARTINE.

Martijn a Dutch masculine form of MARTIN.

Martin a masculine first name meaning 'of Mars; warlike' (*Latin*). The name was adopted by several popes. A variant form is Martyn. A diminutive form is Marty.

Martina feminine forms of MARTIN. A diminutive form is Marti.

Martine the French feminine form of MARTINA, now used as an English-language form. A diminutive form is Marti.

Martino an Italian and Spanish masculine form of MARTIN.

Martita a feminine variant form of MARTA. A diminutive form is Tita.

Marty a masculine diminutive form of MARTIN.

Martyn a masculine variant form of MARTIN.

Marvin an anglicised masculine form of Welsh MERFYN.

Marwood a surname, meaning 'bigger or boundary wood' (*Old English*), used as a masculine first name.

Mary a feminine first name meaning 'bitter'; 'their rebellion'; 'star of the sea' (*Hebrew*). In the New Testament Mary was (1) the mother of Jesus, (2) the sister of LAZARUS and MARTHA and a friend of Jesus, and (3) Mary Magdalene, a woman from Galilee from whom Jesus cast out an evil spirit and who was the first to see him after the resurrection. Variant forms are MARION, MIRIAM. The Arabic form is Maryam. Diminutive forms are Mamie, May, Minnie, Mollie, Polly.

Maryam the Arabic form of MARY.

Maryann or **Maryanne** a feminine first name formed from a combination of MARY and ANN or ANNE.

Marylou a feminine first name formed from a combination of MARY and LOUISE.

Massan a Scottish Gaelic masculine first name and the name of a saint, of uncertain origin, preserved in Glen Masan.

Massimiliano the Italian masculine form of MAXIMILIAN.

Mat a masculine diminutive form of MATTHEW. A feminine diminutive form of MARTHA, MATHILDA.

Mateo the Spanish masculine form of MATTHEW.

Mather a surname, meaning 'mower' (*Old English*), used as a masculine first name.

Matheson or **Mathieson** a surname, meaning 'son of MATTHEW', used as a masculine first name.

Mathias a masculine variant form of MATTHIAS.

Mathieu a French masculine form of MATTHEW.

Mathilda a feminine variant form of MATILDA.

Mathilde the French feminine form of MATILDA.

Matilda a feminine first name meaning 'mighty war' (Germanic). A variant form is Mathilda. Diminutive forms are Mat, Mattie, Tilda, Tilly.

Matilde the Italian and Spanish feminine form of MATILDA.

Matt a masculine diminutive form of MATTHEW. Matt Dillon is an American film actor.

Mattaeus a Danish masculine form of MATTHEW.

Matteo the Italian masculine form of MATTHEW.

Matthais a Greek masculine form of MATTHEW.

Matthäus a German masculine form of MATTHEW.

Mattheus a Dutch and Swedish masculine form of MATTHEW.

Matthew a masculine first name meaning 'gift of Jehovah' (*Hebrew*). In the New Testament Matthew (formerly LEVI) was a tax collector who became one of Christ's apostles. Matthew Parris is an English journalist. Diminutive forms are Mat, Matt, Mattie.

Matthias a Latin masculine form of MATTHEW. In the New Testament Matthias was the apostle who was elected to replace Judas Iscariot. A variant form is Mathias.

Matthieu the French masculine form of MATTHEW.

Mattie (1) a feminine diminutive form of MATILDA. (2) a masculine diminutive form of MATTHEW.

Maud or **Maude** a medieval feminine form of MATILDA.

Maughold (pronounced *maw-hald*) a Manx masculine first name from that of a legendary Manx saint who converted from being a pirate to the life of a holy hermit.

Maura an Irish feminine form of MARY.

Maureen (1) an Irish feminine first name meaning 'little Mary'. Originally a diminutive, it has long been a name in its own right. The Gaelic form is Máirín. (2) a feminine anglicised form of MÓIRIN.

Maurice a masculine first name meaning 'Moorish, dark-coloured' (*Latin*). St Maurice (died *c*.286) was a soldier and early martyr. A variant form is MAURUS. A diminutive form is Mo.

Mauricio a Spanish masculine form of MAURICE.

Maurits a Dutch masculine form of MAURICE.

Maurizio an Italian masculine form of MAURICE.

Mauro the Italian masculine form of MAURUS.

Maurus a masculine variant form of MAURICE. St Maurus was a sixth-century Benedictine monk.

Mave a diminutive form of MAVIS.

Mavis an alternative name of the song thrush used as a feminine first name (*English*). A diminutive form is Mave.

Mavourneen or **Mavourna** a feminine first name meaning 'darling little one', from *mo*, 'my', and *mhuirnín*, 'little darling' (*Irish Gaelic*). Originally and still a term of endearment, it has also gone independent as a name.

Max a masculine diminutive form of MAXIMILIAN, MAXWELL, also used as an independent name. A diminutive form is Maxie.

Maxie (1) a masculine diminutive form of MAX, MAXIMILIAN, MAXWELL. (2) a feminine diminutive form of MAXINE.

Maximilian a masculine name meaning 'the greatest', a combination of *Maximus* and *Aemilianus* (*Latin*). Diminutive forms are Max, Maxie.

Maximilien the French masculine form of MAXIMILIAN.

Maxine feminine form of MAX.

Maxwell a surname, meaning 'spring of MAGNUS', used as a masculine first name. A diminutive form is Max. Maxwell Anderson (1888–1959) was an American playwright and screen writer.

May feminine diminutive form of MARGARET, MARY; the name of the month used as a feminine first name. A variant form is Mae. A diminutive form is Minnie.

Maybelle (1) a feminine first name formed by a combination of MAY and BELLE. (2) a variant form of MABEL.

Mayer a surname, meaning 'physician' (*Old French*) or 'farmer' (*Germanic*), used as a masculine first name. Variant forms are Meyer, Myer.

Maylise a feminine variant form of MALISE.

Maynard a surname, meaning 'strong, brave' (*Germanic*), used as a masculine first name.

Mayo a place name, meaning 'plain of the yew tree' (*Irish Gaelic*), used as a masculine first name.

McGee a masculine variant form of MAGEE.

Meave an anglicised feminine form of MEDB.

Medb (pronounced *mave*) a feminine first name meaning 'intoxicating', 'bewitching' (*Irish Gaelic*). The name is probably cognate with Welsh *meddw*, 'drunk'. It was the name of the legendary queen of Connaught who coveted the Brown Bull of Cooley. The legends invest her with magic powers and an intense attraction for men, few of whom however can stand up to her warlike nature. The source of the name is unclear. It has numerous forms, including Madhbh, Maebh, and the anglicised (and most often used) form Maeve. Another anglicised form is Meave.

Meave an anglicised feminine form of MEDB.

Medea a feminine first name meaning 'meditative' (*Greek*). In Greek mythology Medea was the princess who helped Jason obtain the Golden Fleece from her father, the king of Colchis.

Medrawd a Welsh masculine first name and that of the bastard son of King ARTHUR, in the Round Table stories, anglicised as Mordred.

Medwin a surname, meaning 'mead friend' (*Old English*), used as a masculine first name.

Meg or **Meggie** feminine diminutive forms of MARGARET. Meg Ryan and Meg Tilly are American film actresses.

Megan a Welsh diminutive form of MARGARET now used independently.

Mehetabel or **Mehitabel** a feminine first name meaning 'benefited of God' (*Hebrew*). In the Old Testament Mehetabel was the wife of an Edomite king.

Meilyr a masculine first name meaning 'man of iron' (*Welsh*). Meilyr of Caerleon was a twelfth-century wizard. Meilyr Brydydd (1100–1137) was chief bard to Gruffudd ap Cynan.

Meironwen a feminine first name meaning 'white dairymaid' (*Welsh*).

Mel a masculine diminutive form of MELVILLE, MELVIN, MELVYN. Mel Gibson is an American-born Australian film actor and producer.

Melangell a feminine first name meaning 'honey angel' (*Welsh*). It was the name of a saint, preserved in Llanfihangel.

Melanie a feminine first name meaning 'black' (*Greek*). Melanie Griffith is an American film actress.

Melbourne a surname, meaning 'mill stream' (*Old English*), used as a masculine first name.

Melchior a masculine name of uncertain meaning, possibly 'king of light' (*Hebrew*); in the Bible, Melchior was one of the Magi, the three wise men from the east who paid homage to the infant Jesus, presenting him with gifts.

Melchiorre the Italian masculine form of MELCHIOR.

Meleri a Welsh feminine first name. This was the name of St David's grandmother.

Melfyn a masculine first name meaning 'from Carmarthen' (*Welsh*).

Melinda a feminine first name meaning 'honey' (*Greek*) plus the suffix -inda.

Mélisande the French feminine form of MILLICENT. It was the name used by the Belgian poet and dramatist Comte Maurice Maeterlinck (1862–1949) for the heroine of his tragic poem *Pelléas et Mélisande* (1892), which was later (1902) the basis of an opera by the French composer Claude Debussy (1862–1918).

Melissa a feminine first name meaning 'a bee' (*Greek*). A diminutive form is Lissa.

Melle the Breton feminine form of MARY. It also has resonances in *mel*, 'honey'.

Melody a word for tune or tunefulness used as a feminine first name.

Melville or **Melvin** or **Melvyn** a surname, meaning 'Amalo's place' (*Old French*), used as a masculine first name. Melvyn Douglas (1901–81) was an American film and stage actor. A diminutive form is Mel.

Merab the name in the Old Testament of Saul's eldest daughter who was promised to David but who married Adriel.

Mercedes the Spanish feminine form of MERCY (as a plural). Mercedes Ruehl is an American film actress.

Mercer a surname, meaning 'merchant' (*Old French*), used as a masculine first name.

Mercy the quality of forgiveness used as a feminine first name.

Meredith an anglicised form of Welsh MEREDUDD or MAREDDYD used as a masculine or feminine first name.

Meredudd a masculine first name meaning 'great lord' (*Welsh*). A variant form is Mareddyd. Anglicised forms include Merideg, Meriadoc and, most commonly, Meredith.

Merfyn a masculine first name meaning 'eminent matter' (*Welsh*).

Meri a feminine variant form of MERRY.

Meriadoc an anglicised masculine form of Welsh MEREDUDD or MAREDDYD.

Merideg an anglicised masculine form of Welsh MEREDUDD or MAREDDYD.

Meriel a Welsh feminine form of MURIEL. Variant forms are Merle, Meryl.

Merle (1) a feminine first name meaning 'blackbird' (*Old French*). (2) a variant form of MERIEL. Merle Oberon (1911–79) was a Tasmanian-born film actress.

Merlin or **Merlyn** the anglicised masculine form of MYRDDIN. Merlin was the name of a celebrated wizard, first recorded in the *Black Book of Carmarthen* (thirteenth century), but going back to a sixth-century original. In the Arthurian legends he was made the tutor of King ARTHUR. A variant form is Mervyn.

Merri or **Merrie** feminine variant forms of MERRY.

Merrill a surname, meaning 'son of MURIEL' (*Celtic*) or 'pleasant place' (*Old English*), used as a masculine first name. Variant forms are Meryl, Merryll.

Merry (1) the adjective, meaning 'cheerful, mirthful, joyous', used as a feminine first name (*Old English*). (2) a diminutive form of MEREDITH. Variant forms are Meri, Merri, Merrie.

Merryll a masculine variant form of MERRILL.

Merton a surname, meaning 'farmstead by the pool' (*Old English*), used as a masculine first name.

Merfyn a Welsh masculine first name the source of which has not been satisfactorily established. The anglicised form is Mervyn, Mervin or Marvin. Merfyn Frych was a ninth-century king of Gwynedd.

Mervin or **Mervyn** (1) a surname, meaning 'famous friend' (*Old English*), used as a masculine first name. A variant form is Marvin. (2) an anglicised masculine form of MERFYN. (3) a variant form of MERLIN.

Meryl a feminine variant form of MERIEL, MERRILL. Meryl Streep is an American film actress.

Meta a feminine diminutive form of MARGARET.

Meyer a masculine variant form of MAYER.

Mia a feminine diminutive form of MARIA. Mia Farrow is an American film actress.

Micah a masculine first name meaning 'who is like unto Jehovah?' (*Hebrew*). In the Old Testament Micah was a Hebrew prophet of the late eighth century BC.

Michael a masculine first name meaning 'who is like unto God?' (*Hebrew*). In the Bible Michael is one of the seven archangels. Michael Caine is a well-known English actor. Diminutive forms are Mick, Micky, Mike.

Michaela feminine form of MICHAEL.

Michaella the Italian feminine form of MICHAELA.

Michal a feminine form of MICHAEL. In the Old Testament Michal was the younger daughter of Saul who married David.

Micheál (pronounced *mee-hoyl*) the Irish Gaelic masculine form of MICHAEL. It is a popular name in Ireland, with diminutive forms Mick, Micky, Mike, Mikey.

Michel (1) the French masculine form of MICHAEL. (2) a German diminutive of MICHAEL.

Michele the Italian masculine form of MICHAEL.

Michèle or **Michelle** French feminine forms of MICHAELA, now used as English-language forms. Michelle Pfeiffer is an American film actress.

Mick or **Micky** or **Mickey** masculine diminutive forms of MICHAEL, MICHEÁL. Mickey Rourke is an American film actor.

Midir (pronounced *mid-eer*) an Irish Gaelic masculine first name and that of a chief of the Tuatha Dé Danann, the lover of ETAÍN, portrayed as a proud and possessive figure.

Mignon a word, meaning 'sweet, dainty', used as a feminine first name (*French*). A variant form is Mignonette. A diminutive form is Minette.

Mignonette a feminine variant form of MIGNON.

Miguel the Spanish and Portuguese masculine form of MICHAEL.

Mihangel the Welsh masculine form of MICHAEL.

Mikael the Swedish masculine form of MICHAEL.

Mike or **Mikey** a masculine diminutive form of MICHAEL, MICHEÁL.

Mikhail a Russian masculine form of MICHAEL. A diminutive form is Mischa.

Mil a feminine diminutive form of MILDRED, MILLICENT.

Míl *see* MILES.

Milcah a feminine first name meaning 'queen' (*Hebrew*). In the Old Testament Milcah was a niece of Abraham and sister of Lot. She married another uncle, Nahor.

Mildred a feminine first name meaning 'gentle counsel' (*Germanic*). Diminutive forms are Mil, Millie.

Miles a masculine first name meaning 'soldier' from *miles* (*Latin*). It has Irish link with Míl, also known as Míl Espáine, 'of Spain', last of the legendary invader/settlers of Ireland and a source point of numerous family genealogies. A variant form is Myles.

Milford a place name and surname, meaning 'mill ford' (*Old English*), used as a masculine first name.

Miller a surname, meaning 'miller, grinder' (*Old English*), used as a masculine first name. A variant form is Milner.

Millicent a feminine first name meaning 'work and strength' (*Germanic*). A diminutive form is Millie.

Millie feminine diminutive form of AMELIA, EMILIA, MILDRED, MILLICENT.

Millward a masculine variant form of MILWARD.

Milne a surname, meaning 'at the mill' (*Old English*), used as a masculine first name.

Milner a masculine variant form of MILLER.

Milo or **Milon** a masculine or feminine first name meaning 'the Greek Samson' (*Greek*). Milo of Crotona was a famous Greek athlete who is said to have carried four-year-old cow through the stadium at Olympia. Milo Anderson (1912–84) was an American dress designer.

Milt a masculine diminutive form of MILTON.

Milton a surname, meaning 'middle farmstead or mill farm' (*Old English*), used as a masculine first name. A diminutive form is Milt.

Milward a surname, meaning 'mill keeper' (*Old English*), used as a masculine first name. A variant form is Millward.

Mima a feminine diminutive form of JEMIMA.

Mimi an Italian feminine diminutive form of MARIA. The Italian composer Giacomo Puccini (1858–1924) used the name for that of the heroine of his famous opera *La Bohème* (1896). Mimi Rogers is an American film actress.

Mimosa the English name of a tropical shrub with yellow flowers used as a feminine first name.

Mina a feminine diminutive form of JEMIMA.

Minerva a feminine first name meaning 'wise one'. In Roman mythology Minerva was goddess of wisdom and patron of the arts and trades, the counterpart of THE GREEK ATHENA.

Minette a feminine diminutive form of MIGNONETTE.

Minna or **Minne** a feminine first name meaning 'love' (*Germanic*). Diminutive forms of WILHELMINA.

Minnie a feminine diminutive form of MARY, MAY, WILHELMINA.

Minta a feminine diminutive form of ARAMINTA.

Mira a feminine diminutive form of MIRABEL, MIRANDA.

Mirabel or **Mirabelle** a feminine first name meaning 'wonderful' (*Latin*). Diminutive forms are Mira, Myra.

Miranda a feminine first name meaning 'wonderful' (*Latin*). William Shakespeare (1564–1616) used the name for Prospero's daughter in his play *The Tempest*. Miranda Richardson is an English actress. Diminutive forms are Mira, Myra.

Miriam variant feminine form of MARY. In the Old Testament, Miriam was a sister of Moses and Aaron who watched over the infant Moses in his basket.

Mischa a masculine diminutive form of MIKHAIL.

Mitchell a surname form of MICHAEL, a surname, meaning 'big, great' (*Old English*), used as a masculine first name. The diminutive form is Mitch.

Mitzi a German feminine diminutive form of MARIA. Mitzi Gaynor is an American actress and dancer.

Mo a masculine or feminine diminutive form of MAUREEN, MAURICE, MORRIS.

Modest a masculine first name from the Russian form of *modestus*, 'obedient' (*Latin*).

Modesty an English word from *modestus* (*Latin*) for the quality of being shy or humble, used as a feminine first name.

Modred a masculine first name meaning 'counsellor'; in Arthurian legend the knight who killed King Arthur (*Old English*).

Modwen a feminine first name from *morwyn*, 'maiden' (*Welsh*)

Moelwyn a masculine first name from 'white, bare' (*Welsh*).

Mohammed a masculine first name meaning 'praise' (*Arabic*). It was the name taken by Abd Allah (*c*.570–632), the prophet and founder of Islam. Variant forms are Mahomet, Muhammad, Muhammed.

Moina a feminine first name perhaps stemming from *moine*, 'peat, moss': 'girl of the peat-moss' (*Irish/Scottish Gaelic*).

Moingionn a feminine variant form of MONGFHIND.

Moira an anglicised feminine form of Irish MAÍRE, although there is also a place and earldom of the same name in Ulster. Moira Kelly is an American film actress. A variant form is Moyra.

Móirin a feminine diminutive form of Mór often anglicised as MAUREEN.

Mollie or **Molly** feminine diminutive forms of MARY, now used independently.

Moneak an American feminine variant form of MONIQUE.

Mona a feminine first name probably stemming from *muadhnaid*, 'noble'

(*Irish Gaelic*). (2) a Welsh and Manx feminine first name from a name given by the Romans to a wide stretch of the west coast of Britain and its islands. From it comes Mon, the Welsh name of Anglesey. The Isle of Man is also known as Mona's Isle.

Mongfhind or **Mongfhionn** (pronounced *mo-finn*) a feminine first name meaning 'of the long fair hair', from *mong*, 'long hair', and *fionn*, 'fair' (*Irish Gaelic*). It is the name of numerous figures in history and legend, of whom the most prominent is the jealous stepmother of NIALL of the Nine Hostages. A variant form is Moingionn.

Monica a feminine first name the meaning of which is uncertain but possibly 'advising' (*Latin*).

Monika the German feminine form of MONICA.

Monique the French feminine form of MONICA, now also used as an English form. A variant form is Moneak.

Monroe or **Monro** a variant form of MUNRO.

Montague or **Montagu** a surname, meaning 'pointed hill', used as a masculine first name. A diminutive form is Monty.

Montgomery or **Montgomerie** (1) a surname, meaning 'hill of powerful man' (*Old French/Germanic*), used as a masculine first name. (2) an anglicised masculine form of Irish MUIRCHERTACH. A diminutive form is Monty.

Monty a masculine diminutive form of MONTAGUE, MONTGOMERY.

Mór a feminine first name meaning 'tall', 'big', from Gaelic *mór* (*Irish Gaelic*). It may have been used as a subsitute for MÁIRE. Its diminutive form, Móirín, is often anglicised as MAUREEN.

Morag the feminine Scottish Gaelic form of SARAH.

Moray *see* MURRAY.

Mordecai a masculine first name meaning 'man of Marduk' (Babylonian), meaning a person who worshipped the main Babylonian god. In the Old Testament Mordecai was a cousin of Esther who prevented a massacre of the Jews.

Mordred the anglicised masculine form of MEDRAWD.

Morfudd see MORWEN.

Morgan a masculine or feminine first name that traditionally originates with a Celtic war-goddess, still known as The Morrigan, from *mor*, 'great', and *gan*, which may mean either 'sea' or 'queen' (*Irish Gaelic/Welsh*). Many powerful women have borne this name. The name of

Morgan Mwynfawr (seventh century) is preserved in Glamorgan. Although seen also as a boy's name, in the Arthurian romances Morgan le Fay is a witch queen. Morgan Freeman is an American film actor.

Morgana a purely feminine form of MORGAN.

Moriarty an anglicised masculine form of Irish MUIRCHERTACH.

Morien a masculine first name meaning 'sea-born', from *mur*, 'sea' (*Welsh*).

Moritz the German masculine form of MAURICE.

Morley a surname, meaning 'moor meadow' (*Old English*), used as a masculine first name.

Morna an anglicised feminine form of Irish MUIRNE.

Morrice or **Morris** masculine variant forms of MAURICE. A diminutive form is Mo.

Mortimer a surname, meaning 'dead sea' (*Old French*), used as a masculine first name.

Morton a surname, meaning 'farmstead moor' (*Old English*), used as a masculine first name.

Morven (1) a feminine first name that is probably related to MORWEN. (2) a feminine first name from the name of a mountain in Argyll, from Gaelic *mór bhéinn*, 'big mountain' (*Scottish Gaelic*).

Morwen or **Morwena** a feminine first name meaning 'maiden' (*Cornish/ Welsh*). An older form is Morfudd, which was the name of the woman loved by the bard DAFYDD ap Gwilym, unfortunately already married to someone else.

Mosè the Italian masculine form of MOSES.

Moses a masculine first name the meaning of which is uncertain, most probably an Egyptian name. In the Old Testament Moses was the Hebrew prophet who led the Israelites out of Egypt to Canaan, the Promised Land. He also gave the Israelites divinely revealed laws. The Arabic form is Musa.

Moyra a feminine variant form of MOIRA.

Muhammad or **Muhammed** a masculine variant form of MOHAMMED.

Muir a Scottish masculine form of the surname Moore, meaning 'moor' (*Old French*), used as a masculine first name.

Muirchertach (pronounced *murr-hertah*) a masculine first name meaning 'seafarer', from Old Gaelic *muir*, 'sea' (*Irish Gaelic*). The name of a legendary high king, and frequently found in literature and records. It is anglicised into Moriarty and Montgomery.

Muirenn or **Muireann** a variant feminine form of MUIRNE.

Muirne (pronounced *moor-na*) a feminine first name whose derivation is probably from Old Gaelic *muir*, 'sea', and means 'sea-bright' (*Irish Gaelic*), as in MURIEL. Muirne Muncháem, 'of the fair neck', was the mother of Fionn macCumhaill. There is a Gaelic diminutive form, Muirneag. Variant forms are Muirenn, Muireann. It is anglicised as Murna, Morna, Myrna.

Mungo a masculine first name possibly from Old Welsh, *mwyn*, 'dear' and *cu*, 'amiable', meaning 'dear friend'. This was a nickname of KENTIGERN, one of the great Celtic saints and patron of Glasgow Cathedral.

Munro or **Munroe** or **Munrow** a Scottish surname of the Easter Ross clan, perhaps originally from Old Gaelic *mon ruadh*, 'red hill', used as a masculine first name. Variant forms are Monro, Monroe.

Murchadh (pronounced *murr-hah*) the Irish Gaelic masculine form of MURDOCH, anglicised to Murrough, as is MURPHY.

Murdo the anglicised masculine form of MURDOCH.

Murdoch a masculine first name meaning 'sea warrior', from *murchaidh*, 'sea warrior' (*Scottish Gaelic*). The Gaelic form is MURCHADH. An alternative anglicised version is Murdo. Had the ambitions of the Albany Stewarts been gratified, Scotland might have had a King Murdoch instead of James I.

Muriel a Scottish and Welsh feminine first name meaning 'sea bright', from Old Gaelic *murgheal*.

Murna an anglicised feminine form of Irish MUIRNE.

Murphy a surname deriving from Gaelic *muir*, 'sea', and *cú*, 'hound' (*Irish Gaelic*), sometimes used as a masculine first name (and sometimes as a feminine, especially in North America). Other forms include MURROUGH.

Murray a surname, a form of Moray, from Old Gaelic *muir*, 'sea', and *ais*, 'edge, border' (*Scottish Gaelic*), used as a masculine first name. Murray Periah is a cellist and conductor.

Murrough the anglicised masculine form of Irish MURCHADH, MURPHY.

Musa the Arabic form of MOSES.

Myer (1) a surname, meaning 'marsh' (*Old Norse*), used as a first name. (2) a variant form of MAYER.

Myfanwy (pronounced *mih-van-wee*) a feminine first name meaning 'my fine one' (*Welsh*).

Myles (1) a masculine variant form of MILES. (2) a masculine first name meaning 'devotee of MARY' (*Irish Gaelic*).

Myra (1) a feminine first name invented by the poet Sir Fulke Greville (1554–1628), possibly as an anagram of MARY, or to mean 'she who weeps or laments' (*Greek*). (2) a feminine diminutive form of MIRABEL, MIRANDA.

Myrddin (pronounced *mirr-thin*) a masculine first name that appears to combine Old Welsh *myr*, 'sea', and *ddin*, 'hill'. It has been anglicised to MERLIN, the name of a celebrated wizard and is preserved in Carmarthen, 'fort of Myrddyn'.

Myrna an anglicised feminine form of Irish MUIRNE.

Myron a masculine first name meaning 'fragrant oil' (*Greek*).

Myrtle the name of the shrub used as a feminine first name. The American writer F. Scott Fitzgerald (1896–1940) used the name for one of the female characters in his novel *The Great Gatsby* (1925).

N

Naamah a feminine first name meaning 'pretty, loved' (*Hebrew*).

Naaman a masculine first name meaning 'pleasant' (*Hebrew*). In the Old Testament Naaman was a grandson of Benjamin who established a family of Israelites.

Nadezhda a feminine first name meaning 'hope' (*Russian*).

Nadia an English, French and Italian feminine form of NADEZHDA.

Nadine a French feminine diminutive form of NADIA.

Nahum a masculine first name meaning 'comforter' (*Hebrew*). In the Old Testament Nahum was an Israelite prophet of the seventh century BC and author of the Book of Nahum.

Naiada a feminine diminutive form of NAIDA.

Naida a feminine first name meaning 'the water nymph' (*Latin*). A diminutive form is NAIADA.

Nairn a masculine first name meaning 'dweller by the alder tree' (*Celtic*).

Nairne a feminine first name meaning 'from the river' (*Gaelic*).

Naísi a masculine variant form of NAOISE.

Nan a feminine diminutive form of AGNES, ANN, NANCY, NANETTE.

Nana a feminine diminutive form of HANNAH.

Nancy a feminine diminutive form of ANN, now used independently. Nancy Travis is an American film actress. Diminutive forms are Nan, Nina.

Nanette a feminine diminutive form of Ann, now used independently. A diminutive form is Nan.

Naoise (pronounced *nay-si*) an Irish masculine first name and that of the eldest of the three sons of Usna and lover of Deirdre in the famous tale from the *Ulster Cycle*. A variant form is Naísi.

Naomh (pronounced *nayve*) a feminine first name from *naomh*, 'saint' (*Irish Gaelic*). The use of this word as a first name is quite modern.

Naomi a feminine first name meaning 'pleasantness' (*Hebrew*). In the Old Testament Naomi was the mother-in-law of RUTH.

Nap a masculine diminutive form of NAPOLEON.

Napaea a feminine diminutive form of NAPEA.

Napea a feminine first name meaning 'girl of the valley' (*Latin*). Diminutive forms are Napaea, Napia.

Naphtali a masculine first name meaning 'my wrestling' (*Hebrew*). In the Old Testament Naphtali was the second son of Jacob and Bilhah, the maidservant of Rachel, Jacob's wife, who gave her to him because of her infertility. Naphtali founded on the of the twelve tribes of Israel.

Napia a feminine diminutive form of Napea.

Napier a surname, meaning 'linen keeper' (*Old French*), used as a masculine first name.

Napoleon a masculine first name meaning 'lion of the forest dell' (*Greek*). A diminutive form is Nap.

Nara a feminine first name meaning 'nearest and dearest' (*English*).

Narda a feminine first name meaning 'fragrant perfume, the lingering essence' (*Latin*).

Nash a surname, meaning 'ash tree' (*Old English*), used as a masculine first name.

Nat a masculine diminutive form of NATHAN, NATHANIEL.

Natal the Spanish masculine form of NOËL.

Natale the Italian masculine form of NOËL.

Natalie a French feminine form of NATALYA now used as an English-language form.

Natalia a Spanish feminine form of NATALYA.

Natalya a feminine first name meaning 'Christmas' (*Latin/Russian*).

Natasha a Russian feminine diminutive form of NATALYA.

Natene a feminine diminutive form of NATHANIA.

Nathan a masculine first name meaning 'gift' (*Hebrew*). In the Old Testament Nathan was (1) a prophet at the court of David and (2) a son of David and Bathsheba. A diminutive form is Nat.

Nathane or **Nathene** feminine diminutive forms of NATHANIA.

Nathanael a masculine first name meaning 'God gave' (*Hebrew*). In the New Testament Nathanael was one of the early disciples of Jesus, often identified with Bartholomew. A variant form is Nathaniel. A diminutive form is Nat.

Nathania a feminine form of NATHANAEL. Diminutive forms are Natene, Nathane, Nathene.

Nathaniel a masculine variant form of NATHANAEL.

Neachtan a masculine variant form of NECTAN.

Neal or **Neale** a masculine variant form of NIALL.

Nebula a feminine first name meaning 'a cloud of mist' (*Latin*).

Nectan or **Nechtan** a Pictish masculine first name that stems from a root-form *nig*, 'to wash', hence 'purified one'. It is an ancient royal name; it was under their king Nectan that the Picts defeated the invading Anglians in AD 685. The Pictish kings had a priestly role. A variant form is Neachtan.

Ned or **Neddie** or **Neddy** masculine (contraction of 'mine Ed') diminutive forms of EDGAR, EDMUND, EDWARD, EDWIN.

Nehemiah a masculine first name meaning 'Jehovah comforts' (*Hebrew*). In the Old Testament Nehemiah was a sixth-century BC leader of the Israelites on the return from the Babylonian captivity. His story is told in the Book of Nehemiah.

Neil or **Neill** a masculine variant form of NIALL.

Nell or **Nellie** or **Nelly** feminine diminutive forms of ELEANOR, ELLEN, HELEN.

Nelson a surname, meaning 'son of NEIL', used as a masculine first name.

Nemo a masculine first name meaning 'grove' (*Greek*).

Nerice or **Nerine** or **Nerissa** a feminine first name meaning 'from the sea' (*Greek*). William Shakespeare (1564–1616) used the name Nerissa for Portia's waiting-maid in his play *The Merchant of Venice*.

Nero a masculine first name meaning 'dark, black-haired' (*Latin*). It was the name of the Roman emperor (AD 37–68) infamous for his cruelty.

Nerys a feminine first name meaning 'lordly', from *ner*, 'lord' (*Welsh*). Nerys Hughes is a well-known Welsh actress.

Nessa (1) a feminine first name meaning 'ungentle' (*Irish Gaelic*). The explanation lies in the traditional story of Nessa, mother of CONCHOBHAR, or Conor, macNessa. Originally called Assa, or 'gentle one', Nessa was so fierce in defence of the kingdom of Ulster that her name was prefixed by *Ní*, meaning 'not'. (2) a feminine diminutive form of AGNES, VANESSA.

Nessie a feminine diminutive form of AGNES.

Nest or **Nesta** a Welsh feminine diminutive form of AGNES.

Nestor a masculine first name meaning 'coming home' (*Greek*). In Greek mythology, Nestor was a leader of the Greeks at the siege of Troy and as such appears in the play *Troilus and Cressida* by William Shake-speare (1564–1616). Nestor Almenedros (1930–92) was a Spanish-born cinematographer and film director.

Netta or **Nettie** feminine diminutive forms of HENRIETTA.

Neven a masculine variant form of NEVIN.

Neville a place name and surname, meaning 'new place' (*Old French*), used as a masculine first name.

Nevin a surname, meaning 'little saint' (*Irish Gaelic*), used as a masculine first name. Variant forms are Nevin, Niven.

Newell a surname, meaning 'new field' (*Old English*), used as a masculine first name.

Newland a surname, meaning 'new land' (*Old English*), used as a masculine first name.

Newlyn the name of a Cornish town, the origin of which is cognate to Gaelic *naomh*, 'holy', and *linne*, 'pool', used as a feminine first name. Nuline is a variant form.

Newman a surname, meaning 'newcomer, new settler' (*Old English*), used as a masculine first name.

Newton a surname, meaning 'new farmstead or village' (*Old English*), used as a masculine first name.

Niall or **Nial** (pronounced nee-al) an Irish and Scottish masculine first name meaning 'champion', from Old Gaelic *nia*, 'champion'. It was common for disputes to be decided by combat between rival champions from either side. Niall Noígiallach, 'of the Nine Hostages', was a celebrated fifth-century high king of Ireland, progenitor of the Ui Néill dynasty. Variant forms include Neil, Neill, Neal, Neale. The English name NIGEL has been associated with Niall but the resemblance is coincidental.

Niamh or **Niam** or **Niav** (pronounced *nee-av*) a feminine first name meaning 'radiant one' (*Irish Gaelic*). Niamh of the golden hair, daughter of the sea-god Manannan, fell in love with Oisin (Ossian) and took him to Tir nan Og.

Niccolò an Italian masculine form of NICHOLAS.

Nichol a masculine variant form of NICOL.

Nicholas a masculine first name meaning 'victory of the people' (*Greek*). St Nicholas was a fourth-century bishop of Myra who became the patron saint of children, merchants, pawnbrokers and sailors as well as of

Russia. He is also strongly associated with Christmas. A variant form is NICOLAS. Diminutive forms are Nick, Nicky.

Nick a masculine diminutive form of NICHOLAS, NICOL. Nick Nolte is an American film actor.

Nickson a masculine variant form of NIXON.

Nicky (1) a masculine diminutive form of NICHOLAS, NICOL. (2) a feminine diminutive form of NICOLE.

Nicodemus a masculine first name meaning 'conqueror of the people' (*Greek*). In the New Testament Nicodemus was a Pharisee who tried to defend Jesus against the other Pharisees.

Nicol a Scottish surname form of NICHOLAS used as a masculine first name. Nicol Williamson is a Scottish actor. A variant form is NICHOL.

Nicola (1) a feminine variant form of NICOLE. (2) an Italian masculine form of NICHOLAS.

Nicolas a masculine variant form of NICHOLAS. Nicolas Cage is an American film actor.

Nicole a feminine form of NICHOLAS. Nicole Kidman is an Australian-born film actress. Variant forms are Nicola, Nicolette, Colette. Diminutive forms are Nicky, Nikkie.

Nicolette a feminine variant form of NICOLE.

Nigel a masculine first name meaning 'black' (*Latin*).

Nigella a femine form of NIGEL. Nigella Lawson is an English journalist.

Nikkie a feminine diminutive form of NICOLE.

Nikolaus a German masculine form of NICHOLAS.

Nils a Scandinavian masculine form of NEIL.

Nina a feminine diminutive form of NANCY.

Ninette a French feminine diminutive form of ANN.

Ninian a masculine first name from the Old Gaelic personal name Ninidh, of uncertain derivation. St Ninian (fourth–fifth century) was one of the fathers of the Celtic Church in Scotland. The modern Gaelic form of the name is Ringean.

Ninon a French feminine diminutive form of ANN.

Nissie or **Nissy** a feminine diminutive form of NIXIE.

Nita a feminine diminutive form of ANITA, JUANITA.

Niven a masculine variant form of NEVIN.

Nixie a feminine first name meaning 'water sprite' (*Germanic*). Diminutive forms are Nissie, Nissy.

Nixon a surname, meaning 'son of NICHOLAS', used as a masculine first name. A variant form is Nickson.

Noah a masculine first name meaning 'rest' (*Hebrew*). In the Old Testament Noah was a Hebrew patriarch who was chosen by God to save himself, his family and a pair of each animal and bird from the Flood by building a ship (Noah's Ark) in which they could float on the water. The Arabic form is Nuh.

Noble a surname, meaning 'noble, famous' (*Old French*), used as a masculine first name.

Noé the French and Spanish masculine form of NOAH.

Noè the Italian masculine form of NOAH.

Noël or **Noel** a masculine or feminine first name meaning 'Christmas' (*French*).

Noëlle or **Noelle** feminine form of NOËL.

Nola a feminine variant form of NUALA.

Nolan a surname, meaning 'son of the champion' (*Irish Gaelic*), used as a masculine first name.

Noll or **Nollie** masculine diminutive forms of OLIVER.

Nominoë (pronounced *nom-in-o-ay*) a masculine first name and that of a ninth-century Breton king who achieved Breton independence from the Frankish empire.

Nona a feminine first name meaning 'ninth' (*Latin*).

Nonnie a feminine diminutive form of ANONA.

Nora or **Norah** a feminine diminutive form of ELEANOR, HONORA, LEONORA, also used independently.

Norbert a masculine first name meaning 'northern hero' (*Germanic*).

Noreen an Irish feminine form of NORA.

Norma a feminine first name meaning 'a rule' (*Latin*), but probably invented as the name of the eponymous heroine of the opera by the Italian composer Vincenzo Bellini (1801–35).

Norman a masculine first name meaning 'northman' (*Germanic*). A diminutive form is Norrie.

Norrie (1) a Scottish surname, stemming from Old Norse *norge*, 'Norway', indicating someone from that land, used as a masculine first name. (2) a masculine diminutive form of NORMAN.

Northcliffe a surname, meaning 'north cliff' (*Old English*), used as a masculine first name.

Norton a surname, meaning 'northern farmstead or village' (*Old English*), used as a masculine first name.

Norval a masculine first name invented by the eighteenth-century writer John Home (1722–1808) in his play *Douglas* (1756), although it has also been found as an old surname, a shortened form of Normanville, from the fourteenth century.

Norville a surname, meaning 'north town' (*Old French*), used as a masculine first name.

Norvin a masculine first name meaning 'northern friend' (*Old English*).

Norward a surname, meaning 'northern guardian' (*Old English*), used as a masculine first name.

Norwell a surname, meaning 'northern stream', used as a masculine first name.

Norwood a surname, meaning 'north wood' (*Old English*), used as a masculine first name.

Nowell an English masculine form of NOËL.

Nuala (pronounced *noola*) a feminine first name that is probably an abbreviated form of FIONNUALA now used independently. Nola is an alternative form.

Nudd (pronounced *nooth*) a masculine first name and that of a legendary Welsh hero, derived perhaps from the Brythonic god-name Nodons.

Nuh the Arabic form of NOAH.

Nuline a feminine variant form of NEWLYN.

Nye a masculine diminutive form of ANEURIN.

Nyree a feminine first name from New Zealand that was brought to the UK by the actress Nyree Dawn Porter.

O

Oakley a surname, meaning 'oak tree meadow' (*Old English*), used as a masculine first name.

Obadiah a masculine first name meaning 'servant of Jehovah' (*Hebrew*). In the Old Testament Obadiah was a Hebrew prophet and author of the Book of Obadiah, the shortest book of the Bible.

Obed a masculine first name meaning 'serving God' (*Hebrew*). In the Old Testament Obed was a descendant of Judah.

Oberon a masculine variant form of AUBERON. William Shakespeare (1564–1616) used the name for the king of the fairies in his comedy *A Midsummer Night's Dream*.

Obert a masculine first name meaning 'wealthy, brilliant' (*Germanic*).

Octavia feminine form of OCTAVIUS. Octavia (died 11 BC) was a Roman widow, the sister of Octavius Caesar (Augustus), who became the wife of Mark Antony in 41 BC. Antony divorced her in 31 BC after meeting Cleopatra. Through her daughters by Antony she was the grandmother of Caligula and the great-grandmother of Nero. She appears in the play *Antony and Cleopatra* by William Shakespeare (1564–1616) and also in *All for Love* (1678) by John Dryden (1631–1700).

Octavian a masculine variant form of OCTAVIUS. The name was used by the German composer Richard Strauss (1864–1949) and his librettist, the Austrian poet and dramatist Hugo von Hofmannsthal (1874–1929) for the young hero of their opera *Der Rosenkavalier* (1211). The role is actually sung by a woman.

Octavie a French feminine form of OCTAVIA.

Octavius a masculine first name meaning 'eighth' (*Latin*). Octavius Caesar (63 BC–AD 14) was a Roman statesman who was adopted by Julius Caesar in 44 BC. He was the brother-in-law of Mark Antony whom he defeated at Actium in 31 BC. Thereafter he became the first emperor of Rome, adopting the name AUGUSTUS. He appears in two plays by William Shakespeare (1564–1616), *Julius Caesar* and *Antony and Cleopatra*. Octavian is a masculine variant form.

Oda a French masculine form of OTTO.

Odd the Norwegian masculine form of OTTO.

Oddo or **Oddone** Italian masculine forms of OTTO.

Oded a masculine first name meaning 'upholder' (*Hebrew*). In the Old Testament Oded is (1) the name of the prophet Azarias and (2) a Samarian prophet who intercepted to save the lives of captives taken from Judah after its defeat by Israel and Syria.

Odelia or **Odelie** feminine variant forms of ODILE.

Odette a feminine diminutive form of ODA.

Odhrán (pronounced *oh-rann*) a masculine first name from *odhra*, 'dark-haired' (*Irish Gaelic*). The name was borne by St Columba's associate and has strong connections with Iona. 'Reilig Odhrain' is the place where many kings and Lords of the Isles were buried.

Odile or **Odille** a feminine first name meaning 'rich, wealthy' (*Germanic*). Variant forms are Odelia, Odelie, Otilie, Ottilie.

Odoardo an Italian masculine form of EDWARD.

Odysseus see ULYSSES.

Oengus *see* ANGUS.

Ofra a feminine variant form of OPHRAH.

Ogden a surname, meaning 'oak valley', used as first name (*Old English*). Ogden Nash (1902–71) was an American humorous poet.

Ogilvie or **Ogilvy** a surname, meaning 'high peak' (*Celtic*), used as a masculine first name.

Oisín *see* OSSIAN.

Olaf or **Olav** a masculine first name meaning 'divine remnant' (*Old Norse*).

Olave (1) a Manx Gaelic masculine form of OLAF, the name of the founder of the Manx kingdom. (2) a feminine variant form of OLIVE or Olivia.

Oleg the Russian masculine form of HELGE.

Olga the Russian feminine form of HELGA. St Olga (*c*.879–969) was a Russian grand-duchess who began the Christianisation of Russia.

Olimpia the Italian feminine form of OLYMPIA.

Olive a feminine first name meaning 'an olive' (*Latin*). Variant forms are Olivia, Olave.

Oliver a masculine first name meaning 'an olive tree' (*Latin*). Oliver and

ROLAND were the most famous of the legendary twelve paladins who attended on Charlemagne. Oliver Cromwell (1599–1658) was an English Puritan statesman and general who was one of the Parliamentary leaders of the English Civil War. Following the execution of King Charles I, he quelled the Royalist forces in Scotland and Ireland and was Lord Protector of the Commonwealth (1653–58). Diminutive forms are Ollie, Olly, Noll, Nollie.

Oliverio the Spanish masculine form of OLIVER.

Olivia a feminine variant form of Olive. William Shakespeare (1654–1616) used the name for 'a lady of great beauty and fortune' in his comedy *Twelfth Night*. A diminutive form is Livia.

Oliviero the Italian masculine form of OLIVER.

Ollie or **Olly** masculine diminutive forms of OLIVER.

Olwen a feminine first name meaning 'white footprint' (*Welsh*). It is the name of the heroine of the legend of 'Culhwych ac Olwen'.

Olympe the French feminine form of OLYMPIA.

Olympia a feminine first name meaning 'heavenly' (*Greek*). Olympia Dukakis is an American actress.

Omar a masculine first name meaning 'first son' (*Arabic*). Omar (died 644) was the second caliph of Islam (634–644). Omar Sharif is an Egyptian film actor and bridge player. A variant form is Umar.

Ona a feminine diminutive form of names ending -ona, for example Fiona.

Onefre a Spanish masculine form of HUMPHREY.

Onefredo an Italian masculine form of HUMPHREY.

Onfroi a French masculine form of HUMPHREY.

Onofrio the Italian masculine form of HUMPHREY.

Onorio the Italian masculine form of HONORIUS.

Oonagh or **Oona** (pronounced *oo-na*) a feminine first name meaning 'the one' (*Irish Gaelic*), a Gaelic form of UNA, the maiden rescued from the dragon in the legend of St George.

Opal the name of the iridescent gemstone used as a feminine first name, precious stone (*Sanskrit*).

Ophelia a feminine first name from *ophis*, 'serpent' (*Greek*). William Shakespeare (1654–1616) used the name for the young and innocent girl in *Hamlet* who is instructed by her father, Polonius, to spurn the eponymous prince's advances.

Ophélie the French feminine form of OPHELIA.

Ophrah or **Ophra** a feminine first name meaning 'fawn' (*Hebrew*). Variant forms are Ofra, Oprah.

Oprah a modern feminine variant of OPHRAH, introduced by the American television presenter Oprah Winfrey.

Oran an anglicised masculine form of ODHRÁN.

Orazio the Italian masculine form of HORACE.

Orchil an Irish Gaelic feminine first name from a mythical name associated with an ancient goddess of twilight.

Oren a masculine first name meaning 'laurel' (*Hebrew*).

Oreste the Italian masculine form of ORESTES.

Orestes a masculine first name meaning 'mountain climber' (*Greek*). In Greek mythology Orestes was the son of Agamemnon, who killed his mother and her lover in revenge for the death of his father.

Orfeo the Italian masculine form of ORPHEUS.

Orfhlaith a feminine variant form of ORLA.

Oriana or **Oriane** a feminine first name meaning 'golden' (*Latin*).

Oriel a feminine first name meaning 'strife' (*Germanic*).

Orin, Orrin an anglicised masculine form of ODHRÁN.

Orion a masculine first name meaning 'son of light' (*Greek*).

Orla or **Orlaith** a feminine first name meaning 'golden girl', from *ór*, 'gold' (*Irish Gaelic*). Other forms are Orlaith, Orfhlaith.

Orlanda feminine form of ORLANDO.

Orlando the Italian masculine form of ROLAND, with OLIVER the most famous of the legendary twelve paladins who attended on Charlemagne. William Shakespeare (1654–1616) used the name for that of the courageous hero of his comedy *As You Like It*. The English writer Virginia Woolf (1882–1941) also used the name for the hero/heroine of her fantastic novel, *Orlando* (1928).

Ormond or **Ormonde** a surname, meaning 'from east Munster' (*Irish Gaelic*), used as a masculine first name.

Orna a feminine first name meaning 'dark-haired' (*Irish Gaelic*), a feminine form of ODHRÁN.

Orpheus a masculine name of uncertain meaning. In Greek mythology, a Orpheus was a poet who sought to retrieve his wife Eurydice from Hades.

Orrin an anglicised masculine form of ODHRÁN.

Orsino a masculine first name meaning 'little bear'. William Shakespeare (1654–1616) used the name for the lovesick duke of Illyria who begins the comedy Twelfth Night with the famous words, 'If music be the food of love, play on.'

Orso a masculine first name meaning 'bear' (*Latin/Italian*).

Orsola the Italian feminine form of URSULA.

Orson a masculine first name meaning 'little bear' (*Latin/Old French*). Orson Welles (1915–85) was an American film actor and director. His most famous film was *Citizen Kane* (1941), which he directed and in which he starred.

Ortensia the Italian feminine form of HORTENSE.

Orvil or **Orville** a masculine first name meaning 'golden place' (*Old French*).

Orwin a masculine variant form of ERWIN.

Osbert a masculine first name meaning 'God-bright' (*Old English*). A diminutive form is Ossie.

Osborn or **Osborne** or **Osbourne** a surname, meaning 'divine bear, or warrior (*Germanic*), used as a masculine first name. A diminutive form is Ossie.

Oscar a masculine first name meaning 'divine spear' (*Germanic*). It was probably taken to Ireland by the Vikings and appears in the later Fenian Cycle of legends as the son of Ossian, and a great poet and warrior. In his Ossianic poems, the Scottish poet James Macpherson (1736–96) was responsible for a new popularity for the name in Europe.

Oskar the German and Scandinavian masculine form of OSCAR.

Osmond or **Osmund** a masculine first name meaning 'divine protection' (*Germanic*). St Osmund (died 1099) was a Norman French bishop of Salisbury who completed and consecrated the cathedral there. A diminutive form is Ossie.

Ossian an Irish and Scottish masculine first name from Oisín, 'little deer', from Gaelic *oisean*. Ossian, bard and warrior, son of FIONN mac-Cumhaill, is one of the great figures of Gaelic legend, who, lured by NIAMH, spent hundreds of years in Tir nan Og, and emerged as young as he went in, only to age three hundred years and die in the space of a day.

Ossie a masculine diminutive form of OSBERT, OSBORN, OSCAR, OSMOND, OSWALD.

Osvaldo the Italian masculine form of OSWALD.

Oswald a masculine first name meaning 'divine rule' (*Germanic*). St Oswald (*c.*605–641) was an Anglo-Saxon king of Northumbria (633–641) who restored Christianity to the region. William Shakespeare (1654–1616) used the name for Goneril's steward in the tragedy, *King Lear*.

Oswin a masculine first name meaning 'God-friend' (*Old English*).

Otilie a feminine variant form of ODILE.

Otis a surname, meaning 'son of Ote' (*Germanic*), used as a masculine first name.

Ottar *see* ARTHUR.

Ottavia the Italian feminine form of OCTAVIA.

Ottavio the Italian masculine form of OCTAVIUS.

Ottilie a feminine variant form of ODILE.

Otto a masculine name meaning 'rich' (*Germanic*).

Ottone an Italian masculine form of OTTO.

Owain a Welsh masculine form of Eugenius, 'well-born', anglicised as Owen. It is a popular name in old Welsh legends and that of the hero of the thirteenth-century poem 'Owain'. Owain Glyndwr was the last independent prince of Wales (*c.* 1350–*c.* 1416).

Owen (1) an anglicised masculine form of OWAIN. (2) an anglicised masculine form of EOGANÁN.

Oxford a place name, meaning 'ford for oxen' (*Old English*), used as a masculine first name.

Oxton a surname, meaning 'place for keeping oxen' (*Old English*), used as a masculine first name.

Oz or **Ozzie** or **Ozzy** masculine diminutive forms of names beginning with Os-.

P

Pablo the Spanish masculine form of PAUL. Pablo Picasso (1881–1973) was a Spanish painter and sculptor and a highly influential figure in twentieth-century art. He cofounded the Cubist movement.

Paddy (1) a masculine diminutive form of PÁDRAIG, PATRICK. Paddy Ashdown was the leader of the Liberal Democratic Party (1988–99). (2) a feminine diminutive form of PATRICIA.

Pádraig (pronounced *paw-rik*) the Irish Gaelic masculine form of PATRICK. Diminutive forms are Paddy, Pat.

Paget or **Pagett** or **Padget** or **Padgett** a surname, meaning 'young page' (*Old French*), used as a masculine first name.

Paige or **Page** a surname, meaning 'page' (*Old French*), used as a feminine first name.

Palmiro a masculine first name meaning 'palm' (*Latin*).

Palmira feminine form of PALMIRO.

Paloma the Spanish word for 'dove' used as a feminine first name.

Pam a feminine diminutive form of PAMELA.

Pamela a feminine first name invented by the English poet Sir Philip Sidney (1554–86) derived from the Greek work for 'honey'. A diminutive form is Pam.

Pancho a masculine diminutive form of FRANCISCO.

Pandora a feminine first name meaning 'gifted' (*Greek*). In Greek mythology, Pandora was the first woman on earth. The gods gave her a box full of blessings for mankind, which she was told not to open. She did, and they all flew away except hope.

Pansy (1) a feminine first name meaning 'thought' (*French*). (2) the name of the garden flower used as a feminine first name.

Paola the Italian feminine form of PAULA.

Paolo the Italian masculine form of PAUL.

Paris a masculine first name meaning 'torch, firebrand' (Greek). In Greek

223

mythology Paris was the second son of King Priam of Troy and Hecuba whose abduction of Helen, wife of the Greek Menelaus, led to the Trojan War. He appears in *Troilus and Cressida* by William Shakespeare (1654–1616). Shakespeare also used the name for that of a young nobleman who is encouraged to woo Juliet in *Romeo and Juliet*.

Pascal a masculine first name meaning 'of the passover' (*Latin/French*).

Pasquale the Italian masculine form of Pascal.

Pat (1) a masculine diminutive form of Pádraig, Patrick. (2) a feminine diminutive form of Patricia.

Patience a feminine first name meaning 'patience' (*Latin*).

Patric a masculine variant form of Patrick.

Patrice (1) the French masculine form of Patrick. (2) the French feminine form of Patricia.

Patricia the feminine form of Patrick. Diminutive forms are Paddy, Pat, Patsy, Pattie, Patty, Tricia.

Patricio the Spanish masculine form of Patrick.

Patricius a masculine variant form of Patrick.

Patrick a masculine first name meaning 'of noble birth, a patrician' from Latin Patricius. St Patrick (*fl*. fifth century) born to a romanised British family on the West coast of Britain, is the great missionary saint of Ireland, and that country's patron saint. The name was so popular in Ireland as for 'Paddy' and 'Irishman' to be synonymous to outsiders. Patrick Bergin is an American actor. A variant form is Patric. The diminutive forms Paddy and Patsy are usually found in Ireland; Pat is more common in Scotland.

Patrizia the Italian feminine form of Patricia.

Patrizio the Italian masculine form of Patrick.

Patrizius the German masculine form of Patrick.

Patsy a feminine diminutive form of Patricia.

Pattie or **Patty** feminine diminutive forms of Martha, Patience, Patricia.

Paul a masculine first name meaning 'little' (*Latin*). In the New Testament Paul (born Saul of Tarsus) was a Jewish persecutor of Christians who underwent a conversion on the road to Damascus and became the Christianity's leading missionary, making three missionary journeys to Cyprus, Asia Minor, Greece and Palestine. He wrote many of the Epistles. He was executed in Rome *c*.67.

Paula feminine form of Paul.

Paulette a French feminine form of PAULA.

Paulina or **Pauline** a feminine diminutive forms of PAULA. William Shakespeare (1654–1616) used the form Paulina for one of the characters in his play *A Winter's Tale*.

Pawl the Welsh masculine form of PAUL.

Payne or **Payn** a surname, meaning 'countryman' (*Old French*), used as a masculine first name.

Peace the word for the condition of tranquillity or calm used as a feminine first name.

Peadar an Irish and Scottish Gaelic masculine form of PETER.

Pearl the name of the lustrous white gem used as a feminine first name.

Pedaiah a masculine first name meaning 'Jehovah ransoms' (*Hebrew*).

Pedr a Welsh masculine form of PETER.

Pedro the Portuguese and Spanish masculine form of PETER. William Shakespeare (1654–1616) used the name for Don Pedro, prince of Arragon, in his comedy *Much Ado About Nothing*. Pedro Almodóvar is a Spanish film director.

Peer a Norwegian masculine form of PETER.

Peg a feminine diminutive form of MARGARET.

Pegeen an Irish feminine diminutive form of MARGARET.

Peggie or **Peggy** a feminine diminutive form of MARGARET.

Peleg a masculine first name meaning 'division' (*Hebrew*).

Pelléas *see* MÉLISANDE.

Pen a feminine diminutive form of PENNY.

Penelope a feminine first name meaning 'duck' (*Greek*). In Greek mythology Penelope was the wife of ULYSSES. During his protracted absence it was assumed that he was dead and Penelope was pestered by suitors whom she put off on the pretext that before she could make up her mind she must first finish a shroud that she was weaving. To gain time, she undid by night the work she had done by day. Diminutive forms are Pen, Penny.

Penny feminine diminutive form of PENELOPE, now used independently.

Peony a feminine first name meaning 'healing' (*Greek*), the name of a plant with pink, red, white or yellow flowers used as a feminine first name.

Pepe a masculine diminutive form of JOSÉ.

Pepin a masculine first name meaning 'enduring' (*Germanic*).

Pepillo or **Pepito** masculine diminutive forms of JOSÉ.

Per a Scandinavian masculine form of PETER.

Perceval or **Percival** a masculine first name meaning 'pierce valley' (*Old French*).

Percy a surname, meaning 'from Perci-en-Auge in Normandy' (*Old French*), used as a masculine first name.

Perdita a feminine first name meaning 'lost' (*Latin*). It was invented by William Shakespeare (1564–1616) for a character in his play *The Winter's Tale*.

Peredur a Welsh masculine first name and the name of the hero of the Arthurian romance *Tair Rhamant*, a seventh son who undergoes magical adventures and may be either a precursor of, or derive from, Sir PERCEVAL, knight of the Holy Grail in the English Arthurian tales.

Peregrine a masculine first name meaning 'wanderer' (*Latin*). Peregrine Worsthorne is an English journalist. A diminutive form is Perry.

Peronel a feminine contraction of PETRONEL.

Peronnik a Breton masculine equivalent of PEREDUR.

Perry (1) masculine diminutive form of PEREGRINE, now used in its own right. (2) a surname, meaning 'pear tree' (*Old English*), used as a masculine first name.

Persephone a Greek feminine first name of uncertain meaning. In Greek mythology, Persephone was goddess of the underworld.

Persis a feminine first name meaning 'a Persian woman' (*Greek*). In the New Testament Persis was a Roman Christian friend of PAUL.

Pet a feminine diminutive form of PETULA.

Pete a masculine diminutive form of PETER.

Peter a masculine first name meaning 'rock' (*Latin*). In the New Testament Peter, originally called Simon, was a Galilean fisherman who was called Peter ('rock') by Jesus. He became the leader of the apostles. He is considered by some Christians to be the first pope. Diminutive forms are Pete, Peterkin.

Peterkin a masculine diminutive form of PETER.

Petra feminine form of PETER.

Petrina a feminine diminutive form of PETRA.

Petronel or **Petronella** feminine form of Petronius, a Roman family name (*Latin*).

Petrucio the Italian masculine form of Peter. William Shakespeare

(1654–1616) used the name for the main male character in his comedy *The Taming of the Shrew* but anglicised it to 'Petruchio' so that it was pronounced almost correctly.

Petrus a German masculine form of PETER.

Petula a feminine first name meaning 'asking' (*Latin*). A diminutive form is Pet.

Petunia the name of a plant with white, blue or purple flowers used as a feminine first name.

Phamie a feminine diminutive form of EUPHEMIA.

Phebe a feminine variant form of PHOEBE.

Phedra a feminine first name meaning 'bright' (*Greek*).

Phèdre the French feminine form of PHEDRA.

Phelim a masculine first name meaning 'always good' (*Irish*).

Phemie a feminine diminutive form of EUPHEMIA.

Phenie a feminine diminutive form of JOSEPHINE.

Phil (1) a masculine diminutive form of PHILIP, PHILLIP. (2) a feminine diminutive form of PHILIPPA.

Philbert a masculine first name meaning 'very bright' (*Germanic*).

Philemon a masculine first name meaning 'friendly' (*Greek*). In Greek mythology was an elderly peasant who, with his wife, Baucis, entertained Zeus and Hermes in their cottage. In the New Testament Philemon was a wealthy Christian in Asia Minor to whom PAUL wrote a letter concerning Philemon's slave, who had run away and been converted by Paul who told him to return to Philemon.

Philip a masculine first name meaning 'lover of horses' (*Greek*). In the New Testament Philip was (1) one of Christ's apostles and (2) one of the seven deacons appointed to tend the Christians of Jerusalem, and (3) a son of King Herod the Great. A variant form is Phillip. Diminutive forms are Phil, Pip.

Philipp the German masculine form of PHILIP.

Philippa feminine form of PHILIP. Diminutive forms are Phil, Pip, Pippa.

Philippe the French masculine form of PHILIP.

Phillip a masculine variant form of PHILIP. Diminutive forms are Phil, Pip.

Philomena a feminine first name meaning 'love and strength' (*Greek*).

Phineas or **Phinehas** a masculine first name meaning 'serpent's mouth' (*Hebrew*). In the Old Testament Phinehas was a grandson of Aaron who became a priest and warrior.

Phoebe a feminine first name meaning 'moon' (*Greek*). In the New Testament Phoebe was a Roman Christian woman to whom PAUL wrote. William Shakespeare (1654–1616) used the name for a shepherdess in his comedy *As You Like It*. Phoebe Cates is an American film actress. A variant form is Phebe.

Phoenix the name of a legendary Arabian bird that at the end of a certain number of years is consumed by fire but then regenerates itself. It has been used as a masculine first name in the USA.

Phyllida a feminine variant form of PHYLLIS. Phyllida Law is a British actress and the mother of the actress Emma Thompson.

Phyllis a feminine first name meaning 'a green bough' (*Greek*).

Pia feminine form of PIO.

Pierce a surname form of PIERS used as a masculine first name. Pierce Brosnan is an Irish-born film actor.

Pierre the French masculine form of PETER.

Piers a masculine variant form of PETER.

Pierse a surname form of PIERS used as a masculine first name.

Pieter a Dutch masculine form of PETER.

Pietro the Italian masculine form of PETER.

Pilar a feminine first name meaning 'pillar' (*Spanish*), an allusion to the Virgin Mary who appeared to St James the Greater standing on a pillar.

Pio the Italian masculine form of PIUS.

Pip (1) a masculine diminutive form of PHILIP, PHILLIP. (2) a feminine diminutive form of PHILIPPA.

Pippa a feminine diminutive form of PHILIPPA.

Pius a masculine first name meaning 'holy' (*Latin*). It was the name adopted by many popes.

Placido a masculine first name meaning 'peaceful' (*Latin/Spanish*). Placido Domingo is a prominent Mexican-born opera singer and director.

Plato a masculine first name meaning 'broad' (*Greek*). Plato (*c.*427–*c.*347) was an Athenian who, with his teacher, Socrates, and pupil, Aristotle, initiated western philosophy.

Polly feminine diminutive form of MARY, now used independently.

Pollyanna a feminine first name formed from a combination of POLLY and ANNA. The North American writer Eleanor Hodgman Porter created a fictional character, called Pollyanna Whittier, whose optimism has become synonymous with the name.

Pomona a feminine first name meaning 'fruitful' (*Latin*).

Poppy the name of the plant that has a bright red flower used as a feminine first name.

Portia a feminine first name meaning 'gift' (*Latin*). Portia, daughter of Cato Uticensis, was the wife of Marcus Junius Brutus, one of the conspirators against Julius Caesar. She appears in the play *Julius Caesar* by William Shakespeare (1564–1616), who also used the name for the heroine of his play *The Merchant of Venice*.

Powel a masculine first name meaning 'son of Hywel', from *ap*, 'son' (*Welsh*).

Presley a surname, meaning 'priests' meadow', used as a masculine first name.

Prima the feminine form of PRIMO.

Primo a masculine first name meaning 'first born' (*Latin*).

Primrose the name of the yellow spring flower used as a feminine first name.

Prisca see PRISCILLA.

Priscilla a feminine first name derived from *prisca*, 'ancient' (*Latin*). In the New Testament Priscilla and her husband, Aquila, were Roman Christians who helped Paul in his missionary work. Paul called her Prisca. Diminutive forms are Cilla, Prissie.

Prissie a feminine diminutive form of PRISCILLA.

Proinséas (pronounced *phron-shas*) the Irish Gaelic masculine version of FRANCIS.

Prosper a masculine first name meaning 'favourable, fortunate' (*Latin*).

Pròspero the Italian masculine form of PROSPER. William Shakespeare (1654–1616) used the name (without the accent) for the rightful duke of Milan in his play *The Tempest*.

Prudence the word for the quality of caution or circumspection used as a feminine first name (*Latin*). Diminutive forms are Prue, Prudie.

Prudie a feminine diminutive form of PRUDENCE.

Prue a feminine diminutive form of PRUDENCE, PRUNELLA. Prue Leith is an English cook and cookery writer and the chairman of the Royal College of Arts.

Prunella a feminine first name meaning 'plum' (*Latin*). Prunella Scales is an English actress. A diminutive form is Prue.

Psyche a feminine first name meaning 'of the soul' (*Greek*).

Pugh

Pugh a surname, meaning 'son of HUGH' (*Welsh*), used as a masculine first name.

Pwyll or **Pwll** (pronounced *pull*) a masculine first name from *pwll*, 'wisdom', 'prudence' (*Welsh*). Pwll, prince of Dyfed, is the hero of the first 'branch' of the *Mabinogion* tales.

Q

Qabil the Arabic form of CAIN.

Queenie a feminine diminutive form of the word 'queen', 'the supreme woman', used as a feminine first name (*Old English*).

Quenby a surname, meaning 'queen's manor', used as a feminine first name (*Old English*).

Quentin a masculine first name meaning 'fifth' (*Latin*). A variant form is Quinton.

Querida a feminine first name meaning 'beloved', a Spanish term of endearment used as a feminine first name.

Quinta feminine form of QUINTO.

Quinto the Italian masculine form of QUINTUS.

Quintus a masculine first name meaning 'fifth' (*Latin*). William Shakespeare (1654–1616) used the name for a character in his play *Titus Andronicus*.

Quenel or **Quennel** a surname, meaning 'queen war' (*Old English*), used as a masculine first name.

Quigley or **Quigly** a surname, meaning 'untidy' (*Irish Gaelic*), used as a masculine first name.

Quinby a masculine variant form of QUENBY.

Quincy or **Quincey** a surname, meaning 'fifth place' (*Latin/French*), used as a masculine first name.

Quinlan a masculine first name meaning 'well formed' (*Irish Gaelic*).

Quinn a surname, meaning 'wise' (*Irish Gaelic*), used as a masculine first name.

Quinton a masculine variant form of QUENTIN.

R

Rab a masculine diminutive form of ROBERT, occasionally found as a name in its own right.

Raban a masculine first name meaning 'raven' (*Germanic*).

Rabbie a masculine diminutive form of ROBERT.

Rachel a feminine first name meaning 'lamb' (*Hebrew*). In the Old Testament Rachel was the younger sister of Leah and the second and best-loved wife of Jacob. She was the mother of Joseph and Benjamin. A variant form is Rachelle. Diminutive forms are Rae, Ray.

Rachele the Italian feminine form of RACHEL.

Rachelle a feminine variant form of RACHEL.

Radcliffe a surname, meaning 'red cliff' (*Old English*), used as a masculine first name.

Radha (pronounced *ra-ha*) a feminine first name meaning 'far-seeing'. The name is related to *radharc*, 'vision' (*Irish Gaelic*).

Radley a surname, meaning 'red meadow' (*Old English*), used as a masculine first name.

Radnor a place name and surname, meaning 'red slopes' (*Old English*), used as a masculine first name.

Rae (1) a Scottish surname, perhaps from Gaelic *rath*, 'grace', used as a masculine or feminine first name. (2) a feminine diminutive form of RACHEL.

Rafe a variant form of RALPH.

Raffaele or **Raffaello** Italian masculine forms of RAPHAEL.

Rafferty a surname, meaning 'prosperous' (*Irish Gaelic*), used as a masculine first name.

Raghnailt (pronounced *ran-ailt*) the Irish and Scottish Gaelic feminine form of RAGHNALL.

Raghnall (pronounced *ren-ull*) a Scottish Gaelic masculine version of an Old Norse name brought by the Vikings, Rognvaldr, 'power in counsel', the Norse equivalent of REYNOLD or REGINALD. It has numerous anglicised versions, including Ranald, Ronald, Randal.

Raheel or **Raheela** a feminine variant form of RAHIL.

Rahel a German feminine form of RACHEL

Rahil the Arabic form of RACHEL. A variant form is Raheel, Raheela.

Rahim a masculine first name meaning 'merciful, compassionate' (*Arabic*).

Rahima or **Rahimah** the feminine form of RAHIM.

Raibeart the Scottish Gaelic masculine form of ROBERT.

Raimondo the Italian masculine form of RAYMOND.

Raimund the German masculine form of RAYMOND.

Raimundo a Spanish masculine form of RAYMOND.

Rainaldo an Italian masculine form of REGINALD.

Raine a feminine variant form of RAYNE.

Rainier a French masculine form of RAYNER.

Raisa a feminine first name meaning 'tolerant' (*Greek*).

Raleigh a surname, meaning 'red or deer meadow' (*Old English*), used as a masculine first name. Variant forms are Rawley, Rayleigh.

Ralph a masculine first name meaning 'famous wolf or hero' (*Germanic*). Sir Ralph Richardson (1902–83) was an eminent English actor. Variant forms are Rafe, Rolph.

Ram a masculine first name meaning 'height' (*Hebrew*). In the Old Testament Ram was a descendant of Judah.

Ramón a Spanish masculine form of RAYMOND.

Ramona feminine form of RAMÓN.

Ramsden a masculine first name meaning 'ram's valley' (*Old English*).

Ramsay or **Ramsey** a place name and surname, meaning 'wild garlic river island', used as a masculine first name (*Old Norse*).

Ranald an anglicised masculine form of RAGHNALL.

Rand a masculine diminutive form of RANDAL, RANDOLF.

Randal (1) or **Randall** an Old English surname and diminutive form of RANDOLPH used as a masculine first name. A variant form is Ranulf. (2) an anglicised masculine form of RAGHNALL.

Randolf or **Randolph** a masculine first name meaning 'shield-wolf' (*Germanic*). Randolph Scott (1898–1987) was an American star of many Western films. A variant form is Ranulf. Diminutive forms are Rand, Randy.

Randy a masculine diminutive form of RANDOLPH, that is also used independently.

Ranee or **Rani** a feminine first name meaning 'queen' (*Hindi*).

Rankin or **Rankine** a diminutive surname masculine form of RANDOLPH used as a masculine first name.

Ransom a surname, meaning 'son of RAND', used as a masculine first name.

Ranulf a masculine variant form of RANDOLF.

Raoul the French masculine form of RALPH.

Raphael a masculine first name meaning 'the healing of God' (*Hebrew*). In the Bible Raphael is one of the archangels with powers of healing.

Raphaela feminine form of RAPHAEL.

Raquel the Spanish feminine form of RACHEL.

Ras a masculine diminutive form of ERASMUS, ERASTUS.

Rasmus a masculine diminutive form of ERASMUS.

Rastus a masculine diminutive form of ERASTUS.

Raul the Spanish masculine form of RALPH. Raul Julia was a Puerto-Rican born film actor.

Rawley a masculine variant form of RALEIGH.

Rawnsley a surname, meaning 'raven's meadow' (*Old English*), used as a masculine first name.

Ray (1) a masculine diminutive form of RAYMOND, now used independently. Ray Liotta is an American film actor. (2) a feminine diminutive form of RACHEL. A variant form is Rae.

Rayleigh a masculine variant form of RALEIGH.

Raymond or **Raymund** a masculine first name meaning 'wise protection' (*Germanic*). A diminutive form is Ray.

Rayne a surname, meaning 'mighty army', used as a masculine or feminine first name. Variant forms are Raine (feminine), Rayner (masculine).

Rayner a masculine variant form of RAYNE (*Germanic*).

Rea a feminine variant form of RHEA.

Read or **Reade** a surname, meaning 'red headed' (*Old English*), used as a masculine first name. Variant forms are Reed, Reede.

Reading a place name and surname, meaning 'people of the red one', used as a masculine first name. A variant form is Redding.

Reardon a masculine variant form of RIORDAN.

Rebecca or **Rebekah** a feminine first name meaning 'noose' (*Hebrew*). In the Old Testament Rebecca was the wife of Isaac and mother of Esau and Jacob. She connived with Jacob to deprive Esau of his birthright. Dame Rebecca West (1892–1983) was an English writer. Diminutive forms are Beckie, Becky.

Redding a masculine variant form of READING.

Redman (1) a surname, meaning 'red cairn or thatcher' (*Old English*), used as a masculine first name. (2) a variant form of REDMOND.

Redmond a masculine first name meaning 'counsel protection' (*Germanic*). A variant form is Redman.

Reece a surname form of RHYS used as a masculine first name.

Reed or **Reede** masculine variant forms of READ.

Rees the English masculine form of RHYS.

Reeve or **Reeves** a masculine first name meaning 'steward, bailiff' (*Old English*).

Reg a masculine diminutive form of REGINALD.

Regan a feminine first name meaning 'king's consort', from *rí*, 'king', and *gan* 'queen' (*Irish Gaelic*). The name gets a bad reputation in *King Lear* by William Shakespeare (1564–1616). Variant forms are Reagan, Rogan.

Reggie a masculine diminutive form of REGINALD.

Regina a feminine first name meaning 'queen' (*Latin*).

Reginald a masculine first name meaning 'counsel rule' (*Germanic*). Diminutive forms are Reg, Reggie.

Reid a Scottish surname that is also found as a masculine first name, from Scots *reed*, 'red'; also Gaelic *ruadh*, 'red'.

Reilly a surname, meaning 'valiant' (*Irish Gaelic*), used as a masculine first name. A variant form is RILEY.

Reinald an early English masculine form of REGINALD.

Reine a feminine first name meaning 'queen' (*French*).

Reinhard a German masculine form of REYNARD.

Reinhold a Scandinavian masculine form of REGINALD.

Reinold a Dutch masculine form of REGINALD.

Remus a masculine first name meaning 'power' (*Latin*).

Renaldo a Spanish masculine form of REGINALD.

Renata a feminine diminutive form of RENÉE.

Renato an Italian and Spanish masculine form of REGINALD.

Renatus the Latin masculine form of RENÉ.

Renault a French masculine form of REGINALD.

René a masculine first name meaning 'born again' (*French*).

Renée feminine form of RENÉ.

Renfrew a place name and surname, meaning 'point of the torrent' (*Celtic*), used as a masculine first name.

Renie a feminine diminutive form of IRENE.

Rennie or **Renny** a diminutive surname form of Reynold used as a masculine first name.

Renton a surname, meaning 'farmstead of power' (*Old English*), used as a masculine first name.

Reuben a masculine first name meaning 'behold a son' (*Hebrew*). In the Old Testament Reuben was the eldest son of Jacob and Leah and the founder of one of the twelve tribes of Israel. A diminutive form is Rube.

Reuel a masculine first name meaning 'friend of God'.

Reva feminine form of REEVE.

Rex a masculine first name meaning 'king' (*Latin*).

Rexanne (1) a feminine first name formed from a combination of REX and ANNE. (2) a variant form of ROXANNE.

Reynard (1) a masculine first name meaning 'brave advice' (*Germanic*). (2) 'fox' (*French*).

Reynold a masculine first name meaning 'strong rule' (*Germanic*).

Rhea a feminine name of uncertain origin and meaning. In Roman mythology Rhea was the mother of REMUS and Romulus. In Greek mythology she was the mother of several gods, including Zeus. Variant forms are Rea, Rheia.

Rhedyn a feminine first name meaning 'fern' (*Welsh*).

Rheia a feminine variant form of RHEA.

Rheinallt a Welsh masculine form of REYNARD. Rheinallt was a fifteenth-century bard.

Rhian a feminine first name meaning 'fair maid', from *rhiain*, 'maiden' (*Welsh*).

Rhiannon a feminine first name meaning 'fair maiden' (*Welsh*), but as the name of a princess in the *Mabinogion* tales it also has the sense 'moon goddess' from the old British goddess Rigantona. A variant form is Riannon.

Rhianwen a feminine first name meaning 'pure maiden' (*Welsh*).

Rhisiart the Welsh masculine form of RICHARD.

Rhoda a feminine first name meaning 'rose' (*Greek*). In the New Testament Rhoda was a Christian servant in Jerusalem who was the first to hear Peter on his miraculous release from prison.

Rhodri (pronounced *rod-ree*) a masculine first name from a root form *rhod*, 'circle', 'disc' (*Welsh*), indicative of a crown or coronet. Rhodri Mawr, 'the great' was a ninth-century king of Gwynedd.

Rhona a feminine variant form of RONA.

Rhondda a feminine first name meaning 'slender', from *rhon*, 'lance' (*Welsh*), and by extension 'slim'. It is the name of a South Wales town in a narrow valley.

Rhonwen a feminine first name meaning 'fair and slender', from *rhon*, 'lance', and *gwen*, 'fair' (*Welsh*).

Rhydderch a masculine first name from *rhi*, 'king', dyrch, 'great', 'exalted' (*Welsh*). It was the name of a famous king of Strathclyde in the sixth century; the ring found for him in a salmon by St MUNGO is incorporated in the arms of the city of Glasgow.

Rhydwen (pronounced *ridd-wen*) or **Rhydian** (*ridd-eean*) a masculine first name meaning 'white, or blessed, ford' (*Welsh*).

Rhys (pronounced *rees*) a Welsh masculine first name, possibly meaning 'ardour', from that of Rhys ap Gruffudd, a twelfth-century prince of Deheubarth (southern Wales). The anglicised form is Rees.

Ria a German feminine diminutive form of MARIA.

Riannon a feminine variant form of RHIANNON.

Rica a feminine diminutive form of RODERICA.

Ricardo a Spanish masculine form of RICHARD.

Riccardo an Italian masculine form of RICHARD.

Rich a masculine diminutive form of RICHARD, RICHMOND.

Richard a masculine first name meaning 'a strong king; powerful' (*Germanic*). It was the name of three kings of England. Richard I, 'Coeur de Lion' or 'Lion-hearted' (1157–99), who spent only six months of his ten-year reign (1189–99) in England. Richard II (1367–1400) succeeded his grandfather as a child in 1377. His reign was marked by discontent and baronial opposition and he was forced to abdicate in 1399. Richard III (1452–85) was originally the brother of Edward IV who, after Edward's death in 1483, seized his nephews and declared himself their protector. After their mysterious deaths, he assumed the throne. He was defeated and killed at the Battle of Bosworth. Diminutive forms are Dick, Rich, Richey, Richie, Rick, Rickie, Ricky, Ritchie.

Richey or **Richie** a masculine diminutive form of RICHARD, RICHMOND.

Richmond a surname, meaning 'strong hill' (*Old French*), used as a masculine first name. Diminutive forms are Rich, Richey, Richie.

Rick or **Rickie** or **Ricky** masculine diminutive forms of ARIC, RICHARD.

Rider a surname, meaning 'knight, rider' (*Old English*), used as a masculine first name. Sir Rider Haggard (1856–1925) was an English author of adventure stories, the best known being *King Solomon's Mines* (1885).

Ridley a surname, meaning 'cleared meadow' (*Old English*), used as a masculine first name. Ridley Scott is an English-born film director best known for his film *Blade Runner*.

Rigantona *see* RHIANNON.

Rigby a surname, meaning 'farm on a ridge' (*Old English*), used as a masculine first name.

Rigg a surname, meaning 'at the ridge' (*Old English*), used as a masculine first name.

Riley a masculine variant form of REILLY.

Rina a feminine diminutive form of names ending -rina.

Rinaldo an Italian masculine form of REGINALD. Rinaldo was a prominent figure in medieval romance as one of the paladins who attended on Charlemagne. William Shakespeare (1654–1616) used the name for a character in his comedy *All's Well That Ends Well*.

Ring a surname, meaning 'wearing a ring' (*Old English*), used as a masculine first name.

Riona a feminine diminutive form of CATRIONA.

Riordan a surname, meaning 'bard' (*Irish Gaelic*), used as a masculine first name. A variant form is REARDON.

Ripley a place name and surname, meaning 'strip-shaped clearing' (*Old English*), used as a masculine first name.

Rita a feminine diminutive form of MARGARITA, MARGHERITA, used independently. Rita Hayworth (1918–87) was a famous American film star of the 1940s.

Ritchie a diminutive and surname masculine form of RICHARD.

Ritter a masculine first name meaning 'knight or rider' (*Germanic*).

Roald a masculine first name meaning 'famous ruler' (*Old Norse*). Roald

Dahl (1916–90) was a well-known English writer, particularly of books for children.

Rob a masculine diminutive forms of ROBERT. Rob Lowe is an American film actor.

Robat the Welsh masculine form of ROBERT.

Robbie or **Robby** a masculine diminutive form of ROBERT that is now being used as a name in its own right. Robbie Coltrane is a well-known Scottish actor.

Robert a masculine first name meaning 'bright in fame' (*Germanic*). Robert De Niro is a well-known American film actor. Diminutive forms are Bob, Bobby, Rab, Rob, Robbie, Robby, Robin.

Roberta feminine form of ROBERT.

Roberto the Italian and Spanish masculine form of ROBERT.

Robin a masculine diminutive of ROBERT, now used as independent masculine or feminine first name. Robin Hood was a traditional hero of a group of Old English ballads. He was said to have been a generous and gallant outlaw and robber, living a happy life with his merry comrades, 'under the greenwood tree', in more than one forest, but especially Sherwood. The Welsh form is ROBYN.

Robina a feminine form of ROBIN.

Robinson a surname, meaning 'son of ROBERT' (*Old English*), used as a masculine first name.

Robyn the Welsh masculine form of ROBIN. This spelling, outside Wales at least, is often nowadays used as a feminine first name.

Rocco a masculine name of uncertain meaning possibly 'crow' (*Germanic*).

Rochelle a feminine first name meaning 'little rock' (*French*).

Rochester a place name, and surname, meaning 'Roman fort at the bridges' (*Old English*), used as a masculine first name.

Rock a masculine first name meaning 'stone' or 'oak' (*Old English*).

Rocky an English masculine form of ROCCO.

Rod a masculine diminutive form of RODERICK, RODNEY.

Rodden a surname, meaning 'valley of deer' (*Old English*), used as a masculine first name.

Roddy a masculine diminutive form of RODERICK, RODNEY.

Roderica feminine form of RODERICK. A variant form is Rodericka. A diminutive form is Rica.

Roderich the German masculine form of RODERICK.

Roderick or **Roderic** a masculine first name from *ruadh*, 'red', and *rí*, 'king' (Scottish Gaelic); the Gaelic form is Ruairidh. It is cognate with Welsh RHYDDERCH, and its diminutive forms include Rod, Roddie, Rory.

Roderick or **Roderic** a masculine first name meaning 'fame powerful' (*Germanic*). Diminutive forms are Rod, Roddy, Rurik.

Rodericka a feminine variant form of RODERICA.

Roderico or **Roderigo** an Italian masculine form of RODERICK. William Shakespeare (1654–1616) used the name for 'a foolish gentleman' in love with Desdemona in his tragedy *Othello*.

Rodger a masculine variant form of ROGER.

Rodney a surname and place name, used as a masculine or feminine first name. A diminutive form is Rod.

Rodolf an Italian and Spanish masculine form of RUDOLPH.

Rodolphe a French masculine form of RUDOLPH.

Rodrigo an Italian and Spanish masculine form of RODERICK.

Rodrigue the French masculine form of RODERICK.

Roger a masculine first name meaning 'famous with the spear' (*Germanic*). A variant form is RODGER.

Rogerio the Spanish masculine form of ROGER.

Rohan a masculine first name meaning 'healing, incense' (*Sanskrit*).

Rohanna feminine form of ROHAN.

Róisín (pronounced *rosh-een*) a feminine first name meaning 'little rose' (*Irish Gaelic*). As Róisin Dubh, 'Dark Rosaleen', from a seventeenth-century Gaelic poem, the name is synonymous with Ireland.

Roland a masculine first name meaning 'fame of the land' (*Germanic*). Roland, also known as ORLANDO, and OLIVER were the most famous of the legendary twelve paladins who attended on Charlemagne. Oliver and Roland once fought for five days without either gaining the advantage. Variant forms are Rolland, Rowland. A diminutive form is Roly.

Rolanda or **Rolande** feminine forms of ROLAND.

Roldán or **Rolando** Spanish masculine forms of ROLAND.

Rolf a contraction of RUDOLF. A variant form is Rollo.

Rolland a masculine variant form of ROLAND.

Rollo a masculine variant form of ROLF.

Rolph a masculine variant form of RALPH.

Roly a masculine diminutive form of ROLAND.

Roma a feminine first name meaning 'a Roman' (*Latin*).

Romeo a masculine first name meaning 'a Roman' (*Latin*), originally referring to a person who had gone on pilgrimage to Rome. William Shakespeare (1654–1616) used the name for the young heir of the Montagues who falls in love with Juliet, the daughter of the Capulets, the enemies of the Montagues, in his tragedy *Romeo and Juliet*, which is probably the world's best-known love story.

Romilly a surname, meaning 'broad clearing' (*Old English*) or 'place of Romilius' (*Old French*), used as a masculine first name.

Romney a place name, meaning 'at the broad river' (*Old English*), used as a masculine first name.

Ròmolo a masculine first name, the Italian form of Romulus, of Etruscan origin and unknown meaning; in Roman legend, Romulus and his brother REMUS founded Rome.

Romy a feminine diminutive form of ROSEMARY.

Ron a masculine diminutive form of RONALD. Ron Silver is an American actor.

Rona a Scottish feminine first name, probably a feminine form of RONAN. There is also the island of Rona, from *hraun-ey*, 'rough island' (*Old Norse*), but as St Ronan lived and died on North Rona, the two names are intertwined. A variant form is Rhona.

Ronald an anglicised masculine form of RAGHNALL. Diminutive forms are Ron, Ronnie, Ronny.

Ronalda feminine form of RONALD. Diminutive forms are Ronnie, Ronny.

Ronan a masculine first name meaning 'little seal'. The likely derivation is *ron*, 'seal', with the diminutive suffix -an (*Scottish Gaelic*). It was the name of several saints.

Ronnie or **Ronny** (1) a masculine diminutive form of RONALD. (2) a feminine diminutive form of RONALDA, VERONICA.

Rooney a masculine first name meaning 'red, red-complexioned' (*Gaelic*).

Rory a masculine first name meaning 'red' (*Irish and Scots Gaelic*).

Rosa a feminine first name meaning 'a rose' (*Latin*). Diminutive forms are Rosetta, Rosie.

Rosabel or **Rosabella** or **Rosabelle** a feminine first named formed by a combination of ROSA and BELLA.

Rosalie or **Rosalia** a feminine first name meaning 'little and blooming rose' (*Latin*).

Rosalind or **Rosaline** a feminine first name meaning 'beautiful as a rose' (*Latin*). William Shakespeare (1654–1616) used the form Rosalind for the heroine of his comedy *As You Like It* and Rosaline for a character in *Love's Labour's Lost*. Rosaline is also an off-stage character in *Romeo and Juliet* with whom Romeo is supposed to be in love. A diminutive form is LINDA.

Rosamund or **Rosamond** (1) a feminine first name meaning 'horse protection, famous protection' (*Germanic*). (2) 'rose of the world' (*Latin*).

Rosanne or **Rosanna** feminine compounds of ROSE and ANNE. Rosanna Arquette is an American actress. A variant form is Roseanne, Roseanna.

Roscoe a surname, meaning 'deer wood' (*Old Norse*), used as a masculine first name. Roscoe Ates (1892–1962) was an American film actor who appeared in many films as a comic character.

Rose the English form of ROSA; the name of the flower used as a feminine first name. St Rose of Lima (1586–1617) was a Peruvian Dominican nun who was the first person in the Western Hemisphere to be canonised. She is the patron saint of South America. Diminutive forms are Rosette, Rosie.

Roseanne or **Roseanna** feminine variant forms of ROSANNE, ROSANNA.

Rosemarie a feminine first name formed by a combination of ROSE and MARIE.

Rosemary the name of the plant associated with remembrance used as a feminine first name. Diminutive forms are Romy, Rosie.

Rosemonde a French feminine form of ROSAMUND.

Rosetta a feminine diminutive form of ROSA.

Rosette a feminine diminutive form of ROSE.

Rosh a masculine first name meaning 'head' (*Hebrew*). In the Old Testament Rosh was a son of Benjamin.

Rosie a feminine diminutive form of ROSA, ROSE, ROSEMARY, now also used independently.

Roslin or **Roslyn** a place name, meaning 'unploughable land by the pool' (*Scots Gaelic*), used as a masculine or feminine first name. A variant form is ROSSLYN.

Rosmunda the Italian feminine form of ROSAMUND.

Ross a place name and surname, meaning 'promontory or 'wood', from *ros* (*Scottish Gaelic*), now widely used as a masculine first name.

Rosslyn a masculine or feminine variant form of ROSLIN.

Rowan (pronounced *rau-an*) a masculine or feminine first name that comes from the rowan tree, *ruadhan*, 'little red one' (*Scottish Gaelic*). In the past rowan berries were a specific against witchcraft, but the spread of the name has been very recent.

Rowe a surname, meaning 'hedgerow' (*Old English*), used as a masculine first name.

Rowell a surname, meaning 'rough hill' (*Old English*), used as a masculine first name.

Rowena a feminine first name, perhaps an anglicised form of Welsh RHONWEN. The name was used by Geoffrey of Monmouth in his *Historia Regum Britanniae* for the daughter of the fifth-century Saxon invader Hengist. The name was used by Sir Walter Scott (1771–1832) for the heroine of his novel *Ivanhoe*.

Rowland a masculine variant form of ROLAND.

Rowley a surname, meaning 'rough meadow' (*Old English*), used as a masculine first name.

Roxanne or **Roxane** a feminine first name meaning 'dawn of day' (*Persian*). A variant form is Rexanne. A diminutive form is Roxie.

Roxburgh a place name and surname, meaning 'rook's fortress' (*Old English*), used as a masculine first name.

Roxie a feminine diminutive of ROXANNE.

Roy (1) a masculine first name from *ruadh*, 'red' (*Scottish Gaelic*). (2) a masculine first name meaning 'king', from *roy* (*Old French*).

Royal (1) a masculine variant form of ROYLE. (2) the adjective meaning 'befitting a monarch, regal', used as a feminine first name.

Royce a surname form of ROSE used as a masculine first name.

Royle a surname, meaning 'rye hill' (*Old English*), used as a masculine first name. A variant form is Royal.

Royston a surname, meaning 'place of Royce' (*Germanic/Old English*), used as a masculine first name.

Ruairidh the Scottish Gaelic masculine form of RODERICK. A diminutive form is Rurik.

Rube a masculine diminutive form of REUBEN.

Rubén a Spanish masculine form of REUBEN.

Ruby the name of the red gemstone used as a feminine first name.

Rudi a German masculine diminutive form of RÜDIGER, RUDOLF.

Rüdiger the German masculine form of ROGER.

Rudolf or **Rudolph** a masculine first name meaning 'famous wolf; hero' (*Germanic*).

Rudyard a masculine first name meaning 'reed enclosure' (*Old English*).

Rufe a masculine diminutive form of Rufus.

Rufus a masculine first name meaning 'red-haired' (*Latin*). In the New Testament Rufus was a son of Simon who was forced to help Jesus' torture stake. A diminutive form is RUFE.

Rugby a place name and surname, meaning 'Hroca's stronghold' (*Old English*), used as a masculine first name.

Ruggiero or **Ruggero** Italian masculine forms of ROGER. Ruggero Raimondo is an Italian opera baritone and actor.

Rupert an anglicized Germanic masculine form of ROBERT.

Ruprecht the German masculine form of ROBERT.

Rurik a masculine diminutive form of RUAIRIDH.

Russ a masculine diminutive form of RUSSELL.

Russell a surname, meaning 'red hair' (*Old French*), used as a masculine first name. A diminutive form is Russ.

Rutger a Dutch masculine form of ROGER. Rutger Hauer is a Dutch film actor, best known for his part in the film *Blade Runner*.

Ruth a feminine first name meaning 'friend' (*Hebrew*). In the Old Testament Ruth was the daughter-in-law of NAOMI who, after the death of her husband, followed Naomi to Bethlehem where she helped support her by gleaning the fields of Boaz, who later married her. Their great-grandson was DAVID. The story is told in the Book of Ruth.

Rutherford a surname, meaning 'cattle ford' (*Old English*), used as a masculine first name.

Rutland a place name, meaning 'Rota's estate' (*Old English*), used as a masculine first name.

Ruy a Spanish masculine form of RODERICK.

Ryan an Irish surname, from an Old Gaelic word meaning 'chief', used as masculine first name. It is an extremely popular first name, helped by the film star Ryan O'Neal.

Rye a masculine first name meaning 'from the riverbank' (*French*).

Rylan or **Ryland** a surname, meaning 'where rye grows' (*Old English*), used as a masculine first name.

S

Saba a feminine Arabic form of SHEBA.

Sabin a shortened masculine form of SABINUS.

Sabina a feminine first name meaning 'Sabine woman' (*Latin*).

Sabine a French and German feminine form of SABINA.

Sabino an Italian masculine form of SABINUS.

Sabinus a masculine first name meaning 'Sabine man' (*Latin*). A shortened form is Sabin.

Sabra a feminine first name meaning 'restful' (*Hebrew*).

Sabrina a feminine name of uncertain meaning, linked to the name of the River Severn (*pre-Celtic*). A variant form is Zabrina.

Sacha a Russian masculine diminutive form of Alexander now used increasingly as a feminine form, with the variant form of Sasha. Sacha Distel is a French singer.

Sadhbh (pronounced *sawv*) an Irish Gaelic feminine first name meaning 'sweetness'. This was the name of the mother of Oisín, 'Ossian', who was turned into a deer.

Sadie a feminine diminutive form of SARA.

Sal a feminine diminutive form of SALLY, SARAH.

Salina a feminine first name meaning 'from the salty place' (*Greek*).

Sally or **Sallie** feminine diminutive forms of SARA, now used independently.

Salome a feminine first name meaning 'peaceful' (*Hebrew*). In the New Testament Salome was a granddaughter of Herod the Great and stepdaughter of Herodias at whose suggestion she beguiled her grandfather by her dancing into giving her the head of John the Baptist.

Salomo a Dutch and German masculine form of SOLOMON.

Salomon the French masculine form of SOLOMON.

Salomone the Italian masculine form of SOLOMON.

Salvador a masculine first name meaning 'Christ the saviour' (*Latin/ Spanish*).

Salvatore the Italian masculine form of SALVADOR.

Salvia a feminine first name meaning 'sage' (*Latin*).

Sam (1) a masculine diminutive form of SAMSON, SAMUEL, now used independently. Sam Neill is a New Zealand-born film actor. (2) a feminine diminutive form of SAMANTHA.

Samantha a feminine first name the meaning of which obscure but possibly 'listener' (*Aramic*) or a compound of SAM and ANTHEA. A diminutive form is Sam.

Sammy a masculine diminutive form of SAMSON, SAMUEL.

Samson or **Sampson** a masculine first name meaning 'like the sun' (*Hebrew*). In the Old Testament Samson was an Israelite warrior who performed great feats of strength against the Philistines until he was betrayed by DELILAH. Samson, Duc de Bourgogne, was one of the legendary twelve paladins who attended on Charlemagne. William Shakespeare (1654–1616) used the form Sampson for a character in *Romeo and Juliet*. A diminutive form is Sam, Sammy.

Samuel a masculine first name meaning 'name of God' or 'heard by God' (*Hebrew*). In the Old Testament Samuel was a Hebrew prophet, priest, judge and military leader who anointed SAUL and then DAVID, the first two kings of the Israelites. The two Books of Samuel chronicle the origin and early history of the ancient Israelites. Samuel L. Jackson is an American film actor. Diminutive forms are Sam, Sammy.

Samuele the Italian masculine form of SAMUEL.

Samuela feminine form of SAMUEL.

Sancha or **Sanchia** feminine variant forms of SANCIA.

Sancho a masculine first name meaning 'holy' (*Spanish*).

Sancia feminine form of SANCHO. Variant forms are Sancha, Sanchia.

Sanders a shortened masculine form of ALEXANDER. A diminutive form is Sandy.

Sandie a feminine diminutive form of ALEXANDRA.

Sandra a feminine diminutive form of ALEXANDRA, now used independently.

Sandy (1) a masculine diminutive form of ALEXANDER, LYSANDER, SANDERS. Once upon a time this name could be used, like Jock, as the synonym for a male Scot. (2) a feminine diminutive form of ALEXANDRA.

Sanford a surname, meaning 'sandy ford' (*Old English*), used as a masculine first name.

Sanson the German masculine form of SAMSON.

Sansón the Spanish masculine form of SAMSON.

Sansone the Italian masculine form of SAMSON.

Santo a masculine first name meaning 'saint' (*Italian*).

Saoirse (pronounced *sair-sha*) an Irish feminine first name meaning 'freedom', which has been used as a personal name from the twentieth century, when Ireland regained its independence.

Sapphire (1) a feminine first name derived from *saphir*, 'beautiful' (*Hebrew*). (2) the name of the blue precious stone used as a feminine first name.

Sarah or **Sara** a feminine first name meaning 'princess' (*Hebrew*). In the Old Testament Sarah was the wife of ABRAHAM and mother of ISAAC. She appeared to be barren but then gave birth to Isaac when she was in her sixties. Diminutive forms are Sadie, Sal, Sally.

Saraid (pronounced *sarr-ad*) an Irish feminine first name meaning 'best one'. In legend, it is the name of the daughter of King Conn of the Hundred Battles, possessed of mystic skills.

Sasha a feminine variant form of Sacha.

Saul a masculine first name meaning 'asked for by God' (*Hebrew*). In the Old Testament Saul became the first king of the Israel when the tribes to unite under a king. He at first defeated the Philistines but became mad and committed suicide. He was succeeded by DAVID. In the New Testament Saul was the original name of PAUL.

Savanna a form of the Spanish word for an open grassland used as a feminine first name.

Saveur the French masculine form of SALVADOR.

Saxon a masculine first name meaning 'people of the short swords' (*Germanic*).

Scarlett a variation of the word 'scarlet', a bright red colour, used as a feminine first name by Margaret Mitchell (1900–1949) in her novel *Gone with the Wind*.

Scáthach (pronounced *ska-hach*) an Irish feminine first name and that of the warrior woman of the Isle of Skye who taught the arts of battle to CUCHULAINN and FERDIA. The source of the name is not clear, but it is not related to that of Skye itself, which comes from Old Norse. It is of historical interest in displaying close links between Scotland (Alba) and Ireland (Erin) long before the emigration of the Scots.

Scota an Old Gaelic feminine first name whose derivation is not clear. It is a generalised Latin name for an Irishwoman; but was borne as a personal name by two significant women of Gaelic legend, both said to be daughters of a pharaoh. The older Scota is said to be the grandmother of Iber, founder of the Gaels; the younger was the second wife of Míl Espáine (*see* MILES).

Scott the surname of a Scottish Border clan, used as a very popular and widely used first name for boys. F. Scott Fitzgerald (1896–1940) was an American writer, whose best-known novel is *The Great Gatsby* (1925). Scott Glenn is an American film actor. The name was, perhaps, spread even further in the later twentieth century by television's *Star Trek*. The diminutive form is Scotty or Scottie.

Scottie or **Scotty** the masculine diminutive form of SCOTT.

Scoular a south Scottish surname, meaning 'schoolmaster', literally 'schooler', sometimes used as a masculine first name.

Seachlainn *see* MALACHY.

Sealey a masculine variant form of SEELEY.

Seamas or **Seamus** Irish Gaelic masculine forms of JAMES. Seamus Heaney is an eminent Irish poet.

Sean (pronounced *shawn*) an Irish Gaelic masculine form of JOHN. Sean Connery is a Scottish-born film actor. Anglicised forms are Shaun, Shawn, Shane. It has also been used as a feminine form. Sean Young is an American film actress.

Searle a surname, meaning 'armed warrior', used as a surname (*Germanic*).

Seaton a place name and surname, meaning 'farmstead at the sea' (*Old English*), used as a masculine first name. A variant form is Seton.

Sebastian a masculine first name meaning 'august, majestic' (*Greek*). St Sebastian (died *c*.288) was a Roman soldier who became an early Christian martyr. He was shot with arrows and then beaten to death. William Shakespeare (1654–1616) used the name in two plays: for the brother of Viola in his comedy *As You Like It*, and the brother of the king of Naples in *The Tempest*. He also used the name as JULIA's name in disguise in *The Two Gentlemen of Verona*.

Sebastiano the Italian masculine form of SEBASTIAN.

Sébastien the French masculine form of SEBASTIAN.

Secondo the Italian masculine form of SECUNDUS.

Secundus a masculine first name meaning 'second born' (*Latin*). In the New Testament Secundus was a Christian who accompanied Paul on part of his third missionary journey.

Seeley a surname, meaning 'blessed and happy' (*Old English*), used as a masculine first name. A variant form is Sealey.

Seigneur a masculine variant form of Senior.

Seirian (pronounced *sye-reean*) a Welsh feminine first name meaning 'bright one', a feminine form of Seiriol.

Seiriol a masculine first name meaning 'bright one', from *serennu*, 'sparkle' (*Welsh*). It was the name of a sixth-century saint, preserved in the Welsh name of Priestholm Island, Ynys Seiriol.

Selby a place name and surname, meaning 'place by the willow trees' (*Old English*), used as a masculine first name.

Selden a masculine first name meaning 'from the valley of the willow tree' (*Old English*).

Selena a feminine variant form of Selina.

Selig a masculine first name meaning 'blessed, happy one' (*Yiddish*). A variant form is Zelig.

Selina a feminine first name meaning 'heavenly' (*Greek*). A variant form is Selena. A diminutive form is Lina.

Selma feminine form of Anselm.

Selwyn or **Selwin** a Welsh masculine form of Julian. *See* Sulien.

Semele a feminine first name meaning 'single' (*Greek*). In Greek mythology Semele was the daughter of King Cadmus of Thebes who was tricked by Hera into persuading Zeus, Hera's husband and Semele's lover, to attend her with the same majesty as he approached Hera. When he did, accompanied by lightning and thunder, Semele was instantly consumed by fire but Zeus managed to save their son, Dionysus.

Sencha (pronounced *senn-ha*) an Irish Gaelic masculine first name meaning 'historian'. The *seanachaidh* was the historian and keeper of the traditions of the *tuath* or clan.

Senga (1) a feminine first name meaning 'slender' (*Gaelic*). (2) backward spelling of Agnes.

Senior a surname, meaning 'lord' (*Old French*), used as a masculine first name. A variant form is Seigneur.

Seóbhrach (pronounced *sho-rach*) a Scottish feminine first name from the Gaelic *seóbhrach*, meaning 'primrose'.

Seonag (pronounced *shon-ak*) the Scottish Gaelic feminine form of JOAN.

Seonaid (pronounced *sho-na*) a Scottish Gaelic form of JANET. The anglicised version Shona is often found. *See also* SINEAD.

Seóras a Scottish Gaelic masculine form of GEORGE.

Seosamh (pronounced *sho-sa*) the Irish and Scottish Gaelic form of JOSEPH.

Septima feminine form of SEPTIMUS.

Septimus a masculine first name meaning 'seventh' (*Latin*).

Seraphina or **Serafina** a feminine first name meaning 'of the seraphim, of burning faith' (*Hebrew*).

Serena a feminine first name meaning 'calm, peaceful' (*Latin*).

Serge the French masculine form of SERGIUS.

Sergei the Russian masculine form of SERGIUS.

Sergio the Italian masculine form of SERGIUS.

Sergius a masculine first name, from that of a Roman family, of Etruscan origin and unknown meaning. It was the name adopted by several popes, including St Sergius I (639–701) who came into conflict with Emperor Justinian.

Sesto the Italian masculine form of SEXTUS.

Sétanta an Irish Gaelic masculine first name and the original name of CU-CHULAINN.

Seth a masculine first name meaning 'appointed' (*Hebrew*). In the Old Testament Seth was a third son of Adam and Eve sent to replace the murdered ABEL.

Seton a masculine variant form of SEATON.

Seumas (pronounced *shay-mas*) an Irish Gaelic masculine form of JAMES.

Sewald or **Sewall** or **Sewell** a surname, meaning 'sea powerful' (*Old English*), used as a masculine first name. A variant form is Siwald.

Sexton a surname, meaning 'sacristan' (*Old French*), used as a masculine first name.

Sextus a masculine first name meaning 'sixth' (*Latin*).

Seymour a surname, meaning 'from Saint-Maur in France' (*Old French*), used as a masculine first name.

Shalom a masculine first name meaning 'peace' (*Hebrew*).

Shamus an anglicized masculine form of SEAMUS.

Shane an anglicised masculine form of SEAN.

Shanel or **Shanelle** a feminine variant form of CHANEL.

Shanley a surname, meaning 'son of the hero' (*Irish Gaelic*), used as a masculine first name.

Shannon the Irish river name, perhaps related to Gaelic *sionn*, 'old', has found a new role as an increasingly popular feminine first name, not inaptly as it had its own goddess, named Sinann or Sionan.

Shari a feminine diminutive form of SHARON.

Sharon a Biblical place name mentioned in the Song of Solomon used as a feminine first name (*Hebrew*). Sharon Stone is an American film actress. A diminutive form is Shari.

Shaw a surname, meaning 'small wood or grove' (*Old English*), used as a masculine first name.

Shawn or **Shaun** an anglicised masculine form of SEAN.

Shea a surname, meaning 'stately, dauntless' (*Irish Gaelic*), used as a masculine first name.

Sheana an anglicised feminine form of SÍNE.

Sheba (1) a feminine diminutive form of BATHSHEBA. (2) or **Saba** the name of a former kingdom in the southwest Arabian Peninsula, mentioned in the Bible, used as a feminine first name.

Sheelagh a feminine variant form of SHEILA.

Sheelah (1) a feminine first name meaning 'petition' (*Hebrew*). (2) a feminine variant form of SHEILA.

Sheena an anglicised feminine form of SÍNE.

Sheffield a place name, meaning 'open land by the Sheaf river' (*Old English*), used as a masculine first name.

Sheila or **Shelagh** or **Sheela** an anglicised feminine form of Sile, the Irish and Scottish Gaelic form of CELIA. This name became highly popular in Australia, to the extent that all girls were 'Sheilas'.

Sheldon a surname, meaning 'heathery hill with a shed, flat-topped hill, or steep valley' (*Old English*), used as a masculine first name.

Shelley a surname, meaning 'clearing on a bank' (*Old English*), used as a feminine first name. Shelley Long is an American film actress best known for appearing in the TV sitcom *Cheers*.

Shepard a surname, meaning 'sheep herder, shepherd' (*Old English*), used as a masculine first name.

Sherborne or **Sherbourne** a surname, meaning 'clear stream' (*Old English*), used as a masculine first name.

Sheree or **Sheri** a feminine variant form of CHÉRIE.

Sheridan a surname, meaning 'seeking' (*Irish Gaelic*), used as a masculine first name. Sheridan Morley is an English writer and biographer.

Sherilyn a feminine first name, a combination of SHERRY and LYNN. Sherilyn Fenn is an American film actress

Sherlock a masculine first name meaning 'fair-haired' (*Old English*).

Sherman a surname, meaning 'shearman' (*Old English*), used as a masculine first name.

Sherrie or **Sherry** a feminine variant form of CHERIE.

Sherwin a surname, meaning 'loyal friend or fast-footed' (*Old English*), used as a masculine first name.

Sherwood a place name and surname, meaning 'shore wood' (*Old English*), used as a masculine first name.

Sheryl a feminine variant form of CHERYL.

Shirl a feminine diminutive form of SHIRLEY.

Shirley a surname and place name, meaning 'thin clearing', used as a feminine first name. Its popularity as a feminine name was established by Charlotte Brontë (1816–55) in her novel *Shirley*. A diminutive form is Shirl.

Sholto a masculine first name meaning 'sower, seed-bearing' (*Scottish Gaelic*).

Shona the anglicised feminine form of SEONAID.

Sian (pronounced *shan*) the Welsh feminine form of JANE. It is cognate with Gaelic SÍNE. Sian Phillips is a well-known Welsh actress.

Siarl (pronounced *sharl*) the Welsh masculine form of CHARLES.

Sib a feminine diminutive form of SIBYL.

Sibeal an Irish feminine form of SYBYL.

Sibyl or **Sibylla** a word meaning 'soothsayer' (*Greek*) used as a feminine first name. In Greek mythology they were certain women endowed by Apollo with the gift of prophecy. Their number is variously stated but is generally given as ten. Variant forms are Sybyl, Sybylla. A diminutive form is Sib.

Sid a masculine diminutive form of SIDNEY.

Siddall or **Siddell** a surname, meaning 'broad slope' (*Old English*), used as a masculine first name.

Sidney a surname, meaning 'wide island' (Old English), used as a masculine or feminine first name. A variant form is SYDNEY. A diminutive form is Sid.

Sidonia or **Sidonie** or **Sydony** a feminine first name meaning 'of Sidon' (*Latin*).

Siegfried a masculine first name meaning 'victory peace' (*Germanic*).

Siegmund the German masculine form of SIGMUND.

Siencyn the Welsh masculine form of English Jenkin, literally 'little JOHN'.

Sierra the word for a mountain range used as a feminine first name (*Spanish*).

Sig a masculine diminutive form of SIGMUND.

Sigismond the French masculine form of SIGMUND.

Sigismondo the Italian masculine form of SIGMUND.

Sigiswald a masculine first name meaning 'victorious ruler' (*Germanic*).

Sigmund a masculine first name meaning 'victory protection' (*Germanic*). A diminutive form is Sig.

Sigrid a feminine first name meaning 'fair and victorious' (*Old Norse*). A diminutive form is Siri.

Sigurd a masculine first name meaning 'victorious guardian' (*Old Norse*).

Silas a shortened masculine form of SILVANUS. In the New Testament Silas was an early Christian missionary and prophet and a companion of PAUL on his journeys.

Sile the Gaelic feminine form of CELIA, CECILY, often rendered in English as SHEILA, SHELAGH, etc.

Sileas (pronounced *shee-luss*) the Scottish Gaelic feminine form of JULIA.

Silvain a French masculine form of SILVANUS.

Silvana feminine form of SILVANO.

Silvano the Italian masculine form of SILVANUS.

Silvanus a masculine first name meaning 'of a wood' (*Latin*). In Roman mythology Silvanus was a god of the fields and forests, the Roman counterpart of the Greek Pan. A variant form is SYLVANUS.

Silvester a masculine first name meaning 'of a wood' (*Latin*). A variant form is SYLVESTER. A diminutive form is Sly.

Silvestre a French and Spanish masculine form of SILVESTER.

Silvestro an Italian masculine form of SILVESTER.

Silvia a feminine first name meaning 'of a wood' (*Latin*). William Shakespeare (1654–1616) used the name for the beloved of Valentine in *The Two Gentlemen of Verona*. A variant form is SYLVIA.

Silvie the French feminine form of SILVIA.

Silvio the Italian and Spanish masculine forms of SILVANUS.

Sim (1) a masculine diminutive form of SIMON, SIMEON. (2) a feminine diminutive form of SIMONE.

Sím (pronounced *sheem*) a Scottish Gaelic form of SIMON, virtually a hereditary name among chiefs of the Clan Fraser, who are known as Mac-Sími.

Simeon a masculine variant form of SIMON. In the Old Testament Simeon was the second son of JACOB and LEAH from whom one of the twelve tribes of Israel was descended. In the New Testament Simeon was a Jew who recognised Jesus as the Messiah.

Simmy a masculine diminutive form of SIMON.

Simon a masculine first name meaning 'hearing with acceptance' (*Hebrew*). In the New Testament Simon was the name of two of the apostles of Jesus: the original name of Peter and Simon the Zealot. Simon was also the name of the man in whose house Mary Magdalene anointed Jesus' feet. A variant form is SIMEON, Symeon. Diminutive forms are Sim, Simmy.

Simona feminine form of SIMON. A diminutive form is Sim.

Simone the French feminine form of SIMONA.

Simwnt the Welsh masculine form of SIMON.

Sinann *see* SHANNON.

Sinclair a surname, meaning 'from St Clair in France' (*Old French*), used as a masculine first name. A variant form is St Clair. Sinclair Lewis (1885–1951) was an American writer.

Síne (pronounced *sheena*) an Irish Gaelic feminine form of JANE or JEAN. An anglicised form is found in Sheena and Sheana.

Sinead (pronounced *shin-aid*) the Irish Gaelic feminine form of JANET. Sinead Cusack, the actress, and Sinead O'Connor, the singer, have kept the name prominent.

Siobhán (pronounced *shiv-awn*) the Irish Gaelic feminine form of JOAN, from Old French Jehane. In the latter form it was introduced to Ireland by the Normans in the twelfth century. The actress Siobhán McKenna (1923–86) helped to establish the name in recent times.

Sion the Welsh masculine form of JOHN. The diminutive is Sionyn.

Sionan *see* SHANNON.

Sioned a Welsh feminine form of JANET.

Sionym the Welsh masculine diminutive form of SION.

Sior the Welsh masculine form of GEORGE.

Siri a feminine diminutive form of SIGRID.

Sis a feminine diminutive form of SISLEY.

Sisley a feminine variant form of CECILY. Diminutive forms are Sis, Sissie, Sissy.

Sissie or **Sissy** a feminine diminutive form of SISLEY.

Siwald a masculine variant form of SEWALD.

Skelton a surname, meaning 'farmstead on a hill' (*Old English*), used as first name.

Skerry a masculine first name meaning 'sea rock' (*Old Norse*).

Skip a masculine diminutive form of SKIPPER.

Skipper a nickname and surname, meaning 'jumping' (*Middle English*) or 'ship's captain' (*Dutch*), used as a masculine first name. A diminutive form is Skip.

Skipton a place name and surname, meaning 'sheep farm' (*Old English*), used as a masculine first name.

Slade a surname, meaning 'valley' (*Old English*), used as a masculine first name.

Sly a masculine diminutive form of SILVESTER, SYLVESTER.

Smith a surname, meaning 'blacksmith' (*Old English*), used as a masculine first name.

Snowden or **Snowdon** a surname, meaning 'snowy hill' (*Old English*), used as a masculine first name.

Sofie the French feminine form of SOPHIE.

Sol (1) a masculine first name meaning 'the sun' (*Latin*). In Roman mythology Sol is the god of the sun, the counterpart of the Greek Helios. (2) a masculine diminutive form of SOLOMON.

Soliman an Arabic masculine form of SOLOMON.

Solly a masculine diminutive form of SOLOMON.

Solomon a masculine first name meaning 'peaceable' (*Hebrew*). In the Old Testament Solomon was the son of David and Bathsheba who succeeded his father as king of Israel. He built the temple at Jerusalem and was reputed to be very wise. Arabic forms are Sulayman or Suleiman, Soliman or Solyman. Diminutive forms are Sol, Solly.

Solveig a feminine first name meaning 'house strong' (*Old Norse*).

Solyman an Arabic masculine form of SOLOMON.

Somerled a masculine first name the source of which is *sumar-lioi*, 'summer warrior' (Old Norse), referring to a Viking raider. Its modern Gaelic form is SOMHAIRLE. Somerled, Lord of Argyll (died 1164) was the ancestor of the Lords of the Isles.

Somerset a place name, meaning 'settlers around the summer farmstead' (*Old English*), used as a masculine first name.

Somerton a place name, meaning 'summer farmstead' (*Old English*), used as a masculine first name.

Somhairle a modern Scottish Gaelic masculine form of SOMERLED. It is anglicised as SORLEY and sometimes mistakenly as Samuel.

Somhairlidh (pronounced *sorr-lee*) the Old Scottish Gaelic masculine form of SOMERLED.

Sonya or **Sonia** a Russian feminine diminutive form of SOPHIA.

Sophia a feminine first name meaning 'wisdom' (*Greek*). Diminutive forms are Sophie, Sophy.

Sophie or **Sophy** feminine diminutive forms of SOPHIA, now used independently.

Sophronia a feminine first name meaning 'of a sound mind' (*Greek*).

Sorcha (pronounced *sorr-ha*) a feminine first name meaning 'bright, radiant' (*Irish/Scottish Gaelic*).

Sorley an anglicised masculine form of SOMHAIRLE. Sorley Maclean (1911–96) was a great Gaelic poet of the twentieth century.

Sorrel a masculine first name meaning 'sour' (*Germanic*), the name of a salad plant used as a masculine or feminine first name.

Spencer a surname, meaning 'steward or dispenser' (*Old French*), used as a masculine first name. Spencer Tracy (1900–1967) was an eminent American film actor.

Spring (1) a feminine first name meaning 'desire' (*Sanskrit*). (2) the name of the season between winter and summer used as a feminine first name.

Squire a surname, meaning 'shield bearer' (*Old French*), used as a masculine first name.

Stacey (1) a masculine diminutive form of EUSTACE, now used independently. Stacy is a variant form. (2) or **Stacie,** feminine diminutive forms of EUSTACIA, ANASTASIA, now used independently.

Stacie a feminine variant form of STACEY.

Stacy a masculine variant form of Stacey. Stacy Keach is an American film actor.

Stafford a surname, meaning 'ford by a landing place' (*Old English*), used as a masculine first name.

Stamford a masculine variant form of STANFORD.

Standish a surname, meaning 'stony pasture' (*Old English*), used as a masculine first name.

Stanford a surname, meaning 'stone ford' (*Old English*), used as a masculine first name. A variant form is Stamford.

Stanhope a surname, meaning 'stony hollow' (*Old English*), used as a masculine first name.

Stanislas or **Stanislaus** a masculine first name meaning 'government and glory' (*Slavonic*).

Stanley a surname and place name meaning 'stony field' (*Old English*), used as a masculine first name.

Stanton a surname, meaning 'stony farmstead' (*Old English*), used as first name.

Star or **Starr** an English feminine form of STELLA.

Stasia a feminine diminutive form of ANASTASIA.

Stefan a German masculine form of STEPHEN.

Stefano the Italian masculine form of STEPHEN.

Steffan the Welsh masculine form of STEPHEN.

Steffi or **Steffie** feminine diminutive forms of STEPHANIE.

Stella a feminine first name meaning 'star' (*Latin*).

Stephan a German masculine form of STEPHEN.

Stephanie feminine form of STEPHEN. A diminutive form is Stevie.

Stephen a masculine first name meaning 'crown' (*Greek*). In the New Testament Stephen was the first Christian martyr. Stephen was also the name adopted by several popes. Stephen Fry is an English comedian, writer and actor. A variant form is STEVEN. Diminutive forms are Steve, Stevie.

Sterling a surname, meaning 'little star' (*Old English*), used as a masculine first name. A variant form is Stirling.

Steuart a masculine variant form of STEWART.

Steve a masculine diminutive form of STEPHEN. Steve Martin is an American comedian and film actor.

Steven a masculine variant form of Stephen. Steven Spielberg is an American film director and producer whose films include *Jaws* and *Schindler's List*.

Stevie a feminine diminutive form of STEPHANIE, STEPHEN. Stevie Smith (1902–71) was an important English poet.

Stewart the surname, meaning 'steward', from *stig-ward*, 'housekeeper' (*Old English*), used as a masculine first name. The name is wholly identified with Scotland through its adoption as a surname by the High Stewards of the kingdom. In the fourteenth century the Stewarts became the royal house. The French form Stuart has also been in use since the sixteenth century, and both forms are used as first names. A variant form is Steuart.

Stirling (1) a masculine variant form of STERLING. (2) a place name, meaning 'enclosed land by the stream' (*Scottish Gaelic*), used as a masculine first name. Stirling Moss is an English racing driver.

St John (pronounced *sinjon*) a masculine first name meaning 'Saint John'.

Stockland a surname, meaning 'land of a religious house' (*Old English*), used as a masculine first name.

Stockley a surname, meaning 'cleared meadow of a religious house' (*Old English*), used as a masculine first name.

Stockton a place name and surname, meaning 'outlying farmstead' (*Old English*), used as a masculine first name.

Stoddard a surname, meaning 'horse keeper' (*Old English*), used as a masculine first name.

Stoke a place name and surname, meaning 'outlying farmstead' (*Old English*), used as a masculine first name.

Storm the word for a meteorological condition of violent winds and rain, hail or snow used as a masculine or feminine first name. Storm Jameson (1891–1986) was an English writer.

Stowe a surname, meaning 'holy place' (*Old English*), used as a masculine first name.

Strachan or **Strahan** a surname, meaning 'little valley' (*Scots Gaelic*), used as a masculine first name.

Stratford a place name, meaning 'ford on a Roman road' (*Old English*), used as a masculine first name.

Struan a territorial name from Perthshire, meaning 'streams', from *sruthan* (*Scottish Gaelic*), used as a masculine first name. It is associated with the Clan Robertson, of the same locality.

Stuart the French masculine form of STEWART.

Sue or **Sukey** or **Sukie** feminine diminutive forms of SUSAN.

Sulayman an Arabic masculine form of SOLOMON.

Sulien a Welsh masculine first name meaning 'sun-born'. This name is sometimes confused with Selwyn, 'Julian', and its Breton form Sulian.

Suleiman an Arabic masculine form of SOLOMON.

Sullivan a surname, meaning 'black-eyed' (*Irish Gaelic*), used as a masculine first name.

Summer a feminine first name meaning 'season' (*Sanskrit*), the name of the season between spring and autumn used as a personal name.

Sumner a surname, meaning 'one who summons' (*Old French*), used as a masculine first name.

Susan the English feminine form of SUSANNA. Susan Sarandon is an American film actress. Diminutive forms are Sue, Sukey, Sukie, Susie, Susy.

Susanna or **Susannah** a feminine first name meaning 'lily' (*Hebrew*). In the Old Testament Susanna was a young Jewish woman saved from death by Daniel. In the New Testament Susanna was one of the women who cared for Jesus and his apostles in Galilee. A variant form is SU-ZANNA.

Susanne a German feminine form of SUSANNA.

Susie or **Susy** feminine diminutive forms of SUSAN.

Sutherland a place name and surname, meaning 'southern land' (*Old Norse*), used as a masculine first name.

Sutton a place name and surname, meaning 'southern farmstead' (*Old English*), used as a masculine first name.

Suzanna a feminine variant form of SUSANNA.

Suzanne a French and German feminine form of SUSAN.

Sven a masculine first name meaning 'lad' (*Old Norse*).

Syb a feminine diminutive form of SYBYL.

Sybille the French feminine form of SYBYL.

Sybyl or **Sybilla** feminine variant forms of SIBYL, SIBYLLA. A diminutive form is Syb.

Sydney a masculine variant form of SIDNEY. Sydney Pollack is an American film director who also acts.

Sylvain a French masculine form of SILVANUS.

Sylvanus a masculine variant form of SILVANUS.

Sylvester a masculine variant form of SILVESTER. Sylvester was the name adopted by several popes, including Sylvester II (*c.*940–1003) who was the first French pope (999–1003). Sylvester Stallone is an American film actor. A diminutive form is Sly.

Sylvia a feminine variant form of Silvia.

Sylvie the French feminine form of Silvia.

Symeon a masculine variant form of Simon. In the New Testament Symeon was (1) an ancestor of Mary, mother of Jesus, and (2) one of the Antioch congregation who chose Paul and Barnabus for missionary work.

T

Tab or **Tabby** feminine diminutive forms of TABITHA.

Tabitha a feminine first name meaning 'gazelle' (*Aramaic*). Diminutive forms are Tab, Tabby.

Tad a masculine diminutive form of THADDEUS, also used independently.

Taddeo the Italian masculine form of THADDEUS.

Tadhg (pronounced *taig*) a masculine first name meaning 'poet', 'bard' (*Irish Gaelic*). It is a frequent name in Old Irish sources, and a tribute to the esteem in which poets were held. Anglicised versions include Thady, Teague.

Taffy Welsh masculine form of DAVID (*Celtic*).

Taggart a surname, meaning 'priest' (*Scots Gaelic*), used as a masculine first name.

Tait a surname, meaning 'cheerful' (*Old Norse*), used as a masculine first name. Variant forms are Tate, Teyte.

Talbot a surname, meaning 'command of the valley' (*Germanic*), used as a masculine first name.

Taliesin (pronounced *tal-ee-sinn*) a masculine first name meaning 'radiant brow' (*Welsh*). This was the name of one of the earliest of the great Old Welsh poets, said to have lived in the kingdom of Strathclyde in the sixth century.

Talitha a feminine first name meaning 'maiden' (*Aramaic*).

Tallulah a place name, meaning 'spring water' (*North American Indian*), used as a feminine first name.

Talorc a masculine variant form of TALORCAN.

Talorcan a masculine first name and that of a Pictish king who defeated the Dalriada Scots in AD 736. It is preserved in the place name Kiltarlity. Variant forms are Talorgan and Talorc or Talorg.

Talorg a masculine variant form of TALORCAN.

Talorgan a masculine variant form of TALORCAN.

Tam a masculine diminutive form of THOMAS (*Scots*).

Tamar a feminine first name meaning 'palm tree' (*Hebrew*). In the Old Testament Tamar was (1) a sister of Absalom who married two of Judah's sons and then Judah himself, and (2) a daughter of Absalom. Diminutive forms are Tammie, Tammy.

Tamara the Russian feminine form of TAMAR. Tamara Karsavina is a Russian ballerina who moved to the United States.

Tammas a Scottish masculine form of THOMAS. The diminutive form is Tam. A further pet form is Tammy, although this has also become a girls' name in its own right, from being an abbreviation of Tamsin or Tamar.

Tammie or **Tammy** (1) a feminine diminutive form of TAMAR, TAMSIN now used as a first name in its own right. (2) a masculine diminutive form of TAMMAS.

Tamsin a Cornish feminine contraction of THOMASINA, now used independently. A diminutive form is Tammie.

Tancred a masculine first name meaning 'thought strong' (*Germanic*). Tancred (died 1112) was a Norman soldier and one of the leaders of the First Crusade who took part in the capture of Jerusalem.

Tancredi or **Tancredo** Italian masculine forms of TANCRED.

Tania or **Tanya** feminine diminutive forms of TATIANA, TITANIA, now used independently.

Tanisha a feminine first name meaning 'born on Monday' (*Hausa*).

Tansy a feminine first name meaning 'immortal' (*Greek*), the name of a medicinal plant bearing yellow flowers used as a feminine first name.

Tara the anglicised form of Temair, the name of the ancient capital of Ireland, used as a feminine first name. It may mean 'mound' and be related to Irish Gaelic *torr*, 'hill', 'tower'.

Tariq a masculine first name meaning 'night star' (*Arabic*).

Tarquin a masculine first name from the Roman family name Tarquinius.

Tate a masculine variant form of TAIT.

Tatiana feminine form of a Roman family name of unknown meaning (*Latin*). Diminutive forms are Tania, Tanya.

Taylor a surname, meaning 'tailor' (*Old French*), used as a masculine first name.

Teague an anglicised masculine form of Irish TADHG.

Tearlach (pronounced *char-lach*) the Scottish Gaelic form of CHARLES.

Tebaldo an Italian masculine form of THEOBALD.

Ted or **Teddie** or **Teddy** masculine diminutive forms of EDWARD, THEODORE, THEODORIC.

Teenie a feminine diminutive form of CHRISTINE.

Tegwen or **Tegan** a feminine first name meaning 'beautiful, fair' (*Welsh*), a feminine version of Tegyn, the name of an early Welsh saint.

Tegyn *see* TEGWEN.

Teilo a masculine first name and that of a sixth-century saint, preserved in Llandeilo and many other places.

Tel a masculine diminutive form of TERENCE.

Teleri a Welsh feminine first name from the River Tyleri in Monmouth.

Temair *see* TARA.

Tempest the word for a violent storm used as a feminine first name.

Tennison or **Tennyson** masculine variant forms of DENISON.

Teobaldo an Italian and Spanish masculine form of THEOBALD.

Teodora an Italian and Spanish feminine form of THEODORA.

Teodorico an Italian masculine form of THEODORIC.

Teodoro an Italian and Spanish masculine form of THEODORE.

Teodosia an Italian feminine form of THEODOSIA.

Terence a masculine first name, from that of a Roman family name of unknown origin (*Latin*). Variant forms are Terrance, Terrence. Diminutive forms are Tel, Terry.

Terencio a Spanish masculine form of TERENCE.

Teresa the Italian and Spanish feminine forms of THERESA. St Teresa of Avila (1515–82) was a Spanish ascetic nun who reformed the Carmelite order. Her works include an autobiography, *The Way to Perfection*. In 1970 she was proclaimed a Doctor of the Roman Catholic Church.

Terese a feminine variant form of THERESA.

Teri a feminine diminutive form of THERESA.

Terrance or **Terrence** masculine variant forms of TERENCE.

Terri a feminine diminutive form of TERESA, THERESA, now used independently.

Terris or **Terriss** a surname, meaning 'son of TERENCE', used as a masculine first name.

Terry (1) a feminine diminutive form of TERESA. (2) a masculine diminutive form of TERENCE.

Tertius a masculine first name meaning 'third' (*Latin*).

Tess or **Tessa** or **Tessie** feminine diminutive forms of Esther, Teresa, Theresa. The English novelist and poet Thomas Hardy (1840–1928) used the form Tess for the eponymous heroine of his novel *Tess of the d'Urbervilles* (1891).

Tewdwr a Welsh masculine first name, anglicised as Tudor, and a royal name long associated with Anglesey.

Teyte a masculine variant form of Tait.

Thad a masculine diminutive form of Thaddeus.

Thaddeus a masculine first name meaning 'gift of God' (*Greek-Aramaic*). In the New Testament Thaddeus was one of the apostles of Jesus. Diminutive forms are Tad, Thad, Thaddy.

Thaddy a masculine diminutive form of Thaddeus.

Thady an anglicised masculine form of Irish Tadhg.

Thaine a surname, meaning 'holder of land in return for military service' (*Old English*), used as a masculine first name. A variant form is Thane.

Thalia a feminine first name meaning 'flourishing blossom' (*Greek*). In Greek mythology Thalia was one of the muses, the goddesses who presided over the sciences and arts.

Thane a masculine variant form of Thaine.

Thea a feminine diminutive form of Althea, Dorothea, now used independently.

Thecla a feminine first name meaning 'god glory' (*Greek*).

Theda a feminine diminutive form of Theodora, Theodosia.

Thelma feminine first name coined in the 19th century by the English writer Marie Corelli (1855–1924) for her novel *Thelma*, perhaps from 'wish' (*Greek*).

Theo a masculine or feminine diminutive form of Theobald, Theodore, Theodora.

Theobald a masculine first name meaning 'bold for the people' (*Germanic*). A diminutive form is Theo.

Theodor a Scandinavian and German masculine form of Theodore.

Theodora feminine form of Theodore. Diminutive forms are Dora, Theo.

Theodore a masculine first name meaning 'the gift of God' (*Greek*). St Theodore (died 690) was the Greek-born seventh archbishop of Canterbury and the first archbishop of the whole English church. Diminutive forms are Ted, Teddie, Teddy, Theo.

Theodoric or **Theodorick** a masculine first name meaning 'people powerful' (*Germanic*). Diminutive forms are Derek, Derrick, Dirk, Ted, Teddie, Teddy.

Theodorus a Dutch masculine form of THEODORE.

Theodosia a feminine first name meaning 'gift of God' (*Greek*).

Theodosius masculine form of THEODOSIA.

Theophila feminine form of THEOPHILUS.

Theophilus a masculine first name meaning 'lover of God' (*Greek*). In the New Testament Theophilus was the Christian to whom LUKE addressed his gospel and the Acts of Apostles.

Theresa a feminine first name meaning 'carrying ears of corn' (*Greek*). Theresa Russell is an American film actress. Diminutive forms are Teri, Terri, Terry, Tess, Tessa, Tessie, Tracey, Tracie, Tracy.

Thérèse the French feminine form of THERESA. St Thérèse of Lisieux (1873–97) was a French Carmelite nun noted for her spiritual autobiography, *The Story of a Soul*.

Theresia or **Therese** German feminine forms of THERESA.

Theron a masculine first name meaning 'hero' (*Greek*).

Thewlis a surname, meaning 'ill-mannered' (*Old English*), used as a masculine first name.

Thibaut a French masculine form of THEOBALD.

Thierry or **Thiery** a French masculine form of THEODORIC. Thiery d'Ardaine was one of the legendary twelve paladins who attended on Charlemagne.

Thirza a feminine first name meaning 'pleasantness' (*Hebrew*). Variant forms are Thyrza, Tirza.

Thom a masculine diminutive form of THOMAS.

Thomas a masculine first name meaning 'twin' (*Aramaic*). In the New Testament Thomas was one of the apostles of Jesus, 'Doubting Thomas', who could not accept Christ's resurrection until he touched the wounds. St Thomas Aquinas (1224–74) was one of the Doctors of the Roman Catholic Church. Diminutive forms are Tam, Thom, Tom, Tommy.

Thomasina or **Thomasine** feminine forms of THOMAS.

Thor a masculine first name meaning 'thunder' (*Old Norse*), in Norse mythology, the god of thunder. A variant form is Tor.

Thora feminine form of THOR.

Thorburn a surname, meaning 'Thor's warrior or bear' (*Old Norse*), used as a masculine first name.

Thordis a feminine variant form of TORDIS.

Thorketit *see* TORQUIL.

Thorndike or **Thorndyke** a surname, meaning 'thorny ditch' (*Old English*), used as a masculine first name.

Thorne a surname, meaning 'thorn tree or hawthorn' (*Old English*), used as a masculine first name.

Thorold a masculine first name meaning 'THOR rule' (*Old Norse*). A variant form is Torold.

Thorp or **Thorpe** a surname, meaning 'farm village' (*Old English*), used as a masculine first name.

Thorwald a masculine first name meaning 'ruled by THOR' (*Old Norse*). A variant form is Torvald.

Thurstan or **Thurston** a surname, meaning 'THOR stone' (*Old Norse*), used as a masculine first name. Thurstan (1078–1140) was an archbishop of York.

Thyrza a feminine variant form of THIRZA.

Tib or **Tibbie** Scottish feminine diminutive forms of ISABEL, ISABELLA.

Tibold a German masculine form of THEOBALD.

Tiebout a Dutch masculine form of THEOBALD.

Tiernan an anglicised masculine form of TIGHERNAC.

Tierney (1) a feminine first name meaning 'lordly', from Gaelic *tighearna*, 'lord' (*Irish Gaelic*). (2) the anglicised masculine form of TIGHERNAC.

Tiffany a feminine first name meaning 'the manifestation of God, the festival of Epiphany' (*Greek*).

Tighernac (pronounced *tyeer-nah*) a masculine first name meaning 'lordly', from *tighearna*, 'lord' (*Irish Gaelic*). This was the name of a celebrated annalist of events in the Celtic world. It is anglicised as TIERNEY or Tiernan.

Tilda or **Tilde** feminine diminutive forms of MATILDA.

Till a German masculine diminutive form of DIETRICH.

Tilly a feminine diminutive form of MATILDA.

Tim a masculine diminutive form of TIMON, TIMOTHY. Tim Robbins is an American film actor and director.

Timmie or **Timmy** masculine diminutive forms of TIMOTHY.

Timon a masculine first name meaning 'reward' (*Greek*). In the New Testament Timon was one of seven men chosen by the apostles of Jesus to look after the Christian congregation. William Shakespeare (1654–1616) used the name for the eponymous hero of his play *Timon of Athens*.

Timothea feminine form of TIMOTHY.

Timothy a masculine first name meaning 'honouring God' (*Greek*). In the New Testament Timothy was a disciple of PAUL who was the leader of the Christian community at Ephesus. Paul addressed two books to him. Diminutive forms are Tim, Timmie, Timmy.

Tina a feminine diminutive form of CHRISTINA, CHRISTINE, etc, also used independently.

Tiphaine a French feminine form of TIFFANY.

Tiree the name of an island, meaning 'land of corn', used as a feminine first name (*Scots Gaelic*).

Tirza or **Tirzah** feminine variant forms of THIRZA. In the Old Testament Tirzah was the name of (1) a daughter of a contemporary of Moses and Joshua, and (2) the name of a city in Samaria that was captured by Joshua.

Tita feminine form of TITUS. A diminutive form of MARTITA.

Titania a feminine first name meaning 'giant' (*Greek*). In medieval folklore Titania was the wife of Oberon and queen of fairies. William Shakespeare (1654–1616) used the two in his comedy *A Midsummer Night's Dream*. Diminutive forms are Tania, Tanya.

Titian an English masculine form of TITIANUS.

Titianus a Roman name derived from TITUS.

Tito the Italian and Spanish masculine form of TITUS. Tito Gobbi (1915–84) was a famous Italian operatic baritone.

Titus a masculine first name meaning 'protected' (*Latin*). In the New Testament Titus was a disciple of PAUL to whom Paul addressed a book. William Shakespeare (1654–1616) used the name for the eponymous hero of his tragedy *Titus Andronicus*.

Tiziano the Italian masculine form of TITIANUS.

Tobey feminine form of TOBY. A variant form is Tobi.

Tobi (1) a masculine variant form of TOBY. (2) a feminine variant form of TOBEY.

Tobias or **Tobiah** a masculine first name meaning 'Jehovah is good' (*Hebrew*). In the Old Testament Tobiah was an opponent of Nehemiah, the Persian king. In the Apocrypha, Tobias was the son of Tobit who was guided on a journey by Raphael. The Scottish playwright James Bridie (1888–1951) based his play *Tobias and the Angel* (1930) on the story. A diminutive form is TOBY.

Toby a masculine diminutive form of TOBIAS, now used independently. A variant form is Tobi.

Todd a surname, meaning 'fox' (*Old Norse*), used as a masculine first name.

Todhunter a surname, meaning 'foxhunter' (*Old Norse/Old English*), used as a masculine first name.

Toinette a feminine diminutive form of ANTOINETTE.

Tom a masculine diminutive form of THOMAS, now used independently. Tom Cruise and Tom Hanks are American film actors.

Tomas the Spanish masculine form of THOMAS.

Tomás a Spanish masculine form of THOMAS.

Tomasina or **Tomina** feminine forms of THOMAS.

Tomaso or **Tommaso** Italian masculine forms of THOMAS.

Tommie or **Tommy** masculine diminutive forms of THOMAS. Tommy Lee Jones is an American film actor.

Tomos a Welsh masculine form of THOMAS.

Toni feminine diminutive forms of ANNETTE, ANTOINETTE, ANTONIA, now used independently.

Tonia a feminine diminutive form of ANTONIA.

Tonie feminine diminutive forms of ANNETTE, ANTOINETTE, ANTONIA, now used independently.

Tony (1) a masculine diminutive form of ANTONY. (2) a feminine diminutive form of ANNETTE, ANTOINETTE, ANTONIA.

Topaz the white gemstone used as a feminine first name.

Tor a masculine variant form of THOR.

Torcuil the Scottish Gaelic form of TORQUIL.

Tordis a feminine first name meaning 'THOR's goddess' (*Old Norse*). A variant form is Thordis.

Torin a Scottish and Irish Gaelic masculine first name, probably from a Norse name incorporating that of Thor, god of thunder and war; 'thunder' in Gaelic is *torrunn*.

Tormod (pronounced *torr-o-mot*) a masculine first name meaning 'Norseman' (*Scottish Gaelic*).

Torold a masculine variant form of THOROLD.

Torquil a masculine first name from Lewis in the Western Isles, from Gaelic Torcuil, a form of Old Norse Thorketil, 'vessel of Thor'. Thor was the Norse god of thunder and warfare.

Torr a surname, meaning 'tower (*Old English*) or bull (*Old French*), used as a masculine first name.

Torvald a masculine variant form of THORWALD.

Tory a feminine diminutive form of VICTORIA.

Townsend or **Townshend** a surname, meaning 'end of the village' (*Old English*), used as a masculine first name.

Tracey (1) a masculine variant form of TRACY. (2) a feminine diminutive form of TERESA, THERESA.

Tracie a feminine diminutive form of TERESA, THERESA, now used independently.

Tracy (1) a surname, meaning 'Thracian' (*Old French*), used as a masculine first name. A variant form is Tracey. (2) a feminine diminutive form of TERESA or THERESA, now used independently.

Traherne a surname, meaning 'iron strength' (*Welsh*), used as a masculine first name.

Travers a surname, meaning 'crossing, crossroads' (*Old French*), used as a masculine first name. A variant form is Travis.

Traviata a feminine first name meaning 'lead astray' (*Italian*), the title of the eponymous opera by Giuseppe Verdi (1813–1901) used as a feminine first name.

Travis a masculine variant form of TRAVERS.

Treasa (pronounced *tres-sa*) an Irish Gaelic feminine form of Teresa, inspired particularly by St Teresa of Avila.

Trefor a place name, from *tref*, 'settlement', and *vawr*, 'big' (*Cornish/Welsh*), that has long been in use as a first name. It is anglicised as Trevor.

Tremaine or **Tremayne** a surname, meaning 'homestead on the rock' (*Cornish*), used as a masculine first name.

Trent a river name, meaning 'liable to flood' (*Celtic*), used as a masculine first name.

Trev a masculine diminutive form of TREVOR.

Trevelyan a surname, meaning 'mill farm' (*Cornish*), used as a masculine first name.

Trevor the anglicised masculine form of TREFOR. A diminutive form is Trev.

Tricia a feminine diminutive form of PATRICIA.

Trilby a feminine first name coined in the 19th century by George du Maurier (1834–96) for the heroine of his novel *Trilby*.

Trina the latter part of CATRIONA that is assuming an identity of its own as a Scottish and Irish feminine first name.

Trisha a feminine diminutive form of PATRICIA.

Tristram or **Tristam** or **Tristan** a variant form of TRYSTAN. The German composer Richard Wagner (1813–83) used the form Tristan for his opera *Tristan und Isolde*.

Trix or **Trixie** feminine diminutive forms of BEATRICE.

Troy (1) a surname, meaning 'of Troyes' (*Old French*), used as a masculine first name. (2) the name of the city in Asia Minor besieged by the Greeks used as a masculine first name. Troy Donahue is an American film actor who starred in many films in the 1960s.

Truda or **Trudie** or **Trudy** feminine diminutive forms of GERTRUDE.

True the adjective for the quality of being faithful and loyal used as a masculine first name.

Truelove a surname, meaning 'faithful sweetheart' (*Old English*), used as a masculine first name.

Trueman or **Truman** a surname, meaning 'faithful servant' (*Old English*), used as a masculine first name.

Trystan a Cornish and Welsh masculine first name that has been linked to *triste*, 'sad' (*French*), but this is unlikely. The tragic romance of the Cornish chief Trystan and ISEULT of Ireland was drawn into the fabric of the Arthurian legends. Variants of the name include Tristan, Tristram, Tristam.

Tudor (1) the anglicised Masculine form of TEWDWR. (2) a Welsh masculine form of THEODORE.

Tuesday a feminine first name meaning 'day of Mars', the name of the second day of the week used as a feminine first name (*Old English*). Tuesday Weld is an American film actor.

Tullio the Italian masculine form of TULLIUS.

Tullius a Roman family name of Etruscan origin and uncertain meaning used as a masculine first name.

Tully (1) a surname, meaning 'flood' (*Irish Gaelic*), used as a masculine first name. (2) an English form of TULLIUS.

Turner a surname, meaning 'worker on a lathe' (*Old French*), used as a masculine first name.

Turpin a surname, meaning 'THOR the Finn' (*Old Norse*), used as a masculine first name.

Twyford a surname, meaning 'double ford' (*Old English*), used as a masculine first name.

Ty a masculine diminutive form of TYBALT, TYLER, TYRONE, TYSON.

Tybalt a masculine variant form of THEOBALD. In *Romeo and Juliet* by William Shakespeare (1564–1616), Tybalt is a cousin of Juliet and enemy of Romeo, who kills him. A diminutive form is Ty.

Tye a surname, meaning 'enclosure' (*Old English*), used as a masculine first name.

Tyler a surname, meaning 'tile-maker' (*Old English*), used as a masculine first name. A diminutive form is Ty.

Tyrone a territorial name, from the ancient kingdom Tir Eógain, 'land of Eogan', still a county in Ireland, made popular as a first name in the twentieth century by the film star Tyrone Power and the drama producer Tyrone Guthrie. A diminutive form is Ty.

Tyson a surname, meaning 'firebrand' (*Old French*), used as a masculine first name. A diminutive form is Ty.

U

Uberto an Italian masculine form of HUBERT.

Uda feminine form of UDO.

Udall or **Udell** a surname, meaning 'yew-tree valley' (*Old English*), used as a masculine first name.

Udo a masculine first name meaning 'prosperous' (*Germanic*).

Ughes *see* UISDEAN.

Ugo or **Ugolino** or **Ugone** Italian masculine forms of HUGH.

Uilleam (pronounced *eel-yam*) the Scottish Gaelic masculine form of WILLIAM. *See* LIAM.

Uisdean (pronounced *oosh-tyan*) a Scottish Gaelic form of Ugues, Norman-French HUGH.

Ulises a Spanish masculine form of ULYSSES.

Ulisse an Italian masculine form of ULYSSES.

Ulmar or **Ulmer** a masculine first name meaning 'wolf' (*Old English*).

Ulric or **Ulrick** a masculine first name meaning 'wolf power' (*Old English*); the English form of ULRICH.

Ulrica an English feminine form of ULRIKE.

Ulrich a masculine first name meaning 'fortune and power' (*Germanic*).

Ulrike feminine form of ULRICH.

Ulysses the Roman form of the name of the Greek god Odysseus, whose name means 'wrathful' (*Greek*), used as a first name. He is the hero of Homer's *Odyssey* and a prominent character in the Iliad. He married PENELOPE and took part in the Trojan War. He was restored to Penelope at Ithaca after twenty years' wanderings. He appears in the play *Troilus and Cressida* by William Shakespeare (1564–1616), and the Irish-born author James Joyce (1882–1941) reincarnated him as Leopold Bloom in his novel *Ulysses* (1922). A diminutive form is LYSS.

Uma a feminine first name recorded by Robert Louis Stevenson (1850–94) in his story 'The Beach of Falesá'. Uma Thurman is an American film actor.

Umar a masculine variant form of OMAR.

Umberto the Italian masculine form of HUMBERT.

Una (1) an anglicised feminine form of OONAGH. (2) feminine form of 'one' (*Latin*) used by Edmund Spenser (*c*.1552–99) in *The Faerie Queene*.

Unity the quality of harmony or concord used as a feminine first name.

Unwin a surname, meaning 'not a friend' (*Old English*), used as a masculine first name.

Upton a surname, meaning 'upper farmstead' (*Old English*), used as a masculine first name.

Urania a feminine first name meaning 'heavenly' (*Greek*) and in Greek mythology the name of one of the muses.

Urbaine the French masculine form of URBAN.

Urban a masculine first name meaning 'town-dweller' (*Latin*). It was the name adopted by several popes.

Urbano the Italian masculine form of URBAN.

Uri a masculine first name meaning 'light' (*Hebrew*).

Uriah a masculine first name meaning 'fire of the Lord' (*Hebrew*). In the Old Testament Uriah was a Hittite soldier in King David's army and husband of Bathsheba. He was killed in battle on David's instructions so that David could marry Bathsheba. Charles Dickens (1812–70) used the name for the character of Uriah Heep, the ''umble' hypocrite, in his novel *David Copperfield* (1849–50).

Urian a masculine first name meaning 'a husbandman' (*Danish*).

Uriel a masculine first name meaning 'light of God' (*Hebrew*). In Judaism Uriel was one of the four chief angels in apocryphal writings.

Urien a Welsh masculine first name and that of a fifth-century king of the land of Rheged, in what is now southern Scotland. He was incorporated into the Arthurian legends, sometimes as the husband of the witch-queen MORGAN le Fay.

Ursula a feminine first name meaning 'she-bear' (*Latin*). St Ursula was a fourth-century virgin martyr. William Shakespeare (1654–1616) used the name for an attendant of Hero's in his comedy *Much Ado About Nothing*.

Ursule the French feminine form of URSULA.

Uther a masculine first name from *uthr*, 'terrible' (*Welsh*). Uther Pendragon, 'head leader', was the second husband of IGRAINE and the father of King ARTHUR.

Uzziah

Uzziah a masculine first name meaning 'Jehovah is strength' (*Hebrew*). In the Old Testament Uzziah was a king of Judah in whose reign Judah reached the height of its power.

Uzziel a masculine first name meaning 'God is strength' (*Hebrew*). In the Old Testament Uzziel was (1) a grandson of Levi and uncle of Moses and Aaron, and (2) a musician in the service of David.

V

Vachel a masculine first name meaning 'little calf' (*Old French*).

Vail a surname, meaning 'valley' (*Old English*), used as a masculine first name.

Val (1) a masculine diminutive form of VALENTINE. Val Kilmer is an American film actor. (2) a feminine diminutive form of VALENTINA, VALERIE.

Valborga a feminine first name meaning 'protecting ruler' (*Germanic*). Diminutive forms are Walburga, Walborga, Valburga.

Valburga a masculine diminutive form of VALBORGA.

Valda a feminine first name meaning 'flower', from a Cornish word cognate with Welsh *blodyn*, 'flower'.

Valdemar a masculine variant form of WALDEMAR.

Valdemaro an Italian masculine form of WALDEMAR.

Valentin a French, German and Scandinavian masculine form of VALENTINE.

Valentina feminine form of VALENTINE. A diminutive form is Val.

Valentine a masculine or feminine first name meaning 'strong; healthy; powerful' (*Latin*). St Valentine was a third-century Christian martyr whose name as become associated with the practice of sending gifts or cards to loved ones on 14 February, St Valentine's Day, a that seems to have been associated with the mating time of birds. William Shakespeare (1654–1616) used the name in two of his comedies: for a gentleman attending the duke in *Twelfth Night* and as one of the two gentlemen in *The Two Gentlemen of Verona*. A diminutive form is Val.

Valentino an Italian masculine form of VALENTINE.

Valeria the feminine form of VALERIO. William Shakespeare (1654–1616) used the name in his play *Coriolanus*.

Valerian masculine form of VALERIE.

Valeriano an Italian masculine form of VALERIAN.

Valerie a feminine first name meaning 'strong' (*Latin*). A diminutive form is Val.

Valerio an Italian masculine form of VALERIA.

Valéry a masculine first name meaning 'foreign power' (*Germanic*).

Valmai a feminine first name meaning perhaps 'mayflower', from *blodyn*, 'flower', and *mai*, 'May' (*Cornish/Welsh*).

Van a masculine first name meaning 'from, of', a prefix in Dutch surnames now used independently as an English-language first name.

Vance a masculine first name meaning 'young' (*Old English*).

Vanessa a feminine first name invented by Jonathan Swift (1667–1745) for his friend Esther Vanhomrigh, created from the prefix of her surname plus the suffix -essa. A diminutive form is Nessa.

Vasili or **Vassily** Russian masculine forms of BASIL.

Vaughan or **Vaughn** a surname, meaning 'small one' (*Welsh*), used as a masculine first name.

Velvet the English name of a rich, soft cloth used as a feminine first name.

Venetia (pronounced *veneesha*) the Italian name of the region around Venice in northern Italy used as a feminine first name.

Venus the name of the Roman goddess of love, especially sensual love, the equivalent of the Greek Aphrodite. William Shakespeare (1654–1616) wrote a poem, *Venus and Adonis* (1593), that tells of the passion of Venus for the youthful Adonis and the killing of the latter by a wild boar.

Vera (1) a feminine first name meaning 'faith' (*Russian*). (2) a feminine first name meaning 'true' (*Latin*).

Vere a surname, meaning 'from Ver in France' (*Old French*), used as a masculine first name.

Vergil a masculine variant form of VIRGIL.

Verity a feminine first name meaning 'truth' (*Latin*).

Verne or **Verna** feminine diminutive forms of LAVERNE.

Vernon a surname, meaning 'alder tree' (*Old French*), used as a masculine first name.

Verona a feminine variant form of VERONICA.

Veronica a feminine first name meaning 'true image' (*Latin*). St Veronica was a woman of Jerusalem who gave Jesus her veil so that he could wipe the sweat from his brown on the way to Calvary. The veil bore a miraculous imprint of his face. A variant form is Verona. Diminutive forms are Ronnie, Ronny.

Veronika a Scandinavian feminine form of VERONICA.

Veronike a German feminine form of VERONICA.

Véronique a French feminine form of VERONICA.

Veryan *see* BURYAN.

Vesta a feminine first name of uncertain meaning. In Roman mythology, Vesta was the goddess of the hearth, the equivalent of the Greek Hestia. Her public sanctuary was in the Forum in Rome where a sacred fire was kept constantly burning by the Vestal Virgins, her priestesses.

Vi a feminine diminutive form of VIOLA, VIOLET.

Vic a masculine diminutive form of VICTOR.

Vicente a Spanish masculine form of VINCENT.

Vicki or **Vickie** or **Vicky** a feminine diminutive form of VICTORIA, now used independently.

Victoire a French feminine form of VICTORIA.

Victor a masculine first name meaning 'conqueror' (*Latin*). The name was adopted by several popes. A diminutive form is Vic.

Victoria a feminine first name meaning 'victory' (*Latin*). Queen Victoria (1819–1901) was queen of the United Kingdom (1837–1901) in an expansionist period and lent her name to describe the period. Diminutive forms are Tory, Vickie, Vicky, Vita.

Vida a feminine diminutive form of DAVIDA.

Vidal a Spanish masculine form of *vitalis* (*Latin*), 'living, vital'. Vidal Sassoon is an English hairdresser who established a chain of shops.

Vilhelm a Swedish masculine form of WILLIAM.

Vilhelmina a Swedish feminine form of WILHELMINA.

Vilma a feminine diminutive form of VILHELMINA.

Vina a feminine diminutive form of DAVINA, ALVINA.

Vince a masculine diminutive form of VINCENT.

Vincent a masculine first name meaning 'conquering; victorious' (*Latin*). St Vincent de Paul (*c*.1581–1660) was a French priest who founded two charitable orders. Diminutive forms are Vince, Vinnie, Vinny.

Vincente an Italian masculine form of VINCENT.

Vincentia a feminine form of VINCENT.

Vincentio an Italian masculine form of VINCENT. William Shakespeare (1654–1616) used the name for characters in two of his plays, *The Taming of the Shrew* and *Measure for Measure*.

Vincenz a German masculine form of VINCENT.

Vinnie or **Vinny** a masculine diminutive form of VINCENT.

Vinson a surname form of VINCENT used as a masculine first name.

Viola or **Violet** a feminine first name meaning 'a violet' (*Latin*). William Shakespeare (1654–1616) used the form Viola for the heroine of his comedy *Twelfth Night* who is required to pretend to be a boy. A diminutive form is Vi.

Violetta the Italian feminine form of VIOLA, VIOLET.

Virgil a masculine first name meaning 'staff bearer' (*Latin*), the name of the Roman poet of the first century BC. A variant form is Vergil.

Virgilia a feminine form of VIRGILIO. William Shakespeare (1654–1616) used the name for the wife of Coriolanus in his eponymous play.

Virgilio the Italian and Spanish masculine form of VIRGIL.

Virginia a feminine first name meaning 'virginal' (*Latin*). Virginia Woolf (1882–1941) was a noted English novelist, critic and essayist whose works include the novels *To the Lighthouse* (1927) and *Orlando* (1928). A diminutive form is Ginnie.

Virginie a Dutch and French feminine form of VIRGINIA.

Vita (1) feminine form of VITO. (2) a feminine diminutive form of VICTORIA. Vita Sackville-West (1892–1962) was an English writer and noted gardener.

Vitale an Italian masculine form of *vitalis* (*Latin*), 'living, vital'.

Vito the Italian masculine form of VITUS.

Vitore an Italian masculine form of VICTOR.

Vitoria a Spanish feminine form of VICTORIA.

Vitorio the Spanish masculine form of VICTOR.

Vittorio an Italian masculine form of VICTOR.

Vitus a masculine first name meaning 'life' (*Latin*).

Viv a feminine diminutive form of VIVIEN.

Vivian or **Vyvian** a masculine first name meaning 'full of life' from *vivere*, 'to live' (*Latin*). A variant form is Vyvian. *See also* BÉIBHINN.

Vivien or **Vivienne** feminine form of VIVIAN. A diminutive form is Viv.

Vladimir a masculine first name meaning 'royally famous', 'a renowned monarch' (*Slavic*). St Vladimir (*c*.956–1015) was a Viking pagan who became the ruler of Kiev in Russia. He converted to Christianity, married Anna, sister of the Byzantine Emperor Basil II, and became the first Christian ruler of Russia.

Vladislav a masculine first name meaning 'great ruler' (*Slavonic*).

Vyvian a masculine variant form of VIVIAN.

W

Wade a surname, meaning 'to go, or at the ford' (*Old English*), used as a masculine first name.

Wadsworth a surname, meaning 'WADE's homestead' (*Old English*), used as a masculine first name. A variant form is Wordsworth.

Wainwright a surname, meaning 'maker of carts' (*Old English*), used as a masculine first name.

Wake a surname, meaning 'alert, watchful' (*Old English*), used as a masculine first name.

Walburga or **Walborga** feminine diminutive forms of VALBORGA.

Waldemar a masculine first name meaning 'noted ruler' (*Germanic*). A variant form is VALDEMAR.

Waldo a masculine first name meaning 'ruler' (*Germanic*).

Walker a surname, meaning 'a fuller' (*Old English*), used as a masculine first name.

Wallace or **Wallas** a masculine first name that is cognate with 'Welsh' and means an inhabitant of the originally Brythonic kingdom of Strathclyde, which existed up to the end of the tenth century. It was the surname of the great defender of Scotland's liberty in the thirteenth/fourteenth century Wars of Independence, William Wallace, it became a popular first name in the twentieth century. A variant form is WALLIS. The diminutive form is Wally.

Wallis a variant form of WALLACE, used as a masculine or feminine first name. Wallis Simpson (1896–1986) was an American divorcée for whom King Edward VIII (1894–1972) gave up the throne of the United Kingdom. A diminutive form is Wally.

Wally a masculine diminutive form of WALLACE, WALLAS, WALLIS.

Walt a masculine diminutive form of WALTER, WALTON.

Walter a masculine first name meaning 'ruler of army, people' (*Germanic*). Diminutive forms are Walt, Wat, Watty.

Walther a German masculine form of WALTER.

Walton a surname, meaning 'farmstead of the Britons' (*Old English*), used as a masculine first name. A diminutive form is Walt.

Wanda a feminine variant form of WENDA.

Ward a surname, meaning 'watchman, guard' (*Old English*), used as a masculine first name.

Warfield a surname, meaning 'field of the stream of the wrens' (*Old English*), used as a masculine first name.

Warne a surname, meaning 'alder wood' (*Cornish*), used as a masculine first name.

Warner a surname, meaning 'protecting army' (*Germanic*), used as a masculine first name.

Warren a surname, meaning 'wasteland' or 'game park' (*Old French*), used as a masculine first name. Warren Beatty is an American actor and husband of Annette Bening.

Warwick a place name and surname, meaning 'dwellings by the weir' (*Old English*), used as a masculine first name.

Washington a place name and surname, meaning 'Wassa's estate' (*Old English*), used as a masculine first name. Washington Irving (1783–1859) was an American writer whose stories include *The Legend of Sleepy Hollow* and *Rip van Winkle*.

Wat a masculine diminutive form of WALTER.

Watkin a masculine diminutive form of WALTER, literally 'little Walter'.

Watty a masculine diminutive form of WALTER.

Waverley a place name, meaning 'meadow or clearing by the swampy ground' (*Old English*), used as a masculine first name.

Wayne a surname, meaning 'a carter', used as a masculine first name.

Webb a surname, meaning 'weaver' (*Old English*), used as a masculine first name.

Webster a surname, meaning 'woman weaver' (*Old English*), used as a masculine first name.

Wellington a place name and surname, meaning 'Weola's farmstead' (*Old English*), used as a masculine first name.

Wenceslas or **Wenceslaus** a masculine first name meaning 'wreathed with glory' (*Slavonic*). St Wenceslas (*c*.907–929), famed in the Christmas carol, was a duke of Bohemia (*c*.925–929) who attempted to Christianise his people but was assassinated by his brother. Wenceslaus

(1361–1419) was king of Bohemia (1378–1419) and Holy Roman Emperor (1378–1400).

Wenda feminine form of WENDEL. A variant form is Wanda.

Wendel or **Wendell** a masculine first name meaning 'of the Wend people' (*Germanic*).

Wendy a feminine first name invented by Sir J. M. Barrie (1860–1937) for the main female character in his play *Peter Pan* (1904). It gained popularity quite quickly.

Wentworth a surname, meaning 'winter enclosure' (*Old English*), used as a masculine first name.

Werner a German masculine form of WARNER.

Wes a masculine diminutive form of WESLEY.

Wesley a surname, meaning 'west wood' (*Old English*), made famous by the Methodists John Wesley (1703–91) and Charles Wesley (1707–88), used as a masculine first name. Wesley Snipes is an American film actor. A diminutive form is Wes.

Whitaker a surname, meaning 'white acre' (*Old English*), used as a masculine first name. A variant form is Whittaker.

Whitman a surname, meaning 'white- or fair-haired' (*Old English*), used as a masculine first name.

Whitney a surname and place name, meaning 'white island or Witta's island' (*Old English*), used as a masculine or feminine first name. Whitney Houston is an American singer.

Whittaker a masculine variant form of WHITAKER.

Wilbert a masculine first name meaning 'well-born' (*Old English*).

Wilbur a masculine first name meaning 'wild boar' (*Old English*).

Wilf a masculine diminutive form of WILFRID.

Wilfrid or **Wilfred** a masculine first name meaning 'will peace' (*Germanic*). A diminutive form is Wilf.

Wilfrida or **Wilfreda** feminine form of WILFRID.

Wilhelm the German masculine form of WILLIAM. A diminutive form is Wim.

Wilhelmina or **Wilhelmine** feminine form of WILHELM. Diminutive forms are Elma, Minna, Minnie, Wilma.

Will a masculine diminutive form of WILLIAM.

Willa a feminine form of WILL, WILLIAM.

Willard a surname, meaning 'bold resolve' (*Old English*), used as a masculine first name. Willard White is a Jamaican-born opera singer.

Willemot a masculine first name meaning 'resolute in spirit' (*Germanic*).

William a masculine first name meaning 'resolute helmet' (*Germanic*). Diminutive forms are Bill, Will.

Williamina feminine form of WILLIAM.

Willie a masculine diminutive form of WILLIAM.

Willoughby a surname, meaning 'farm by the willows' (*Old Norse/Old English*), used as a masculine first name.

Willson a masculine variant form of WILSON.

Willy a masculine diminutive form of WILLIAM.

Wilma a feminine diminutive form of WILHELMINA; feminine form of WILLIAM.

Wilmer (1) a masculine first name meaning 'famous will or desire' (*Old English*). (2) a masculine form of WILMA.

Wilmot a diminutive surname form of WILLIAM used as a masculine first name.

Wilson a surname, meaning 'son of WILL' (*Old English*), used as a masculine first name. A variant form is Willson.

Wilton a place name and surname, meaning 'floodable place' (*Old English*), used as a masculine first name.

Wim a contraction of WILHELM.

Win a feminine diminutive form of WINIFRED.

Windham a masculine variant form of WYNDHAM.

Windsor a place name and surname, meaning 'slope with a windlass' (*Old English*), used as a masculine first name.

Winifred a feminine first name meaning 'joy and peace' (*Old English*). Diminutive forms are Freda, Win, Winnie, Wynn, Wynne.

Winnie a feminine diminutive form of WINIFRED.

Winona a place name, in Minnesota, USA, used as a first name. Winona Ryder is an American film actress.

Winslow a place name and surname, meaning 'Wine's burial mound' (*Old English*), used as a masculine first name.

Winston a place name and surname, meaning 'friend's place or farm' (*Old English*), used as a masculine first name.

Winter the name for the cold season of the year used as a masculine first name.

Winthrop a surname, meaning 'friend's farm village' (*Old English*), used as a masculine first name.

Winton a surname, meaning 'friend's farm' (*Old English*), used as a masculine first name.

Wolf or **Wolfe** a masculine first name meaning 'wolf' (*Old English*).

Wolfgang a masculine first name meaning 'bold wolf' (*Germanic*).

Wolfram a masculine first name meaning 'wolf raven' (*Germanic*).

Woodrow a surname, meaning 'row (of houses) in a wood' (*Old English*), used as a masculine first name. A diminutive form is WOODY.

Woodward a surname, meaning 'forest guardian' (*Old English*), used as a masculine first name.

Woody a masculine diminutive form of WOODROW, now used independently. Woody Guthrie (1912–67) was an American folksinger and songwriter. Woody Allen is the adopted name of the American actor, writer and film director.

Wordsworth a masculine variant form of WADSWORTH.

Worth a surname, meaning 'farmstead' (*Old English*), used as a masculine first name.

Wyman a surname, meaning 'battle protector' (*Old English*), used as a masculine first name.

Wyn a masculine first name from *gwyn*, 'white, pure' (*Welsh*). A variant form is Wynn.

Wyndham a surname, meaning 'homestead of WYMAN' (*Old English*), used as a masculine first name. A variant form is Windham.

Wynn or **Wynne** (1) a surname, meaning 'friend' (*Old English*), used as a masculine or feminine first name. (2) a masculine variant form of WYN. (3) a feminine diminutive form of WINIFRED.

X

Xanthe a feminine first name meaning 'yellow' (*Greek*).

Xavier a place name, meaning 'new house owner' (*Spanish/Basque*), used as a masculine first name.

Xaviera feminine form of XAVIER.

Xena or **Xene** or **Xenia** a feminine first name meaning 'hospitality' (*Greek*).

Xenos a masculine first name meaning 'stranger' (*Greek*).

Xerxes a masculine first name meaning 'royal' (*Persian*).

Y

Yahya the Arabic form of John. In the Koran Yahya is the counterpart of John the Baptist.

Yale a surname, meaning 'fertile upland' (*Welsh*), used as a masculine first name.

Yann the Breton masculine form of JOHN.

Yasmin or **Yasmine** feminine variant forms of JASMINE.

Yehuda a feminine variant form of JEHUDA.

Yehudi a masculine first name meaning 'a Jew' (*Hebrew*).

Ygraine and **Yguerne** feminine variant forms of IGRAINE.

Yolanda or **Yolande** a feminine variant form of VIOLA.

Yorath a Welsh masculine form of IORWETH, usually found as a surname.

York or **Yorke** a place name and surname, meaning 'estate of Eburos or of the yew trees' (*Celtic/Latin/Old English*), used as a masculine first name.

Yseult a feminine variant form of ISEULT.

Yunus the Arabic form of Jonah.

Yuri a Russian masculine form of GEORGE.

Yusuf the Arabic form of Joseph.

Yves a masculine first name meaning 'yew tree' (*French-Germanic*).

Yvette a feminine diminutive form of YVES.

Yvonne feminine form of YVES.

Z

Zabdiel a masculine first name meaning 'gift of God' (*Hebrew*).

Zabrina a feminine variant form of SABRINA.

Zaccheus a masculine first name meaning 'innocent, pure' (*Hebrew*). In the New Testament Zaccheus was a tax collector in Jericho met Jesus on his visit to Jericho and was his host.

Zach a masculine diminutive form of ZACHARY.

Zachary or **Zachariah** or **Zacharias** or **Zecheriah** a masculine first name meaning 'Jehovah has remembered' (*Hebrew*). In the New Testament Zachary was the father of St John the Baptist. St Zacharias (died 752) was a Greek-born pope (741–752). Diminutive forms are Zach, Zack, Zak.

Zack a masculine diminutive form of ZACHARY.

Zadok a masculine first name meaning 'righteous' (*Hebrew*). In the Old Testament Zadok was a priest who worked closely with King David. 'Zadok the Priest' was the first of four anthems composed by George Handel (1685–1759) for the coronation of George II (1727). It is still performed at British coronations.

Zak a masculine diminutive form of ZACHARY.

Zara a feminine first name meaning 'flower' (*Arabic*).

Zeb a masculine diminutive form of ZEBADIAH, ZEBEDEE, ZEBULON, ZEBULUN.

Zebadiah or **Zebedee** a masculine first name meaning 'gift of the Lord' (*Hebrew*). In the New Testament Zebedee was a fisherman on the Sea of Galilee and the father of James the Great and John, two of the apostles of Jesus.

Zebulon or **Zebulun** a masculine first name meaning 'elevation' (*Hebrew*). In the Old Testament Zebulun was the sixth son of Jacob and Leah and founder of one of the twelve tribes of Israel. Diminutive forms are Lonny, Zeb.

Zed a masculine diminutive form of ZEDEKIAH.

Zedekiah a masculine first name meaning 'justice of the Lord' (*Hebrew*). In the Old Testament Zedekiah was the last king of Judah whose reign ended with the deportation of the Jews to Babylon. A diminutive form is Zed.

Zeke a masculine diminutive form of EZEKIEL.

Zelda a feminine diminutive form of Grizelda also used independently. Zelda Sayre was the wife of the American writer F. Scott Fitzgerald.

Zelig a masculine variant form of SELIG.

Zelma a feminine variant form of SELMA.

Zenas a masculine first name meaning 'gift of Zeus' (*Greek*). In the New Testament Zenas was friend of Paul.

Zenobia a feminine first name meaning 'having life from Zeus' (*Greek*).

Zeph a masculine diminutive form of ZEPHANIAH.

Zephaniah a masculine first name meaning 'hid of the Lord' (*Hebrew*). In the Old Testament Zephaniah was a Hebrew prophet and author of the Book of Zephaniah. A diminutive form is Zeph.

Zinnia the name of a plant with brightly coloured flowers used as a feminine first name, named after the German botanist JG Zinn.

Zoë or **Zoe** a feminine first name meaning 'life' (*Greek*).

Using Numerology to Choose a Name

Introduction

We all know that a name can affect how you are perceived as a result of its socio-cultural connotations, but some people believe that the number that a name represents can crucially affect all aspects of one's life. This study of names (and birth dates) is known as numerology.

This section is a lighthearted inclusion to perhaps provide one more avenue of choice as you make your decision in a choice of baby name.

What is numerology?

Numerology is the name given to an ancient method of studying numbers that has been in use for thousands of years. It is used to give insight into people's personalities and their motivation in life. It is an ancient science that is used to analyse people's characters.

The most popular form of numerology in use today is based on the work of Pythagoras, the famous Greek mathematician and philosopher who lived during the sixth century BC. This book employs a system which is based on the work of Pythagoras.

It was Pythagoras's belief that numbers were the first of all things in nature. It was his belief that numbers were the basis of everything, in the natural, spiritual and scientific world. He believed that everything could be reduced to mathematical terms and that everything had a numerical value. Through studying the world in numerical form, he sought to achieve greater understanding of the world he lived in. Pythagoras, who believed that numbers created order and beauty, founded a school for students to follow his philosophy, and this was known as the Italic or Pythagorean School.

The Pythagoreans believed that numbers could represent religious and holy things, for example, one represented unity (and therefore God), two was duality (the Devil), and four was a sacred and holy number on which they could swear oaths. Numbers were also thought to represent the planets and elements: one represented the sun, two stood for the moon, five was fire, six stood for the earth and eight represented the air.

Pythagoras formulated the concept called the Music of the Spheres', based on the idea that all the planets in the universe formed a harmonious whole consisting of a musical chorus. He discovered that there was a relationship between sound and numbers, and developed this discovery to form his metaphysical concept. He suggested that every planet was a certain distance from a central point in the universe and that if an invisible string connected each planet to the central point, when plucked the string would emit a certain tone or vibration. Each sound or vibration could be associated with a particular number. He also believed that the sound or vibration of the universe dictated by the position of the planets would have a strong influence on the character of an individual born at that particular time.

Numerologists believe that the numbers one to nine have specific characteristics, and these characteristics are the basis for the methods of analysis described here. The numbers one to nine are the only numbers that are believed to be significant to numerology. All numbers greater than nine can be reduced to a single digit by the process of fadic addition, for example:

> 12 is reduced to 3 by adding 1 and 2;
> 49 is reduced to 4 by adding 4 and 9 which equals 13
> and subsequently adding 1 and 3 to make 4.

The numbers one to nine have different characteristics and therefore different influences on the characters and personalities of individuals. The influences of the numbers one to nine are examined in the following chapters. Each number is different. No one number is better or worse than any other. They are simply different.

Numerologists believe that through studying your date of birth and your name it is possible to analyse your character. They believe that it is possible to identify the potential that exists within you, your motivation, the way you interact with other people and the main characteristics asscociated with your date of birth and name.

By studying your personality through numerology, numerologists believe that it is possible to know yourself better, learn to accept yourself for who you are and modify your behaviour where appropriate.

Name numbers

Numerologists believe that a great deal can be interpreted about your personality and life by analysing your birth date. and by studying your name. Name numbers are not tied to you in the same way that you are to your birth date. It is possible to change your name. It is not possible to alter your date of birth.

Your name affects how other people react to you. On simply hearing a name people make assumptions about the person that owns it before they even meet. This is because your name is a word, and words form the basis of communication in our society. Every word means something to somebody. Your name is no exception.

Your name is a personal symbol that is inseparable from you. It has been chosen for you and you will react to it in your own individual way.

The name that you choose to work with for purposes of numerology is entirely up to you. Some numerologists insist that you must use the full name that is on your birth certificate as they believe that this is the true name. Other numerologists argue that the name most commonly used should be the one that is analysed. The choice is yours, but it is probably best to use the name that you identify most strongly with.

If you are known by more than one name and are unsure which one to analyse, try working with both names and see which is the one that you think gives you most insight into yourself. It could be that you are a mixture of the two names and do not really truly belong to either one.

If you have changed your name, it is interesting to analyse the name you are known by now and compare it with the name you used to be known by. This often reveals a process of change and development.

Your first name affects your personal life and has the strongest influence on your personality. Your surname indicates the traits and characteristics that you have inherited and has less effect on your personality. If you are always known by your surname it will have greater significance and should be treated as a first name. Your full name provides the complete picture of you and how other people view you.

There are three numerical aspects of your name that can be analysed:

the vowel number, the consonant number and the full name number.

To analyse the name, it is first necessary to break down the alphabet so that every letter has a number associated with it. This is done by the process of fadic addition. A = 1 because it is the first number in the alphabet, M = 4 because M is the thirteenth number in the alphabet and 1 + 3 = 4 and Z = 8 because Z is the twenty-sixth number in the alphabet and 2 + 6 = 8, and so on.

The complete alphabet and the numbers associated with each letter are recorded in the chart below:

1	2	3	4	5	6	7	8	9
A	B	C	D	E	F	G	H	I
J	K	L	M	N	O	P	Q	R
S	T	U	V	W	X	Y	Z	

The Vowel Number

The vowel number is also known as the motivation number, the ambition number, the heart's desire number and other names. We shall simply refer to it as the vowel number.

In terms of the numerology of names, the vowel number is second only in importance to the whole name number. The vowel number indicates your ambitions and desires. From analysing the make-up of your name, it is possible to identify areas of conflict in your life that arise from incompatible numbers. Your vowel number, for example, may not be the same as your birth date number, and so your vowel number dictates that you have an ambition that your birth date number dictates will not be achieved.

The vowels are A, E, I, O and U. If you have no vowels in your name but do have a Y, the Y can be interpreted as a vowel. If you have vowels and a Y in your name, you can analyse your name twice, once using the Y as a vowel and once using it as a consonant.

The numbers that represent each vowel are listed below.

A = 1   E = 5   I = 9   O = 6   U = 3   Y = 7

To find your vowel number follow the steps listed below.
Step 1: Write out the name that you have chosen to work with.

Example: CAROLINE MACDONALD

Step 2: Place the number for each vowel above the appropriate letter.
Example:

```
1    6    9    5       1         6      1
C  A  R  O  L  I  N  E    M  A  C  D  O  N  A  L  D
```

Step 3: Add all the numbers together.

Example: $1 + 6 + 9 + 5 + 1 + 6 + 1 = 29$

Step 4: Using the process of fadic addition (continuing to add the numbers together until a single digit number remains) reduce this figure to a number between 1 and 9.

Example: $2 + 9 = 11 > 1 + 1 = 2$

In our example the vowel number for Caroline Macdonald is 2.

Vowel Number One
People with vowel number one want to take charge and to be in control. Freedom and independence are very important to people with vowel number one. They do not like to be dictated to by others. They need to be in charge of their own lives. They are generally optimistic people who have a great deal of inner strength. They are often a source of inspiration to other people.

People with vowel number one are determined individuals who occasionally overlook the wants and needs of others in the pursuit of their own goals.

Vowel Number Two
People with vowel number two do not have any desire to take the lead or be in control. They want to follow others. They want balance and harmony in their lives. They achieve this through negotiation and compromise, at which they are extremely skilled. They need to be able to get on with other people. They want to avoid conflict and competition in their lives.

People with vowel number two are easy-going individuals who are well liked but occasionally taken advantage.

Vowel Number Three

People with vowel number three want life to be enjoyable. They seek to bring pleasure into their own and other people's lives. They are cheerful and optimistic people, and they are usually lively conversationalists and entertaining company. They need to feel popular and want people to like them. They are hard-working but know when to stop and how to enjoy themselves in their spare time.

People with vowel number three are confident and outgoing and other people occasionally regard them as being full of themselves.

Vowel Number Four

People with vowel number four want orderly and conventional lives. They need organization in their lives and want 'a place for everything and everything in its place'. They are very practical and efficient individuals who work hard in pursuit of security and stability. They are dependable and reliable people who need to have a purpose in life.

People with vowel number four can overwork themselves and need to allow themselves time to relax.

Vowel Number Five

People with vowel number five want variety and change in their lives. They need to feel free and unrestricted to explore life and have adventures. They need to be able to expand their knowledge by having new experiences. They are adaptable and versatile people who enjoy the challenge of adjusting to a new environment. They need to travel to broaden their horizons.

People with vowel number five can become restless and frustrated if they find that life does not move at a fast enough pace to meet their needs.

Vowel Number Six

People with vowel number six want peace and harmony in their lives. They have a strong sense of responsibility for the wellbeing of others. They need to believe that justice is being done and cannot abide injustice. They are very caring people and need the opportunity to give and receive love. They need to be able to create a home environment where they can feel safe and secure.

People with vowel number six can be overprotective and may become anxious and nervous.

Vowel Number Seven

People with vowel number seven need to be able to spend a great deal of time alone with their thoughts. They need a peaceful and private space in which they can contemplate life. They are very independent individuals and do not want to be told what to do by others. They are great thinkers and are often very perceptive. People with vowel number seven are more likely than most to have psychic powers. They have a love of natural beauty and need to spend time in natural surroundings, away from civilization.

People with vowel number seven may become frustrated and unhappy if they are not allowed to have enough personal space and freedom.

Vowel Number Eight

People with vowel number eight have a burning desire to succeed and are very ambitious individuals. They need to be self-reliant and independent. They do not want to feel at the mercy of anyone else. They are usually great organizers and are confident in their own abilities. They want to be in responsible positions and have no fear of making decisions.

People with vowel number eight may set themselves unachievable goals and become frustrated if they are not able to meet them.

Vowel Number Nine

People with vowel number nine want life to meet their ideals. They want the world to be a better place. They want everyone to be happy and at peace. They are compassionate and caring individuals who have romantic notions. They have a great love of life and want to live life to the full. They have a great fondness for their fellow humans and want to spend a great deal of their time talking and sharing thoughts.

People with vowel number nine tend to try to do too much at one time and can let themselves become exhausted.

Consonant Number

The consonant number is also known as the external image number, the impression number, the inner self number and other names. We shall simply refer to it as the consonant number. The consonant number indicates how you present yourself in public. It gives you insight into how other people regard you. The consonant number does not reflect who you actually are but shows what other people think you are like. The consonant number is the least important of the numbers that are found by analysing your name but helps to build up a complete picture of you.

The consonants are all the letters in the alphabet that are not vowels. The numbers associated with each consonant are listed below:

B = 2   C = 3   D = 4   F = 6   G = 7   H = 8   J = 1   K = 2
L = 3   M = 4   N = 5   P = 7   Q = 8   R = 9   S = 1   T = 2
V = 4   W = 5   X = 6   Y = 7   Z = 8

To find your consonant number, simply follow the steps listed below:

Step 1: Write out the name that you have chosen to work with.

Example: CAROLINE MACDONALD

Step 2: Place the appropriate number beneath each consonant in the name.

Example:
C A R O L I N E   M A C D O N A L D
3   9   3   5   4   3 4   5   3 4

Step 3: Add all the numbers together.

Example: 3 + 9 + 3 + 5 + 4 + 3 + 4 + 5 + 3 + 4 = 43

Step 4: Using the process of fadic addition reduce this number to a single unit.

Example: 4 + 3 = 7
In our example the name Caroline Macdonald has the consonant number 7.

Consonant Number One
People with consonant number one present a cool, calm and collected image. They appear to be unique individuals who stand out from the crowd. They send out signals of confidence and self-reliance saying that they do not

want anyone's help. They project an air of being in control of every situation. They appear to be determined to face life alone and do not want to work closely with other people. They seem to be happy people who find it easy to make friends.

Consonant Number Two

People with consonant number two seem to want not to be noticed. They seem to make an effort to merge in with the background. They seem to be uncomfortable if they are the centre of attention. They appear to want to avoid conflict, and they project an image of being a diplomat and negotiator who seems to be able to find a compromise in any situation. They seem to be approachable and friendly and willing to listen. They seem to be warm and comforting people who are trustworthy and reliable.

Consonant Number Three

People with consonant number three appear to be the life and soul of the party. They appear to be bright, enthusiastic and entertaining individuals. They seem to live life to the full and know how to enjoy themselves fully. They appear to thrive on the company of others and seem always to be willing to make new friends. They seem to be intelligent people who have the ability to make others laugh. They seem to need excitement in their lives and enjoy a hectic social life. They seem to be popular individuals and are often the first people to be invited to any social events.

Consonant Number Four

People with consonant number four appear to be practical and organized individuals who have no fear of hard work and responsibility. They seem to be trustworthy individuals who are 'as straight as they come'. They appear to be the type to play everything by the book and never bend the rules or leave anything to chance. They seem to be disciplined and in charge of their emotions. They appear to be confident of their own abilities and to know what they want from life. They appear to have a fondness for traditions and seem conservative in their approach to life. They seem to be admired for their honesty and hard work.

Consonant Number Five

People with consonant number five appear to be multi-talented individuals who can turn a hand to whatever takes their fancy. They seem to be adaptable individuals who have the ability to captivate an audience. They appear to be constantly on the move and looking for new challenges. They seem to be constantly in pursuit of new experiences and opportunities to broaden their horizons. They seem unpredictable and transient. They appear to need a great deal of independence and personal freedom, and seem not to want to become too involved with anyone.

Consonant Number Six

People with consonant number six appear to be responsible and nurturing individuals who are willing to offer support and protection to other people. They seem to be calm and balanced people who are content with their lives. They seem to be blessed with creative talents and appear to have the ability to make anywhere feel like home. People seem to be drawn to people with birth date number six and seek their advice and opinions. They seem to have near-perfect lives.

Consonant Number Seven

People with consonant number seven appear to be distant and mysterious. They seem to be absorbed in their own thoughts for much of the time and appear to be unapproachable. They seem to be secretive and unwilling to share their thoughts with others. It seems that they enjoy their own company and are not particularly interested in making new friends. They appear to be intelligent and perceptive people who are considered to be philosophical and observant. They appear to live their lives outwith the norms of society.

Consonant Number Eight

People with consonant number eight appear to be almost larger than life. They seem to be self-assured and completely confident. They seem to dominate the company that they are in. They appear to be strong characters who have a great deal of power that they know how to use. They have an air of success and project an image of being at ease with themselves and their surroundings. They seem to want to be regarded as a figure of authority and want to be in control. They seem to be respected for their ambition and abilities.

Consonant Number Nine

People with consonant number nine seem to be non-judgmental and open-minded individuals who are happy to accept everyone whom they meet as their equal. They appear to love everyone and have a great deal of compassion and tenderness towards their fellow human beings. They appear to have many creative talents and unique abilities. They seem to be determined to live their lives as they choose. They appear to be emotional and understanding individuals who enjoy the company of others and always have time to talk and listen. They seem to be popular and regarded as good friends.

Whole Name Number

The whole name number is also known as the expression number, the destiny number, the life mission number and the character number. We shall simply call it the whole name number. The whole name number is the most important number that can be derived from your name. The whole name number indicates what you actually do and gives insight into your ability to interact with others. The whole name number is very important because you have the power to change it. By changing your name you can change your whole name number and so change what you do.

The whole name number is calculated by adding together all the numbers in your name. To do this we should again refer to the chart that shows which numbers correspond with the letters of the alphabet.

1	2	3	4	5	6	7	8	9
A	B	C	D	E	F	G	H	I
J	K	L	M	N	O	P	Q	R
S	T	U	V	W	X	Y	Z	

Step 1: Write out the full name that you have chosen.

Example: CAROLINE MACDONALD

Step 2: Place the appropriate numbers above the vowels and below the consonants.

Example:

```
  1   6   9   5       1       6   1
C A R O L I N E   M A C D O N A L D
3   9   3   5     4   3 4     5   3 4
```

Step 3: There are two ways to do this next step.

(1) Add together all the vowel numbers. Add together all the consonant numbers. Then add both totals together.
Example:
$1 + 6 + 9 + 5 + 1 + 6 + 1 = 29$
$3 + 9 + 3 + 5 + 4 + 3 + 4 + 5 + 3 + 4 = 43$
$29 + 43 = 72$

(2) Add all the numbers together.
Example:
$1 + 6 + 9 + 5 + 1 + 6 + 1 + 3 + 9 + 3 + 5 + 4 + 3 + 4 + 5 + 3 + 4 = 72$
The end result should be the same no matter which method you use.

Step 4: Now use the process of fadic addition to reduce this number to a single unit.
Example: $7 + 2 = 9$
In our example the whole name number is 9.

Whole Name Number One—The Leader
People with the whole name number one are assertive and confident in their interaction with other people. They are happy to take on the role of leader and are comfortable with responsibility and making decisions. They are open-minded and willing to experiment with new experiences. They are bold in their actions and are often the first to take a step in a new direction. They believe in themselves and in their ability to succeed.

People with the whole name number one can be self-centred and may disregard the desires and needs of others. They can be too ambitious and become impatient in waiting for success.

Whole Name Number Two—The Mediator
People with the whole name number two are friendly and approachable in their interaction with other people. They are tactful and diplomatic individuals who are able to cooperate well with other people. They have valuable negotiating skills and are able to find ways in which to achieve compromise. They enjoy peaceful surroundings and often have an appreciation of the arts. They are sympathetic towards others and appreciate the support of others in return.

People with the whole name number two can be indecisive. They also are sometimes guilty of dishonesty. In their attempts to keep the peace they will sometimes fail to tell the truth.

Whole Name Number Three—The Optimist
People with the whole name number three are lively and entertaining in their interaction with other people. They are great communicators and often have a brilliant command of language. They are witty and intelligent people who make full use of their talents. They are fun-loving individuals who love to socialize. They are often blessed with creative talents that they need to be able to utilise.

People with whole name number three can lack organization in their lives and they may find that they try to do too many things at any one time.

Whole Name Number Four—The Builder
People with the whole name number four are down to earth and practical in their interaction with other people. They are organized and efficient individuals who work hard to achieve their ambitions. They are respected and admired by other people because of their commitment and determination. They are thoughtful people who never rush into situations without considering the consequences. They have a very logical approach to life and know what they want to achieve. They are conservative with a fondness for tradition.

People with the whole name number four can work too hard and push themselves too far. They can also be narrow-minded and find it hard to accept people different from themselves.

Whole Name Number Five—The Chameleon
People with the whole name number five are open and adaptable in their interaction with other people. They have a versatile approach to life and are happy to embrace change. They do not like to have restrictions imposed upon them and have a strong need for personal freedom and independence. They are interested in discovering about the various theories relating to the purpose of life and are always receptive to new input from other people. They have an optimistic approach to life and view every new experience as an opportunity to learn something new.

People with the whole name number five may find that they are constantly on the move and lose touch with friends and family. They may find that some people are distrustful of their unconventional approach to life.

Whole Name Number Six—Home Lover

People with the whole name number six are kind and caring in their interaction with other people. They are balanced and calm individuals who enjoy harmonious surroundings. They are responsible people who take on the role of protecting others. They are always willing to offer a helping hand to anyone in need. They create warm and comfortable home environments, which are very important to them and which they will defend strongly.

People with the whole name number six can sometimes be patronizing to other people and offer help where it is not wanted.

Whole Name Number Seven—The Thinker

People with the whole name number seven do not feel bound by the conventions of society and will interact with other people as they see fit at any given time. They are self-reliant and independent individuals. They do not want to learn from the experiences of others or to listen to other people's advice. They enjoy their own company and need time and space to be alone.

People with the whole name number seven may become lost in their own thoughts and eventually lose touch with reality. They are not confident in their decision making and sometimes opportunities will pass them by while they consider their options.

Whole Name Number Eight—The Success Story

People with the birth date number eight interact with other people in a businesslike fashion. They are ambitious and confident individuals who are sure of themselves and their ability to succeed in whatever they choose to do. They are respected and admired by others because of their hard work and commitment. They are strong-willed and determined individuals who persevere in the face of adversity.

People with the whole name number eight can become obsessed with material wealth and become greedy and miserly.

Whole Name Number Nine—The Humanitarian

People with the whole name number nine are tolerant, kind and compassionate in their interaction with other people. They are charitable and forgiving individuals who are willing to give anyone a second chance. Other people's opinions are important to them, and they rarely take any form of action without consulting someone else first. They pursue equality and harmony in their lives and are accepting of everyone's uniqueness.

People with the whole name number nine may become disillusioned by the lack of harmony in the world.

Name Chart

The use of a name chart helps to reveal more evidence about the influence that your name has on your character. The name chart reflects the strengths and weaknesses that may exist in your personality.

The numerical value of each letter that appears in your name is placed each time it appears in the appropriate section of the grid.

3	6	9
2	5	8
1	4	7

To find the numbers that relate to the letters in your name, we use the chart that shows which numbers correspond with the letters of the alphabet.

1	2	3	4	5	6	7	8	9
A	B	C	D	E	F	G	H	I
J	K	L	M	N	O	P	Q	R
S	T	U	V	W	X	Y	Z	

Step 1: Write out the name that you have chosen to work with. If working with the full name, it can be interesting to work out the name chart for your first name alone before adding in your surname and take note of the difference your surname makes to your reading of your character.

Example: CAROLINE MACDONALD

Step 2: Place the appropriate numbers above the vowels and below the consonants.

Example:

```
  1     6     9     5         1         6         1
C A R O L I N E   M A C D O N A L D
3     9     3     5         4   3 4     5     3 4
```

303

Step 3: Record the numbers in the empty grid

Example:

Significance can be drawn from complete and incomplete lines in your name chart. These lines are known as the Arrows of Pythagoras and reflect strengths and weakness in your personality.

1–5–9 The Line of Determination

The presence of this complete number line in a birth chart indicates resoluteness, persistence, dedication, strong will, tenacity, firmness of purpose, conviction, fortitude and stamina.

1–5–9 missing The Line of Resignation

The lack of any numbers present in this line indicates lack of motivation, submission, lack of enthusiasm, unwillingness, lack of determination and lack of originality.

3–5–7 The Line of Compassion

The presence of this line in a birth chart indicates sympathy, consideration, humanity, kindness, understanding, benevolence and intuition.

3–5–7 missing The Line of Scepticism

The lack of any numbers present in this line indicates, lack of trust, sus-
picion, disbelief, incredulity and cynicism.

3–6–9 Line of the Intellect

The presence of this line in a birth chart indicates intelligence, creative
thought, the ability to solve problems and mental agility.

3–6–9 missing The Line of Eccentricity

The lack of any numbers present in this line indicates unconventional
thought, nonconformity, individuality and lack of logic.

2–5–8 The Line of Emotion

The presence of this line in a birth chart indicates sensitivity, spirituality, balance, harmony, calm and love.

2–5–8 missing The Line of Sensitivity

The lack of any numbers present in this line indicates a lack of self-confidence, shyness, a sense of inferiority, a tendency to be introverted.

1–4–7 The Line of Physicality

The presence of this line in a birth chart indicates good health, manual dexterity, action, skill, practicality and ability.

1–4–7 missing The Line of Illusion (figure 77)

The lack of any numbers present in this line indicates insecurity, weakness, uncertainty, a tendency to be accident-prone, a non-materialistic approach to life and a lack of practicality.

1–2–3 The Line of the Planner

The presence of this line in a birth chart indicates consideration, neatness, administrative skills, organizational abilities and leadership qualities.

1–2–3 missing The Line of Confusion

The lack of any numbers present in this line indicates disorder, chaos, a lack of balance, muddle and disorganization.

4–5–6 The Line of Will

The presence of this line in a birth chart indicates ambition, determination, single-mindedness, clarity of purpose and sense of direction.

4–5–6 missing The Line of Frustration

The lack of any numbers present in this line indicates a lack of fulfilment, dissatisfaction, disappointment, discontent, resentment and a lack of success.

7–8–9 The Line of Action

The presence of this line in a birth chart indicates enthusiasm, zeal, energy, vitality, power, activity and decisiveness.

7–8–9 missing The Line of Inertia

The lack of any numbers present in this line indicates inactivity, stagnation, passivity, idleness and contemplation.

Intensity Numbers

Intensity numbers are numbers that dominate your name chart. Any number that occurs more frequently than any other in your name chart is known as the intensity number. The intensity number reveals your hidden character and aspects of your personality that are not immediately obvious from the initial analysis of your name. The intensity number is not of primary significance in the analysis of your character through numerology but adds further information.

If there is one number that is dominant in your chart, your intensity number is quite strong. If more than one number is dominant then the effect of the intensity number is weakened.

In the example that we used of Caroline MacDonald's name number the number three is dominant in the chart. Therefore, Caroline's has the intensity number three. Three is the number that appears more frequently than any other so the intensity number is quite significant in the analysis of her character.

Below are listed the traits and characteristics associated with each intensity number:

Intensity Number One
Self-aware, strong-willed, assertive, original, confident, able to take control and self-reliant.

Intensity Number Two
Diplomatic, cooperative, thoughtful, tactful, able to negotiate and compromise, sensitive and noncompetitive, listens to the views of others.

Intensity Number Three
Happy, confident, entertaining, creative, sociable, joyous, optimistic and gregarious.

Intensity Number Four
Practical, traditional, conservative, organized, efficient, hard-working, committed, patient, focused and determined.

Intensity Number Five
Independent, free-spirit, versatile, adaptable, open-minded, skilled in communicating, open to new experiences and change and fond of travel.

Intensity Number Six
Sensitive, balanced, responsible, protective, just, creative, home builder, harmonious, caring, loving and nurturing.

Intensity Number Seven
Loner, thinker, independent, solitary, mysterious, creative, philosophical, observant, secretive, self-contained, content and self-reliant.

Intensity Number Eight
Efficient, ambitious, successful, powerful, determined, wealthy, strong-willed, organized, responsible, trustworthy and dependable.

Intensity Number Nine
Tolerant, compassionate, open-minded, non-judgmental, emotional, sensitive, caring, loving, romantic, idealistic and humanitarian.

Missing Numbers

Missing numbers are sometimes referred to as karmic numbers. They represent qualities that you naturally lack in your personality. They are called karmic numbers because some numerologists believe that your purpose in life is to develop these qualities to achieve happiness and balance.

There are various numbers that influence your character: the birth date number, the vowel number, the consonant number, the full name number and the intensity number. To find your missing number, you must record all these numbers and see which numbers from one to nine are not represented.

Bith date number
The calculation that needs to be done to find your birth date number is relatively simple:

First: Write out your full date of birth.
Example: 21 June 1967
Second: Write your date of birth in its numerical form.
Example: 21/06/1967

Step 1: Add together the numbers in each section of your birth date.
Example: $2 + 1 = 3; 0 + 6 = 6; 1 + 9 + 6 + 7 = 23$

Step 2: Add together the three totals.
Example: $3 + 6 + 23 = 32$

Step 3: Add these two numbers together to reduce the number to 1 in the range of 1 to 9 (using the process of fadic addition).
Example: $3 + 2 = 5$

Step 4: This should now be a number between 1 and 9 and will be the birth date number.
Example: Hence the person in our example has the birth date number 5.

Example 2: 14 September 1941

14/09/1941

Step 1: $1 + 4 = 5; 0 + 9 = 9; 1 + 9 + 4 + 1 = 15$

Step 2: $5 + 9 + 15 = 29$

Step 3: $2 + 9 = 11; 1 + 1 = 2.$

A further procedure had to be carried out at step three because did not reduce the number to one digit between 1 and 9.

Birth chart
In this example it was necessary to do a further step at Step 3 as the one Your birth date number is calculated using the series of numbers that formulate your date of birth. Each number within this series has an influence on your relationship with your birth date number. Two people who share the same birth date number may have very different birth charts and therefore different characteristics.

To find out more about yourself from your birth chart use the simple process shown below.

For reference, look at the complete birth chart below, which indicates the way in which numbers are recorded in it.

3	6	9
2	5	8
1	4	7

Step 1: Write out your date of birth in numerical form.
e.g. 27th August 1965, 27.08.1965
Step 2 : Discard any zeros from the series of numbers.
e.g. 27.8.1965
Step 3: Record the numbers in the birth chart, e.g.

	6	9
2	5	8
1		7

It is important to record a number every time it appears, even if you have four or more of one number.

Missing numbers

The example below shows the final set of numbers for Caroline Macdonald born 27.08.1965.

Birth Date Number—2
First Name Vowel Number—3
Surname Vowel Number—8
Full Name Vowel Number—2
First Name Consonant Number—2
Surname Consonant Number—5
Full Name Consonant Number—7
First Name Whole Name Number—5
Surname Whole Name Number—4
Full Name Whole Name Number—9
Intensity Number—3

These are the most significant numbers but to find missing numbers we must also compare the birth chart and the name chart.
Example:

Name Chart		
33 33	66	99
	55 5	
11	44 4	

Birth Chart		
	6	9
2	5	8
1		7

It can be seen from the two charts that Caroline does not have any entirely missing lines but the numbers that are not represented in the charts represent weaker aspects of her character that could be developed. The significance of those is explained in the following pages.

There is space below for you to fill in the final set of numbers for your name and date of birth.

Birth Date Number—
First Name Vowel Number—
Surname Vowel Number—
Full Name Vowel Number—
First Name Consonant Number—

Surname Consonant Number—
Full Name Consonant Number—
First Name Whole Name Number—
Surname Whole Name Number—
Full Name Whole Name Number—
Intensity Number—

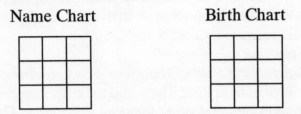

Name Chart   Birth Chart

If after the final analysis you find that there is one or more numbers that are not represented then you have a missing number. The significance of missing numbers is examined below.

Missing Number One
People who are missing number one from their numerological make-up lack the ability to take the lead and have difficulty in getting themselves heard. They find it difficult to be assertive and are not confident about giving their opinion on matters.

People who are missing number one should try to build up their self-confidence and take more chances in life.

Missing Number Two
People who are missing number two from their numerological make-up tend to lack the ability to cooperate with other people. They often find it difficult to listen to other people's opinions and ideas and are usually convinced that their position is the correct one to take. They frequently find it difficult to see the opportunity for compromise when they are involved in disputes.

People who are missing number two should try to hear what other people are saying and should try to be less stubborn.

Missing Number Three
People who are missing number three from their numerological make-up

lack the ability to communicate effectively with other people. They often find that they are not able to express themselves in the way that they would like to. They frequently find that they are misunderstood by other people because of their inability to say what they mean. They tend to have a rather pessimistic view of life and generally have the expectation that things will go against them.

People who are missing number three should try to adopt a more optimistic approach to life and be more open in their interaction with other people.

Missing Number Four

People who are missing number four from their numerological make-up lack order and control in their lives. They tend to float along through life without self-restraint and often end up in financial difficulties. They often have no concept of structure and find it difficult to fit into a working environment.

People who are missing number four should try to be more organized in their daily lives and to practise more self-control. They could also benefit from acting less impulsively.

Missing Number Five

People who are missing number five from their numerological make-up lack the ability to accept change. They tend to live closed lives and are often reluctant to widen their horizons or incorporate new experiences into their lives. They are generally set in their ways and are frequently suspicious of people who have unorthodox lifestyles.

People who are missing number five often find that they become stuck in a rut because of their fear of change. In order to avoid stagnation in their lives they should occasionally make conscious efforts to embrace change. They should try to have an optimistic outlook and not regard change as something that will cause them grief.

Missing Number Six

People who are missing number six from their numerological make-up lack the ability to empathize with other people. They are often rather self-centred individuals who do not always take other people's thoughts and feelings into consideration. They generally dislike responsibility and like to live their lives for themselves. They sometimes have difficulty in expressing their emotions to the people closest to them.

People who are missing number six should try to be more considerate of other people and not always assume that their own needs have highest priority.

Missing Number Seven

People who are missing number seven from their numerological make-up lack the ability to spend time alone with their thoughts. They are often very active people who spend most of their time in the company of other people. They generally live very hectic lives and do not usually allow themselves time to stop and reflect on their actions. They sometimes are overly concerned with material wealth.

People who are missing number seven should try to slow down and take time to think about their lives. They should try to be less concerned with material gains and should turn their attention to expanding their minds.

Missing Number Eight

People who are missing number eight from their numerological make-up lack any sort of business sense. They are generally lacking in organizational skills and are frequently inefficient individuals who lack motivation and ambition. They tend to be easily put off any course of action by the slightest obstacle in their way.

People who are missing number eight should think about what they want from life and how they can achieve the goals they set themselves. They should try to be more determined to achieve their goals and should not give in so easily.

Missing Number Nine

People who are missing number nine from their numerological make-up lack vision. They tend to be rather narrow-minded and often live sheltered lives. They generally disapprove of lifestyles different from their own. They often lack compassion and tend to have no real interest in the wellbeing of others. Their outlook on life is generally pessimistic and they do not expect much from life.

People who are missing number nine should try to be more open-minded and should not be too judgmental of other people. They should try to understand other people better and look for common ground rather than focusing on differences.

Names and Numbers

Choosing a name for a child is something that people spend a great deal of time thinking about. Numerologists believe that by calculating the number associated with the name being considered, the people choosing a name can determine whether it is appropriate or not. This section looks at the characteristics associated with each number and gives examples of names.

Compatibility with birth date number

When choosing a name it is best first to establish the birth date number as described on page 310, and then decide on a complementary name number, i.e. you should choose a name that has a name number indicating characteristics that will not cause conflict with the birth date number.

The characteristics of birth date numbers are summarised as follows:

Birth Date Number One
Decisive and independent, Number Ones make strong and effective leaders as they are assertive, confident, perceptive, self-motivated and focused on success. Can tend to be self-centred and have narrow vision as a result of their self-confidence and determination to succeed.

Birth Date Number Two
They have the ability to compromise and negotiate. Number Twos are charming and considerate of others. They are peace-loving and are able to maintain harmony. Naturally shy away from conflict, which can result in issues not being resolved. Often lack motivation.

Birth Date Number Three
Charming with a childlike quality of innocence, they have a good sense of humour and a real interest in other people. Number Threes enjoy talking, making others laugh and living life to the full. Can be show-offs and may have a tendency to be a little shallow.

Birth Date Number Four

Hard-working, loyal and ambitious, Number Fours have common sense and a practical approach to life. They are careful and are unlikely to make a decision without giving the matter a great deal of thought. They are reliable friends though have a tendency towards intolerance.

Birth Date Number Five

Number Fives are free spirits who have a sense of adventure and a curiosity about life. They have a desire to expand their horizons and gain insights into the lifestyles of other cultures. Number Five people are easy going and happy-go-lucky but can be too impulsive.

Birth Date Number Six

Number Six people are stylish and have the ability to command the attention of others. Number Sixes have charisma, and are trustworthy and tolerant. They are able confidants but are sometimes unable to deal with their own difficulties and put a brace face on problems.

Birth Date Number Seven

Sensitive and compassionate, Number Sevens have a natural wisdom and ability to see to the truth of matters. They are exceptional people, able to offer warmth, sympathy and understanding. Number Sevens often lack confidence, are romantics, and can tend to daydream.

Birth Date Number Eight

Content and sure of themselves, Number Eights know what they want from life and know how they are going to achieve their goals. They are realistic, dependable, strong-willed, responsible and loyal, but they can become stubborn and unbending and sometimes have a tendency to be tactless.

Birth Date Number Nine

Number Nines are independent, courageous and resilient. Optimists by nature, Number Nines are sure of themselves, determined, enthusiastic and are non-judgmental of others. However, quick tempers are common amongst Number Nines, as is a tendency to lash out at whoever is nearest to hand.

Name Numbers

Number One
Confident—assertive—independent—strong-willed—original—determined—pioneering—powerful—innovative.

Adam	Dan	Jayne	Monica
Agnes	Edith	Joanna	Natasha
Alan	Emily	Juan	Nicolas
Barry	Erin	Kate	Pablo
Bob	Edith	Kay	Rebecca
Bobby	Haleb	Lois	Ralph
Cilla	Hannah	Loren	Tessa
Cindy	Ivor	Lorne	Tyne
Claude	Jackson	Lynus	Zara
Clarissa	Jamal	Mae	Zoe

Number Two
Cooperative—diplomatic—friendly—kind—supportive—calm—understanding—quiet

Adrian	Dennis	Jaclyn	Page
Andrew	Desmond	Jamie	Paulo
Andria	Dianne	Jarrett	Sadie
Ann	Gail	John	Sarah
Asha	Glen	Loyd	Stefan
Dana	Hatty	Nadia	Tony
Denise	Jade	Oscar	Ursula

Number Three
Creative—joyful—charming—communicative—expressive—open—lively—fun-loving

Alec	Clare	Jessica	Natal
Alun	Eamon	Joe	Raja
Amber	Ella	Jock	Sara
Amos	Ellen	Julie	Sasha
Amy	Isabel	Mandy	Scot
Angel	James	Marcus	Sean
Anna	Jane	Mary	Tom
Austin	Jasmin	Mel	Wallace
Celia	Jean	Nancy	Zelda

Number Four
Practical—self-disciplined—stable—hard-working—organized—efficient

Abdul	Carol	Gill	Nathan
Albert	Clint	Graeme	Neil
Allan	Daisy	Hamish	Tracey
Angela	Danny	Harold	Wilma
Annabel	Delia	Haydon	Winona
Anthea	Emmett		

Number Five
Carefree—curious—communicative—versatile—sensual—independent

Aldo	Frank	Joanne	Paul
Blossom	Isla	Joy	Rossalyn
Donald	Janet	June	Scott
Drew	Jason	Lara	Shelley
Eileen	Jenny	Lloyd	Tommy
Emma	Jim	Maureen	Wayne
Euan			

Number Six
Harmonious—creative—responsible—domestic—loving—caring—sensitive

Ailsa	Cybil	Isaac	Lesley
Alex	Dane	Janice	Lydia
Andre	Diane	Jasper	Malcolm
Arden	Dougal	Jered	Maria
Billy	Fred	Joel	Petra
Blair	Gary	Judy	Rae
Bryan	Grant	Karl	Sally
Camilla	Ian	Kim	Selina
Claudia	Ina		

Number Seven
Refined—quiet—individualistic—intuitive—thoughtful—contemplative

Amanda	Carmel	Grace	Sheena
Amon	Cassandra	Hazel	Simon
Andrea	Chloe	Isabella	Sinead
Anne	Douglas	Jill	Stewart
Ashley	Ewan	Jodie	Todd
Basil	Flora	Lilly	Trudy
Bonny	Freda	Lynne	Walter
Brad	Giles	Mark	Wanda
Carl	Glenn		

Number Eight
Powerful—independent—ambitious—organized—successful—authoritative

Abraham	Colette	Heidi	Laura
Alicia	Colin	Helen	Leah
Alistair	Cynthia	Hugh	Liam
Allen	Danielle	Isobel	Ray
Bernard	Deborah	Jeanette	Ross
Bill	Dudley	Julia	Tina
Brian	Gaby	Justine	Samuel
Carla	Gerard	Keith	Toby
Clara			

Number Nine
Compassionate—idealistic—dramatic—romantic—wise—caring—empathetic

Alastair	Daniel	Fiona	Roger
Anita	Debbie	Holly	Sandy
Beatrice	Deirdre	Matthew	Sheila
Betty	Dick	Mick	Shelley
Bret	Eddie	Morag	Tiffany
Carmen	Eliott	Nicola	Valerie
Carrie	Erica	Patsy	Vicki
Catriona	Ernest	Reilly	Willy